# Steam and Cinders

# Steam and Cinders

## The Advent of Railroads in Wisconsin
## 1831–1861

### Axel S. Lorenzsonn

**Wisconsin Historical Society Press**

Published by the Wisconsin Historical Society Press
*Publishers since 1855*

© 2009 by State Historical Society of Wisconsin

For permission to reuse material from *Steam and Cinders: The Advent of Railroads in Wisconsin*, (ISBN 978-0-87020-385-5), please access www.copyright.com or contact the Copyright Clearance Center, Inc. (CCC), 222 Rosewood Drive, Danvers, MA 01923, 978-750-8400. CCC is a not-for-profit organization that provides licenses and registration for a variety of users.

**wisconsinhistory.org**

Photographs identified with WHi are from the Society's collections; address inquiries about such photos to the Visual Materials Archivist at Wisconsin Historical Society, 816 State Street, Madison, WI 53706.

Front cover: WHi 62336
Back cover, from left to right: WHi 62554, WHi 62556; both maps courtesy of the Library of Congress

Printed in the United States of America

Designed by 2econd Shift Production Services

13 12 11 10 09    1 2 3 4 5

**Library of Congress Cataloging-in-Publication Data**

Lorenzsonn, Axel S.
  Steam and Cinders : the advent of railroads in Wisconsin, 1831–1861 / Axel S. Lorenzsonn.
       p. cm.
   Includes bibliographical references and index.
    ISBN 978-0-87020-385-5 (hbk : alk. paper)  1. Railroads—Wisconsin—History—19th century.  2. Milwaukee and Mississippi Railroad Company—History.  I. Title.

  HE2771.W6L67 2009

  385.09775'09034—dc22

2009018219

∞ The paper used in this publication meets the minimum requirements of the American National Standard for Information Sciences—Permanence of Paper for Printed Library Materials, ANSI Z39.48–1992.

*To Nandini, Faye, and Erik*

# Contents

| | |
|---|---:|
| **Acknowledgments** | **viii** |
| **PART ONE: BEGINNINGS** | **1** |
| **Chapter 1**    A Proposal<br>1831 | **3** |
| **Chapter 2**    Lead Railroads Come to Western Michigan Territory<br>1831–1836 | **15** |
| **Chapter 3**    Railroads and the Creation of Wisconsin Territory<br>1836 | **29** |
| **Chapter 4**    The Territorial Years<br>1837–1848 | **42** |
| **PART TWO: THE FIRST RAILROAD** | **61** |
| **Chapter 5**    Establishing a Company<br>1848–1849 | **63** |
| **Chapter 6**    Milwaukee to Waukesha: Picking the Route<br>1849 | **73** |
| **Chapter 7**    Construction Begins<br>1849 | **81** |
| **Chapter 8**    Rails and Locomotives<br>1850 | **93** |
| **Chapter 9**    A Railroad is Born<br>January–April 1851 | **106** |
| **Chapter 10**    Growing Pains<br>May–December 1851 | **115** |
| **Chapter 11**    Wisconsin's Only Railroad<br>1852 | **125** |

## PART THREE: NEW GROWTH — 137

**Chapter 12**    In the Rock River Valley
1848–1852 — **139**

**Chapter 13**    The New Contenders
1852 — **147**

**Chapter 14**    The Scramble for New Routes
1853 — **163**

**Chapter 15**    Complete to Madison
1854 — **179**

## PART FOUR: THE GREAT BUILDING BOOM — 191

**Chapter 16**    Western Goals and Eastern Connections
1855 — **193**

**Chapter 17**    An Explosion of Railroads
1856 — **206**

**Chapter 18**    The Struggle for Land Grants
1856 — **222**

**Chapter 19**    Reaching the Mississippi
1857 — **230**

## PART FIVE: HARD TIMES AND RECOVERY — 249

**Chapter 20**    A Peculiar Hardship
1858 — **251**

**Chapter 21**    Reorganization
1859 — **269**

**Chapter 22**    New Beginnings
1860–1861 — **284**

**Epilogue** — **297**
**Afterword** — **308**
**Notes** — **310**
**Index** — **330**

# Acknowledgments

*History* and *story* are the same word differently written.
—Moses M. Strong

We are more eager to have railroads than we are to get to heaven.
—Anonymous Wisconsin pioneer

I have long loved history. My childhood summers were spent at the beach lying on a damp towel and reading books about Revolutionary War heroes, frontiersmen, and Native Americans. In college I was taken by Juliette McGill Kinzie's *Wau-bun: The Early Day in the Northwest*, her account of living in Wisconsin in the 1830s. And for the last ten years I have been collecting stories of Wisconsin's early railroads.

Why railroads? The train bug bit me a number of years ago while I was shopping for a toy train for my son. I then became curious about the origin of railroads in Madison, where I live. A trip to the Wisconsin Historical Society Library revealed to me that the first train to arrive in Madison came from Milwaukee on May 23, 1854. It had two locomotives, thirty-two cars, and one thousand passengers and was met at the depot by some two thousand Dane County residents, most of whom had never seen a train before. At the Madison Public Library in the 1858 city directory I found advertisements for railroads with fascinating names such as the Milwaukee and Mississippi, the La Crosse and Milwaukee, and the Chicago, St. Paul and Fond du Lac. I was hooked.

When I first began collecting early Wisconsin railroad stories, I found that they were few and scattered. Pictures and photographs are rare. There are several summaries of early railroad development in local Wisconsin histories, but no book exists on the topic. With the encouragement of family and friends, I decided to try

# ACKNOWLEDGMENTS

to write such a book. The result is *Steam & Cinders*, the story of the first thirty years of railroads in Wisconsin.

I would like to thank the people who helped make this book possible, although I regret I cannot name them all. I thank my wife, Nandini, my daughter, Faye, and my son, Erik, for being supportive and for reviewing sections of the manuscript. Thanks to my parents, Edgar and Vilja Lorenzsonn, for insisting that I was a railroad historian and giving me confidence. Thanks to my mother-in-law, Josephine Sarkar, for giving me a copy of Stephen Ambrose's *Nothing Like It in the World*, which became the model for this book. Thank you to Dr. Stephen Weiler for helping me keep my focus. Thank you to the Madison Public Library's Sue Koehler, a now-retired librarian who helped me find and use reference guides; to the staff at the Wisconsin Historical Society Archives for helping me locate maps and other materials; to the volunteers in the society's microfilm room for their assistance and good cheer; to freelance editor John Toren for reading the manuscript thoroughly and offering many valuable suggestions; and to Wisconsin Historical Society Press editors Kate Thompson and Sara Phillips for their editing, guidance, and support. Thanks to all of the folks at the local historical societies for digging for those elusive pre–Civil War railroad items—I was touched by their attention and courtesy. And finally, a special thank you to former Wisconsin Historical Society Press editor J. Kent Calder for giving me encouragement, direction, and so much of his time.

# PART ONE: BEGINNINGS

# Chapter 1

## A Proposal
### 1831

In 1831 the United States was forty-two years old; its lands stretched from the Atlantic Ocean to the Rocky Mountains, and Andrew Jackson was president. There were twenty-four states in the Union at the time, and all but Louisiana and Missouri lay east of the Mississippi river. Slavery was practiced in the twelve southern states and prohibited in the twelve northern states. The United States owned and administered the areas known as Florida Territory, Arkansas Territory, and Michigan Territory, from which future states were expected to emerge. The remaining areas of the United States—the lands west of Arkansas Territory, Missouri, and the upper Mississippi River, and extending to the Rocky Mountains—were Indian Territory. There, settlement by whites was prohibited. Both the United States and Britain claimed the Pacific Northwest, while Texas, the Southwest, and California belonged to Mexico.

There were thirteen million people living in the United States in 1831. Eleven million of them were white, two million were African American, and 330,000 were aboriginal Native American. Most of those African Americans were slaves in the South. Both whites and African Americans had been increasing in numbers; their combined population had doubled in less than twenty years. As a result, many whites, and, in the south, their attendant black slaves, had moved from the settled areas of the East to cheaper, more fertile lands between the Appalachian Mountains and the Mississippi River. Native Americans, meanwhile, had been declining in number. The Indian Removal Act of 1830 called for those living east of the Mississippi to be moved west to the Indian Territory, a directive the United States would carry out over the next decade.[1]

Three-quarters of Americans lived on subsistence farms at this time, consuming most of what they grew and marketing the surplus nearby. But as roads and waterways were improved, more and more of these individuals turned to commercial farming, growing crops or raising livestock for shipment and sale at distant markets and buying food and other necessities for themselves and their families rather than growing or producing them. What they produced varied by region. In New England they raised sheep, in Ohio they grew wheat, in Tennessee and Kentucky they grew tobacco or corn and raised pigs and cattle, and across the South they grew cotton. In all of these regions, farmers found that they could achieve a better life through commercial farming than they had experienced with subsistence farming.[2]

It was improved transportation—transportation that was faster, cheaper, and more readily available—that allowed these new commercial farmers to produce more, sell more, and buy more. The earliest land transportation had been conducted over the Indian trails that connected villages and crossed streams at fordable shallows. Settlers soon "improved" these trails by widening them into wagon roads. These roads were primitive—often consisting of little more than stakes marking the way across open areas and cleared forest paths littered with one-foot-high tree stumps—but they enabled hundreds of settlers to first move west and then ship their produce back east.

In many regions canals augmented or competed with wagon roads. The first canals were opened around 1800. These were generally two or three miles long and allowed vessels to pass around falls and rapids on otherwise navigable rivers. Longer canals were built parallel to rivers. Their construction was expensive, but they reduced the cost of shipping to one-third of what it was by wagon. By 1831 there were some forty canals operating or being built in the United States. The longest, New York State's 363-mile Erie Canal, had opened in 1825 and earned a substantial profit every year thereafter. Canal projects were underway in Maryland, Pennsylvania, Ohio, and Indiana, where investors hoped to achieve similar results.[3]

Lakes and rivers were the main routes of transportation for most travelers and goods. Canoes, flatboats, and keelboats carried much of the trade. After 1810 they were joined by steamboats. Steamboats were the first form of transport to be powered by engines, and they had a definite advantage traveling upstream—charging one-tenth of what keelboats charged to carry freight in that direction. In 1831 steamboats ran from New Orleans to Nashville and Knoxville, Tennessee;

# A PROPOSAL

Louisville, Kentucky; Peoria, Illinois; Indianapolis, Indiana; and Pittsburgh, Pennsylvania. Steamers were making regular runs on the Great Lakes between Buffalo, New York, and Detroit, Michigan Territory, charging passengers as little as three dollars for a one-way fare.⁴

Though steamboats represented an important shift toward affordable mechanized travel, they were about to compete with an even more powerful animal: the Iron Horse, otherwise known as the steam-powered locomotive.

By 1831 Americans were witnessing the emergence of a new form of improved transportation—the steam-powered railroad. Horse-powered railroads, typically short tracks at quarries and mines, had been used in America since approximately 1800. A more developed form appeared in 1830 with the Baltimore and Ohio Railroad in Maryland, which offered freight and passenger service over thirteen miles of track, all powered with horses. But a steam-powered railroad held more promise. Steam locomotives could pull long trains at high speeds. Although they would require large monetary investments, they had the potential to be practical alternatives to canals and turnpikes.

The idea for steam-powered railroads had been developed in Britain, where the first commercial steam engines, designed by Thomas Newcomen, began pumping water out of mines in 1700. Steam engines were further improved in the 1700s by James Watt. In 1804 the first working steam locomotive, designed and built by Cornishman Richard Trevethick, pulled a train carrying ten tons of iron and a handful of passengers a distance of ten miles. In 1819 rolled iron rails, which were invented and produced by John Birkinshaw, supported the weight of the new locomotives for the first time. And on September 25, 1825, the Stockton and Darlington Railroad—the first steam-powered railroad to offer passenger and freight service to the public—opened for business.

The idea had developed in Britain. Now it was about to arrive in America.⁵ In August of 1830, the Tom Thumb, Peter Cooper's one-ton locomotive, pulled a car carrying thirty-six passengers for twenty-six miles at speeds approaching eighteen miles per hour on the Baltimore and Ohio Railroad in Maryland. On Christmas day of that year, E. L. Miller and C. E. Detmold's four-ton locomotive Best Friend of Charleston pulled a train with 141 passengers twelve miles at speeds over twenty miles per hour on the Charleston and Hamburg Railroad in South Carolina. In 1831 two more steam-powered railroads were about to open for business—the Mohawk and Hudson Railroad in New York State and the Camden and Amboy Railroad in New Jersey. Clearly, something new was underway in America. Never before had people and goods traveled at such high, sustained speeds. Six years of steam-rail development in Britain indicated that the steam-powered railroad in America could be profitable and expansive. There was reason to be excited.

In 1831, as rails were being laid in the East, "Wisconsin" was little more than the name of a river. The land we call Wisconsin today was part of what was then known as the Michigan Territory. "Western Michigan Territory" or "the part of Michigan Territory west of Lake Michigan," would not be known as Wisconsin for another five years.

This land was and is distinctly different in its northern parts than in its southern. In the north, granite lay exposed on the earth's surface, crystal-clear lakes numbered in the hundreds, and pine forests covered the rest.[6] In the southern region, where our story takes place, the climate was warmer, the soil richer, and the growing season longer. Airy woodlands of beech, basswood, and maple alternated with wetlands and prairies of grass and wild flowers. Some of the prairies were dotted with oak trees and had a parklike appearance; these were known as "oak openings." In the eastern and central sections of this southern region were many marshes and bogs, the legacy of a great glacier that had retreated 14,000 years earlier. The western parts, untouched by the glacier, were well-drained "ridge and coulee" country.[7]

At this time Western Michigan had some thirty thousand residents, with Indians outnumbering whites eight to one.[8] The Chippewa (Ojibwa) and Menomonee people lived in the north, the Potawatomi along Lake Michigan, and the Winnebago (Ho Chunk) inhabited the central and western regions. Most of the men of these tribes were trappers by profession. Families supplemented their income with hunting, fishing, growing corn, and harvesting wild rice. The three thousand white people in Western Michigan were evenly divided between those living along the Fox-Wisconsin waterway and those living in the southwestern lead-mining region. The former consisted of French and British fur-trading families, their French-Canadian hired men, 200 new American arrivals, and the troops stationed at the forts at Green Bay, Portage, and Prairie du Chien.[9] The residents of the lead-mining district were mostly Southerners from Missouri, Kentucky, and Tennessee who had come up in the previous five years to work the mines.

Transportation in Western Michigan was mostly by water. With a canoe and a set of strong shoulders on which to carry it, one could go almost anywhere. On the Fox and Wisconsin rivers, some traders used larger vessels—thirty-foot French bateaux or sixty-foot Durham boats. The Fox-Wisconsin waterway was the main thoroughfare through the territory, but it did have obstacles. There were several rapids that required portaging, and it was long and winding in its upper reaches. At the portage between the Fox and Wisconsin rivers, boats and cargo had to be carried one and a quarter miles on carts pulled by oxen. The Wisconsin River, on the other hand, had many shallows and shifting sandbars, making navigation difficult. Most of the traffic on this waterway carried trade goods to and from Native American communities. Eastern manufactured goods went west to tribes as far away as the Rocky Mountains, and bales of fur went east to New York and Europe. By 1831 several steamboats were also plying the lower Wisconsin River, a few traveling as far upriver as Portage.

Land transportation in Western Michigan was primitive. For the most part people still used Indian trails, some of which were worn a foot or two into the ground. One such trail that had subsequently been widened into a wagon road ran from Green Bay to the Grand Kakalin rapids of the Fox River. Such roads were more numerous in mining areas, where they connected villages, mines, and smelt-

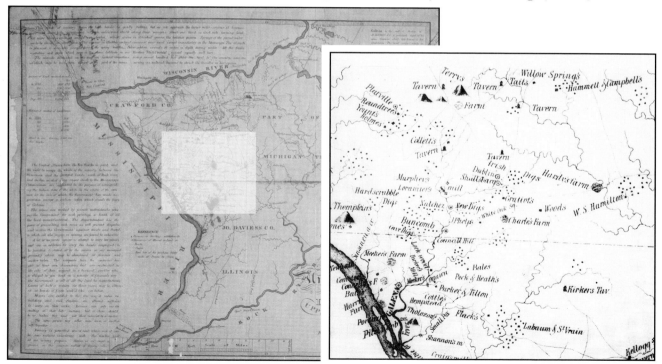

R. W. Chandler, an early settler in Galena, Illinois, pruduced this map to publicize the lead-mining area of Illinois and Wisconsin in 1829. The inset map shows the names and locations of many of the early settlers and their mines.
(MAP) WHI IMAGE ID 39775; (INSET) WHI IMAGE ID 42834

ers. Getting lead to market was no easy task—large-wheeled "waggons" pulled by eight to ten yoke of oxen had to carry 70 pounds of cast iron lead, or "pigs," from the smelters to the river landings. As lead mining became a staple of the economy in western Michigan Territory, these roads became an important conduit for overland transportation.

Beginning in 1825, lead mining transformed the landscape of southern Michigan Territory. Five-foot-square pit openings, marked with primitive winches that lowered and raised miners and ore, dotted the horizon. Picks and blasting powder were used to get at the ore. One miner could extract 150 pounds of ore in a day. At the smelter, ore sold for one to two cents per pound. Half to three-quarters of this ore contained lead. The smelter would extract the lead from the ore and channel it into cast-iron forms to make the 70-pound pigs. The pigs would then sell for four or five cents per pound. From the nearest river landing—on the Fever, the Mississippi, or the Wisconsin Rivers—the pigs were shipped to New Orleans. They were then shipped again, this time by sailing vessel, around Florida to the final market at New York, where they were processed in factories that manufactured weights, print type, shot, paint, and other items.

This burgeoning industry was not without its problems. As the lead-mining industry grew, tensions between settlers and natives arose over land use. The lead-mining region—bordered by the Wisconsin River on the north, the Mississippi on the west, the Illinois state line on the south, and the Sugar River on the east—had experienced a turbulent six-year history. In 1825 the United States had recognized its ownership by the Chippewa, Ottawa, Potawatomi, and Winnebago tribes. But that same year, white miners from Missouri, Kentucky, Tennessee, and southern Illinois began arriving to mine lead.[10] Tensions grew. Then in 1827 two attacks by Winnebago near Prairie du Chien caused almost the entire white population of the region to evacuate to Galena. Local militia under General Henry Dodge and troops from Jefferson Barracks, Missouri, restored order in what became known as the Winnebago War. Yet despite this turmoil, in 1828 some ten thousand miners were back, once again mining on Indian land.

In 1829 the United States government finally purchased the land in this area from the various tribes that had previously held ownership. The area was subsequently administered by the Army Ordinance Bureau, which leased plots to individuals for the purposes of mining and smelting. Farming, which was thought to interfere with mining, was prohibited. Yet some farming was done, and settlements grew at Mineral Point, Dodgeville, Potosi, Hazel Green, Shullsburg, and Platteville.

In 1829, with the United States flooded with lead imported from Europe, the bottom dropped out of the lead market. The price of lead in the region dropped from four cents a pound to only one cent per pound. Miners rushed to get out of

The center panel of the Wisconsin Centennial Mural, painted by W. A. McCloy in 1948, celebrates the lead mining that brought settlers to the southwestern region of Michigan Territory in the 1820s and 1830s.
WHI IMAGE ID 40753

the district, and the population dropped from ten thousand individuals to three thousand in one year. For two years, the people of the region eked out a living, waiting for better times; by 1831, the price of lead was finally returning to what it had been.[11]

It is against this background of uncertainty and risk that, in 1831, a man named Henry Rowe Schoolcraft came to the Wisconsin lead-mining region, interested to see what expertise he could offer to the struggling Wisconsin mines. A nationally recognized authority in lead mining, Schoolcraft was born in Hamilton, New York, in 1793 and attended Middlebury College in Vermont. During 1818 and 1819 he visited many of the lead mines of Missouri and thereafter developed a plan for their reorganization. He published his plan, *A View of the Lead Mines of Missouri*, and presented it to President James Monroe. It was favorably received, and many of its recommendations were later incorporated into federal legislation.

Schoolcraft first visited "Western Michigan" in 1820, when he served as a geologist for an exploratory expedition led by Michigan Governor Lewis Cass, although at that time there were few lead mines in the territory for him to visit. In 1822 he was appointed United States Indian Agent to the Ojibwa tribe on Lake Superior, a position he would hold for many years. In 1827 he was elected to Michigan's Territorial Council.[12] In 1830 that council granted a railroad charter to the Detroit and Pontiac Railroad Company. It was the first railroad charter in the Northwest Territory and the first contact Schoolcraft had with railroads.

In May of 1831 Schoolcraft, in his capacity as Indian Agent, received special instructions from Washington to visit the tribes of the upper Mississippi to hear complaints, council peace, vaccinate against smallpox, and take a census. The party accomplished its mission and arrived at Prairie du Chien on August 12. Schoolcraft decided to indulge his interest in mineralogy and visit the Galena and Wisconsin lead mines before returning to Saulte St. Marie.[13]

Schoolcraft left Prairie du Chien alone, by canoe, on August 14 at four o'clock in the afternoon. He paddled until nightfall, then spent the night on a sandbar. The following day he passed Cassville and Dubuque, then ascended the Fever River

Henry Rowe Schoolcraft, mineralogist and Indian agent, proposed a railroad to serve the lead region in 1831.
WHi Image ID 23557

This engraving depicts Schoolcraft's first visit to western Michigan Territory in 1821, when he traveled along the Ontonagon River.
WHi Image ID 4953

to Galena, which was the main depot of the lead-mining district. It was from there that Schoolcraft would begin his tour of the Wisconsin lead mines. As always, he kept a journal:

> On the following day [August 16] I dispatched my canoe back. . . . I then hired a light wagon to visit the mine country. . . . Mr. Bennet, the landlord, went with me to bring back the team. We left Galena about ten o'clock in the morning [August 17], and, passing over an open, rolling country [we then] reached Gratiot's Grove, at a distance of fifteen miles. The Messrs. Gratiot received me kindly and showed me the various ores, and their mode of preparing and smelting them. . . .
>
> Having examined whatever was deemed worthy of attention here, I drove on about fifteen miles to Willow Springs. In this drive we had the Platte Mounds, a prominent object, all the afternoon on our left. We stopped at Irish diggings, and I took specimens of the various spars, ores, and rocks. . . .
>
> The face of the country is exceedingly beautiful, the soil fertile, and bearing oaks and shagbark hickory. Grass and flowers cover the prairies as far as the eye can reach. The hills are moderately elevated and the roads excellent, except for short distances where streams are crossed. . . .
>
> We reached Mineral Point . . . and then drove on two or three miles to General Dodge's. The General received me with great urbanity. I was introduced to

his son Augustus, a young gentleman of striking and agreeable manners. Mrs. Dodge had prepared in a few moments a cup of coffee, which formed a very acceptable appendage to my late dinner. We then continued on our way.[14]

At this point in his journal, Schoolcraft records his idea for diverting the Wisconsin River into a canal that would be used to ship lead from the mines to Green Bay and the East:

The River of Galena rises in the mineral plains of Iowa County, in that part of the Northwestern Territory which is attached, for the purposes of temporary government, to Michigan. . . . The town of Galena, the capital of the mining country, occupies a somewhat precipitous semicircular bend, on the right [or north] bank of the river . . . and admits steamboat navigation thus far. . . . Lead is brought in from the smelting furnaces on heavy ox teams capable of carrying several tons at a load. I do not know that water *has been*, or that it *cannot* be made subservient in the transportation of this article from the mines. . . . It is to be feared the supply of water would be inadequate. To remedy this deficiency, the Wisconsin itself might be relied on. Could the waters of this river be conducted in a canal along its valley from the portage to the bend at Arena, they might, from this point, be deflected in a direct line to Galena. This route would cut the mine district centrally, and afford the upper tributaries of the Pekatonika and Fever Rivers as feeders. Such a communication would open the way to a northern market, and merchandise might be supplied by the way of Green Bay, when the low state of water in the Mississippi prevents the ascent of boats. It would, at all times, obviate the tedious voyage, which goods ordered from the Atlantic cities have to perform through the straits of Florida and the Gulf of Mexico.[15]

In one short sentence Schoolcraft makes first mention of a railroad for Wisconsin: "A railroad could be laid upon this route with equal, perhaps superior advantages."

Schoolcraft wasn't new to railroads. He served on the Michigan Territorial Council which had been considering a petition for a Detroit and Pontiac Railroad. Nonetheless, making this proposal at a time when America had but one steam railroad, which had been operating for only eight months, was a bold idea. He concluded by saying:

These things may seem too much like making arrangements for the next generation. But we cannot fix bounds to the efforts of our spreading population and spirit of enterprise. Nor, after what we have seen in the way of internal improvement in our own day and generation, should we deem anything too hard to be accomplished.[16]

## A PROPOSAL

Schoolcraft's proposal for a canal or railroad that would travel from the Fox-Wisconsin portage through the mining district never became a reality, but it did start people thinking about a railroad that could carry the lead of the mining district to Lake Michigan.

# Chapter 2

## Lead Railroads Come to Western Michigan Territory

**1831–1836**

In the years following Schoolcraft's visit, white residents in western Michigan Territory continued trading with Native Americans and mining lead, giving little thought to railroads. That changed when the United States government began selling land in the territory during 1834. New arrivals came and commenced farming, wheat joined lead as an item marketable by rail, and interest in railroads grew once again. The motivation to build a railroad in the territory was enhanced by news of the rapid expansion of railroads in the East.

What did the residents of western Michigan Territory know of railroads during this time? Most of them, like people in other parts of the country, knew that railroads with steam locomotives had been developed in England in the 1820s and had come to the United States in the 1830s. They had seen pictures of locomotives in periodicals like the *American Traveler*, which in 1826 published a detailed picture of a steam locomotive pulling coal cars on the Hetton Rail-Road in Britain. Some of them might have read Thomas Earle's *Treatise on Rail-Roads Compiled from the Best and Latest Authorities*, which was published in 1830, or taken a look at William Brown's widely distributed but erroneously titled 1831 lithograph *The First Steam Passenger Train in America*, which showed the locomotive and carriages of the Mohawk and Hudson Railway in New York. Those with an interest in the subject were surely pleased when, on January 2, 1832, the *Rail-Road Journal* began publication with a picture on the first page of a locomotive with two operators pulling a carriage.[1] Images such as these,

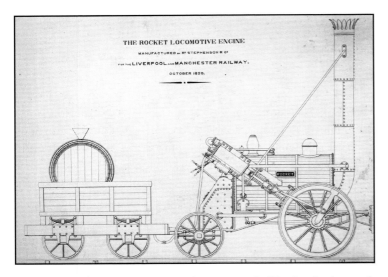

A mechanical drawing of Robert Stephenson's "Rocket," winner of the 1829 Rainhill Trials in England. The Rocket was considered the first reliable steam locomotive.
WHI Image ID 62048

popularized by the literature of the day, were prevalent in the American mind.

By 1834 and 1835 some people in the territory had started to consider the feasibility of constructing small railroads to run from mills or mines to nearby rivers; others were beginning to consider the advantages that would be created by longer railroads that could carry lead from the Mississippi region to Lake Michigan. These early train advocates began to associate themselves politically and geographically with others who shared their views, forming railroad-based alliances that would play a role in the movement for separation of Wisconsin from Michigan Territory. In the fall of 1831 Lucius Lyon began the government survey of the public lands west of Lake Michigan— a step toward putting them up for sale. Surveying as he traveled, Lyon located the Wisconsin-Illinois line, then ran a line north to the Wisconsin River, and using these two lines as axes, proceeded to divide the territory into six-mile-square townships, each township divided into thirty-six numbered, one-mile-square sections. With this grid one could describe the location of any point in the territory—Mineral Point, for example, was located in range 3 west, town 5 north, section 14. In 1832 Lyon began to survey the land east of Mineral Point in a similar fashion.[2]

Not the first steam passenger train in America, but the first run by the Mohawk and Hudson Railroad company of New York. Woodcut by Thomas Earle, 1831.
WHI Image ID 62487

# LEAD RAILROADS COME TO WESTERN MICHIGAN TERRITORY

Early in 1832, Territorial Delegate Austin E. Wing introduced a bill in Congress calling for a new "Wisconsin Territory." The bill failed, but it established "Wisconsin" as the name for the territory-to-be.³ Meanwhile, in Detroit, the Michigan Legislative Council chartered the Detroit and St. Joseph Railroad Company and authorized it to build a railroad across Michigan's lower peninsula. When complete, this railroad would make the long water journey up Lake Huron and then back down Lake Michigan obsolete, saving two days of travel on the journey between New York and western Michigan Territory. Henry Rowe Schoolcraft and Morgan L. Martin of Green Bay were on the council.

The onset of the Black Hawk War overshadowed all other events of 1832, putting a stop to discussions concerning the new Wisconsin Territory. In April, Sauk leader Black Hawk and twelve hundred of his followers, including women and children, crossed the Mississippi River from Iowa to their former lands in Illinois, violating a treaty agreement. In attempting to surrender, they were fired upon by white militia. Black Hawk's warriors retaliated with scattered raids northward as far as the lead region of western Michigan Territory. On July 21 at Wisconsin Heights, above the Wisconsin River, Black Hawk and his warriors held off the Michigan militia under Henry Dodge, now a colonel, while their women and children escaped across the river. On August 2, combined troops under General Henry Atkinson, Colonel Henry Dodge, and Colonel Zachary Taylor caught up with what remained of Black Hawk's party as they were attempting to cross the Mississippi. They massacred one hundred of the Sauk tribe members in what is known as the battle of the Bad Axe, while across the Mississippi in Iowa the Sioux, allied with American troops, killed two hundred more. Only fifty of the original twelve hundred Sauk survived. Two hundred and sixty white soldiers and settlers were killed as well.⁴

After the conflict, the fifty-year-old Dodge became immensely popular as the "hero of the Black Hawk War."⁵ Dodge had come from Missouri to the lead mining district in 1827 with his wife, nine children, and a family of slaves. They had settled at what would become Dodgeville and there began mining and smelting lead. Dodge was the leader of the Michigan Militia, a group of lead miners who had been at the fore of most of the fighting.⁶

The war made the lands between Lake Michigan and the Mississippi safer for settlers and hastened the transfer of their ownership from the Native American tribes to the United States. At the Treaty of Rock Island in September 1832, the United States purchased the Winnebago lands between the Wisconsin River and

Chief Black Hawk, painted by Robert M. Sully.
WHi Image ID 11706

the Illinois line and the Sauk and Fox lands across the Mississippi in Iowa in a sale known as the Black Hawk Purchase. The Potawatomi would sell their lands along Lake Michigan the following year.

In 1833 settlers and speculators began claiming these newly ceded lands. In October Morgan L. Martin and Solomon Juneau of Milwaukee agreed with a handshake to develop the Milwaukee site on Lake Michigan as a village and a port. Juneau had preemptive rights to purchase the land, while Martin would supply the money. In December Juneau also welcomed Albert Fowler, R. J. Currier, Andrew J. Lansing, and Quartus Carley, all of whom had come from Chicago to stake claims.

The year 1834 saw more settlers trickling into the newly opened lands along Lake Michigan. On February 5 the *Green Bay Intelligencer* reported: "Not a mail arrives but brings to some of our citizens letters showing the deep interest of the writers in the character of our country and proposing various questions in regard to the soil, climate, health, productions, settlements, markets, etc."[7] In Green Bay James Doty platted the new village of Astor, and Daniel Whitney boasted of two hotels in Navarino. On the Sheboygan River, Oliver Crocker and William Paine erected a sawmill. At the rapids of the Fox River (Waukesha) Morris D. and Alonzo R. Cutler staked their claims.[8] At the mouth of the Root River (Racine), Captain Gilbert Knapp staked his claim, named it Port Gilbert, built a cabin, and stayed the winter. And at Prairie du Chien on the Mississippi, two new suburbs had sprouted—Uppertown and Lowertown—and were being occupied by newly arrived Easterners.[9] In Milwaukee, Juneau and Martin hosted Byron Kilbourn, business partner of U.S. Surveyor General Micajah T. Williams. Eight months later Kilbourn, Williams, Juneau, and Martin would purchase most of what is now Milwaukee.

Meanwhile, in the lead region, economic growth continued, with the price of lead rising to over four cents per pound. At Mineral Point Abner Nichols, a Cornish immigrant and prominent resident of the village, opened the Mansion House, an inn that catered to a rowdy mining clientele. In August people came from miles around to celebrate the two-year anniversary of the Battle of the Bad Axe. Dodge was the guest of honor and there was an ox roast followed by a dance. On November 10 the United States government's first Wisconsin District land sale took place in Mineral Point. All of the non-mineral lands south of the Wisconsin River and west of the fourth principal meridian were put up for sale. Almost all of the land sold for the minimum $1.25 per acre.

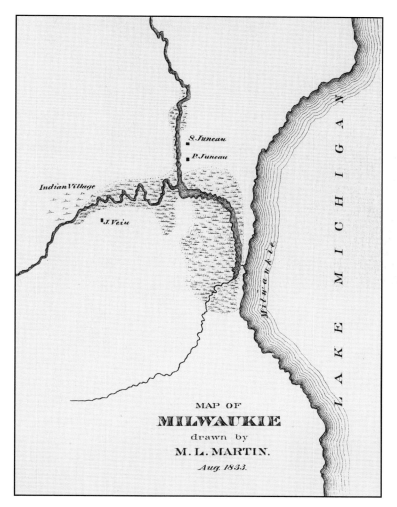

Morgan L. Martin's 1833 map of Milwaukee. Labeled on the map is an Indian village and the cabins of Jacques Veiu, Solomon Juneau, and Peter Juneau. Martin and Solomon Juneau would become partners in developing the city of Milwaukee between the river and the lake.
WHi Image ID 53894

Across the Mississippi settlers were flocking into the Black Hawk Purchase lands (Iowa), and the cities of Dubuque, Bellevue, Muscatine, Burlington, Fort Madison, and Keokuk mushroomed into existence. On June 30 Congress gave the unorganized lands between the Mississippi and Missouri rivers (Iowa, Minnesota, and parts of the Dakotas) to Michigan Territory; in September it created Des Moines and Dubuque counties therein. For the next four years these two trans-Mississippi counties would weigh heavily in territorial politics.[10]

Did western Michigan Territory have any railroads during these early years? The answer, surprisingly, is yes, though they were very different from modern rail lines, and when and where they were built is unknown. Underground "tramways" were built by lead miners in the late 1820s or early 1830s. Tramways carried "trams"—small, boxlike wagons in which miners transported lead inside mines. Out of sight and unnoticed, tramways carried lead ore, otherwise known as galena, to hillside mine entrances or locations where it could be hoisted outside with a winch. Installing tramways was a dangerous business, and required bracing of the quickly dug tunnels:

> When all the mineral is raised that can be found in sinking a shaft, the miner commences drifting east or west in the crevice for more mineral. For this purpose it is sometimes necessary to brace the aperture with timbers to prevent caving. Sometimes a lead is worked out by means of a level; that is, a tunnel being dug in the bottom of the crevice through the hill, and in this tunnel is constructed a cheap railroad for carrying out the contents of the crevice.[11]

These mining tramways were the first "railroads" to operate in Wisconsin. Their immediate antecedents were mine tramways in Britain, which had come into use around 1600, and those of central Europe, which had been operating since the Middle Ages. Their earlier ancestors were Roman tramways, whose tracks consisted of parallel, stone-lined ruts. These were used at rock quarries throughout the Roman Empire, including in Britain. Motive power for all of these early tramways was provided by people or animals.

One variation on tramway technology was seen at Daniel Whitney's shot tower at Helena on the Wisconsin River, built in 1834. A precursor to modern ammunitions plants, the shot tower was a tower inside which molten lead was dropped into a pool of water to form musket balls. Helena, originally known as Arena, had been established by Dodge in 1827 as a place from which to ship his lead. In 1830 Whitney purchased several lots there and began work on the tower. Whitney, who in

1819 had walked from New Hampshire to Green Bay carrying housewares to sell, now owned lumber mills along the Fox and Wisconsin rivers and was developing the village of Navarino at Green Bay. In 1832 construction of the shot tower was interrupted by the Black Hawk War. On July 28 militia under Colonel Dodge tore down the village and used the lumber to build rafts to ferry troops across the river. Only the shot tower was spared. The tower was finished in 1833, and Whitney began to manufacture lead shot in 1834. Whitney shipped his finished product via Green Bay to the east. Subsequent owners would ship it overland to Milwaukee.[12]

The railway in the shot tower was only ninety feet long, miniature in comparison to the steam locomotive rails that would follow it in the coming years. It was used to carry the lead shot from the bottom of the tower to the finishing rooms outside. The rolling stock was a single rail wagon, and the motive power was provided by a single horse. William R. Smith of Mineral Point described the shot tower and its railway in the summer of 1837:

Daniel Whitney's Shot tower at Helena, drawn in 1831.
WHi Image ID 32207

A small rail-way is erected within the lateral drift, communicating with the well, and extending to the finishing house, which is built on the bank of the creek, immediately opposite the entrance to the shaft. On this rail-way the shot is carried in small boxes or cars from the basin or well, by a horse power, into the finishing house; this same power by various machinery is employed in drying the shot in a cylinder over an oven; from the oven the shot is carried into the polishing barrel, and thence the various sizes are passed over the several inclined floors for separation, and taken to the separating sieves; after which the several sizes are weighed, bagged, and put into kegs; a steamboat can lie at the door of the finishing house for the purpose of taking the commodity to market.[13]

Yet another tramway was being installed on Lake Superior's Madeleine Island. There, American Fur Company agent Lyman Warren was moving the village of La Pointe—made up of his trading post and the adjacent cabins—to a new location on the north side of the island (its present site). There he built a four-hundred-foot-long dock that stretched from the company warehouse far out over the deep lake water. On the dock he installed a light railway, which he used to transport cargo to and from the boats.

While these primitive railways were not powered by steam, the ingenious use of such early technologies helped to pave the way for later innovative uses of steam-powered locomotives.

A flood of new arrivals came to western Michigan Territory in 1835. In Milwaukee they arrived on lake steamers from Buffalo or in wagons from Chicago. Bigelow's Sawmill ran day and night to supply the lumber for new buildings. The editor of Green Bay's *Intelligencer* and *Democrat* wrote:

> There is already a town laid out at the mouth of the Milwauky [sic], where they are selling quarter-acre lots at $500 and $600. This fall there will be one hundred buildings up. Fifty people are living there, and a gentleman supports a school at his own expense. A clergyman is about taking up his abode there; Albert Fowler is appointed Justice of the Peace, and the county courts will be organized at the next session of the Territorial Council. Land speculators are circumambulating the country and the Milwauky [sic] is all the rage.[14]

At the end of the year Milwaukee had 130 residents and twenty-eight buildings. Other sites along the Lake Michigan shoreline and in Green Bay were also being developed. At Sheboygan, William Farnsworth closed his trading post, purchased the land at the rapids, and bought Crocker and Paine's mill. At Root River (now Racine), Knapp, Hubbard, and Barker claimed 140 acres. Late in the year they built a sawmill and a store at the Root River's lower rapids. On June 5 the first settlers arrived at Pike (now Kenosha), having left Buffalo on March 25, taken a steamer to Detroit, walked to Chicago, taken a schooner to Milwaukee, and walked back to Pike. By the end of the year there were nine families, including thirty-two people in total, at Pike River Village.[15] At Green Bay, Doty was building the Astor House, a twenty-thousand-dollar hotel. It would be three stories high—the largest hotel in the West—and painted white with green shutters. At the Fox-Wisconsin portage, Whitney's Portage Canal Company constructed a towpath, and then dug a channel through which small boats could pass in times of high water between the Fox and Wisconsin rivers.[16] Meanwhile, lead miners were enjoying record production and a good price of five cents per pound. Mineral Point's six hundred residents raised $575 for a new county courthouse, and local resident John Philips built a brewery.

# LEAD RAILROADS COME TO WESTERN MICHIGAN TERRITORY

The government land sales held in Green Bay in August included the coveted tracts at Milwaukee.[17] Among the buyers were Martin (for himself and Juneau), William B. Ogden, and George Smith of Chicago. Even Schoolcraft participated:

> The rage for investment in lands was now manifest in every visitor that came from the East to the West. Everybody, more or less, yielded to it. I saw that friends, in whose prudence and judgment I had confided for years, were engaged in it. . . . I . . . yielded partially, and in a moderate way to the general impulse, by making some investments in Wisconsin. . . . I embarked in a steamer for Green Bay—where I attended the first land sales, and made several purchases.[18]

It also looked to be a profitable investment for the principle financiers, bringing in money at a quick turnaround. Elizabeth T. Baird recalled:

> Mr. William Ogden, who in after years was called the railroad king, was the most prominent man among the speculators. He bought largely of land at government prices, and would sell the same property at auction in the evening. The purchases were very largely made for speculation.[19]

Out of those speculators vying for land in Milwaukee, one man in particular rose to prominence. Byron Kilbourn, who bought on behalf of himself and his partner, Micajah T. Williams, would emerge as a key player in the transformation of Milwaukee from a plot of undeveloped swampland along the Milwaukee River to a full-fledged, densely populated city. Born in Connecticut and raised in frontier Ohio, Kilbourn followed in his father's footsteps to become a land surveyor.[20] When Kilbourn was sixteen years old, his father, an Episcopalian deacon, went bankrupt. Kilbourn left home with his father's permission, virtually penniless, to find work. In time he was hired as a surveyor on the ambitious Ohio canal projects that were to connect Lake Erie with the Ohio River. Under the supervision of canal commissioner Williams, he rose to the position of resident engineer.[21]

Kilbourn was offered an opportunity to work in the West in 1833 when Williams left the canal service to become U. S. Surveyor General of the Northwest Territories. Williams offered Kilbourn a job surveying in western Michigan Territory south of Green Bay. In addition to surveying, Williams wanted Kilbourn to look for an optimal site for a port city on Lake Michigan between Green Bay and Chicago that the two of them could develop together. Kilbourn accepted the job and arrived in Green Bay by boat on May 8, 1834. Over the following ten months, he laid out fifteen townships in the region of today's Manitowoc. Suffering with rheumatism, he wrote Williams of the "excessive fatigue of traversing Cedar Swaps—sinking through their mossy surface into the water and mud . . . the continual wetness of the feet and legs. . . ." This was Kilbourn's introduction to what would become Wisconsin, the territory and state that he would in large part develop.[22]

Kilbourn took time off from surveying to explore the Lake Michigan shore on horseback, looking for a harbor site that he and Williams could claim and develop. The best site was where the Milwaukee River emptied into Lake Michigan. But when he arrived there in November 1834, he found it was already occupied by American Fur Company trader Juneau—the only white resident between Green Bay and Chicago at that time. Kilbourn called on Juneau and found that he was only claiming the east side of the river. That left the west side free for Kilbourn and

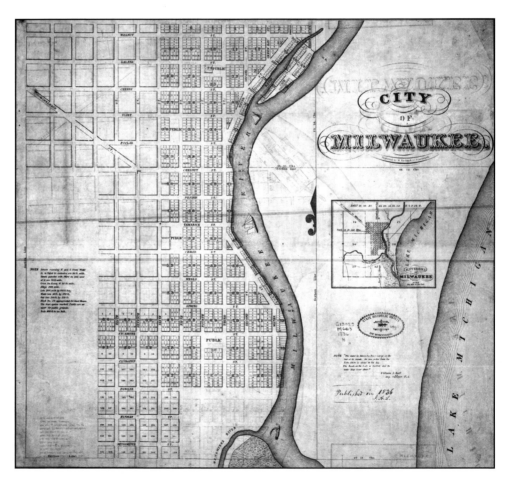

A map of Byron Kilbourn's Milwaukee in 1836. Note that the competing Milwaukee of Solomon Juneau, between the Milwaukee River and Lake Michigan, is blank.
WHi Image ID 9524

# LEAD RAILROADS COME TO WESTERN MICHIGAN TERRITORY

Williams. Kilbourn got back on his horse, rode all the way back to Ohio, and told Williams about what he had found.[23]

Kilbourn returned to Green Bay for the government land sale held from July 30 to August 9 of 1835. Settlers who had squatted on and improved government land were given priority to purchase it; if two settlers claimed the same tract of land, each was allowed to purchase half and was then given a "floating right" to purchase the equivalent of the other half anywhere in the land district. Kilbourn used the "floating rights" of such settlers to purchase some three hundred acres that were largely swampland on the west side of the Milwaukee River. He later transferred the titles into his own name.[24]

In 1836 and the years that followed, Kilbourn and Williams developed Kilbourntown west of the Milwaukee river while Juneau developed Juneautown east of it. The work in Kilbourntown consisted of lowering the bluffs to fill the swamps, grading streets, and selling lots. Single-minded and almost ruthless, Kilbourn made and distributed a map that pictured Kilbourntown as a thriving village, while it showed Juneautown as being almost nonexistent. He laid out his streets so that they misaligned with those of Juneautown in order to isolate his competitor by preventing the building of bridges (which is why Milwaukee's bridges are askew to this day). He built a bridge over the Menomonee River to ensure that arrivals from Chicago came only to Kilbourntown, and he operated a steam launch, the *Badger*, that ferried immigrants from incoming vessels to a single destination—Kilbourntown, of course.[25]

With expansion and speculation becoming the norm, the time was ripe for the discussion concerning a separate "Wisconsin Territory"—and of the railroads that might be built there—to be reopened.

Rail travel had made significant headway in the five years since its introduction into the United States. By 1835 there were some 800 miles of railroad in the East, with new lines being projected frequently. In Massachusetts the Boston and Lowell and the Boston and Providence opened in June. In New York the Mohawk and Hudson and the Utica and Schenectady prospered alongside the Erie Canal. In New Jersey the Camden and Amboy linked New York City and Philadelphia. The Baltimore and Ohio opened its line to Washington, DC, on August 25, 1835, with four trains carrying one thousand passengers. President Andrew Jackson had even dismissed his cabinet in order to watch the trains' arrival. West of the Appalachians, the state of Ohio chartered the Ohio Railroad Company to build a 177-mile link on the Great Western Railway—the railway that Dewitt Clinton had conceived in 1829 to connect New York with the Mississippi. Also in Ohio, the Mad River and Lake Erie began construction at Sandusky. In Indiana and Illinois, the legislatures began to formulate internal improvement bills for the building of roads, canals, and railroads.[26] And in Michigan Territory the Detroit and St. Joseph, which had been chartered in 1831 to build a line across the lower peninsula, had organized and was securing right-of-way.[27]

In western Michigan Territory—which was not yet called Wisconsin—there were cautious proposals for railroads running inland from Lake Michigan and a growing belief that a railroad from the western lead mines to the lake would be built. In April Surveyor General Williams wrote contractor H. Burnham that a railroad should be built westward from Milwaukee toward navigable streams leading to the Mississippi. Milwaukee now actually boasted a Railroad Street (today's Greenfield Avenue). And at Port Gilbert (Racine), Gilbert Knapp was planning a railroad to run inland beside the Root River. Milwaukee County agreed to petition the Territorial Council to aid in the building of this railroad.[28]

Plans for the separation of Wisconsin from Michigan were also underway by October 1835, but these were complicated by Michigan's own plans for statehood. Michigan had already declared itself a state, but Congress would not admit it to the Union because of its boundary dispute with Ohio.[29] Without the area that would become the state of Michigan, Michigan Territory consisted of what was left—today's Wisconsin, Iowa, Minnesota, and the eastern Dakotas, with John S. Horner of Virginia serving as the acting governor.

Michigan Territory elections were held to choose one delegate to Congress, as well as the thirteen territorial council seats. The resulting Seventh Legislative Council of the Territory of Michigan convened at Green Bay on New Year's Day, 1836. Nine of the thirteen councilmen—enough to constitute a quorum—met in a small wooden building on Main Street in Navarino. They elected William S. Hamilton, son of Alexander Hamilton, of Iowa County as president, and Albert G. Ellis of Green Bay as secretary. Unfortunately, the council had its hands tied. Congress would need to approve any legislation it passed, yet Congress could not recognize the council without the representation of Michigan proper, which it did not have. For the time being, the council had to limit itself to making resolutions and sending memorials (requests for money) to Congress.

Even at this early date, railroad interests played an important role in the political maneuvering at the Green Bay Session, particularly in regard to choosing the site for the territorial capital. It began with Iowa County's representative James Vineyard moving that the capital be on the Mississippi River.[30] Since half the population of the "rump" territory—that is, territory left over when Michigan proper was removed from statehood—lived west of the river, this made sense. But representatives from the mining district advocated Mineral Point, while those from Green Bay voted for their own village. President Hamilton, agreeing with Vineyard, called for Cassville (on the Mississippi) to be the capital. The representatives from west of the Mississippi, with four votes, supported Hamilton's choice. One more vote was needed, and it came from Milwaukee County. According to historian Joseph Schafer, the "cement" that held this coalition together was "a project for uniting the Mississippi to Lake Michigan by means of a railway traversing the lead region."[31] A memorial was sent to Congress on January 8 proposing Cassville as the capital.

The proposed railroad from the Mississippi to Lake Michigan was the next item of business at the session. Benjamin H. Edgerton of Milwaukee County, the chairman of the committee on internal improvements, presented his report on transportation needs. Edgerton, who would become one of Wisconsin's leading railroad pioneers, was born in Connecticut in 1811. He was a first cousin of Millard Fillmore, who later became president of the United States. Edgerton's father had moved his family to western New York, then the frontier, where he commenced farming. Edgerton left at the age of twelve for Buffalo, where he took up surveying and began studying to become a civil engineer. In 1834 he came to Green Bay as a surveyor of public lands. Having finished this work in the spring of 1835, he, according to one account, "Rolled his earthly possessions into a bundle, strapped it on the back of an Indian pony, and traveled southward through the wilderness, following Indian trails through woods, prairies, streams, and swamps" until he reached Milwaukee.[32] There he was hired by Juneau to survey the new east side. He lived in the Juneau household, "Laying out and naming the streets of Milwaukee during the day and enjoying Mrs. Juneau's acorn pies in the evenings." He also showed an interest in the village's civic affairs, which was how he came to represent Milwaukee County on the council.[33]

Edgerton's committee report would result in a memorial to Congress that would serve as Wisconsin's transportation blueprint for years to come. The memorial requested an appropriation for surveying harbors in order to build light houses; for surveying the Fox and Wisconsin Rivers in order to remove obstructions at the rapids of the Mississippi; and for building a road from Chicago to Green Bay. But the bulk of the memorial dealt with a Lake Michigan–Mississippi River railroad:

> The subject of constructing a railroad from Lake Michigan, passing through the mining district, terminating at or near Cassville on the Mississippi River, is one which claims the attention of all who take an interest in the prosperity and growth of our country; and we would pray your honorable body to make provision for the survey and examination of the route. . . .

Something may be judged of the importance of this railroad by calculating the immense saving that through its means might be made in transporting lead by way of the Erie Canal to New York. The average cost of transporting this lead to the navigable waters of the Mississippi is thirty-one cents per hundred pounds. From thence to New York it is one dollar and twenty-five cents per hundred pounds. By means of a railroad running directly through this heart of the mining country, the cost of transporting this amount to Lake Michigan would but little exceed the present cost of transporting it to the Mississippi. From Lake Michigan, by way of the Erie Canal to New York, the cost of transportation is but forty-two cents per hundred pounds. By allowing the cost of transportation by the way of the railroad to Lake Michigan to be thirty-five cents per hundred pounds, which t'will not exceed, the cost of transporting the fourteen million pounds of lead by the different routes would stand thus:

> I. By the way of New Orleans.
> 31¢ per 100 for delivering it upon the Mississippi
> $43,400.00
> $1.25 per 100 from thence to New York
> $175,400.00
> $218,800.00
> II. By the way of the Erie Canal.
> 35¢ per 100 to Lake Michigan
> $49,400.00
> 42¢ per 100 from thence to New York
> $58,800.00
> $107,800.00
> Making a saving in the transportation by way of the Erie Canal, of $110.000.00[34]

Edgerton's argument that a railroad would cut the cost of shipping lead to market by more than half was well received. His memorial was adopted by the council on January 13, 1836. Two days later the council dispatched it and other memorials to Congress and adjourned without setting a date for their next meeting. Those seven members from out of town, who had enjoyed Green Bay's warm hospitality for two weeks, rode off in the January cold to their homes—fifty, one hundred, and two hundred miles away. Those from Crawford, Iowa, and Des Moines Counties had to ride through the central, uninhabited stretches of the territory where "camping out was a necessity."[35]

# Chapter 3

# Railroads and the Creation of Wisconsin Territory

### 1836

On January 7, 1836, while the "rump council"—the council overseeing the rump territory—was meeting in Green Bay, Delegate George Wallace Jones presented his memorial for Wisconsin Territory in Washington. Jones had come from Missouri to mine lead at Sinsinawa Mound by the Mississippi in western Michigan Territory in 1827. He served as an aide-de-camp to Colonel Dodge during the Black Hawk War and had been elected Michigan Territory's delegate to Congress the previous October. After presenting his memorial, he obtained a private audience with President Jackson, where he conveyed the wish of many of the residents of the territory that Dodge be appointed their governor. In March, Missouri Senator Thomas Hart Benton wrote the president that Dodge was "prudent, firm, generous, frank, brave, honorable & thoroughly acquainted with Western character; accustomed to Indian character in all its phases; and being in the habit of acting with the regular troops on the frontier & always harmoniously & efficiently." He could as well have been describing Jackson himself.

Senator John Clayton of Delaware introduced the bill for the creation of the Territory of Wisconsin, which the Senate approved on March 29. It went to the House, where Jones drew attention to the fact that the territory had to date contributed 70,000,000 pounds of lead to the U.S. treasury. The House passed the bill, and on April 20 Jackson signed it into law. Wisconsin Territory would officially come into existence on July 3, 1836, with Dodge as its governor.[1] The territory was characterized by rapid population growth, rampant speculation, and an avid interest in who would gain control of the state's earliest big venture: the railroad charter.

During the spring of 1836 people were drawn to Wisconsin like bears to honey. In Milwaukee, steamboat arrivals were double those of the previous year. Some newcomers headed inland to stake claims, while others stayed in the village. Milwaukee was in a state of speculative madness. One observer wrote:

> Every body had a fortune in his pocket, in land or in his mind. Buildings went up like magic. . . . Stores with three sides enclosed and slab roofs went up in a single day. . . . Stocks of goods were frequently retailed in a week and some invoices were sold at fabulous profit without even being opened. This did not last simply for a few days or weeks, but continued uninterruptedly from early Summer until Winter. About sixty buildings were erected and people were half-dazed by the rapid progress the place made toward a city.[2]

Towns and villages all over Wisconsin were expanding at rapid rates. In Green Bay's village of Navarino, Emmons Follett opened a furniture factory. Up the Fox River at Bridgeport (today's Wrightstown), Hoel Wright opened a ferry service and hotel.[3] At Sheboygan William Farnsworth platted the village, and Asael Dye built a two-story warehouse and a 160-foot dock. Lots were selling for $500 to $600—approximately $35,000 to $43,000 in today's dollars. At Pike (Kenosha), the main body of the Western Emigration Company—a joint-stock association headquartered in Hannibal, New York, whose purpose was settlement in the West—arrived on June 1. They had made the difficult journey via Canada to Michigan during a harsh winter.[4]

At Prairie du Chien on the Mississippi, resident Hercules Dousman wrote:

> We are overrun here with land speculators, sharpers, etc., etc. They are buying up the whole country—they have got the people here perfectly *delirious*—there are two or three opposition towns in contemplation on the Prairie alone.[5]

One such sharper, a Mr. Charles Van Dorn, bought 525 acres at the confluence of the Wisconsin and Mississippi Rivers and laid out a courthouse square, parks, and streets named after presidents. He sold shares in the venture at two hundred dollars each. When his investors discovered that most of the land was under water, Mr. Van Dorn and the money disappeared.[6]

# RAILROADS AND THE CREATION OF WISCONSIN TERRITORY

Henry Dodge, first governer of Wisconsin Territory, signed Wisconsin's first railroad charters into law at Belmont in 1836. Painted by James Bowman in 1834.
WHi Image ID 27177

Meanwhile, in the sparsely inhabited central region of the territory known as the Rock River Valley, scattered bands of Indians continued to trade furs for goods and whiskey. There, in April, partners James Doty of Green Bay and Stevens T. Mason of Detroit purchased the isthmus between Third and Fourth Lakes (Madison) for $1,500.[7]

Wisconsin Territory was born on July 3, 1836. On that day hundreds of people lined the road to Mineral Point, welcoming home Colonel Henry Dodge, who was returning from service on the western frontier to be sworn in as governor. Thousands gathered in Mineral Point the next day to celebrate the birth of the nation and to attend the inauguration of the new governor and the secretary, John S. Horner. Robert Dougherty, Justice of the Peace for Iowa County, administered the oath of office to the two men.

Governor Dodge set up his executive office in Mineral Point, making that village the first, albeit temporary, capital of Wisconsin. His first order of business was to complete the territorial government by establishing the legislative and judicial branches. To that end he ordered a census and announced on September 9 that Wisconsin Territory had 22,218 white inhabitants—11,613 east of the Mississippi and 10,605 west. He announced that the territorial legislature would have 13 seats in the Council (the upper house, or Senate), 26 in the House of Representatives (the lower house), and specified the number of seats each county would have in each body. Elections for the seats were held in October, and the first session was opened on October 25 at Belmont.[8]

Many people questioned Dodge's choice of Belmont. Why hadn't he chosen Cassville, recommended by the Green Bay Council, or Mineral Point or Platteville, established communities in the lead-mining region? Belmont, after all, had been platted only four months earlier and lacked buildings and amenities—not an ideal setting for a large meeting. The answer may have been that Dodge was doing a favor for John Atchinson, Belmont's promoter and a successful speculator. The ties between Dodge and Atchinson went back to the Black Hawk War, during which Dodge had ridden to Galena to obtain food for the miners and their families, who were holed up in forts. Atchinson had been the only merchant there willing to give Dodge credit, providing the supplies for the forts. Dodge may also have chosen Belmont to avoid favoring any of the other towns vying to become the new territory's capital. Whatever Dodge's reason may have been, Atchinson's role in the matter became an object of public—and legal—scrutiny. During the following year, Atchinson would take an oath before Judge David Irwin stating that he had made no deals with the governor.

Against the backdrop of Dodge's inauguration and the area's rapid expansion and speculation, excitement was growing about creating railroads in the new territory. Economic conditions seemed favorable. There was record lead production, lead prices were high, and the territory was experiencing unprecedented immigration along with a real estate boom. That fall the new territorial government would

# RAILROADS AND THE CREATION OF WISCONSIN TERRITORY

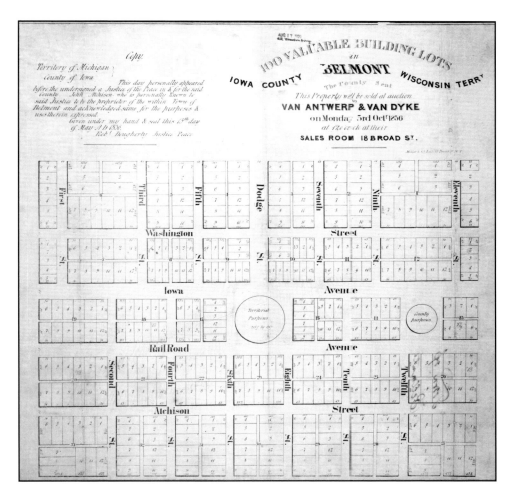

Many of Belmont's newly platted lots were sold at auction on October 3, shortly before the meeting of the first territorial legislature.
WHi Image ID 41792

be granting railroad charters at Belmont. Charters were necessary for anyone wishing to build a railroad outside their own property, and as such they were the prize that all railroad promoters hoped to win.

A charter is a grant of special rights and privileges given by a sovereign power—a king, a state, or a country—to an individual or to a company. Put simply, a charter granted the holder rights to build a public way across privately owned land. In eighteenth-century England, canal companies needed charters to build across private lands held by different owners. English horse-powered railroad companies also obtained such charters, the first being the Middleton Colliery

Railway in 1758. The first charter to an American railroad company was granted by the Commonwealth of Massachusetts to the Granite Railway Company on April 3, 1826, for a two-mile-long track connecting a quarry to a dock. It required the company to carry stone for any person willing to pay a toll, making it the first common-carrier railroad company in America.

Railroad charters in the United States were given by states or territories and adopted much of the English form. They typically named a number of persons who would act as commissioners and sell shares in the company. When a specified number of shares had been sold, the commissioners convened a meeting of the shareholders. The shareholders elected a specified number of directors, who in turn elected the company's officers (president, vice president, treasurer, etc.). The directors authorized surveys, acquired property, hired contractors, and made general business decisions. Railroad charters usually specified the amount of capital stock that would be issued, the price per share, when construction of the railroad had to begin or end, the termini or route of the railroad, and sometimes the amount of tolls or fares. Once a person or group had been granted a charter, they held the right to build and therefore held great influence over the speculators and investors whom they solicited to help build their project—a position of power that many in the new Wisconsin Territory hoped to acquire.

Atchison was one such hopeful. He was planning a 23-mile-long railroad in the lead-mining region from Belmont to the Mississippi River—the Belmont and Dubuque Railroad. The railroad was to transport pigs of lead from smelters along the line to the Mississippi for shipping to St. Louis and New Orleans. Atchinson and his friends saw that such a railroad would be a great improvement over the existing Galena–Mineral Point wagon road. That road, like most others at the time, lacked grading (to reduce the climb over hills), fill (to make low, wet areas passable), and bridges over streams. It was described by Strange M. Palmer as follows:

> The road from Galena by way of Elk Grove and Belmont to Mineral Point, then the great thoroughfare fore [sic] the transportation of a very large portion of the mineral raised in that region, was cut up and rendered almost impassable by immense trains of heavily laden wagons, drawn in most cases by oxen, numbering from four to twelve in a team.[9]

The Belmont and Dubuque was to run parallel to this wagon road between Belmont and Elk Grove. But where the wagon road went south to Galena, the railroad would veer southwestward to Jamestown and Mississippi City. The grade between Belmont and the Mississippi was almost entirely downhill—a definite advantage, since lead would be shipped in that direction. The promoters were also planning a 23-mile branch line running north from Belmont to Mineral Point and Dodgeville. The branch would serve additional smelters and connect with the proposed Milwaukee and Mississippi railroad.

The Belmont and Dubuque had formidable supporters. Two of them, William I. Madden and Pachall Bequette, were sons-in-law of the governor. Madden was a miner, smelter, and farmer at Elk Grove. Bequette was a miner, farmer, and store owner at Diamond Grove. Then there was Charles Bracken, an aid-de-camp to Dodge during the Black Hawk War, who was also a miner and farmer at Elk Grove. John Foley, who had come to the district in 1825 after serving as sheriff of Jo Daviess County, Illinois, was another railroad supporter who was influential in Dubuque County. Other supporters were James Gilmore, a miner at Menomonee diggings; Richard McKinn, a smelter and sawmill operator at New Baltimore; and Francis K. O'Farrall, a mysterious investor who would soon be the largest shareholder of the Bank of Milwaukee. With such backers, the success of the Belmont and Dubuque Railroad seemed assured.[10]

James Doty was also hoping to receive a charter. He was promoting Green Bay's interests, including a proposed railroad—the La Fontaine Rail Road—that would improve shipping on the Fox-Wisconsin Rivers route. The La Fontaine would carry goods and passengers around the Kakalin rapids, where the Fox River drops 145 feet over fifteen miles. It would also tie together Doty's town sites at Astor (today's Green Bay) and Fond du Lac. The La Fontaine Rail Road was to run from the village of La Fontaine at the foot of the rapids to Winnebago City, which was soon to be established on the northern shore of Lake Winnebago. The length of the railroad would only be some sixteen miles. Freight and passengers would have to transfer between the cars and the boats at both ends, but those who had experienced the earlier difficulties of portaging would not, in all likelihood, mind this inconvenience.[11]

Plans for railways seemed to be brewing in every corner of the state, heightening both the sense of competition and the possibility for less-than-honest politicking. In Milwaukee in midsummer, negotiations concerning a Milwaukee and Mississippi railroad usually took place in Albert Fowler's office, a twelve-foot-square board hut. But on Saturday, September 17, Milwaukeeans crowded into the Shanty Tavern in Kilbourntown—twenty-two feet wide with dirt floors, it was the west side's new public house—to continue the discussion. Awaiting them were village president Byron Kilbourn and Benjamin Edgerton, who had advocated the railroad at the legislative session in Green Bay. The attendees adopted Edgerton's plan for a railroad running from Milwaukee, via Mineral Point, to Cassville on the Mississippi. Some pointed out that grading for such a line would be easy for the first fifty miles, since timber and gravel were readily available. There was also discussion of whether this railroad should be built from local resources only or whether capital should be sought from Eastern investors. The possibility of land being granted by Congress for the railroad was also brought up. The meeting then adjourned for one week.

During that week, Kilbourn's newspaper, the *Milwaukee Advertiser*, reported that the meeting had been favorably noticed outside of the territory. New York papers spoke of it as being of great importance to Wisconsin and to New York. This report was, however, a ploy. The editors had placed advertisements in Eastern papers, which they were now proclaiming to be news. There was another item in the *Advertiser* that week that may also have been a ploy—this one about a charter for another railroad, from Milwaukee to Superior. The *Advertiser* claimed its piece originated from an unknown source in Chicago. The newspaper's editor claimed not to know where the town of Superior was, and disapproved of someone promoting a fictitious railroad. Superior turned out to be a paper town on the Wisconsin River adjacent to the 1832 battleground (Wisconsin Heights, near present-day Sauk City) and was a logical terminus for a canal from the Four Lakes to that river. It was never discovered who placed the ad, and nothing more was heard of the Milwaukee and Superior Railroad. But it did generate some excitement that week, resulting in a meeting at the Shanty Tavern that had even more attendees than the previous week's. These are the minutes of that meeting:

> Captain Samuel Brown was called to the chair, and Byron Kilbourn appointed Secretary, when, after due consideration, it was on motion
>
> *Resolved*. That it is expedient to petition the Legislature, at its next session, to pass an act incorporating a company for the purpose of constructing a railroad, by the nearest and best route, from the town of Milwaukee to the Mississippi River, making Mineral Point a point on said road, if practicable; if not, then so near that place as a feasible route can be found.
>
> *Resolved*. That a committee consisting of fifteen members, including the President and Secretary of this meeting, be appointed, whose duty it shall be to correspond with the people of other parts of the Territory, upon this subject, and to draw up a petition, circulate it for signatures, and present the same to the Legislature, and in general to take such measures as they may deem proper and needful to carry into effect the objects of this meeting.
>
> *Resolved*. That, in addition to the President and the Secretary, the following named persons shall constitute such committee, viz: N. F. Hyer, Hans Crocker, S. Juneau, Wm. A. Prentiss, D. S. Hollister, S. W. Dunbar, Horace Chase, Wm. R. Longstreet, Colonel A. B. Morton, Jas. H. Rogers, B. H. Edgerton, Wm. N. Gard-

# RAILROADS AND THE CREATION OF WISCONSIN TERRITORY

ner, and Thomas Holmes, and that a majority of said committee may transact business.

*Resolved.* That the proceedings of this meeting be signed by the President and Secretary, and published in such papers as are friendly to the project.

Byron Kilbourn, Secretary[12]

The petition drive for the Milwaukee and Mississippi railroad was underway.

Wisconsin's first legislative assembly convened at Belmont on October 25. Legislators had been arriving for days, most of them staying at Atchinson's boarding house. The accommodations for Brown County's five representatives and their unknown number of lobbyists were typical—a 15 x 20 foot unheated, unfurnished room without beds.[13] The session began with Reverend Mazzuchelli delivering an opening prayer. Henry S. Baird of Green Bay was elected the president of the council and Peter Engle of Dubuque was voted speaker of the house. Governor Dodge delivered the opening address. He reminded the legislators that they were to lay out the judicial districts and recommended that they memorialize Congress for preemption laws, improved waterways, surveys for harbors, lighthouses, and a railroad from Lake Michigan to the Mississippi. Regarding the latter, the governor stated that

> the construction of a rail-road, commencing at some suitable point on the Mississippi, in this Territory, passing through the mining country to the Rock river, and direct to lake Michigan, is a subject of great interest to the citizens of this Territory, who have strong claims on the patronage of the Government in granting a donation in land for that important purpose.[14]

The "claims on the patronage of the government" he referred to came from taxes paid in lead for seven years. The "granting a donation in land" would follow what Congress had already done in several states where proceeds of the sale of alternate sections of government land were used to fund construction projects. After further recommendations, the governor concluded his address by saying he would agree to whatever the legislature decided in choosing a territorial capital.[15]

The choosing of a capital was the main item of business, but here again, railroads would play a role in determining the battle lines. The nominated cities were Burlington, Dubuque, Cassville, Mineral Point, Milwaukee, Helena, Racine, Belmont, Platteville, Astor, Fond du Lac, Wisconsinapolis, Wisconsin City, Madison City, and City of the Four Lakes. The most noticeable promoter was Doty, who had arrived on November 2 with plats for Fond du Lac, City of the Four Lakes, and Madison City and had made himself popular by distributing buffalo robes among the legislators.[16] Doty realized that the railroad-based alliance of Des Moines County, Iowa County, and Milwaukee County—which had successfully promoted Cassville at the Green Bay session—no longer held sway. Dubuque County, which had been absent at the Green Bay meeting, was now present and supporting its own city, Dubuque. Doty convinced Dubuque County to join with Brown County (home of Green Bay) to support Fond du Lac (Doty's development) as the permanent capital, with Dubuque to serve as the temporary capital until the permanent capital was ready. From these machinations it seemed certain that Fond du Lac would become the capital—but it was not to be.

On November 10, John P. Arndt of Brown County introduced the bill nominating Fond du Lac and Dubuque as the capital and temporary capital, respectively, but it was defeated seven votes to six. Joseph Teas of Des Moines County moved

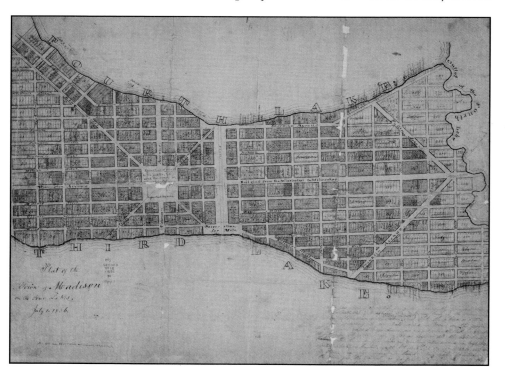

Original Madison Plat Map dated July 1, 1836. It was laid out by James D. Doty and surveyor John Suydam en route to the first Wisconsin legislative session at Belmont. There, Doty succeeded in having Madison designated as the territorial capitol.
WHi Image ID 32207

# RAILROADS AND THE CREATION OF WISCONSIN TERRITORY

to substitute Madison for Fond du Lac and Burlington for Dubuque. This was the old Des Moines–Iowa–Milwaukee County alliance striking back. Doty had played the two trans-Mississippi counties against each other in order to get his preferred choice, Madison, approved. On November 23 the bill designating Madison as the capital and Burlington as the temporary capital passed, seven votes to six. The winning votes from Des Moines, Iowa, Brown, and Milwaukee Counties then went on to defeat motions for substitutions of Cassville, Mineral Point, Milwaukee, Portage, Helena, Racine, Belmont, Platteville, Astor, Belleview, Koshkonong, Wisconsinapolis, and Wisconsin City. On November 28 the bill passed the House of Representatives and Governor Dodge signed it into law.

The selection of Madison as the new capital of Wisconsin Territory was a victory for Milwaukee, for the lead-mining region, and for Des Moines County. On December 10 Milwaukee's *Advertiser*, predicting that the separation of Dubuque and Des Moines Counties from Wisconsin Territory was not far off, described Madison as "the most judicious selection that could be made, when . . . this territory will . . . be divided . . . Madison will be nearly the geographical center of the new state."[17] The selection of Madison as the new capital was also a victory for the proposed Milwaukee and Mississippi railroad. It had been the choice of the lead-mining region, whose residents assumed that a Milwaukee-Mississippi railroad would be more promising for shipping lead to Lake Michigan than the still-to-be-improved Fox-Wisconsin waterway. Proof of the railroad's complicity in the winning alliance is found in a letter written by Brown County Representative Albert G. Ellis of Green Bay on November 10:

> This measure has been brought about by an arrangement between the Des Moines and Milwaukee members, agreed to by the *Iowans* (Iowa County, e.g. lead region representatives). The idea of your Milwaukee and Mississippi Railroad has had great influence in determining the question, and determining it, too, to the great prejudice of the county of Brown. The bill will no doubt become a law; unless the Executive should veto it; this is confidently expected by some—but I rather doubt it.[18]

❖ ❖ ❖ ❖ ❖ ❖

In December, as promised, railroad charters were taken up by the legislature at Belmont, and according to one observer, "There were many desired."[19] The results were at least as surprising as the final choice of Madison as capital. Of the several charters requested, the territory granted only two. The first went to Doty's La Fontaine Rail Road Company, and was signed into law on December 3. It dictated that the termini of the railroad would be Winnebago City and La Fontaine and specified three directors (commissioners): Doty, his cousin Morgan L. Martin, and one David Jones.[20] It authorized the company to acquire capital stock in the amount of fifty thousand dollars, to be sold in shares of fifty dollars each. Construction was required to begin before July 4, 1837, and the railroad was to be completed within five years of that date. The legislature reserved the right to limit the rates charged by the company once the railroad began operation.

The second charter, granted on the last day of the session, was for Atchinson's Belmont and Dubuque Rail Road Company. Atchinson had been the fiscal agent for the legislative session, and had been authorized on December 3 to advance money to defray its costs. Conceivably, this may have had some bearing on this railroad being chartered.[21] It wasn't the first time Atchinson's name had been associated with possible favoritism by Wisconsin's ruling body. But the situation had changed in light of Madison's promotion as state capital. The railroad's promoters had been counting on the village of Belmont becoming the capital in order to supply the railroad with passenger traffic. That having failed, they now claimed to be dependent on a railway to transport lead. The charter gave the Belmont and Dubuque Rail Road Company the power to

> construct a single or double track railroad from the town of Belmont, in Iowa County, to the nearest and most eligible point on the Mississippi River within the Territory; and they (the company) shall have power to extend the railroad if they shall deem it expedient, from Belmont to Mineral Point, and from thence to Dodgeville in the said county of Iowa, with power to transport, take and carry property by the power and force of steam, of animals, or of any other mechanical or other power, or of any combination of them; and they shall also have power to make, construct and erect such warehouses, toll-houses, carriages, cars, and all other works and appendages necessary for the convenience of said company in the use of said railroad . . . provided, that the toll on any species of property shall not exceed fifteen cents per ton per mile, nor upon any passengers more than six cents each per mile.[22]

Nine commissioners would handle the affairs of the company until it organized. Then a board of seven directors would be elected. The company was to be capitalized at $250,000 by selling shares of $100 each—a much larger venture than Doty's. Any disputes over expropriation (obtaining right-of-way) were to be referred by a justice of the peace to the sheriff of the county in question, who would summon a jury of 18 persons to hear the case. The company was only to own land sufficient for construction; holding and speculating in other lands was forbidden.[23]

# RAILROADS AND THE CREATION OF WISCONSIN TERRITORY

Surprisingly, the proposed Milwaukee and Mississippi Railroad did not receive a charter. Milwaukeeans had submitted bundles of petitions "as thick as your arm."[24] But their Green Bay opponents, who still hoped to develop the Wisconsin-Fox waterway for the shipment of lead, and the promoters of the Belmont and Dubuque, who were opposed to any attempt to ship lead over the lakes in favor of their proposed overland route, kept the measure from ever reaching the table. Councilman Ellis was truculently opposed to its consideration, while Milwaukee County Representative Alanson Sweet was indifferent, saying the petition was "Kilbourn's speculation," and that Milwaukee County Representative Sheldon, to whom the petitions had been entrusted, lived in Janesville and therefore handled the task ineffectively on purpose. He supposed that Sheldon, who handled the petitions for the Milwaukee and Mississippi Railroad, did not support the petitions as actively as he could have.

The Milwaukee and Mississippi railroad, which had helped to make Madison the capital of Wisconsin, was put back in what some considered its proper place. Although it did not receive a charter, a legislative committee chaired by Charles Durkee of Pike (Kenosha) drafted a memorial to Congress requesting an appropriation for a survey of the route. The memorial stated that Wisconsin was "unable to determine which is the most eligible route for a road from the various points which have been suggested for the commencement and termination."[25] The legislature had, however, fixed the Four Lakes area (Madison) and Blue Mounds on the route and had suggested the line diverge from the Four Lakes east with one branch running to Green Bay and the other to Milwaukee or Racine—"a compromise," according to historian Joseph Schaffer, "that didn't really satisfy anyone."[26] This memorial passed in the House on November 30 and in the council on December 1. On the ninth day of December, Wisconsin's first territorial legislature adjourned.[27]

# Chapter 4

# The Territorial Years
### 1837–1848

During the spring of 1837 Wisconsin residents began to notice that their paper money—both bills and bank notes—was rapidly loosing its value. This should not have come as a surprise. During the previous summer, President Jackson had instituted his specie circular act, which dictated that government land offices were only to accept specie (gold or silver coin) in payment for land. While this had impeded land speculators, the general public seemed unaffected, and business continued to boom. Then, on May 10, 1837, there was a run on New York City banks, with people demanding specie for their paper. As Senator Henry Hubbard of New Hampshire wrote Moses Strong of Mineral Point, "There is a general and fearful panic abroad in the land. God only knows what will be the final result."[1] Banks around the nation folded, and a six-year economic depression set in.[2] In Wisconsin, specie was scarce, while paper, which was often worthless, was abundant. No one would accept paper notes, especially in payment of debts. Those that owed money and lacked specie, which included most businessmen, were forced into bankruptcy. People who had thought themselves rich suddenly found themselves poor. Wisconsin was without currency and was reduced once again to barter.

Yet railroads continued to be promoted during these difficult years. After all, it cost little to project or propose a railroad, and since such proposals lifted spirits, many people felt the better for it. William R. Smith toured the lead-mining region

THE TERRITORIAL YEARS    43

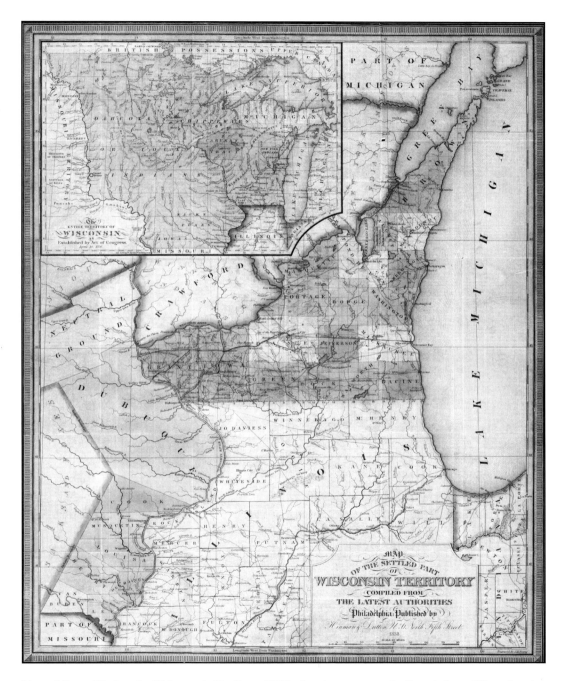

Map of the settled part of Wisconsin Territory, 1838, showing proposed railroads from Milwaukee to the Mississippi with a branch to Lake Kegonsa and from Dodgeville to the Wisconsin River.
WHI IMAGE ID 39785

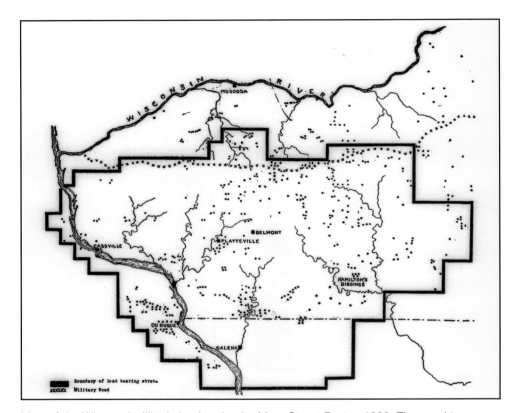

Map of the Wisconsin-Illinois lead region by Mary Stuart Foster, 1839. The need to transport lead was one argument for a railroad.
WHi Image ID 42835

during the summer of 1837 and published an account of his journey in which he mentioned several proposed railroads, one of which connected with the proposed Belmont and Dubuque Railroad at Dodgeville:

> [O]ne [town is] nearly opposite Pine [R]iver and Long Island called "Buchanan"; from this town, which is at the mouth of Mineral [C]reek, there is a proposed railroad to Dodgeville, passing through a mineral region, and thus giving the means of transportation of heavy material to water carriage on the Wisconsin.[3]

Smith's book included a map showing the Belmont and Dubuque, the La Fontaine, and several other unnamed railroads. One, labeled "proposed railroad," was the Milwaukee and Mississippi. It was depicted as running westward from Milwaukee, passing north of Prairie Village (Waukesha), crossing the Rock River at its junction with the Crawfish, and arriving at Madison City. From there the line ran north around Fourth Lake (Lake Mendota) to the projected City of the Four Lakes (near Middleton). From there it was shown running west to Moundville (Blue Mounds), crossing the Belmont and Dubuque at Dodgeville, and then forking in Grant County with a northern branch to Mississippi Landing—another projected city that failed to materialize—and a southern branch to Cassville. A branch line left the main line between the City of the Four Lakes and Moundville and headed southeasterly to First Lake (Lake Kegonsa). Smith's map of these routes was not, of course, entirely accurate, as plainly evidenced by the fact that the Milwaukee and Mississippi had yet to obtain a charter. Smith was indulging in boosterism—promoting Wisconsin and encouraging people to settle there, even if it meant stretching the truth.

Though building a railroad would have been an expensive undertaking, merely promoting a railroad was not costly. Proposing a route and a name, petitioning Congress for surveys or for grants of land, and obtaining railroad charters from the territorial legislature could all be done quite reasonably. During the years of the economic downturn, many memorials were put before Congress for a survey of the proposed Milwaukee and Mississippi Railroad. The representatives at the Green Bay rump council had sent the first of these memorials early in 1836. Delegate George W. Jones drafted another at about that same time. Both requests were taken into consideration by Congress that summer, but no action followed. That fall Wisconsin's first legislature at Belmont sent another memorial, but again there were no results.

In 1837 Jones presented Congress with a petition from the village of Sinipee on the Mississippi requesting a survey for a railroad from Milwaukee, via Sinipee, all the way to the Pacific Ocean. Its reading "produced a great laugh and hurrah in the House," but it also set some wheels turning.[4] The next spring, citizens of the lead-mining region and of Milwaukee memorialized Congress for a survey from Milwaukee to Dubuque. The memorial was signed by over 250 people, including Charles Bracken and Peter Parkinson of the lead-mining region and Solomon Juneau, Hans Crocker, and Lemuel W. Weeks of Milwaukee. It referred to two subjects the memorialists felt helped Wisconsin's cause: the lack of a need for inclined planes (grades on which railroad cars are pulled up an incline by cables powered by stationary steam engines) and the idea for a transcontinental railroad:

*Memorial To Congress By Grand Jurors Of Iowa County And Others*
April 19, 1838

To the Honorable Senate and House of Representatives of the United States in Congress Assembled:

[Y]our petitioners . . . represent that the connexion [sic] of Lake Michigan with the Mississippi River . . . by means of a Rail Road is of such importance . . .

that your honorable bodies will grant our prayer by immediately appointing an Engineer to locate a route. . . .

The length of the . . . Rail Road would only be about one hundred and fifty miles, passing over a country so admirably adapted by nature for its construction as not to require a single plane upon which locomotive power would not be most advantageously applied. . . . This Road would . . . constitute a permanent link in the great chain of direct steam communication between the extreme East and Far West, which the determined spirit of American enterprise has decreed shall speedily connect the waters of our two opposite oceans. . . .

Your memorialists conclude . . . in consideration of the . . . sale and settlement . . . of the public domain, and in . . . keeping in check the formidable number of Indians, now congregated by order of the United States, west of the Mississippi River.[5]

Responding to these requests, Congress passed a law in July 1838 that appropriated two thousand dollars for a survey of a railroad from Milwaukee to Dubuque.[6] Two months later a party of United States topographical engineers arrived in Milwaukee. The *Milwaukee Sentinel* of September 18, 1838, reported the news in hopeful tones:

*Lake Michigan & Mississippi Railroad*
Three government engineers arrived here last evening, with the necessary apparatus, and will immediately commence the survey of a route for a railroad from this place to the Mississippi River, for which purpose the government made an appropriation of $2,000, at the last session of Congress. Of the vast importance of this work to the Territory, as well as the whole Northwest, we have before spoken, and are pleased to see this early attention paid by the government to this important work.[7]

Unfortunately, this work was soon suspended. Byron Kilbourn explained the reasons behind this decision in a letter to John Plumbe of Sinipee:

The Engineers assigned to this work, after locating about twenty miles of the line, were directed to take charge of the roads for which appropriations had been made, in consequence of which their further operations on the Rail Road have been suspended.[8]

This aborted 20-mile survey was the first railroad survey to be undertaken in Wisconsin. For several years, the territory would ask Congress for money to continue the survey—requests Congress would continue to ignore.

Despite Congress's continued denials to fund railroad surveys, and despite the economic depression that by itself prevented the selling of railroad stock and the actual building of a railroad, Wisconsin Territory continued to grant railroad charters, beginning with one for the Root River Rail Road Company, signed by Governor Dodge at Burlington, Iowa, on January 11, 1838. This charter authorized the company to build a railroad from Ball's Mill on the Root River to the head of the river's lower rapids, with the privilege of later extending the line to Racine. Capitalization was set at $25,000, with shares at $50 each; there were to be five commissioners, and construction was to begin on or before July 4 of that year, and to finish within five years.

There was also at this time a petition for a charter for a railroad from Racine to Janesville.[9] The petitioners included Lorenzo Janes, Bushnell B. Cary, Elias Smith, Consider Heath, Eugene Gillespie, H. D. Wood, Charles Leet of Racine County, Samuel F. Phoenix of Walworth County, and Henry F. Janes of Rock County, for whom Janesville is named. Given the village's relative lack of development, a railroad to Janesville was a brash undertaking—Edward D. Holton, who visited Janesville at this time, wrote:

> At what is now the site of Janesville, I tarried a number of days. There were there then three log houses and one log blacksmith shop. John P. Dickson, Esq., just elected a member of the Legislature from the city of Janesville, entertained travelers in his more than usually ample log house. Old Squire Janes, a frontier man from whom the town took its name, was then residing there. At that time there were no bridges, and but few roads in the whole country.[10]

The promoters of the proposed Racine and Janesville line felt that a survey would help their request for a charter; because of Congress's reticence in granting funds for other surveys, they undertook to perform one themselves. Unfortunately, they ran out of funds before the survey was completed.

If funds were lacking in the territory at this time, the granting of charters was not. In January 1839 Wisconsin Territory granted its fourth railroad charter, this time to the Michigan and Rock River Railroad Company, authorizing the building of a railroad "from Rock River at Illinois State line [Beloit]" to a "point on Lake Michigan in the town of Southport [Kenosha]." The company was capitalized at one hundred thousand dollars with shares of one hundred dollars each. Construction was required to start within three years and to finish within ten.[11] But this company too failed to develop beyond the charter stage, again due to a lack of funds.

48    STEAM AND CINDERS

The territory's fifth charter, granted to the Pekatonica and Mississippi Railroad Company on March 6, 1839, authorized the company to construct a railroad from Mineral Point to some point on the Mississippi River in Grant County. Capital was set at fifty thousand dollars in shares of one hundred dollars each; construction was to begin within three years and finish within ten. The company was to charge three cents per mile for passengers and five cents per ton-mile for freight. As with a toll road, the company would be required to allow any person using suitable and proper carriages to use the railroad, in this case for a rate of one and a half cents per ton-mile. This idea of a toll railroad was popular at the time, but it never became a reality for this or any railroad. The territory or future state had the power to purchase the railroad at any time upon payment of the full cost of construction and equipment, plus a bonus in the amount of seven percent of those costs. Sadly, this railroad was yet another enterprise that never went beyond receiving a charter.

In addition to new charters, proposed railways that had failed to gain a charter continued to receive support, sometimes from high places. On December 3, 1839, Governor Dodge used his opening address to the legislature to show his favor for the Mississippi and Milwaukee railway, saying:

> The country between the Mississippi and the lake is well adapted to the construction of a railway. . . . The surface of the country is generally level. . . . It would has-

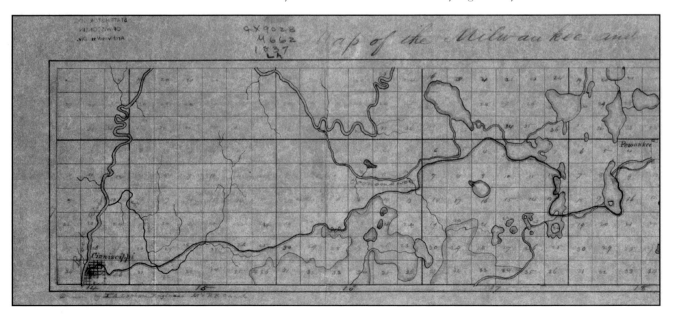

Map of the proposed route of the Milwaukee and Rock River Canal by Increase Lapham, 1837.
WHi Image ID 53818

ten the formation of dense settlements throughout the whole extent of the road, advance the sales of the public lands, afford increased facilities to the agricultural, commercial, and mining interests of the country, and further, it would enable the government to transport troops . . . for the protection of the border settlements against the encroachments of a savage enemy.[12]

These were essentially the same arguments that had been voiced three years earlier, and as then, no action followed. Despite Dodge's and other promoters' continued efforts, the charter for the Pekatonica and Mississippi would be the last railroad charter granted within Wisconsin Territory for the next eight years.

❖ ❖ ❖ ❖ ❖ ❖

Why was it so difficult for the Milwaukee and Mississippi Railroad to gain a charter at this time? A major reason was that many people felt that canals were a more economical and efficient mode of transport than rails. The Milwaukee and Rock River Canal project vied with the proposed Milwaukee and Mississippi railroad as the territory's harbinger of prosperity. Both were undertakings of Kilbourn, who had petitioned for both the canal charter and the railroad charter at Belmont in 1836, though neither was granted. He succeeded with the canal charter the

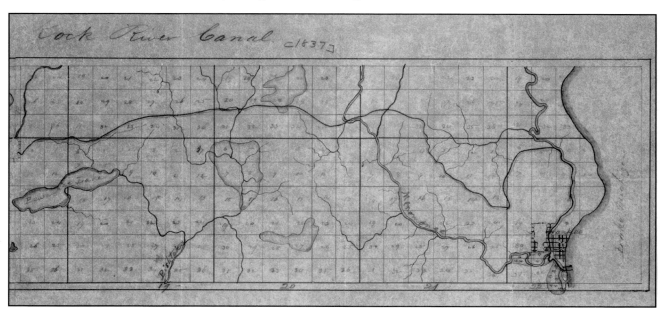

following year at Burlington, where Governor Dodge signed it into law on January 5, 1838. The charter set capital at one hundred thousand dollars, shares at one hundred dollars, and called for construction to begin within three years and end within ten.

Kilbourn and his associate, Increase Lapham, had surveyed the canal route themselves the previous summer. Lapham had proposed using existing lakes and rivers so that the canal itself would be only fifty-two miles long. He had estimated that the cost of a four-foot-deep, forty-foot-wide canal with fifty locks would be eight hundred thousand dollars.[13]

On February 3, 1838, members of the canal company met at Kilbourn's office in Milwaukee. The directors elected Kilbourn president, and Lapham was appointed chief engineer. The new board approved Kilbourn's petition to Congress for the granting of public lands to aid the canal and authorized him to deliver it in person. Kilbourn made the sleigh and stagecoach journey to Washington, arriving in March. A bill for the canal grant was introduced, passed, and signed into law by President Martin Van Buren on June 18. Kilbourn returned to Wisconsin in July, a hero to many but opposed by the settlers of the canal lands, who were unhappy with the legislation for obvious reasons. Congress nevertheless conveyed the necessary lands to the territory early in 1839. According to the stipulations in the grant, the territory would be allowed to sell 139,191 of those acres to the public.

On July 4, 1839, groundbreaking ceremonies for the canal took place in Milwaukee. As president of the company, Kilbourn turned the first spade of earth; numerous speeches followed. The territory's sale of canal lands took place at the same time. All but 210 of the 43,677 acres offered were sold despite the high $2.50-per-acre price.

Enthusiasm for the Milwaukee and Rock River Canal was high, but that enthusiasm soon subsided. As only ten percent down had been required at the land sale, only $12,337 had been realized—not enough to begin construction. Stock sales were slow, and territorial canal bonds hadn't sold at all. Kilbourn's popularity plummeted, even in his own Milwaukee County—he ran for Congress in the fall, but lost.[14]

Construction for the canal finally began in Milwaukee in April 1841. Contractor John Anderson began work on the feeder dam across the Milwaukee River, while William W. Brown began digging the canal near the Chestnut Street Bridge, working north. In December the last section of the dam was closed up. Onlookers watched with excitement as the waters behind the dam slowly rose ten feet. John Hustis delivered an oration and then, with cheers from the crowd, the waters were let into the mile-long canal. Lapham described the water power as follows:

# THE TERRITORIAL YEARS

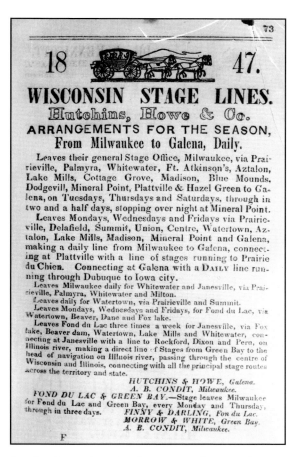

Another form of overland transportation was the stagecoach, still common in 1847.
WHi Image ID 8669

At the head of this navigable portion of the river, [the] dam . . . raises the water twelve feet above high water, and causes a slack water navigation extending two miles further up the stream. A canal of one mile and a quarter brings this water into the town on the west side of the river, and creates there a water power which is estimated to be equal to about one hundred runs of mill-stones; and the canal has a width and depth sufficient to pass almost the whole body of water into the river.[15]

Sadly, although it had a grand beginning, this was to be the extent of the progress that would be made on the Milwaukee and Rock River Canal. It wasn't just lack of funds that brought the project to a halt; profiteering by parties that benefitted from the dam's power was also evident. The dam provided water power for Milwaukee and profit to the Milwaukee Hydraulic Company, in which Kilbourn held shares. On December 10, 1841, Governor James Doty addressed the issue in the legislature:

[T]he work ought not to be continued. . . . The work has progressed to this time to create a water power in the town of which this company or its members are the principal proprietors. . . . I hope it will be in your power to rescue our Territory from the control of this soulless corporation and to cause the fund which was granted by Congress to be employed for the general good.[16]

Kilbourn pointed the finger at others but held himself blameless for the failure of the canal project. Whatever controversy it might have caused, the project had allowed him to sell more lots, establish a water-powered grain mill, sell water rights to incoming manufacturers, provide water power to other industries, and create jobs.[17] During the canal's six years he had built up a loyal following, gained experience as the president of a large corporation, and proven that he could go to Washington and bring back a land grant—valuable skills that he would later use to help create a railroad.

Promoters of the Milwaukee and Mississippi Railroad held a large and enthusiastic meeting at the Milwaukee House, a prominent hotel, on January 22, 1842.

William A. Prentiss chaired the meeting, James H. Rogers and Maurice Pixley served as vice presidents, and Joshua Hathaway and Harrison Ludington acted as secretaries. A committee consisting of Paraclete Potter, George D. Dousman, F. Randall, and William Brown Jr. drew up forceful resolutions that were unanimously adopted. At the subsequent session of the legislature a bill incorporating a Milwaukee and Mississippi Railway Company was introduced but failed to pass. General hostility towards corporations, the opinion that the bill was premature, and opposition from competing lake ports combined to defeat the measure.[18]

Despite this resistance, the best rationale for the railway was economic, in part due to the upswing that by 1843 had lifted Wisconsin—and the rest of the country—out of its long depression. Later that year at a railroad meeting in Madison, Moses M. Strong of Mineral Point maintained that the transportation of lead alone would pay six percent on the proposed Milwaukee and Mississippi Railroad. As he explained,

> The present output of lead is twenty million pounds annually; shipped by way of New Orleans, it costs $2.50 per hundred; from Lake Michigan to the east, it would cost but 50 cents; hence the smelter could well afford to pay 75 cents per hundred to the railroad, saving thereby $1.25, and still give the railroad an annual revenue of $150,000.[19]

Lapham also maintained that lead would justify the cost of a Milwaukee and Mississippi Railroad:

> The great object . . . is the transportation of the fifty-five millions of pounds of lead, copper, and shot . . . to . . . Lake Michigan. . . . This . . . can be best accomplished by means of a railroad from Milwaukee to the Mississippi [R]iver. The two great obstacles . . . are the difficulty of deciding upon the points at which it shall terminate . . . and the want of adequate funds. . . .
>
> The cost of transportation of lead by waggons [sic] from Mineral Point to Milwaukee . . . is about fifty cents per hundred pounds. At this lowest rate the fifty-five millions of pounds, if transported on a railroad, would yield an income of two hundred and seventy-five thousand dollars per annum, which would be sufficient to pay the whole cost of the road in a few years.[20]

Lapham believed it was only a matter of time before Eastern capitalists took notice of this opportunity:

> [I]f we take into account the increase of business consequent upon this improvement, the merchandize [sic] that would be carried from Milwaukee to the mineral

country, the agricultural and other products that would be transported on the road, and the toll derived from passengers, we cannot resist the belief that this project is one that must soon attract the attention of capitalists, even if the people of Wisconsin should now exert themselves much to accomplish so desirable an improvement.[21]

In 1844 a select committee in the Territorial House of Representatives finally prepared a report concerning the feasibility of constructing a railroad from Potosi, on the Mississippi, to Lake Michigan for the purpose of transporting lead. The committee's estimate of the cost to build and equip this road with locomotives, cars, and other materials was four million dollars. So confident was the committee of the economic feasibility of such a plan that they went so far as to project the receipts:

| | |
|---|---|
| 25,000,000 lbs. lead at 37½ cts. per 100 lbs. | $93,750 |
| 1,000,000 lbs. copper at 37½ cts. per 100 lbs. | 3,750 |
| 10,000 tons merchandize [sic] and return freights at $10 | 100,000 |
| 100,000 bushels grain at 12½ cents per bushel | 12,500 |
| 4,000,000 feet pine lumber at $2.50 per M[ile] | 10,000 |
| Total | $220,000[22] |

The committee members who prepared the optimistic figures above believed that passengers and freight receipts would cover the operating costs for the Milwaukee and Mississippi Railroad and that lead was the commodity that would make the railroad pay. But they would be among the last to put forth such a view concerning railroads in Wisconsin. By the mid 1840s it was recognized that wheat, not lead, would justify any new railroad construction—and those promoters who acknowledged that shift would be first in line when the legislature was ready to discuss new charters.[23]

By 1843 wheat production had superseded lead production in gross value in the territory. The population had doubled four times since 1836, and most of those newcomers had come to the state in order to grow wheat. Many had been wheat farmers back in Vermont and western New York during the 1830s. Faced with a growing population and deteriorating soil, they had sold their land at a good price to livestock producers who needed pasture, then packed up to start anew in the West—that is, Wisconsin Territory. In the 1840s these Northeastern transplants were joined by European immigrants from England, Norway, and Germany.

By 1845 it was clear that wheat had replaced lead as the territory's most profitable product. That year, 133,000 thousand bushels of wheat were shipped from Milwaukee. In 1846 the estimated receipts on agricultural products coming into the city were fifty-seven percent of the total, while those of lead were only twelve percent. Wheat had become king in Wisconsin, and many farmers, businessmen, merchants, and wholesalers were convinced that a railroad was needed to carry it to market.

Wisconsin wheat farmers typically broke soil during their first year, planted wheat during their second, then broke and planted twenty to thirty additional acres each year after that. Their farming methods were a mixture of old and new. They broadcast seeds for planting, cut grain with a sickle, and gleaned and threshed the grain with oxen—methods that had been used for thousands of years. But they also made use of a newer device for cutting called a cradle—a scythe on a long handle with tines that caught the wheat stems, allowing the farmer to stand upright while cutting. By the late 1840s horse-drawn mechanical reapers and threshing machines came into use as well, allowing farmers to purchase more land and grow even more wheat. This eventually led to questions about how best to market the surplus that was being produced.

Wisconsin farmers could sell their wheat locally, or they could haul it by wagon to markets at Milwaukee, Racine, or Southport (Kenosha). Such transport, however, was time and labor intensive, often requiring several trips. In a letter to her brother in 1844, Betsey Lucas remarked that the fifteen wagons and forty yoke of oxen that had passed her Genesee dwelling the previous day had left the road "cut up and Muddy." Historian Joseph Schafer described some of the difficulties of early road transport as follows:

> [I]t was a long, tedious, costly business to market a big crop of wheat. Forty bushels made a load weighing 2,400 pounds. With a team of horses this might be hauled, at the rate of twenty to thirty miles per day, over the rough, rutty, dusty, or muddy roads. The number of days consumed in marketing a load of wheat depended on the distance from market and the condition of the roads. For the farmer in the more westerly counties, it was easy to see that a week or even ten days would be required. Multiply the number of days, whatever it was in a given case, by twenty-five, the number of loads in a crop measuring 1,000 bushels, and see what becomes of the wheat farmer's fall and winter.[24]

When farmers reached their destinations, they were met by buyers, with whom they then agreed on a price. The grain was then taken to warehouses, some of them massive in size and scale of operation, and stored for future export.[25] E. D. Holton recalled one of the warehouses of Milwaukee:

# THE TERRITORIAL YEARS

> Mr. Sweet built the Red Warehouse . . . the first warehouse built with . . . better handling of wheat by elevators. . . . Mr. Sweet entered upon the construction of his mammoth warehouse . . . in the year 1847. . . . This building contained the first steam engine employed for the elevation of grain.[26]

Despite their use of the latest technology, these clearinghouses were only part of the solution for dealing with Wisconsin's booming cash crop. As farms and villages proliferated and the lower portion of the state filled in, the need for a rail system became more pressing. On September 5, 1846, an editor at the *Grant County Herald* wrote:

> [A] tide of emigration is moving westward, with "the spray of the [l]ake still on their garments," and another is moving eastward from the Mississippi. There was a "suture" between these two waves. Their edges had not yet united. The river and the lake had been "feeling for each other," and the railroad must unite them, even though "Sin and Death" should get the contract.[27]

Still, Wisconsin Territory's legislature was slow to act. On January 5, 1846, the fourth session of the Legislative Assembly convened in Madison. Numerous petitions for railroad charters were presented. Councilman Moses Strong, who represented Iowa County, later wrote that there was much bickering, that only four charters were taken up, that these were not acted upon for lack of time, and that had there been more time, the charters would probably nonetheless have been defeated.[28]

The inaction of the Wisconsin Legislature and the cutting comments of one Illinois reporter didn't change the fact that Wisconsin was producing mountains of wheat that needed a better means of getting to market. Transportation had become the bottleneck slowing the territory's growth. Legislators could postpone action for only so long when wheat farmers were crying long and loud for better transportation and businessmen and promoters wanted to provide it. Wisconsin was becoming ripe for railroad development.

❖ ❖ ❖ ❖ ❖ ❖

The time was finally right for railroads in Wisconsin.[29] Although eight years had elapsed since the territory had granted a railroad charter, the legislators who convened in the territorial capitol in Madison on January 4, 1847, recognized the changes that had taken place, saw that transporting wheat would make a railroad profitable in a way that transporting lead never could, and were finally willing, if not eager, to establish a railroad in Wisconsin.

Councilman Strong of Mineral Point was involved in the railroad-related events at this session. As he stated in his account of the proceedings, written years later, "The subject of railroads . . . excited more interest than any other matter except . . . [s]tate government."[30] Strong went on to describe the legislators' first railroad charter grant at this session, as well as the reasoning behind it:

> The first bill upon this subject . . . incorporated the Sheboygan and Fond du Lac Railroad Company. . . . The bill . . . passed . . . without serious opposition . . . probably in consequence of a prevalent opinion that a railroad from Sheboygan to Fond du Lac was a visionary chimera, and that if ever built, it could not come in competition with a road extending west from Milwaukee, Racine, or Southport.

The ease of the first charter's passage was followed by a much more difficult decision. Milwaukee, Racine, and Southport were all vying for a charter for a railroad across the territory, but it was widely recognized that with limited resources available, only one such railroad could be built. Each of these communities wanted that railroad for itself. In Strong's words, "A proposition to authorize one to be built from either Milwaukee, Racine, or Southport westward, was by many of the citizens of the points not named, regarded as a direct blow at their prosperity."[31]

The legislators attempted to redress this problem by chartering a transterritorial railroad without specific end points:

> [T]he joint committee reported a bill to incorporate "the Lake Michigan and Mississippi Railroad Company." . . . The company was authorized to locate and construct a railroad from such eligible point south of township number 8, on Lake Michigan, to such eligible point on the Mississippi River, in the county of Grant, as shall be determined upon by a vote of the stockholders.[32]

Although the charter was granted, the resulting company would ultimately fail to incorporate because it needed to specify specific endpoints from which to draw investors.

Meanwhile, another charter had taken center stage. Milwaukeeans—led by Kilbourn, who had petitioned for the Milwaukee and Mississippi Railroad in 1836 and led the failed and controversial Milwaukee and Rock River Canal Company—had realized the difficulties they would face in obtaining a charter for a Milwaukee and Mississippi Railroad at this session. As a result they were playing a low hand—asking only for a twenty-mile-long railroad from Milwaukee to Waukesha. If they anticipated later extending this railroad to the Mississippi,

# THE TERRITORIAL YEARS

they kept quiet about it. Their bill passed, but not without serious contention in the House, as evidenced by the following passage from Moses Strong's *History of the Territory of Wisconsin*:

> The bill [to incorporate the Milwaukee and Waukesha Railroad Company] introduced by Mr. Turner passed the Council without serious opposition. When the bill came into the House, it met with serious opposition and repeated delays; it was finally ordered to a third reading by a vote of 14 to 11, but when the vote was taken on its passage it was defeated by a vote of 12 to 14. Its friends, however, obtained a re-consideration and it finally passed by a vote of 13 to 12.[33]

Their ruse had worked, but barely. Though no one knew it at the time, the promoters of the Milwaukee and Waukesha Railroad had received their golden ticket—the charter from which Wisconsin's first actual railroad, the Milwaukee and Mississippi Railroad, would be built.

On February 3 the last charter of the session was granted to the Fond du Lac and Beaver Dam Railroad Company with no opposition. Thus four new railroad companies emerged from the 1847 legislature: the Sheboygan and Fond du Lac, the Lake Michigan and Mississippi, the Fond du Lac and Beaver Dam, and the Milwaukee and Waukesha.

The charter for the Milwaukee and Waukesha had been drafted by Alexander Randall of Waukesha, who would be governor of Wisconsin by the time of the Civil War and for whom Camp Randall in Madison is named. It was similar to the territory's eight previous railroad charters, although it referred to Waukesha by its former name of Prairieville:

> *An Act To Incorporate The Milwaukee And Waukesha Railroad Company*
> Be it enacted by the Council and House of Representatives of the Territory of Wisconsin:
> SEC. 1. That William A. Barstow, Norman Clinton, Alexander W. Randall, and Alexander F. Picett, of Waukesha county, and Paraclete Potter, Daniel Wells, Edward D. Holton, Byron Kilbourn, and Lemuel W. Weeks, of Milwaukee [C]ounty, be and they are hereby appointed commissioners, under the direction of a majority of whom, subscriptions may be received to the capital stock of the Milwaukee and Waukesha Railroad Company....
> SEC. 2. That the capital stock of said company shall be one hundred thousand dollars, in shares of one hundred dollars each; and as soon as one thousand shares of stock shall be subscribed, and five dollars on each share actually paid in ... the subscribers of such stock ... shall be and are hereby declared and created a

body corporate and politic, by the name and style of "Milwaukee and Waukesha Railroad Company."

SEC 8. The said company shall have power to locate and construct a single or double track railroad, from such eligible point in the city of Milwaukee, to such eligible point in the village of Prairieville, Waukesha [C]ounty, as shall be determined upon by a vote of the stockholders . . . and shall have power to transport, take, and carry property and persons upon the same, by the power or force of steam, animals, or of any mechanical or other power, or of any combination of them; and they shall also have power to make, construct, and erect all such side-tracks, turn-outs, and connecting-tracks, and also all such warehouses, toll-houses, machine-shops, carriages, cars, and other works and appendages as may be necessary for the convenience of said company to the use of the said railroad; and also to connect said railroad, and operate the same with other railroads and branch railroads in the territory or State of Wisconsin. . . .

SEC. 10. It shall and may be lawful for said company, their officers, engineers, and agents, to enter upon any land . . . take possession of, and use such lands, not exceeding four rods in width, along the line of said route, subject, however, to the payment of such compensation as the company may have agreed to pay. . . .

WILLIAM SHEW, Speaker of the House of Representatives
MASON C. DARLING, President of the Council
Approved February 11th, 1847, HENRY DODGE (Governor)[34]

Wisconsin's territorial period ended with the attainment of statehood on May 29, 1848. With nine railroad charters granted by that time, the people of the territory might have expected to be able to boast of at least one operating railroad—or, if not, that they should have at least one under construction, as the terms of the charters specified. But they had neither. The panic of 1837 and the six-year depression that followed it were partly to blame. But even after the depression lifted in 1842, there had been too few people, too little capital, and too little product in the territory to make building or operating a railroad a profitable venture.

Still, throughout these years the people of Wisconsin continued to discuss, promote, and dream about railroads. Historian Alice E. Smith wrote that "[d]uring the twelve years of territorial existence, it is doubtful if any subject was more widely discussed than railroads."[35] Wisconsin's population had grown twenty-fold during these years, and the acreage planted in wheat had grown accordingly.

With wheat at a premium and exports of wheat to the East growing year by year, the time seemed ripe for the construction of a railroad.

But who would fund it? The people of Wisconsin? They owned land but had little capital. Eastern investors? They might gain control and appropriate profits. Who in the fledgling state would benefit from a railroad—or be hurt by it? Would it be built in time for Wisconsin to keep pace with neighboring states and territories? And would any of the newly chartered railroad companies—especially the Milwaukee and Waukesha, whose charter had been amended at the last meeting of the territorial legislature early in 1848 to allow building to the Mississippi River—catch up with the wheat fervor in time to jump aboard? Seventeen years of proposals, discussions, and dead end charters were enough. It was time to finally raise capital and get to work building a railroad for the brand-new state of Wisconsin.

# PART TWO: THE FIRST RAILROAD

# Chapter 5

## Establishing a Company
### 1848–1849

In February 1847 the Milwaukee and Waukesha Railroad Company had been granted a charter. But six months later there was nothing to show for it beyond a railroad map Byron Kilbourn had made and hung up on the wall of his Chestnut Street office in Milwaukee. To be fair, it *was* an impressive map, depicting railroads radiating from Milwaukee to Dubuque, St. Louis, La Crosse, and St. Paul, all of which, Kilbourn claimed, would eventually be built.

On November 23, 1847, the company's commissioners met at the City Hotel in Milwaukee and elected Dr. Lemuel W. Weeks president and Alexander Randall secretary in order to open the books of subscription to the capital stock. Two and a half months later, on February 7, 1848, in Milwaukee, these officers officially opened the books and received and entered the first subscriptions. Then began the hopeful wait for more subscriptions. The next few weeks and months would tell whether the project would move forward—or be halted in its tracks.

Financing frontier railroads was a challenge. An immense amount of capital was required, but most of the nation's capital was inaccessible, tucked away in pockets back East. Yet railroads in the old Northwest (in what is now Ohio, Indiana, Illinois, and Michigan) had found several sources of funding for building their lines. Foremost among these were private investors who had bought the railroad companies' stocks and bonds. These were largely farmers, tradesmen, and businessmen, and—if their willingness to invest in such a risky proposition was any proof—they were not faint of heart. Their investments, individually and in total, were large, but no dividends were guaranteed. There was always the risk that the railroad would fail and the money invested would be lost. As a railroad matured, it typically had half of its funding in stocks (representing owner equity) and half in bonds (representing money borrowed by the railway against its existing equity). Other sources of investment included U. S. government land grants, state funding, local government funding, and money paid by Eastern banks for securities (stocks and bonds).

By the time Wisconsin started building its railways, there were lessons to be learned from the experiences of other states. State funding of railroads had proven disastrous in Michigan, Indiana, and Illinois, where the states had borrowed and lost heavily on railroads. Wisconsin, in consequence, had placed a clause in its constitution that prohibited borrowing for internal improvements. But local funding was still a possibility. Funding of railroads by local governments had been successful elsewhere and would be legally permitted in Wisconsin. Bonds, on the other hand, were not as easy to acquire. The selling of securities to Eastern banks was difficult until a company had built equity against which to borrow. How the Milwaukee and Waukesha fared in the push for funding would tell investors much about the viability of railroad investments in Wisconsin in general.

On March 11, 1848, Wisconsin's last territorial legislature amended the Milwaukee and Waukesha's charter, authorizing the company to extend its railroad "from the village of Waukesha, in the county of Waukesha, to such point in the village of Madison, in the county of Dane, and thence west to such point on the Mississippi [R]iver, in Grant [C]ounty, as the said company may determine."[1] The amendment extended the original charter all the way from Milwaukee, by way of Waukesha and Madison, to the Mississippi. This was no small gesture—the change granted the company their long-sought approval to build the Milwaukee and Mississippi Railroad!

For Milwaukeeans, it had indeed been a long wait. They had proposed the Milwaukee and Mississippi Railroad in 1835, then failed to obtain a charter in 1836 and 1842. In 1847 they had obtained a charter for a twenty-mile long railroad to Waukesha. Now they could build all the way to the Mississippi. True, the Lake Michigan and Mississippi Railroad Company had received such approval in its own charter at the same time as the Milwaukee and Waukesha, but that company had been unable to move forward.

Other parts of the amendment would help the project make progress. The requirement that the line terminate in Grant County was intentional, made in the interest of the lead miners, whose works were mainly located in the southwestern part of the territory. Part of the amendment authorized the company, when it undertook to build the extension, to increase its capital stock to three million dollars, this larger amount being deemed necessary to build the longer line.[2]

Later that month Kilbourn was elected mayor of the newly incorporated city of Milwaukee, the two parts of which, Kilbourntown and Juneautown, had merged in 1846. Kilbourn's record of service and his entrepreneurial efforts were well-known. In addition to founding the west side of the city in 1835 and his efforts in 1840 to bring water power to the city through the Milwaukee and Rock River Canal, he had also served as village president and city councilman. Fresh in Milwaukeean's minds was Kilbourn's service as a delegate to the state constitutional convention in Madison in 1847 and 1848, where he had served as chairman of the Committee of General Provisions. In this role he had helped to write the Preamble and the Declaration of Rights for Wisconsin's constitution. Now, as mayor of Milwaukee, Kilbourn hoped to usher the railroad into Wisconsin.[3]

In his inaugural address on April 12, Kilbourn attempted to alleviate some of the public's fears regarding the railroad:

> There is in the minds of many an unaccountable misapprehension as to the effect of railroads upon the prosperity of the country through which they pass and the places at which they terminate. Some look upon them as a monopoly, for the sole benefit of those who build and control them. Others admit that they are beneficial to the country, for the farming interests, but injurious to the business towns where they terminate, while others still claim that they contribute to the wealth of commercial points where they terminate at the expense of the whole country, and especially to the destruction of inland villages. None of these views is correct. It may be laid down as a general maxim that whatever facilitates and cheapens intercourse among men, in all their pursuits of business, must be to each and to all beneficial. It is beneficial to the producer, especially to the farmer and the miner, for the price of his commodity will be enhanced in value to the same extent that the cost of transportation is diminished. To the consumer it is beneficial, for the commodities, which he is compelled to purchase from a foreign market, come to him charged with less expense, as facilities are increased and transportation reduced. These propositions . . . are so obvious that every reflecting mind will readily embrace them.[4]

Kilbourn also stressed the need to act promptly in building the railroad, pointing out that Chicago had already started building its own railroad:

Boston enterprise compelled New York to build her Erie Railroad. Will not Chicago enterprise induce Milwaukee to build the Mississippi Railroad? Unless she is content to see the business of the finest region of the country wrested from her grasp, she must do it without delay.

Despite Kilbourn's arguments, "every reflecting mind" did not embrace his views—as was evidenced by the many contrary opinions that appeared in Milwaukee's newspapers.[5]

On May 29, 1848, after twelve years as a territory, Wisconsin finally became a state in its own right.

For most of the territorial years, residents had been opposed to statehood. They were unwilling to shoulder the territorial debt—Congress had given generous support to Wisconsin Territory for internal improvements, including improving territorial roads and building territorial and county government facilities—or engage in boundary disputes with neighboring Illinois or parent Michigan (Wisconsin's original boundaries would have included northern Illinois and Chicago and Michigan's upper peninsula). In an 1845 referendum, the territory's residents registered their opposition, voting against statehood three to one.

However, in the months following that vote, Congress began cutting back appropriations. As President James K. Polk began vetoing bills for internal improvements in the territory, the mood among the area's citizens regarding statehood changed. The benefits of becoming a state—such as a gift of five hundred thousand acres from the government and the right of citizens to vote in national elections—became more appealing. Also important to many was the fact that Wisconsin's admission as a free state would balance the recent admissions of Florida and Texas as slave states.

On April 7, 1846, Wisconsin voters endorsed statehood six to one. A year later they rejected a first draft for a state constitution; one year after that, on April 10, 1848, they adopted a second draft; two weeks after that and two weeks before admission, they elected their first representatives to Congress, their first state officials, their first members of the state assembly and senate, and their first governor, Nelson Dewey. Wisconsin was admitted to the union on May 29. On June 5, the state legislature elected the first U.S. senators from Wisconsin, Henry Dodge and Isaac P. Walker.[6]

The main effect of statehood on Wisconsin's prospective railroads would be financial. Having seen the costly failed investments of Michigan, Indiana, and Illinois in railroads and canals and its own failure with the Milwaukee and Rock River Canal, Wisconsin wrote severe restrictions into its new constitution concerning giving or loaning the credit of the state to individuals or corporations. It established a one hundred thousand dollar limit on Wisconsin's total debt and prohibited the state legislature from borrowing for works of internal improvement of any kind, including railroads.[7]

In the months before statehood was established, there was a surprising lack of support from Milwaukee investors for the Milwaukee and Waukesha Railroad. This had little to do with statehood and everything to do with the latest investment craze, plank roads. Supporting plank roads over railroads was popular idea at the time, as shown in this letter to the editor of the *Milwaukee Sentinel and Gazette* of January 6, 1848:

> Mr. Editor: I have seen much in your city papers on the subject of roads; many are advocating Railroads; that is well; but have you capital to build them, and can you for a great number of years to come induce foreigners to invest in so new a country as yours? If not, why do you not advocate Plank Roads? Ten mile of which can be built for the cost of one Rail Road, and in my opinion they would enhance the value of the farming interest as well as the general prosperity of your city more than Rail Roads. Each farmer could take a small interest in the stock, and pay for it in materials for building, and do much of the labor, thus building up your own prosperity instead of waiting for "dead men's shoes." It is a subject that the present state of the roads admonishes one should be agitated.[8]

Plank roads, also known as "farmers' railroads," resembled large wooden sidewalks; they generally had only a single lane, with occasional turnouts for passing, and they were sturdy enough to support heavy wagons. The first plank road was built in Toronto, Canada, in 1836.[9] The first such road in the United States, the sixteen-mile Syracuse and Central Square Plank Road, was built in New York State in 1846.

The advantages of plank roads were apparent. They were smoother than dirt or gravel roads, they allowed horses and oxen to pull twice the load, and they were usable year-round. Plank roads cost approximately $1,500 per mile to build, while railroads cost ten times that amount.[10] To investors, they seemed like a safer bet. There is no question that they were popular at the time; in fact, Wisconsin Territory had already chartered one such road, the Milwaukee and Lisbon Plank Road

Company (later the Milwaukee and Watertown Plank Road Company), in 1846. Early in 1848, sixteen more plank road companies were chartered as well. In July a legislative committee on internal improvement reported that 1) in time, Wisconsin would have many railroads; 2) that the business to sustain them did not yet exist; and 3) that "a class of thoroughfares less costly in their construction and more practical for every-day use than the railroads was needed in all portions of the Territory of Wisconsin."[11]

1858 ambrotype of the Wade House, a stagecoach inn on the Sheboygan and Fond du Lac plank road (seen in foreground). The road was opened in July of 1852. Shortly after it opened, the Rock River Valley Union Railroad transported its first locomotive, the Winnebago, to Fond du Lac via this road, pulled by as many as 40 horses and oxen.
WHI IMAGE ID 2962

The popularity of plank roads among Milwaukee investors made such roads a serious, competitive threat to the Milwaukee and Waukesha Railroad Company. In the fall of 1848, the Milwaukee and Watertown and the Milwaukee and Janesville plank road companies started construction; meanwhile, the commissioners of the Milwaukee and Waukesha Railroad Company were still looking at empty subscription books. By December the railroad company was in a state of crisis. The commissioners began to consider the possibility that they might fail to raise the amount of money required by the charter to organize. It was then that Commissioner Edward D. Holton stepped forward, as he would do many times in the future. Holton launched a stock subscription drive that he initiated with a personal subscription of five thousand dollars. Over the next three months he canvassed all the potential investors in Milwaukee County, sharing with them his belief that the railroad would be a good long-term investment. He enlisted Deacon Edmond D. Clinton, a farmer and blacksmith in Prairieville (now Waukesha), to do the same in Waukesha County. A trickle of subscriptions began to flow in, and as the weeks went by, that trickle grew into a stream. By April 1849 it appeared that the one hundred thousand dollars needed to organize the railroad company would be reached.

Holton would be a steady, leading presence at the railroad company. Born in Lancaster, New Hampshire, in 1813, he grew up attending local grammar schools while avidly reading books about the West. In the fall of 1838, at the age of 25, Holton came to Milwaukee. Unfortunately, his arrival coincided with the start of the depression. "I spent one day in Milwaukee," he wrote. "Surely a more desolate, down-to-the-heel [*sic*], slip-shod looking place could scarcely be found than was Milwaukee in October 1838."[12] Holton journeyed into the interior for two years to evaluate the country's resources. He returned to Milwaukee in November 1840 and set up as a merchant. In the spring of 1841 he sent the first shipment of wheat ever to be shipped from Milwaukee. Shortly after, he received "a small subscription with which . . . to open a wagon track north-west through to Fond du Lac"—his first experience with road building.[13] During the 1840s, Holton would serve as sheriff of Milwaukee County, help found the Liberty Party in Wisconsin, and work actively as an abolitionist.[14]

Meanwhile, a new source of funds for the planned railroad had been made available. The state had not wanted to go into debt for railroads or canals, as Illinois and Indiana had. But while Wisconsin's constitution forbade the state from funding or undertaking "works of internal improvement," its constitution did not deny local units of government, such villages, towns, cities, and counties, from doing so. So in February 1849, Milwaukee and Waukesha commissioners Kilbourn, Weeks, Alexander Mitchell, John Tweedy, and James Kneeland drafted and conveyed to the legislature a bill that would allow the city of Milwaukee to subscribe to the Milwaukee and Waukesha's stock. The bill, which became law on March 17, 1849, allowed the city to subscribe to $100,000 of railroad stock, which amount could later be increased to $250,000.

Thinking its startup funding was now in place, the Milwaukee and Waukesha Company met to organize in Waukesha on May 10, 1849. Holton had called the stockholders together, but then to his and everyone else's dismay, he discovered that the subscriptions were still two thousand dollars short. He immediately took action. Suspecting that Elisha Eldred, the president of the Milwaukee and Watertown Plank Road Company, might see reason in investing in the railroad, Holton visited Eldred. Holton's suspicions were confirmed—Eldred signed for the needed two thousand dollars. Though a firm supporter of the plank roads, Eldred likely saw plank roads as a feeder to long-distance railroads.

The business of the meeting proceeded, with the stockholders electing the Milwaukee and Waukesha's first directors: Kilbourn, Weeks, Holton, Mitchell, Erastus B. Wolcott, Anson Eldred, James Kneeland, John H. Tweedy, and Edmond D. Clinton. Many of the stockholders wanted Holton to serve as the company's president, but he declined. The directors then elected the forty-eight-year-old Kilbourn as president.

Just as in his mayoral election, Kilbourn seemed the natural choice. He was the only man truly qualified for the job. Lingering concerns about his purchases of Milwaukee land with floating rights in 1835, his questionable tactics promoting

Kilbourntown over Juneautown, and his handling of funds for the Milwaukee and Rock River Canal Company had for the most part been set aside with his election as mayor of Milwaukee. In 1836 he had sponsored the building of Milwaukee's first tavern, Leland's Pavilion, and it was there, under his direction, that the push for a Milwaukee and Mississippi Railroad Company began. Failing to obtain a charter, he then devoted himself to the Milwaukee and Rock River Canal project, bringing to Wisconsin a federal land grant of 166,000 acres that would eventually be used in 1848, when Wisconsin achieved statehood, to pay off the territorial debt. Now, just one year after being elected mayor, he had also been elected president of Wisconsin's first railroad company to go beyond obtaining a charter by selling stock and organizing. Kilbourn was a man who could get big things done, and that was what the new railroad, the new city of Milwaukee, and the new state of Wisconsin needed.

Byron Kilbourn by Samuel Brooks, 1848.
WHi Image ID 2739

Along with Kilbourn, the directors appointed Benjamin H. Edgerton, who had presented the concept of a Milwaukee and Mississippi Railroad at the Green Bay "rump session" early in 1836, as secretary and Walter P. Flanders as treasurer. The directors called for a plan for building the railroad, and they appointed a committee of three—Kilbourn, Holton, and Wolcott—to draft it.[15] Dr. Wolcott was a respected physician in Milwaukee married to Elizabeth Dousman, daughter of Michael Dousman, an investor in Milwaukee land. Wolcott had served as a career surgeon in the U.S. army before retiring to Milwaukee, where he established a private practice and became a partner in the city's first flour mill. He was a highly regarded doctor, as well as a charitable one—he often attended patients who had no means of paying him for his services. As a railroad director, Dr. Wolcott would encounter challenges of a different sort.[16]

After nine days the committee presented their plan in a four-page document authored by Byron Kilbourn, E. B. Walcott, and Edward Holton and entitled "Acts Incorporating the Milwaukee, Waukesha, and Mississippi River Rail Road Company: Together with a Report of the Committee Relating to a Plan of Operations, Adopted by the Board of Directors, Milwaukee, May 19, 1849." The document began with a statement of belief:

> We believe, and we lay it down as a first and fundamental maxim, that the people of Wisconsin, who are or will be directly interested in the construction of a rail road from Milwaukee to the Mississippi, are able within and of themselves, to construct it—And we believe, and lay it down as a second proposition, that being *able* to do it, the true policy of the country is to be consulted by the accomplishment of this great enterprise from our own resources.[17]

The authors of this plan believed that the pioneers of Wisconsin could build and own their own railroad, and that they did not need Easterners to fund it for them. Considering the cost of a railroad and the dearth of capital in Wisconsin at the time, this was a bold statement.

The plan then went into specifics. The road would be divided into five divisions—Milwaukee to Waukesha; Waukesha to Rock River; Rock River to Madison; Madison to (near) Mineral Point; and Mineral Point to the Mississippi in Grant County—all of which were to be built one at a time.

The tasks for building the first division to Waukesha were fivefold, and would need to be followed in order. First, the company would fix the starting and the ending points in Milwaukee and Waukesha, a decision that would be made by a vote of the stockholders, as specified by the charter. Next, the company would survey the country between Milwaukee and Waukesha and choose the route for the railroad. After this, they hoped to grade and gravel the entire division before winter. This would allow for settling during the freezing and thawing cycles, thus producing a more stabile roadbed for the superstructure (wooden ties) and rails. Once the road was graded and graveled, they would lay the ties and complete the bridgework as soon as the frost was out of the ground in the spring. Last, and most exciting, they would lay the track. If all of these steps were completed on time, the first Wisconsin railroad would begin operation by June 1, 1850.

The charter required that a minimum of twenty thousand dollars be expended by February 11, 1850, in order to assure the state that the company was financially established and could raise and expend such funds, and that the Waukesha section of the railroad would be completed by February 11, 1852. They recommended that five hundred thousand dollars be subscribed for each division before beginning its construction. To cut down on expenses, they also recommended that iron rails be bought secondhand and paid for with company stock or purchased on credit. They anticipated that the company would build one section of the railroad per year, reaching the Mississippi River within five years. The authors of the plan concluded:

> Every citizen of Milwaukee, and every citizen in the surrounding country and along the route of the road and within five to twenty miles of it, ought to be a stockholder and interested in the work, if only to the amount of one share, or to a larger amount according to his ability. . . . Every portion of the people on the whole line being equally and deeply interested in the early progress of the work, ought to unite in swelling the capital stock to an amount which will justify the directors in making a commencement.[18]

The Milwaukee and Waukesha Railroad Company had been chartered, authorized to build to the Mississippi River, had sold stock, organized, elected a board of directors, and developed a plan of construction. The time had finally come to build a railroad for Wisconsin.

# Chapter 6

## Milwaukee to Waukesha: Picking the Route

### 1849

Mighty oaks from tiny acorns grow—but only when those acorns are planted in the right location. By the same token, choosing the right route was critical in order for a railroad to get underway and stay solvent. Failing at this critical task would likely cause it to go under. Construction costs needed to be weighed against future ease of operation and profitability when choosing the route. The amount of stock that could be sold along a given line was also a factor. And with resources being scarce, as they were at this time in Wisconsin, choosing a route that could be built cheaply and quickly in order to start bringing in revenues as soon as possible was also paramount.

On June 4, 1849, the Milwaukee and Waukesha's stockholders met in the new Board of Trade building in Milwaukee to address the plan devised by Byron Kilbourn, E. B. Walcott, and Edward Holton. They first decided on the location of the terminal points in Milwaukee and Waukesha and ordered surveys done for the first division. These surveys would help them determine a route between the termini. The directors also increased the company's capital stock to five hundred thousand dollars. To expedite the surveys, the company's board of directors

> adopted the most ready and effective means of organizing a suitable Corps of Engineers, by appointing the President of the Company to be Chief Engineer, and authorizing the employment of such assistants and laborers as might be

necessary to conduct the field surveys and prepare the line of the road for construction at the earliest practicable period.¹

Choosing the president of the company to serve as its chief engineer as well was unusual, but Kilbourn appeared to be the person best qualified for both jobs. He had learned surveying from his father at an early age and had for eight years been a surveyor and resident engineer on the state of Ohio's canal projects. He had superintended the building of Ohio's Milan Ship Canal. And he had helped survey the 52-mile route of the Milwaukee and Rock River Canal. The railroad industry was still in its infancy, and Wisconsin did not have a single railroad engineer at this time, so a qualified canal engineer was the next best thing.²

By this time several routes had been identified between Milwaukee and Waukesha. One of these, the southern route, followed the town line between towns six and seven (along today's Greenfield Avenue) straight west to Waukesha. Another possibility, the northern route, followed the valleys of the Menomonee and Fox Rivers to Waukesha. There were also several routes in between. The directors decided that all of these options should be examined.

On the morning of June 7, engineers Kilbourn, Benjamin H. Edgerton, and Jesper Vliet assembled their crews in Milwaukee at the junction of the Milwaukee and Menomonee Rivers. This beginning point was ideal for several reasons. The land situated at the northwest corner of the junction had been donated to the project, and it had already been determined that the station grounds and depot would lie there. The Milwaukee River would allow vessels on Lake Michigan to access the company's docks, and the valley of the Menomonee River would provide a rail route inland.

Moving west from the meeting point, the survey parties covered the country between the villages along the Menomonee, a process that took several weeks. The directors would report that these surveys were "very minutely made over every part of the intervening country."³ Though thorough, these surveys were preliminary, and were meant only to give a general understanding of the proposed routes' topography. They lacked the detailed measurements of final surveys.

Elevations, even on preliminary surveys, were measured with care. With Waukesha 225 feet higher than Milwaukee, choosing the best climb was important. If a climb was too steep, trains would have to be shortened, lightened, or use helper locomotives. But a gentler route sometimes meant a route that was excessively long and had too many curves. An acceptable balance was found by measuring elevations, a procedure known as "running levels." An axe man, two rod men, and an instrument man would start at the beginning of the line, where the elevation was already known. One rod man would proceed to a forward position, the axe man clearing the way as necessary, while the instrument man would set up his equipment between the two. His instrument, known as a *level*, was a telescope with an attached bubble level mounted on a tripod. Once in position, it was then simply a matter of sighting on the first rod to establish the elevation of the instrument, then sighting on the forward rod to establish that rod's elevation. The rear rod man then moved ahead to a new forward position, the instrument man moved to a new midway point, and a second level reading was taken. The procedure was repeated over many miles with little loss of accuracy.[4]

Kilbourn chose his preferred route based on these first levels, writing in the annual company report, "I superintended them in person for some two weeks or more, until I learned, by levels taken, the general features of the country, and recommended the adoption of a line between the present road and one further south."[5] His surveyors would work several more weeks before finishing and filing their reports. Kilbourn, in the meantime, had been called back to the never ending task of selling stock subscriptions.

❖ ❖ ❖ ❖ ❖ ❖

Beginning in late June 1849, Kilbourn traveled west to the country around the Rock River, "preaching the Railroad to the unbelievers and endeavoring to convince the people that it was in their interest to subscribe to the Stock of the Company."[6] His target audience was farmers, who made up four fifths of the company's stockholders. He offered them several reasons to underwrite the enterprise. The investment itself would be repaid, he claimed, with interest, and the cost of hauling their wheat to market would also drop. Milwaukee's *Daily Wisconsin* backed up his offer:

> A word to Wheat Growers—Saving of transportation on a Railroad—During the week . . . at least 100,000 bushels of wheat were brought into this city by [wagon] teams . . . Most of the wheat comes from a distance of from fifteen to one hundred and twenty miles . . . allowing the average cost . . . 12½ cents per bushel . . . by railroad, 7 cents per bushel . . . such a saving would build a road which the people might own in a few years.[7]

Another advantage was that the value of the farmer's land would increase. According to the October 26 *Milwaukee Sentinel and Gazette*, "Every Farmer who subscribes $500 to this great State enterprise would receive back more than that sum in the increased value of his Real Estate, in consequence of the construction of the Road."[8]

Yet many farmers remained skeptical. They saw that the railroad would have a monopoly on their business and thus be in a position to charge excessive tolls. Railroads were corporations, which to many people meant large, faceless entities that would ignore them when they voiced their needs. Director Edward D. Clinton had addressed these concerns in a letter published June 6, 1849, in the *Milwaukee Sentinel and Gazette*, first acknowledging the farmer's concerns and then assuring them of the value—and necessity—of taking out stock in the company:

> The interests of farmers have always been subject to a ruinous monopoly, which monopoly, as used by the capitalists, has always been diametrically opposed to the ultimate success of the farmer. No one will for a moment contend that we have not had to contend with this monopoly; and yet the farmers of this country are those who hold the power to do away with this burden upon their energies. . . . The design of this railroad is ultimately to benefit the farmers of the country, in common with our commercial interests; and how is this to be effected? The farmer owning stock owns also a share in each depot on the line, and the person who has the charge of the depot is *his* agent. Now supposing *your* agent in Milwaukee telegraphs to any agent on the line where your wheat is stored, that wheat buyers will give so much for a boat load of wheat; the cars will deposit that wheat in Milwaukee in six hours at the farthest from the time the order was received. Thus you will, by taking stock in this railroad, ruin this accursed monopoly, and at the same time obtain the highest price for your wheat. . . . The railroad must be built, and it remains for you to say whether the stock-holders shall consist of enterprising farmers or eastern capitalists. If you refuse to take stock, there is no alternative—eastern capital will step in and we shall forever be cursed with monopolies. . . . Let every farmer who has the interest of the farming community at heart step in ere it is too late.[9]

Clinton and Kilbourn's work was well rewarded. The company's largest sale of stock occurred on July 19. On that day Milwaukee's city council members voted twelve to one to subscribe to one hundred thousand dollars' worth of the company's stock, as allowed by the recent state law.[10] The city would borrow money to pay for the subscription, then pay for the loan with a one percent property tax. City residents who paid property tax would receive receipts that could be exchanged for actual railroad stock. In other words, they would be taxed to finance a private corporation that was expected to benefit all.[11]

On July 30 the directors met to review the survey reports submitted by Kilbourn. His recommended middle route had lost favor with the directors, who now favored either the northern or southern routes. Waukesha was 16.6 miles from

# MILWAUKEE TO WAUKESHA: PICKING THE ROUTE

Milwaukee as the crow flies. The more direct southern route added only one mile to that distance. But it traversed an up and down terrain that would be expensive to build on. The circuitous northern route added four miles, but utilized river valleys that were cheaper to build in. Detailed surveys with cost estimates were called for. Kilbourn would recall:

> I put two parties into the field; Mr. B. H. Edgerton having charge of that on the Southern route, and Mr. Richard P. Morgan of that on the Northern route, with instructions to each to run and report on their respective lines as soon as they could. They were both experienced in running lines, and especially Mr. Morgan.[12]

Edgerton, an engineer in the preliminary survey, had long been active in Milwaukee's civic affairs. A member of St. Paul's Episcopal Church, he had been a foreman for Milwaukee's volunteer fire department and had served on the town council and the harbor committee. Earlier in 1849, when Kilbourn's term as mayor of Milwaukee ended, Edgerton had run for that office as a member of the People's Party, but had been defeated by Democrat Don A. J. Upham. Now he was faced with the difficult job of surveying the southern, or "town line," route to Waukesha.

Morgan, who was surveying the northern route, had joined the Milwaukee, Waukesha, and Mississippi River engineering corps (as they were informally known) during the preliminary surveys in June. He was a civil engineer with substantial railroad experience. He had worked for the Hudson River Railroad in New York and had supervised surveys of the Galena and Chicago Union Railroad, a project that had brought him a great deal of familiarity with the terrain of northern Illinois. The directors of the Galena had liked his estimate of $14,553 per mile and his reduced figure of $8,000 per mile if secondhand strap rail—the thin iron strip that was nailed onto the wooden beams that connected to the ties—was used. The Galena had purchased the strap rail and Morgan had stayed on to helping during the summer of 1848, laying the first rails out of Chicago. Morgan was the only person with the Milwaukee and Waukesha with prior railroad experience. Despite this, he was made responsible for the survey of the easier northern route.[13]

These surveys of the northern and southern routes would be final—the directors and engineers assumed that the railroad would be built on one of the lines being measured. With compass and transit (a surveyor's instrument for measuring horizontal and vertical angles), the surveyors broke the route into straight lines called *courses*. Axe men would clear as needed in order for the surveyors to take sights. Chain men with one-hundred-foot-long engineering chains measured the courses, driving stakes at two-hundred-foot intervals to mark "stations."

Levelers measured the elevation of each station. Transit men followed, measuring the angles where courses changed direction and laying in curves to smooth them. Engineers calculated the volumes of earth that would have to be removed from cuts or dumped in fills and calculated the distances the earth would need to be moved.[14]

Edgerton soon realized that following a straight line, the southern route incurred too many obstacles. It would consequently be too costly to build along that path.[15] Meanwhile, Morgan, ascending the Menomonee River valley, found the grades favorable. His concern was that many curves would be required. Ten miles from Milwaukee, Morgan ran the line northward, into the valley of Underwood's Run (a tributary of the Menomonee River) to maintain grade in climbing the Niagara Escarpment (a limestone formation found in eastern Wisconsin, the Door Peninsula, and Canada; it also underlies Niagara Falls). In southeastern Wisconsin, this escarpment forms the divide from which waters run either east to Lake Michigan or west to the Mississippi River. Morgan and his men crossed this divide near Brookfield, then descended seven miles along the Fox River to Waukesha.

With the surveys complete, the time had come to finalize the route. To this end, six of the company's nine directors—Kilbourn, Holton, Lemuel Weeks, John Tweedy, Anson Eldred, and Alexander Mitchell—met in Milwaukee on September 22. As chief engineer, Kilbourn presented the survey reports accompanied by large-scale plats, profiles (maps showing ascents, levels, and descents of the line), and construction estimates. The directors took time to study these. Then Mitchell, the youngest, proposed a resolution that "the route passing through the valley of the Menomonee and Fox Rivers, and denominated the north route, as the same has been amended and perfected by Messrs. Morgan and Vliet, be adopted as the route of the Railroad from Milwaukee to Waukesha."[16] At two o'clock in the afternoon the board adopted this resolution and the line was fixed. The northern route would be used for Wisconsin's first railroad.

It was fitting that Mitchell, who would later in life be in charge of more miles of railroad than anyone at the meeting, would play such an important role in the beginnings of Wisconsin's first railroad. Born in Scotland, he had come to America in 1839 as an employee of a Scottish banking firm. He was soon put in charge of one of their ventures, the Wisconsin Marine and Fire Insurance Company of Milwaukee. On October 6, 1841, Mitchell married Martha Reed of Milwaukee, a "dashing equestrienne who had one day caught his eye as she rode along a Milwaukee path." When he joined the directorate of the Milwaukee and Waukesha Railroad Company, he was already recognized as the state's leading financial authority, with over one million dollars of the Wisconsin Marine and Fire Insurance Company's certificates of deposit circulating in the state as currency.[17]

One week later the stockholders met at Barstow's Hotel in Waukesha to settle the location of the depot at that end of the route. Had the southern route been chosen, it would have been placed on the eastern side of the Fox River, but instead it was placed on the western.[18]

At the end of the year, President Kilbourn, writing his annual report to the stockholders, understandably praised the route to excess, saying it was

> a line of almost unrivalled excellence in its principal features of grades, curves and cost. The maximum grades ascending westward (or from the Lake) being twenty-five feet to the mile; the maximum grades ascending eastward (or towards the Lake) being only six feet to the mile; and few of the curves being less than three thousand feet radius, presents in these respects an unusually fine line; and what is perhaps of equal importance, these advantages are all obtained on a line of rare cheapness of construction. On the whole line, there is not a deep cut, nor high embankment—not a yard of rock excavation—but few bridges, and those of small dimensions and cheap structures; and a general absence of all those expensive items which constitute the bulk of the cost of Rail roads in eastern states.[19]

The route was criticized by some because of the many curves necessary, but Kilbourn adamantly defended the choice:

> This line is as straight as it could be consistently with its general design, which was to follow the valleys of the Menomonee and Underwood's Run, and of the Fox River. The object in following these valleys was to obtain easy grades and a cheap line. We could not run a straight line in a crooked valley; and our only alternative was, either to take this, with its curves, or take a straighter but more expensive line, over the table land. The question was one of *policy*, and the Board decided in accordance with true policy, beyond a doubt. Had we taken the other route, with our feeble means, we should have failed before we reached Waukesha; and the predictions of the faithless would have been verified by our failure, and our enterprise would have been stigmatized, as it had already been, as a Milwaukee humbug. We took the course of prudence, and adopted the cheapest and most feasible route.[20]

Kilbourn's comments capture a dilemma faced by many railroad builders in nineteenth-century America: that there was a trade-off between the cost of building a railroad and the cost of operating it. A company with ample resources could build a straight, evenly graded line that would cost little to run on. But few companies had such resources when starting out. So they built their lines as quickly and cheaply as possible. Later, when trains were running and money was coming in, they could try to improve them.

# Chapter 7

## Construction Begins
### 1849

In August 1849, while the surveys were still underway, the company advertised in newspapers for construction bids. Under the heading "Notice to Rail-Road Contractors!" it stated that the Milwaukee, Waukesha, and Mississippi River Railroad Company was receiving sealed proposals for grading, bridging, and laying of the railroad's superstructure (the ties and rails). Yet in mid September the company found it had sold subscriptions to only four hundred thousand dollars' worth of its stock—one hundred thousand dollars short of what was called for to begin construction. With winter fast approaching, the directors feared further delay. They proceeded to let the contracts despite the shortfall.

The directors had several choices for how to go about building the railroad. They could simply hire laborers and direct them; they could allow the owners of the road—the stockholders—to build the road; or they could hire contractors with the needed men and tools to do the job. Although the latter option was the most common for large construction projects such as railroads or canals, the directors of the Milwaukee and Waukesha Railroad chose a mixture of the last two methods. They divided the twenty and one half mile route into thirty-four sections, each of which could be bid and contracted for separately. The contracts specified grubbing (removing trees and roots), grading (building the roadbed), ballasting (topping with gravel), laying culverts to allow drainage, and building bridges. The sections nearest Waukesha were reserved for the stockholders, while the rest were to be bid by contractors.

Sales of stock subscriptions became robust as bids for construction were about to be let. On September 24 the *Daily Wisconsin* noted that Byron Kilbourn was promoting a new strategy. We learn from the *Rock County Badger* that on September 17

> a large meeting was held . . . to listen to an address from Mr. Kilbourn. . . . He propose[d] that farmers who choose [buy stock] . . . should contribute stock in labor of grading the road. The idea of people building their own Railroads is an excellent one.[1]

The contracts for grading were let on September 28 at Waukesha, each having been awarded to the lowest bidder. The contract amounts varied. The lowest was for $614, and the highest was $3,029. They totaled $44,374, which was slightly lower than the estimated cost of building the road. While some contractors may have underbid, the directors maintained that all of the contractors would make a healthy profit.[2] The November 28 *Milwaukee Sentinel* reported:

> We also learn that Mr. Clinton, acting under the instructions of the Board, has let a number of contracts for clearing and grading the line of the road at prices very much below the estimated cost of such work. These contracts have been let to Farmers along the line who propose to *work out* their subscriptions in this way. It is gratifying to know that the people of the interior evince the most lively interest in the success of this great enterprise.[3]

One week later, the *Watertown Chronicle* reported:

> Milwaukee and Waukesha Railroad—Contracts for the grubbing and grading of the road were let last week. We understand that M. L. O'Conner, Esq., the enterprising plank road contractor, was the successful bidder for 13 sections, or some six or seven miles—the heaviest of the contracts. He is an engine of himself, and if supplied with the motive power, will be sure to "go ahead."[4]

Construction began in October. Contractors and their crews, farmers along the line, stockholders, and anyone else wishing to lend a hand pitched in. Surveyors had marked the line with wooden stakes. The first job was clearing the line—removing brush and felling trees. Next came the work of grubbing—removing the roots and stumps from the roadway. The most stubborn roots were those of the prairie oaks, the roots of which had grown deeper over many years while prairie fires repeatedly burnt off the tops.

Grubbing was made easier by the use of a plow. A breaking plow pulled by ten yoke of oxen was ideal, but more common was a plow pulled by one or two oxen that would stop whenever it struck a large root. When that happened, the grubbers had to remove the root by hand. When possible, work on culverts and bridges was begun early. This was so that the grading would properly line up with them. Grading was the main work. With picks, shovels, wheelbarrows, horses, oxen, and plows, men moved dirt and built up the roadbed. On level ground they would simply dig the drainage ditches that were necessary on either side of the roadbed, casting the dirt to the middle. A head grader would stand on the grade and indicate with his shovel where the next shovelful should land to keep the grade even. Where there were hills and valleys, the work was far more difficult. The hills would be dug through to make the "cut" for the roadway, and the dirt and gravel removed from the cut would be dumped to build up the embankments over the adjacent valleys. Ideally, the amount of dirt from the cut was exactly what was needed to level out the course, but more often than not extra dirt would have to be brought in. The final step in the grading process was applying gravel, which was brought in on wagons. Gravel gave the road stability and good drainage. It was found in abundance along the first division between Milwaukee and Waukesha, and the men were instructed to apply it generously, to a depth of two feet.

The first section—just next to the station grounds in Milwaukee and along the Menomonee River—was one of the more difficult. *Menomonee* means "wild rice," a plant that grows in water—and much of the line here was in fact being built on land that was under water, up to two to six feet deep in some places. Across the river was a bluff on which men loosened the dirt with picks and shovels and loaded it into dumpcarts. Teamsters would then take the carts across the river, then to the end of the grade, where they would dump the load. As the bluff became lower, the grade became longer—where there had been water, there was now a roadway. Many of the men employed as graders had done similar work cutting down the bluffs and filling swamps to build the city of Milwaukee.[5]

Edward D. Holton, in an 1858 address, recalled the initial building of the roadbed, noting the "sober earnest purpose" of those involved and the common practice of paying for subscriptions in goods or labor:

> It was a great undertaking for that day, under the circumstances. We were without money as a people, either in city or country. Every man had come to the country with limited means—and each had his house, his store, his shop, his barn to

build, his land to clear and fence, and how could he spare anything from his own individual necessities? Some wise men looked on and shook their heads, and there were many croakers. But in the minds of those who had assumed the undertaking, there was a sober earnest purpose to do what they could for its accomplishment. It was demanded of our own people that they should lay aside all their feuds and personalities, and one and all join in the great work. To a very great extent this demand was complied with, and gentlemen were brought to work cordially and harmoniously together who had stood aloof from each other for years. The spirit of union, harmony and concord exhibited by the people of the city was most cordially reciprocated by those of the country along the contemplated line of road. Subscription books were widely circulated, and the aggregate sum subscribed was very considerable. I said we had no money, but we had *things*, and subscriptions were received with the understanding that they could be paid in such commodities as could be turned into the work of constructing the road. This method of building a railroad would be smiled at now, and was, by some among us, then. But it was, after all, a great source of our strength and of our success; at any rate, for the time being.

The work was commenced in the fall of 1849, and for one entire year the grading was prosecuted and paid for by orders drawn upon the merchants, payable in goods—by carts from wagon makers, by harnesses from harness makers, by cattle, horses, beef, pork, oats, corn, potatoes and flour from the farmers, all received on account of stock subscriptions, and turned over to the contractors in payment of work done upon the road. A large amount of the grading of the road from here to Waukesha was performed in this way. Upon seeing this work go on, the people began to say everywhere—why, there is to be a railroad, surely, and the work rose into consequence and public confidence.[6]

Indeed, public confidence not only bolstered spirits, but padded the subscription books, ensuring that the difficult work of grubbing, grading, and building bridges and culverts could keep on. On October 16 the editor of the *Waukesha Democrat* reported:

Operations have commenced on this end of the line in good earnest. The foundation for the depot at this place was laid up last week, and the superstructure will be pushed forward without delay, and covered in this fall. The grading on this end will be commenced in a short time.[7]

The editor then proceeded with uncanny accuracy to recommend lines that would eventually be built (this before a single rail had been laid in Wisconsin):

# CONSTRUCTION BEGINS

> Complete your road to the Mississippi, and you secure the trade and mineral of the central and western counties. Start from your angle north of this place [Brookfield] running northwest, and tap the heart of the Fox River Improvement [Portage], from thence on through the now howling wilderness to the Capital of Minnesota, with your iron road, and Milwaukee controls the trade of the whole Northwest, Minnesota included. With a line to Chicago, Milwaukee has all the railroads she needs. Plank roads will do the rest. Ten years will see these suggestions in process of fulfillment.[8]

On October 23, the *Waukesha Democrat* followed up on their earlier article, reporting on the steady output of labor:

> The work too, under contract, goes on steadily. The fine Stone Depot at Waukesha is rising apace. The grading on several of the sections between this city and that town is under good head-way. We see no reason indeed to doubt that a year hence the trains will be running regularly twice a day between Milwaukee and Waukesha.[9]

The dimensions of this early work on the Milwaukee and Waukesha Railroad are apparent in this article from the *Milwaukee Sentinel* of December 18:

> Our Rail Road—Between four and five hundred men are at work on the different sections of the Milwaukee and Waukesha Rail Road. The Directors are pushing ahead as vigorously as possible, and if backed up, as we doubt not they will be, by the stockholders, are bound to have the road finished and in operation to Waukesha next Summer.[10]

In the same paper, a weather report followed describing the conditions under which the men were working—not cold enough to merit a work stoppage, but cold enough to make for a great deal of discomfort:

> A Cold Snap—The weather changed suddenly from moderate to very cold Sunday night, and at 8 A.M. yesterday, the Mercury was within one degree of zero.[11]

Kilbourn's railroad stock promotions had gained ground very quickly, with farmers buying labor subscriptions in droves. The October 31 *Milwaukee Sentinel* reported that:

The Farmers along the line of the Milwaukee and Mississippi Rail Road are subscribing liberally to the Stock. In the five towns of Whitewater, Waukesha, Palmyra, Genesee and Eagle, these subscriptions exceed $260,000. This amount, added to the sums previously subscribed, including the City subscription of $100,000, swells the aggregate to near $420,000. For a beginning this is indeed promising, and the ball will be "kept in motion."[12]

The trend continued through the fall, as reported by the *Milwaukee Sentinel and Gazette*:

November 17
    At a meeting of the directors . . . on the 14th . . . it is expected by the close of the week . . . the books . . . to be returned with . . . a sum total of Half-A-Million of dollars, including the City Subscription . . . James Kneeland, Secretary Pro-tem.[13]
    November 28. Our Railroad to the Mississippi—We learn from Mr. E. D. Clinton, one of the Directors of the Milwaukee and Mississippi Rail Road Company, that he has obtained within the last fortnight subscriptions to the amount of *seventy nine thousand nine hundred dollars* in the single town of Milton, Rock County. Most of the subscribers are Farmers, who take from $500 to $1,500 worth of stock in the road. The aggregate subscriptions, and all among our own people, to this great State enterprise, now amount to *five hundred and sixty thousand dollars*. This is, indeed, encouraging progress, and makes the eventual success of the undertaking more and more certain. It is worth while to state in this connection, that according to the Chicago Journal of Monday last, the whole amount subscribed to the Chicago and Galena R.R. Company thus far is but $350,000, nearly $200,000 short of the sum subscribed to the Milwaukee and Mississippi Road.[14]

In October two locating parties were sent to explore the country west of Waukesha ahead of the more detailed surveys that would take place the following spring. They found the country generally favorable for railroad construction, although the section through the Scoopenong Bluffs, between Eagle and Palmyra, appeared formidable. They ran their lines west to the railroad's anticipated crossing point over the Rock River (near present day Edgerton). Then they continued two miles further to the village of Fulton, where the line would go northward to Madison ascending alongside the Catfish (Yahara) River. At this point one of the parties proceeded to survey a branch route between Milton and Janesville. The directors at this early date had thought this branch important, though it was not in the scope of the company's charter. In December the weather took a turn for the worse, and the men decided to return to Milwaukee.[15]

# CONSTRUCTION BEGINS

One surveyor, twenty-eight-year-old Anson Buttles, had something more on his mind than his fellow workers. The year before, the Jacob Mullie family had arrived in Milwaukee, having come all the way from Holland. The fact that Mr. Mullie's daughter, Cornelia, spoke little English had not prevented young Anson from making her acquaintance. Because Anson was away on the job much of the time, he and Cornelia corresponded. In a letter dated December 4, he wrote:

> Dearest Cornelia,
> We are very busy now, indeed we shall have to work on next Sunday and every day next week and this week too, all the time, just as hard as we can. One of our men has left, and he was a good one, and I will have to work the harder for it . . . but you know, dear girl, that I must attend to my business. . . . I have thought that when Mr. Kilbourn came back I would get some money from him and we would get married now.[16]

Apparently, the railroad was laying ground for more than just a train route, at least for one young couple.

❖ ❖ ❖ ❖ ❖ ❖

The *First Annual Report of the Directors of the Milwaukee, Waukesha, and Mississippi Rail-Road Company, to the Stock-holders*, issued on the last day of the year, was the first such report in Wisconsin. In it the directors expressed their pleasure in the progress made during 1849, especially with stock subscriptions, which had exceeded six hundred thousand dollars. They predicted that these would reach the one million dollar mark by April, at which time they would no longer solicit them, having gained

> the full amount which the board deem it advisable to receive; and when this amount shall have been subscribed, the books will be finally closed, and no further subscriptions will be received. With this amount and a sound system of finance, the entire road can be completed without any further direct contributions of the stockholders.[17]

The directors also used the annual report to state the estimated costs of building and equipping the road to Waukesha, "based on actual contract prices . . . and on actual proposals for iron by the most responsible parties":

| | |
|---|---:|
| Cost of grubbing, grading, ballasting, and bridging | $ 44,374 |
| 20½ miles Superstructure as per contracts @ $1,350 | 27,060 |
| Fitting and laying down 20½ ms. track (chairs & spikes incl) | 10,250 |
| Depots, Stations, Passenger and Freight Cars, as per estimate | 38,000 |
| Engineering, superintendence and incidental expenses | 12,918 |
| Total for road bed, &c | $132,652 |
| 80 tons iron per mile @ 50—$4000; or 20½ miles | $ 85,000 |
| 2 first-class locomotives (wide gauge) | 15,000 |
| | 100,000 |
| Total 20½ miles, finished | $232,652[18] |

The numbers were reassuring. They showed the cost to be $11,348.88 per mile—less than that of most other railroads (New England railroads averaged $39,000 per mile at this time, and other Western railroads as much as $30,000 per mile).[19] One might wonder, however, whether the directors lowered estimates to make buying railroad stock more attractive.

For rails, the directors decided

> to adopt the best and most approved style of H rail (commonly called T rail) at the outset of this work, and also the wide gauge of six feet (being the same as that adopted by the New York and Erie Rail Road Company), as being far superior to the narrow gauge in general use on most of the eastern roads—For high speed, and for long heavy trains with produce, and for general transportation, it is found that such a road possesses many and decided advantages over the ordinary road.[20]

The "H" or "T" rail chosen was similar to what we see on railroads today, but smaller and lighter. The gauge (distance between the rails) of six feet was new and popular at this time. The directors would, fortunately, change their minds and have the track built in "English," or "standard" gauge (four feet, eight and a half inches), which is still commonly used today. Virtually all broad gauge railroads of the time—including New York's Erie Railroad—would eventually convert to standard gauge, and the conversion was expensive. It involved narrowing the track, rebuilding the trucks on all the cars to bring the wheels closer together, and rebuilding or retiring locomotives.

The directors went on in their report to estimate dates of completion for the first division between Milwaukee and Waukesha, predicting that the railroad would be completed by August 1850:

# CONSTRUCTION BEGINS

> Grading and bridging will be completed . . . middle of June. By the time that iron can be shipped up the Lakes in the Spring, the road bed and superstructure will be ready to receive it. . . . It is expected to complete this division of the road within the month of August next.[21]

Then the directors let the proverbial "other shoe" drop—they informed the stockholders that they (the directors) had put the railroad up as collateral for a loan. Before divulging this fact, they made a case for what they saw as the necessity of doing so:

> [N]egotiations have been opened with . . . iron manufacturers . . . and . . . proposals of the most favorable character have been received. . . . But to obtain this . . . it is necessary to go into the market *with cash*. . . . To draw upon the stockholders . . . would . . . be burthensome. About four-fifths . . . are farmers. . . . Owing to the general failure of the wheat crop . . . there is a . . . pressure . . . which would render it impolitic to make . . . draughts . . . until they shall have . . . another crop. But in order to subserve those interests . . . with this improvement (the railroad), it ought to be completed, and in use, before the maturity of that other crop. . . . To effect this, resort must be had to a loan, based on the general credit of the Company, and a pledge of the road and its resources.[22]

Despite the directors' arguments, such a loan was not a necessity at that time. In Illinois, the Galena and Chicago Union Railroad had been building without needing to resort to borrowing. Possibly the Milwaukee and Waukesha's directors wanted to catch up with the Galena in the race to the Rock River valley. If so, such a loan would help.

The directors concluded their report by restating their maxim, that the railroad should be owned and controlled by the people of Wisconsin. And they reminded their readers that this would only be possible if they bought more company stock.

❖ ❖ ❖ ❖ ❖ ❖

The year 1849 had been eventful in other ways. In March, Zachary Taylor, who had been the commandant at Fort Crawford on the Mississippi near Prairie du Chien, became the twelfth president of the United States. In April, Don A. J. Upham, a supporter of the Milwaukee and Waukesha Railroad, became the third mayor of Milwaukee. In November, Nelson Dewey, first governor of the state of Wisconsin, was elected to a second term.

With the discovery of gold in California, that state was in the news almost daily, and many Wisconsin residents decided to relocate there. The admission of California to the union, and whether it would be a slave state or free, was being hotly debated in the Senate.

Cholera had arrived in Milwaukee in July. It killed its victims quickly, often within a day, and one out of every two people infected died of the disease. It was spread by contaminated food and water, but this was not common knowledge at the time. Newspaper editors trod a fine line between warning readers and downplaying the disease because it was bad for business. A note by the editor of the *Waukesha Democrat* from July 31 was typical:

> Three or four deaths from Cholera occurred in this village and nearby during the past week. At present we believe there is no symptom of the disease manifest in our midst, and it is to be hoped that this dreaded plague is no longer hanging over us. . . . A cheerful spirit, with quietness, temperance, and cleanliness, is the safest and best precaution.[23]

By September, 105 deaths had been reported, though the actual total was higher. Then, mercifully, cold weather ended the plague.[24]

On Thanksgiving Day there had been a run on Milwaukee and Waukesha Railroad director Alexander Mitchell's Wisconsin Marine and Fire Insurance Company to redeem deposit certificates for gold. For two days Mitchell and his associates took in certificates and paid out gold. When the public realized the company was not going to go under, it brought back the gold and received new certificates. As a result, the company acquired an even greater reputation for dependability, as well as more customers.[25]

In other railroad events, the Galena and Chicago Union Railroad in Illinois had 21 miles of road in operation with two daily trains in each direction. The Galena was to connect Chicago with the Mississippi and was seen by many in Wisconsin as an indicator of what the Milwaukee and Waukesha Railroad might do. Nationally, at the end of 1849 there were some seven thousand miles of railroad, all east of the Mississippi. The dream of a transcontinental railroad continued to gain traction. Asa Whitney had issued a booklet entitled "Project for a Railroad to the Pacific" that included a map depicting a railroad from Prairie du Chien, Wisconsin, to Puget Sound. A bill for a land grant for this road was to be brought before Congress. In Wisconsin, it was hoped that the Milwaukee and Waukesha Railroad might become a feeder to this line.

In October a "Pacific Railroad Convention" was held in St. Louis, Missouri. Milwaukee's Board of Trade sent Kilbourn, Holton, Osgood Putnam, and George H.

# CONSTRUCTION BEGINS

Walker as delegates.[26] They of course favored a northern route to the Pacific. The *Milwaukee Sentinel* of October 19 addressed the issue:

> It will be found necessary . . . to carry the line . . . much farther north . . . in order to avoid the numerous streams subject to heavy floods and therefore difficult and expensive to bridge, which are to be found lower down. . . . The Mississippi terminus would have to be as far North as Prairie du Chien.[27]

Meanwhile, work on the shortest of transcontinental lines, the Panama Railroad, had been put under contract by the Panama Rail Road Company of New York, which had purchased exclusive building rights from the government of New Grenada (today's Columbia and Panama).

With events such as these capturing the nation's attention, one might think that the people of Wisconsin would deem the grading of a twenty-mile roadbed insignificant. They did not. Most of them had left their lives and loved ones in the East or in Europe to come to Wisconsin to forge a better life. The railroad promised to help them do this. It promised to make scarce goods abundant, to make the unaffordable affordable, and to transform some of life's drudgery into free time. It would allow them to visit friends and family in the East. This twenty-mile roadbed, now covered by snow, was solid evidence that those promises would be kept.

# Chapter 8

## Rails and Locomotives
### 1850

At mid-century, Wisconsin had a population of over three hundred thousand people. Milwaukee had grown into a metropolis with some twenty thousand residents, and settlements were scattered across the southern third of the state. What sort of a place was southern Wisconsin? Nine out of ten people lived on farms, and wheat was the main crop, for both domestic use and export. Orchards and dairy farms were still rare. Cows, pigs, and dogs roamed free, even in the cities, and fields and gardens were fenced to keep them out. Wisconsin was new—as a state, it was less than two years old, its people were young, and its villages and farms had only been there five, ten, or at most fifteen years. The southern lead miners, fur trading families, and Indians of fifteen years before had been buried by an avalanche of newcomers who identified each other as *Yankees* or *foreigners*. Yankees were Americans from the East, although English immigrants were generally included in the category, too. Foreigners were all other immigrants, who could be identified because they spoke with an accent, be it German, Norwegian, Irish, etc. The proportion of foreigners was steadily increasing, especially in Milwaukee, where immigrants would soon constitute a majority of the population—but Yankees continued to hold the prominent positions in society.

Foremost among the issues now facing the state of Wisconsin was whether its school fund could be tapped to finance railroads. Under the Northwest Ordinance, a section was defined as one square mile; a school section was necessary

Drawing of Milwaukee, circa 1850, by John B. Wengler.
WHi Image ID 11220

as one of the thirty-six sections constituting a township. The school fund's monies were derived from the sale of lands in the state's "school" sections, and the law stated explicitly that this fund was to be used for educational purposes. Yet the law also stipulated that until such a time as money from the sale of these lands was directed toward education, it was to be invested in the "most profitable manner."[1] And what manner could be more profitable, some asked, than investing it in the Milwaukee and Mississippi Railroad? In January 1850 the matter came before the legislature, and Byron Kilbourn submitted a memorial that requested a one hundred thousand dollar loan from the fund to the Milwaukee and Mississippi Railroad Company. According to the *Sheboygan Democrat*, which had a less than favorable opinion of the company's president:

> Byron Kilbourn, the projector of a canal that never was made, went up to the capitol with his picked men, made speeches, ate oysters, and drank beer to influence legislators to support his memorial.[2]

Despite this characterization, the population of southern Wisconsin supported the loan for the most part, although the newspapers of northern communities such as Fond du Lac and Sheboygan—communities that had railroad plans of their own—opposed it. Kilbourn's memorial was referred to a select committee, which gave it a favorable report before the legislature. Its supporters remained hopeful. On February 1, Milwaukee and Mississippi lobbyist and Speaker of the Assembly Moses Strong pleaded with legislators for two hours to vote for the measure.[3] But it was defeated 41 to 21. The editors of the *Sheboygan Democrat* fired their parting shot:

> We wish our friends of Milwaukee god-speed in every laudable enterprise for the growth and improvement of their town, but when they seek to clog up the fountain of learning and intelligence to increase their wealth and power, we can but congratulate them, and especially their children, in their failure.[4]

On February 1, the same day that the school fund measure was defeated, the Milwaukee and Waukesha Railroad was officially renamed the Milwaukee and Mississippi Railroad Company. Governor Nelson Dewey signed the amendment bestowing the new name that fit the route described in the charter.

A major obstacle now faced by the company was the fact that it had no money. Until this time it had built the road through a system of barter. It had exchanged shares of its stock for labor, allowing the builders of the road to become the owners of the road. It also exchanged shares of stock for orders from merchants and tradesmen, and then used those orders to pay the contractors (who in turn paid their laborers). These methods worked well for building the roadway, but in order to buy hardware that was only available in the East—rails, locomotives, etc.—cash was required, and the Milwaukee and Mississippi had very little of that. Since iron rail was imported from England, the amount of money needed was staggering. One mile of track would cost $5,000, meaning the fifty miles of track from Milwaukee to Whitewater would cost $250,000—more money than was readily available in the entire state.[5] The directors called a meeting to address the problem.

On February 28, 1850, the directors met with three hundred stockholders at the court house in Waukesha. A committee was formed consisting of Directors John H. Tweedy and James Kneeland and stockholders W. O. Underwood, George Lawrence, J. Parsons, David J. Powers, S. E. Cobb, Joseph Goodrich, and E. Cawker. President Kilbourn instructed the committee to "devise a plan for obtaining a loan of money sufficient to purchase iron and locomotives for the road."[6] The committeemen retired to discuss the problem. Solutions were offered and rejected. Then Goodrich spoke. His words, as recalled by E. D. Holton, were this:

> See here, I can mortgage my farm for $3000 and go east, where I came from, to get the money for it. Now, are there not one hundred men between Milwaukee and Rock River that can do the same? If so, here is your money. I will be one of them.[7]

Goodrich's idea was simple and workable. While Wisconsin's farmers did not have much money, they owned land that was of considerable value. If they were willing to put up their land as collateral, they could borrow the needed money and invest it in the railroad. It would be a gamble—if the railroad failed, they might lose their farms—but it was a gamble many were willing to take. Several committee members opposed the idea, but it was the only viable plan they could present to the main body of stockholders. Committee chair Tweedy reported the plan to the stockholders. The stockholders approved it overwhelmingly and instructed the board of directors "to make arrangements for holding meetings along the line of the railroad, for the purpose of taking up the proper securities."[8] This

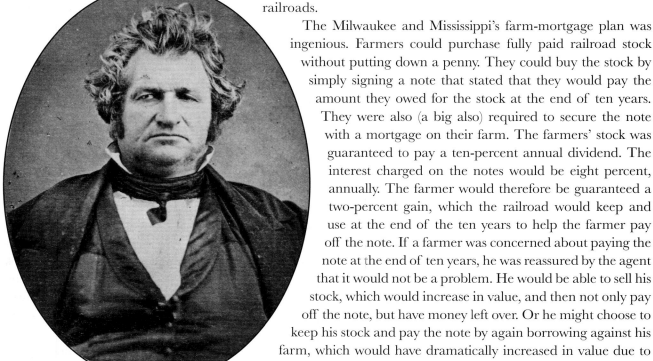

In 1850, Joseph Goodrich of Milton conceived of the idea to finance railroads with farm mortgages. His Milton House became a station on the underground railroad, helping runaway slaves escape to Canada.
WHi Image ID 62358

was the beginning of Wisconsin's farm-mortgage plan for financing railroads.

The Milwaukee and Mississippi's farm-mortgage plan was ingenious. Farmers could purchase fully paid railroad stock without putting down a penny. They could buy the stock by simply signing a note that stated that they would pay the amount they owed for the stock at the end of ten years. They were also (a big also) required to secure the note with a mortgage on their farm. The farmers' stock was guaranteed to pay a ten-percent annual dividend. The interest charged on the notes would be eight percent, annually. The farmer would therefore be guaranteed a two-percent gain, which the railroad would keep and use at the end of the ten years to help the farmer pay off the note. If a farmer was concerned about paying the note at the end of ten years, he was reassured by the agent that it would not be a problem. He would be able to sell his stock, which would increase in value, and then not only pay off the note, but have money left over. Or he might choose to keep his stock and pay the note by again borrowing against his farm, which would have dramatically increased in value due to the presence of the railroad. Either way, the farmer would benefit.

❖ ❖ ❖ ❖ ❖ ❖

When work resumed on the railroad in the spring of 1850, it was clear that the purchase of rails and locomotives was imminent. By the end of May, the one hundred men needed to mortgage their farms for the railroad had been found. Goodrich, the originator of the plan, had been the first, mortgaging his farm for ten thousand dollars. The company listed the notes and mortgages as "money paid in," but it still needed to turn them into cash. Its job would now be to sell the notes and attached mortgages to Eastern investors. These investors would in effect be loaning Wisconsin's farmers the cash to buy the railroad stock. They, the investors, would receive interest on the money loaned, which would be paid by the Milwaukee and Mississippi Railroad Company. The investors expected to receive full payment of principle from the farmers at the end of ten years. If either interest or principle were not forthcoming when due, the investors could foreclose on the farmers' property. Of course neither the farmers, nor the railroad agents, nor the investors, when making the loan, expected that to happen.

Nevertheless, the fact that the one hundred men had been found was of no help unless their notes and mortgages could be sold for cash—and there was no precedent for anyone doing that. On May 22 Kilbourn, carrying notes and mortgages worth $250,000, left Milwaukee on a four-day journey to the East. He took a steamer across Lake Michigan to New Buffalo, a train (the Michigan Central) to Detroit, another steamer to Buffalo, and a series of trains across central New York to Schenectady. There he made tentative arrangements for the purchase of two locomotives. He then continued by train to Albany and then by river packet, down the Hudson, to New York City. There Kilbourn received a shock. No one would buy his note/mortgage securities because they were a type of security that had not been seen before. Kilbourn realized he would have to return to Milwaukee empty-handed.

Or would he? Kilbourn soon discovered an invaluable piece of information: while he could not find buyers for the type of securities he had brought with him, municipal bonds from Western cities *were* marketable in the East. He began developing a new plan based on this knowledge. When he stepped back onto the dock in Milwaukee on June 10, he knew what he was going to do. He would ask the city of Milwaukee's common council to accept the Milwaukee and Mississippi's farm mortgages in lieu of cash for its bonds. Then he would return to the East and sell those bonds for cash for the railroad.

Kilbourn scheduled a public meeting at the court house for the evening of June 14. A large crowd, including representatives of the press, gathered on that evening. The next day the *Daily Wisconsin* reported:

> RAILROAD TO THE MISSISSIPPI WILL BE COMPLETED! ENTHUSIASTIC DEMONSTRATION.—Company's Proposition Accepted.—A large assemblage . . . met at the Court House last evening. . . . The Company now asked the city to increase their stock . . . to take $150,000 additional.
>
> Hon. Byron Kilbourn, President of the Railroad . . . proceeded to recapitulate the progress already made. . . . The road between this place and *Waukesha* (21 miles) was now in such state that in a very few days it could be in readiness for the laying of the rail.
>
> The question, to the mind of Mr. Kilbourn, was whether Milwaukee should retain the business . . . in the Rock River valley. . . . The Chicago railroad . . . was being extended towards our own state line, with the intention of controlling a large section of our State. Now was the time to rouse ourselves and finish the Milwaukee and Mississippi road to Whitewater by the time the Chicago and Galena Company had extended their road to Belvidere.

> It is proposed that the city make a further subscription . . . to provide security . . . the Company will cause to be . . . placed in the hands . . . of the City . . . with certain real estate mortgages in their possession.⁹

This was the crux of Kilbourn's new plan. The city would take the farm mortgages and use them to back municipal bonds that the railroad would then sell in the East. Milwaukee's "railroad ordinance" became final on June 21 when the city council approved it ten to four. The editor of the *Sentinel and Gazette* wrote:

> We congratulate the citizens of Milwaukee and of the state generally on the result of these proceedings. . . . The city of Milwaukee has . . . secured beyond contingency the speedy completion of the road."¹⁰

❖ ❖ ❖ ❖ ❖ ❖

The first annual meeting of the Milwaukee and Mississippi Railroad Company was held on July 1 in Milwaukee. The directors reported the results of the first year's operations to the stockholders:

> The primary subjects which engrossed the attention of the Board were the prosecution of surveys and location of the line; and enlargement of the stock by subscription to . . . an amount of nearly a million of dollars; which amount has been fixed as the maximum of the first subscriptions to be received, previous to the completion of the first division of the road. . . .

| | |
|---|---:|
| *Capital Stock Subscribed* | $991,900.00 |
| *Capital Stock Paid in Expenditures:* | 603,472.00 |
| Grading, Bridging, &c | 31,197.25 |
| Right of Way | 7,994.92 |
| Personal Property Taxes | 650.69 |
| Salaries | 2,923.27 |
| Engineering | 8,994.51 |
| Incidental Expenses | 1,834.66 |
| Total | $ 53,525.40 |

> . . . [T]he Board entertain the gratifying belief that the iron rails, locomotives, etc., will be obtained speedily, and on very favorable terms, and that we

hope to see this division completed and in full and successful operation before the opening of the Spring of 1851.[11]

Kilbourn again left for the East, this time carrying Milwaukee's municipal bonds. On July 16 he telegraphed from New York to say that he had disposed of the entire bond issue at the expected price. That night, in the streets of Milwaukee, "Bonfires blazed and cannons roared."[12] The *Sentinel* predicted that, "[T]he day is not far distant when our Milwaukee Iron Horse, starting betimes from the shores of Lake Michigan, will slack his thirst at eve in the brimming Mississippi."[13]

With money to spend, Kilbourn proceeded to Schenectady, where he was met by Walter Phelps, an employee at the Schenectady Locomotive Works. Kilbourn and Phelps shopped for locomotives in several New York cities before returning to Schenectady and purchasing the two that Kilbourn had made tentative plans to purchase during his previous trip. Kilbourn also saw to the purchase of rails. Almost all American railroads purchased rails imported from England at this time, despite the sixteen dollar per ton duty, because rolled English wrought iron was of better quality than what was available in America. The Milwaukee and Mississippi had purchased 1,860 tons of iron rail, paying forty eight dollars per ton. At forty five pounds per yard, there was enough to lay twenty-three miles of track. The rails would be shipped up the Hudson River to Albany, then over the Erie Canal to Buffalo. There they would be transferred to schooners and shipped over the lakes.

The first locomotives were shipped from Buffalo on the brig *Abiah* and the schooner *Patrick Henry*. Rails and hardware would travel with the locomotives, and had been loaded first, followed by the partially disassembled, crated locomotives. The *Abiah* and the *Patrick Henry* left Buffalo together, sailed westward over the length of Lake Erie, ascended the Detroit and St. Clair rivers, and entered Lake Huron. There they encountered a storm in which the *Patrick Henry* was struck by lightning and suffered extensive damage. She put into Mackinac for repairs while the *Abiah* continued southward on Lake Michigan to Milwaukee.

On the morning of September 12, the *Abiah* made her way one and one-quarter miles up the main channel of the Milwaukee River. She put in at the landing of a lumberyard by the Milwaukee and Mississippi station grounds. She was so heavily laden that the river had to be dredged "close to the shore, so we could put long timbers to shore to vessel."[14] When that was done, some rails were unloaded. Robert Shields, who had come to Milwaukee in 1835, spiked the first one in place. Then, with some difficulty, the locomotive was hoisted. By ten o'clock in the morning it was on the ground—the first locomotive in Wisconsin.

This locomotive had been built two years earlier by the Norris Locomotive Works of Philadelphia. It weighed 46,000 pounds, a respectable weight for its time, and was an "eight-wheeler," having four large driving wheels in back and four small pilot wheels on a truck in front. Its boiler and firebox were of the Bury, or "haystack," design—a design which originated in England in the 1830s—with the horizontal boiler having at the rear a large vertical steam dome that also housed the firebox. By the late 1840s, Bury boilers were going out of fashion, principally because they were expensive to build. But they remained unsurpassed in producing dry steam—the type of steam that was easy on valves and cylinders. Further dimensions of this locomotive were as follows:

| | | | |
|---|---|---|---|
| Diameter of smokebox | 40 in. | Width of water spaces | 2½ in. |
| Diameter of barrel | 36 in. | Length of boiler, overall | 204 in. |
| Diameter of dome (Bury) | 45 in. | Cylinders | 4 in. x 2 in. |
| Diameter of flues | 2 in. | Diameter of driving wheels | 54 in. |
| Length of flues | 22½ in. | Centers of driving wheels, apart | 66 in. |
| Number of flues | 108 | Total weight of engine | 46,000 lbs. |
| Material of flues | copper | Radius of hooks | 69 in. |
| Length of firebox, inside | 39 in. | Upper 11 in., lower 9½ in. | 9½ in. |
| Width of firebox, inside | 35½ in. | Spread of cylinders | 72 in. |
| Height of firebox, inside | 48 in. | Centers of valve rods, apart | 57 in.[15] |

The outer side of each pair of guides was elliptical in form and bore in its center, in letters of cast-iron, the inscription "Norris Works." Wisconsin's first locomotive would eventually carry the names Bob Ellis and Iowa, but initially she was simply No. 1.[16]

On the day after the landing, the *Milwaukee Sentinel* jubilantly reported:

Hurrah for the Rail Road! The first rails of the Milwaukee and Mississippi Rail Road were laid down yesterday, and the first Locomotive is of the largest size and best pattern, weighing some twenty tons, and built in excellent style. It will whisk a train of passenger cars from here to Waukesha next month, in ten minutes less time than Puck required to put a girdle round about the earth.[17]

Following the landing of the No. 1, the first half mile of track was laid with the rails that had accompanied its voyage. Engine No. 1 was reassembled and placed on this track. On September 25, spectators gathered to watch Kilbourn climb into the cab and drive the engine to the end of the track and back. He repeated the performance five times.

# RAILS AND LOCOMOTIVES

The Milwaukee and Mississippi's Engine No. 1 was the first railroad locomotive in Wisconsin.
WHi Image ID 62849

By this time the *Patrick Henry* had arrived with the locomotive Wisconsin, along with the car wheels, castings, and other hardware. With this hardware and local lumber, the company's car builders put together some platform cars, or "flat cars," to attach to the engine. With a half mile of rails laid, Wisconsin's first train, the Wisconsin, pulled men and materials on these platform cars to the railhead to work. Deacon Chandler was the conductor. The Wisconsin soon became the pet of Milwaukee, with the *Sentinel and Gazette* singing its praises:

September 25: The stout *Wisconsin* stands in the temporary depot, impatiently waiting for the laying down of a few more rods of iron, when it will commence its labors for the good of the public. Its shrill whistle awoke the slumbering echoes Tuesday night.

Look Out for the Engine when the Bell Rings. . . . We learn that the *Wisconsin* will fire up for a start toward Waukesha this afternoon. . . . Owing to unavoidable circumstances, it will not be able to reach that place this trip, but our friends there may be sure there's a good time coming shortly.

According to previous notice the locomotive fired up yesterday afternoon for a trip towards the Mississippi. Quite a crowd of our citizens, in compliance with the polite invitation of the engineer of the R. R., Mr. Vliet, mounted to the dizzy heights of the tender, where the accommodations were good, though rather crowded for those of us who took notes.

Leaving the Milwaukee river at about 3 o'clock, amicst the cheers of the assembled multitude, we passed quickly out along the shores of the Menominee, leaving the city on the right and left, and sped on amidst the pealing of the bell, and the screaming of the whistle. Time fails to tell the sights we saw, or of the enthusiasm created by the appearance of the locomotive as we passed westward.

The party returned at an early hour, highly pleased with the trip, and left with their best wishes for the success of the great work thus commenced.[18]

STEAM AND CINDERS

❖ ❖ ❖ ❖ ❖ ❖

Even at this exciting stage of construction, the work of railroad building was not without its hardships. As track-laying proceeded out of Milwaukee and into the countryside, workers encountered hostility. Thugs in the employ of stage coach operators or innkeepers confronted and intimidated them. Often the rails laid the previous day were torn up. Rail workers had to be hired that were a match for the stage coach thugs. Eventually it became obvious that the violence was not going to stop the railroad, and the fighting died down.[19]

In October a late-season, all night thunderstorm jeopardized a portion of graded line. When morning came Milwaukeeans looked out in disbelief. Where there had been a rail line between Eighth Street and Muskego Avenue, there was only a great expanse of water. The entire roadbed, ballast, and track had sunk out of sight. In the days following, Merrill, Superintendent Holton, and as many others as could be summoned struggled to raise the track back up. Earth was brought in with wheelbarrows. Men raised the submerged ties with long bars while others pressed the earth beneath. The track and embankment had been laid over marshy ground and so required a large amount of fill to restore it. It was a long time before locomotives were able to reach the site, and until they did, this work was done by hand. As a consequence, the rails would not reach Waukesha that year and work on the line would be pushed into winter.[20]

❖ ❖ ❖ ❖ ❖ ❖

By November the Milwaukee and Mississippi Railroad Company had completed its first five miles of track—from Milwaukee to Wauwatosa. The directors felt that a celebration was in order. When they heard that Solomon Juneau, the fur trader who was once the sole white resident of Milwaukee and also its first mayor, was coming to town, they decided to host a rail excursion over the newly completed line with Juneau as the guest of honor. And it *was* an honor, as this was to be the first run of a passenger train in Wisconsin. Adding dignity to the affair, the company had just finished its Milwaukee depot—a modest, one-story, gothic-revival-style building, complete with board-and-batten siding, barge boards, and finials on the gables. The date of the excursion was set for November 20.

When the guests arrived at the depot on the morning of the twentieth, the locomotive Wisconsin was ready and waiting with steam hissing from its valves. Hooked behind it were two open platform cars with side rails and benches bolted on. Edwin Bridgeman would be the conductor, and Joseph Cochrane, the engineer. The hosts—Kilbourn and the directors of the company—and the guests—Juneau, Mayor D. A. J. Upham, and others—all bundled up as for a sleigh ride, climbed aboard. At the signal, Engineer Cochrane opened the throttle. The Wisconsin, huffing and puffing, slowly pulled the cars out of the station, then picked up speed as she ran between the Menomonee River and the adjacent bluffs. The November 20 *Sentinel and Gazette* reported:

This lithograph of an early Milwaukee and Mississippi locomotive (artist and date unknown) was kept for many years by the Old Settlers Club in Milwaukee. The closely spaced wheels of the leading truck with the inclined cylinder over them identify this as an early locomotive.
WHi Image ID 25353

> The track was laid as far as Wauwatosa, a distance of five miles, and the Mayor and Council of Milwaukee, the President and Directors of the Company, a representative from each of the city papers, and "a few other invited guests" enjoyed "an excursion" to the end of the track, the Locomotive *Wisconsin* "going at the rate of thirty miles an hour, without any special effort."[21]

As the train moved westward over the newly laid track, Juneau commented on the many changes that had taken place along the route since the days when he carried trade goods to the Indians camps over it. He confessed that he had never seen a railroad or a train before, much less ridden on one.

Unfortunately, despite the excitement caused by the railroad's first journey, by December track laying was behind schedule. The directors had hoped to have the 20.5-mile line to Waukesha finished by this time, yet only 6 miles of track had been laid. They decided that the work would have to continue through the winter, hoping that Waukesha could be reached by February. The track layers then surprised them with a burst of energy in which they laid four miles of track in little over two weeks, arriving at Elm Grove in Waukesha County on December 17. This was significant: the charter allowed the company, with ten miles of track down, to begin serving the public and charging for freight and fares. The Milwaukee and Mississippi was now a functioning railroad. Appropriately, the directors came out with rules and a rate table:

> *Resolved*, That the following Rules be adopted relative to passengers to be conspicuously posted in each Passenger Car:

There is to be no free list: no persons whomsoever shall be entitled to a free passage on any train, except by order of the Board, or by a free pass signed by the President of the Company, or Superintendent of the road; and except also in cases of persons on Company business—which exceptions will be specially communicated to each Conductor.

The following low rates shall be established for Passengers Fare, until otherwise ordered, viz:

| | |
|---|---|
| MILWAUKEE TO SPRING STREET ROAD | 10 CENTS |
| CHASE'S MILL | 15 CENTS |
| WAUWATOSA | 20 CENTS |
| BLANCHARD'S | 25 CENTS |
| UNDERWOOD'S | 30 CENTS |
| ELM GROVE | 35 CENTS |
| DIXON'S ROAD | 45 CENTS |
| POWER'S MILL | 50 CENTS |
| TEW'S ROAD | 55 CENTS |
| PLANK ROAD | 60 CENTS |
| FOX RIVER COTTAGE | 65 CENTS |
| WAUKESHA | 75 CENTS |

In cases of Passengers being taken up between any of the aforesaid points, the fare will be the same as if taken at the point back of that at which such passengers may be received. Children under ten years of age, at half the above rates.[22]

On December 31, President and Chief Engineer Kilbourn finished his report—*Engineer's Report on the Milwaukee and Mississippi Rail Road for the year 1850*—to the directors. It reported the completion of grading between Milwaukee and Waukesha, the laying of track on half that distance, and the expectation that the entire line would be in operation by February of 1851. The cost of construction had been only $9,495 per mile and the emphasis had been on stability, not elegance. He concluded:

The opening of the road to Waukesha will be an era in the history of Wisconsin, of more importance than is dreamed of by the mass of our citizens, or even by some of the most sanguine friends of the measure.

Only one Motto should now be inscribed on the banner of the Company, and that should be "Onward"—and each and every individual Stockholder, however small or humble, and every citizen of Wisconsin, should feel a pride in sustaining and carrying aloft that banner, with his best efforts, until the Lakes of the North be bound by links of iron to the Father of Rivers, and the commercial prosperity of both sides of the great valley, be placed upon a permanent and sure foundation.

Very respectfully submitted,
BYRON KILBOURN, Chief Engineer,
Milwaukee, Dec. 31st 1850[23]

# Chapter 9
## A Railroad is Born
### January–April 1851

With Waukesha just ten miles away, the men laying track on the Milwaukee and Mississippi pushed on. Surprisingly, the January cold seemed to help their efforts—each day they laid more track than the day before. These workers had all started "green" in October. They had never before laid track, and they had had to teach themselves how. They had laid the first rails slowly, even awkwardly; however, with practice they had developed skill and rhythm. Now they were picking up the tempo, laying one-third of a mile of track per day—two miles of track in a week. The track layer's job consisted of unloading rails, carrying them forward, lowering them into position, and spiking them down. The wooden ties on which they laid the rails were always there, stretching on ahead of them, having been placed by other workers. Track layers also bent rails to shape for the curved sections of the track. They did this by sliding them across two heavy wooden blocks with one man steadily hammering the rail midway between.

The rails were brought from Milwaukee to the end of the tracks on a construction train—usually one or two platform cars pulled by a locomotive. Each rail was twenty-four feet long and weighed 408 pounds. After two rails were set in place, a man called a gauger checked the space between them using a wooden rod that was exactly 4 feet, 8½ inches long. Then the rails were spiked down—three hammer blows to each spike. A completed section of track was a sight to behold, beautiful in the way it blended into the countryside and beautiful in its regularity. Each mile of track contained 68,000 cubic feet of gravel, 2,640 oaken railroad ties, 440 iron rails, and 11,440 iron spikes.[1]

The men had been laying track at Elm Grove, ten miles from Milwaukee, at the beginning of the year. From there they followed the graded roadway up the valley of Underwood's Run, a headwater of the Menomonee River. Then they swung westward to cross the divide that separated the Lake Michigan and Mississippi watersheds. This section of the divide was a level area with the hills of Brookfield to the south and a marshy plateau to the north. When they had laid the tracks midway across it, they saw the smoke rising from Powers Mill. Powers Mill was the saw mill that supplied lumber to the railroad. It was, as often happened during these years, a side-venture of several of the directors of the railroad. Directors J. L. Bean, Edmund D. Clinton, David J. Powers, and Edward D. Holton had put up buildings, brought in a fifty-horsepower steam engine, installed the machinery for it to work the saw, and began operating. The lumber from their mill was used in railroad cars, bridges, and cattle guards. But its main use was for the oaken ties of the track, which were nine inches by nine inches and nine feet long. Every twelfth tie was cut eighteen inches wide. These double-wide ties were used under the rail-ends—where two rails butted—which were held in alignment solely by spikes. It would be another year before "iron chairs"—rail-holders fastened to the ties—would be available for the purpose.[2]

Leaving Powers Mill, the track layers worked westward, then southwestward, as the grade descended into the valley of the Fox River. This was not the Fox River that empties into Green Bay—this was the "Fox River of the Illinois," which flows southward through Waukesha into Illinois and empties into the Illinois River, which in turn empties into the Mississippi. The men were working in the upper reaches of the Fox, where it was a small stream, meandering from one side of the roadway to the other. Soon they passed Fox River Cottage (later Forest House), a stage coach house whose proprietors looked forward to sheltering and feeding passengers transferring between the stage coaches and the trains. In mid-February the track layers approached Waukesha, and the ringing of their hammers was heard in the village.

Waukesha began as Prairie Village, then became Prairieville, then Waukesha. The land where the village lay, at the rapids of the Fox River, was first claimed by Alonzo and Morris Cutler, accompanied by their father, in 1834. The Cutlers went back East to get the money with which to purchase it and then returned the following spring to settle. It was said that Morris Cutler provided the first ferry service when he carried people on his back across a shallow part of the river. In 1839 the Cutlers sold the part of their land that was on the rapids to brothers Samuel H. and William A. Barstow. The Barstows built a large flouring mill there, and the village quickly grew up around it. In the mid-1840s William Barstow and Alexander Randall (both future governors of Wisconsin) became enthusiastic promoters of the Milwaukee and Waukesha Railroad. In 1847 they were designated commissioners to receive its stock subscriptions. Those duties ended when the company organized in 1849. Finally, in 1851, with the arrival of the tracks, they were seeing the fruits of their labors. In 1851 Waukesha had two thousand inhabitants. It also had two mills, two foundries, two breweries, eight churches, and—the pride of the village—four miles of limestone sidewalks.

With the tracks nearing Waukesha, more and more railroaders, from the president of the company to the laborers on the line, were coming into town. Anson Buttles, a surveyor for the railroad and a personal friend of Byron Kilbourn, was among them. On January 21 he wrote his wife:

> Dear Wife
>
> Since I started from home, it has seemed an age to me but I get along very well. I did not leave Milwaukee until Thursday and from there we came to Waukesha and here we have been ever since waiting for Mr. Kilbourn to come out but the weather did not let him come[.] [I]t was too cold and I was glad he did not come for it was so cold we could not stay out very long but he came out on Sunday and we went down to the Rail Road to work and was walking around the Depot and just as I turned around Mr. Kilbourn fell down (by stepping on a small stick) and broke his right arm. We took him up to the town and I went after a doctor and he said his arm was broke [sic]. So we telegraphed in to Mrs. Kilbourn and Doctor Wolcott and they came out in two hours. So that has kept us here some time longer, he has sent for a man to come and go out with us. He will be here tomorrow and then we will go. . . .
>
> The weather has been very cold until today, and now I am afraid it will rain soon and make it very bad walking for us. We will have a ride out in a waggon [sic] which Mr. Kilbourn has got for us, which will be better than walking, don't you think?
>
> Your loving husband,
> Anson[3]

The influence of the railroad could be seen in Waukesha's railroad facilities. The buildings, erected in 1849 and 1850, were imposing. The two-story stone depot was larger and more substantial than Milwaukee's single-story frame depot. Two tracks ran through the structure's middle so that passengers could get on and off the trains with a roof over their heads. Next to the depot was an even larger stone building—the 120-foot by 80-foot car-building shop where the company's passenger and freight cars were built. A full 20 miles from the port of Milwaukee, the shop was a statement of optimism. Until the first segment of the railway was complete, all the wheels, axles, and frame components had to be brought from the rail-head by teams and wagons. The Milwaukee and Mississippi Railroad Company had spent $19,135 on its facilities at Waukesha—and only $1,073 on those at Milwaukee.[4]

The car-building shop was fortunate in having experienced car builders John Bailie, Walter Kittredge, and Edwin Kittredge working there. Bailie had practiced his trade in New York before coming to Waukesha. The Kittredges (probably brothers) had built cars in Detroit for the Michigan Central Railroad. In 1841 Walter Kittredge was hired by the Michigan Central Railroad as a master car builder. In 1850 he moved with his family to Waukesha, where he began work at the new Milwaukee and Mississippi car-building shops. At the time only three or four miles of track had been laid at Milwaukee. Edwin Kittredge, who had learned carpentry and car building in the shops of the Michigan Central during the 1840s, was hired in the fall of 1850. Edwin built the company's first passenger car, which was the first railroad passenger car in Wisconsin.[5]

By the time the tracks reached Waukesha, the shops had completed four passenger cars. The cars were typical of their time. They were forty feet long (including the outside platforms), made of wood, painted cream-yellow, and covered by low, arched roofs. Inside were thinly upholstered, tightly spaced seats for forty passengers—comfort on railroads had not yet arrived. However, there were some amenities. The windows by the outside seats could be opened to let in fresh air or closed to keep out smoke and ashes, and the arched roof gave six feet of headroom in the center aisle—enough to allow most people to walk through the car without stooping. By all accounts, these cars were built as well as any in the East.[6]

❖ ❖ ❖ ❖ ❖ ❖

On February 15, 1851, the Milwaukee and Mississippi Railroad Company announced that in ten days time, the first trains would begin to run on a regular schedule: "Trains for freight and passengers leave the Depot on Second Street, regularly every morning and afternoon."[7] The company then posted the following announcement to proclaim the opening of the railroad:

MILWAUKEE & MISSISSIPPI RAIL ROAD PROGRAMME
    For the Occasion of opening the Rail Road to Waukesha on Tuesday, Feb. 25th, 1851.

> The cars will leave the Depot at Milwaukee at 10 o'clock A. M. precisely.
> Fare for each Passenger out and returning $2.50.
> All Passengers by the Train will receive a Dinner Ticket free of Charge.
> HESS' BAND WILL ACCOMPANY THE TRAIN.
> DINNER
> Will be served in the Company's new and spacious Car House, under the direction of the Committee of Arrangements at 1 o'clock P. M. Precisely.
> AFTER THE REMOVAL OF THE CLOTH
> Addresses will be made. Among those who will address the Company, it is expected will be Judge Hubbell, Mayor Upham and Governor Tallmadge.
> Ladies are expected to participate in the festivities of the Occasion.
> THE RETURN TRAIN
> Will leave Waukesha at 4 o'clock p.m. precisely.
> AN EVENING TRAIN
> Will leave at 6 o' clock p. m. to take out those who desire to participate in the festivities of the evening. Fare for single gentlemen, the usual rates. For a gentleman and lady, out and back, two dollars.–E. D. Holton, Supt.[8]

On the morning of the 25th the snow that had been on the ground had melted and Milwaukee's streets were muddy. Despite these conditions people found their way to the depot, at the foot of Second Street, to partake in the opening of Wisconsin's first railroad. There the train—engine No. 1, four newly finished passenger cars, and a platform car fitted with benches—stood waiting. Over two hundred ticketed passengers boarded and took their seats. Hess's Band filled the air with festive music. The "outside passengers," seated on the platform car, wrapped themselves in blankets and prepared for a cold ride. Most of the passengers had never ridden on a train before. Some were nervous about traveling at twenty-five or thirty miles per hour. Yet all knew that they were participating in an historic event—the opening of Wisconsin's first railroad. Many of them would, in the years to come, tell their children and grandchildren about this day.[9]

At twenty minutes past eleven o'clock Conductor Edwin Bridgeman signaled for the train to start. As the engineer opened the locomotive's throttle, steam, at a pressure of one hundred pounds per square inch, rushed down the pipes to the two fourteen-by-twenty-six-inch cylinders, mounted on either side of the boiler at the front of the locomotive. On one side, as the steam pushed the piston in the cylinder forward, the connecting rods pulled the tops of the driving wheels on that side forward. On the other side the steam pushed the piston backward and the rods pushed the bottoms of the driving wheels backward. The wheels on both sides turned, and the 46,000-pound locomotive moved forward. After travel-

This advertisement for the Milwaukee & Mississippi appeared in Samuel Freeman's 1857 *Emigrants Handbook and Guide to Wisconsin*.
WHI IMAGE ID 64016

ing two inches, the iron connecting-link at the rear pulled taut and jerked the 44,000-pound tender (the car directly behind the locomotive that supplied it with cord-wood fuel and the water for the boiler) into motion. The locomotive and tender, moving as a unit, jerked the cars into motion one by one, each with more force than the one before. And then the train was moving. The crowd of onlookers cheered, gentlemen threw their hats into the air, and before anyone fully grasped what was happening, the train left the station.[10]

The inaugural train steamed westward, slowly ascending the Menomonee River valley. Farmers and their families, many dressed in their Sunday best, lined the way, cheering and waving. Conductor Bridgeman had the train make all the proper stops—Spring Street Road, Chase's Mill, Wauwatosa, Blanchard's, Underwood's, Elm Grove, Dixon's Road, Power's Mill, Tew's Road, Plank Road, and Fox River Cottage—all "flag-stops" without platforms or stations—taking on passengers at each. One hour and forty-five minutes after leaving Milwaukee, the train arrived in Waukesha. As the passengers descended from the train inside the sizeable, covered depot, they were greeted by a large crowd of their "country cousins."

Some five hundred people walked from the depot to the car-building shop at Waukesha, where the celebration was to take place. The work of the reception committee was evident: the shop equipment had been cleared and the room fitted up with tables, chairs, and a speaker's platform. After the guests were seated, announcements were made and a letter from President Kilbourn was read in which he conveyed his regret at not being able to attend due to his recent arm injury. Then came a sumptuous dinner. It was followed by speeches from Mayor Upham, Milwaukee and Mississippi Superintendent Holton, and J. Brown of Milwaukee; Alexander Randall of Waukesha; Joseph Goodrich of Milton; and Rufus Cheney of Whitewater. At four o'clock the train returned to Milwaukee. At six o'clock a second train arrived with those coming for the evening celebrations and the dance. The reduced fare for gentlemen bringing ladies had the desired effect. The food, the music, the dancing, the speeches, and especially the train rides—it had been a day to remember.[11]

Regularly scheduled rail service between Milwaukee and Waukesha, with one train daily in each direction, began on March 4, 1851. At the end of the month the directors reported the costs of building the 20.5-mile railroad:

| | |
|---|---:|
| Bridging | 9,472.36 |
| Grading and ballasting | 76,936.67 |
| Amount to complete ballasting, less amount since paid | 19,193.87 |
| Ties | 14,704.26 |
| Laying track | 9,508.46 |
| Miscellaneous items, chargeable to superstructure | 5,880.00 |
| Nineteen hundred tons of iron rail, $50 | 95,000.00 |
| Spikes, estimated at $250 per mile | 5,125.00 |
| Engineering expenses | 8,000.00 |
| Other expenses | 25,000.00 |
| Total 20½ miles, finished, | $268,820.62[12] |

Thus, the cost of the road proper, not including locomotives, cars, buildings, etc., was $13,132.20 per mile. The directors pointed out that the expenditures, though exceeding estimates, were not above the cost of similar roads and did not exceed the average cost of the Galena and Chicago Union road.[13] Their best news, however, was that during March the company had earned revenues averaging $45 per day!

On April 15 the Milwaukee and Mississippi expanded its services by providing one passenger train and one freight train, daily, in each direction. Westbound trains left Milwaukee at 7:40 a.m. and 3:40 p.m.; eastbound trains left Waukesha at 10:00 a.m. and 6:00 p.m. The new schedule was met with acclaim by the business community, and revenues grew. For April the company reported revenues averaging $60 per day—up from the $45 of March.[14]

The Milwaukee and Mississippi's honeymoon period continued through April and May. During this time Milwaukee's newspapers received letters from people who had ridden the trains. On May 5 the following appeared in the *Sentinel and Gazette*. It was written at Waukesha by a traveler from New Hampshire:

> Gentlemen: Having occasion to pass through your State, I rode over the Milwaukee & Mississippi Rail Road en route from your beautiful city to this village, and I cannot forbear offering a word, through your paper, to the public, in relation to the railroad, as I am inclined to opinion there is a misapprehension abroad upon the subject. From what I had heard, I expected to find the road rough and uneven, the cars inferior and uncomfortable, and the whole affair a very sorry imitation of what a well constructed, well conducted railroad ought to be.

But to my great surprise I found the road as smooth as the average Eastern Trunk Railroads. The car I rode in was spacious, plainly but well finished, the upholstery done in modern and most approved manner. The locomotive apparently new, in fine order, of large size, with four driving wheels. Several stops were made upon the route, and from the perfect ease with which the stops and starts were made, I would judge an excellent engineer had charge of the engine. Upon one point I wish to speak particularly, that is the quiet and unobtrusive manner in which the business of the road is carried on. The courteous manner of the attendants would do well to be patterned after by many older companies.

In fine, the morning was bright, quite a number of ladies were along, and the ride was delightful; and as a traveler through your young and beautiful State, I feel that I have been laid under obligation by the projectors and managers of the Milwaukee & Mississippi Rail Road, and would recommend to all fellow travelers going West, instead of taking the dust and sweat of the stagecoaches, or private carriages, to take the railroad.[15]

Another letter, printed in the *Sentinel and Gazette* of May 10, chronicles a trip to the end of the line and beyond:

In Company with several friends we took a ride, Thursday, over the Railroad from this city [Milwaukee] to Waukesha; partly to see for ourselves the condition of the track, and partly to enjoy a brief holiday in the country . . . Taking our places as "outsiders" on one of the Platform Cars, we were enabled to scrutinize quite clearly the appearance and condition of the road-bed and superstructure. . . . The road is wonderfully improved. . . . The road-bed, made almost wholly of gravel, is one of the best we have ever seen, and the superstructure, composed of the heavy T rail resting on substantial oak ties, is well laid, solid and enduring. The cars, though not as elegant as some of those on the older Eastern roads, are neat, airy, and comfortable. The Locomotives are of ample power; the Engineers careful and competent; and the Conductor, Mr. E. Bridgeman, a model of civility. . . .

The approach to Waukesha, down the valley of the Fox, is beautiful. Waukesha itself is a beautiful village, and the country round it fertile, inviting, well settled, and under good cultivation. . . .

The ride home was speedy and pleasant; the train making the schedule time (an hour and a half including all stops) *to a minute*. So much was the excursion enjoyed by all, that before separating it was agreed to repeat the experiment with a larger party, not forgetting the ladies, next week.[16]

❖ ❖ ❖ ❖ ❖ ❖

At the end of May the company announced that its revenues for the month had averaged $114 per day—almost double those of April. The stockholders could breathe a sigh of relief. There had been no guarantees that their railroad, new and untried, would succeed. Two plank roads, running parallel to the railroad, offered competition and had been a concern. But with May's figures, the stockholders knew that the railroad would pay. After receiving the news, Secretary Benjamin Edgerton told a newspaper reporter that he felt "confident that the road would be a great success." For the month of June, the company reported $2,104 in freight revenues and $4,088 in passenger revenues. The total—$6,192—was again almost double the previous month's.[17]

And so it was that Wisconsin received its first railroad. Conceived by Milwaukee pioneers in 1835, presented to the territorial legislature in 1836, chartered by that legislature in 1847, and built in 1849, 1850, and 1851, it became a fully functional railroad in February 1851. This only happened because many people had persevered for many years. Company President Kilbourn deserved much of the credit. So too did Edgerton, Solomon Juneau, John Tweedy, Randall, William Barstow, Richard P. Morgan, Buttles, Sherbourne S. Merrill, Alexander Mitchell, James Kneeland, Holton, Clinton, Goodrich, and countless others. Special recognition was due to the stockholders, most of whom were farmers, who had had the courage to buy into the venture with money, goods, labor, or mortgages on their properties—they *were* the Milwaukee and Mississippi Railroad Company. As that first train left the station, many of them were no doubt very proud of the wonder they had created—and looking forward to the benefits they hoped it would bring.

# Chapter 10

## Growing Pains

### May–December 1851

Amid the progress and enthusiasm surrounding the opening of the railroad, a single troubling note rang out: in April the company had been unable to pay the interest on its bonds. When news of the failure was announced in Milwaukee's newspapers, President Byron Kilbourn sprang to the defense of the company. According to Kilbourn the company was paying interest on all bonds that had been *legitimately* sold, but the bonds in question—$34,000 of a $100,000 issue sold by Treasurer Walter P. Flanders the previous fall—had been purchased through misrepresentation and thus had *not* been legitimately sold.

A few days later Kilbourn and financial agent Jacob L. Bean left for New York to try to resolve the matter. Before leaving they were given instructions by the board to use their stay out East to sell more securities, hoping this would help to secure the company's precarious finances. But the company's inability to pay interest on its bonds was hardly an encouragement for others to invest. What is more, Kilbourn's claim that the bonds were not legitimate lost credibility when he, on arriving in New York, borrowed money to pay the interest. More disturbing, however, was the manner in which Kilbourn blamed Flanders for these troubles.

During the previous summer, in 1850, Kilbourn had gone to New York to sell the company's first farm-mortgage bonds. But as these were a new commodity, he was unable to interest any buyers. Then in October Flanders went to New York and received from the company's agent, Charles Crocker, one hundred thousand dollars of farm-mortgage bonds that he, Crocker, had been unable to sell. Flanders promptly negotiated the sale of these bonds to Cryder, McKay, and Jaudon, a trio of New York investors. Not authorized to conclude the transaction, Flanders returned to Milwaukee and presented the details of the sale to the company's directors. The directors, including Kilbourn, gave it their approval. Flanders then returned to New York, closed the sale, and received the first installment of cash. He had been proud of his accomplishment. He was the first to sell the new farm-mortgage bonds.

So why, four months later, did Kilbourn blame Flanders for the company's embarrassment? As president, Kilbourn could have shouldered responsibility for the mistake, but he didn't. The seriousness of the matter—that it might sink the company—may have had something to do with it. It was clear that the company needed to regain the trust of its investors, something that was more easily accomplished if one person—and not the head of the company—were at fault. Kilbourn claimed that Flanders's assertion, that he had met the buyers of the bonds through his (Flanders's) wife's relations, had lulled the directors into accepting the loan. Had Flanders "admitted that he did not know who they were," the directors would have investigated the buyers further and rejected the loan. Kilbourn began to refer to the loan as "the fraud perpetrated upon Flanders," and then "the Flanders Fraud." The latter insinuated that Flanders had committed fraud, which he hadn't.[1]

After paying the overdue interest in New York, Kilbourn found the credit of the company only partially restored. He reported:

> The apprehensions on this subject were so great that the payment of that interest was not sufficient to restore our credit; and the holders of several of our bonds then requested, nay, begged of me, even after paying the interest, to purchase the bonds of them at 90 per cent., for which amount they offered to surrender the bonds held by them. Considering the small amount of our securities in the market, the panic was very great; and although money was then abundant and easily obtained on all western securities, I found it impossible to negotiate our bonds until something more could be done to restore our credit.[2]

The "something more" Kilbourn proposed was buying back the problem bonds. But in this Kilbourn was frustrated, and negotiations dragged on for months. Again Kilbourn shifted the blame to external factors, saying:

> I soon learned that there were evil designing persons making themselves busy with our affairs, either for the purpose of discrediting us, so as to prevent our raising funds, and thus arresting our operations, or for the purpose of coercing us

# GROWING PAINS

into a settlement with the parties holding our securities, through those who had obtained them by the aforesaid fraud.³

It would not be until mid-August that Kilbourn settled with circus magnate P. T. Barnum and Charles T. Cromwell, the holders of the disputed bonds. He recovered $9,482 of the $34,000, the company suffering a loss of $14,518. Kilbourn later wrote of the affair, of Flanders, and of himself, "In the different stages of this business, the difference between Flanders and myself was, chiefly, that, *without my aid*, he got the Company into the difficulty; and *without his aid*, I got them out of it"—again insinuating the blame fell on Flanders. By the time Kilbourn got the company out of the situation, loan opportunities had been lost and construction work had been delayed several times during the precious summer months.⁴

At the beginning of the summer of 1851, with the line to Waukesha some three months in operation, the directors found time to review some of the problems they had encountered and to come up with solutions for them. At the top of their list was the problem of contractors doing inferior work—work that sooner or later would need to be fixed or re-done, resulting in lost time and added expenses. The situation stemmed from the company's policy of awarding contracts to the lowest bidders. Contractors underbid in order to be awarded jobs; they would then cut corners in their work to stay within costs. The solution, the directors decided, was for the company to monitor all contracted work and to withhold payment until approving such work. To that end they created a new position—constructing engineer—and appointed Benjamin H. Edgerton, the company's secretary, to fill it. Edgerton was to oversee all surveys, locations, plans, and estimates and to develop and enforce standards for construction work. The directors had chosen wisely. Edgerton was an experienced civil engineer and was intelligent, honest, and hardworking. Most importantly, he was persevering—and he would need to be, if the rails were ever to reach the Mississippi.

Edgerton found the ten miles beyond Waukesha difficult. "The grading," he wrote, "is extremely heavy . . . is probably the most formidable . . . this side of Madison."⁵ The men dug cuts as deep as forty-eight feet through hills and built up embankments as high as thirty-five feet across valleys. The roadway was twenty-four feet wide in the cuts and fourteen feet wide on the embankments. Fortunately, there was little rock excavation, most of the digging being of sand or gravel. On the western part of the division Edgerton encountered the steepest grade of the entire road—the half-mile ascent, on which the roadway climbed 17 feet, before Hinkley's

Summit. This would be the governing grade for all westbound trains—the grade that determined how heavy a train could be or how much power it would need to pass over the line. At the top of this grade was the summit pass; at 370 feet above Lake Michigan, it was the highest point between Milwaukee and the Mississippi.[6]

Despite these challenges, Edgerton laid in a railroad of quality, especially in terms of its curves. Sharp curves that would force trains to slow down were avoided. While some Eastern railroads had curves with radii of as little as 500 feet, Edgerton could report that on his road "the least radius of curvature is 3,800 feet, except in the approach to the Whitewater Depot, where a curve of 1,900 feet has been admitted, but occurring where the speed of the trains must of necessity be slackened, it will not be found objectionable."[7]

Early in June a telegram arrived from Kilbourn in New York in which he stated that he had issued $150,000 in bonds and backed them with a mortgage on the road from Milwaukee to Waukesha. The directors gave his act an after-the-fact approval, although several felt a greater sum of money could have been borrowed using the same collateral.[8] These were the company's first road-mortgage bonds. They set a precedent. From this time forth the Milwaukee and Mississippi Company would mortgage as much of its property as it could to borrow as much money as it could, leaving little actual property in the hands of the company itself. This policy would put the company in perpetual danger of losing its property to its Eastern creditors. But it would also allow the company to build faster, reach the next paying destination sooner, and beat the competition. The president and the directors felt that it was critical for the road to reach the Rock River valley before the "Chicago roads"—the Galena and Chicago Union and Rock River Valley Union—did. For Edgerton the $150,000 bond issue meant that there would be funds with which to continue building.

And continue Edgerton did. In July the rails reached Jenkins' Station, seven miles beyond Waukesha. The Milwaukee and Mississippi's agents had earlier approached the residents of Jenkinsville, two miles to the south of the station, and asked for right-of-way and station grounds. They had been refused. The people there had done well enough being on the stagecoach line, and they didn't want that changed. But Benjamin A. Jenkins, the founder of the village, who at one time had been forced to make fifty-mile shopping trips to Milwaukee pushing a wheelbarrow, thought differently. He offered the railroad agents what they were asking for, free of charge, on property he owned north of the village. The *Milwaukee and Mississippi* accepted Jenkins's offer, rerouted its line, and built a depot there. Jenkins then erected a warehouse and a store next to the depot, platted a village, and sold lots. Thus Jenkins founded two Wisconsin communities, Jenkinsville and Jenkin's Station, which are today known as Genesee and Genesee Depot.[9]

North Prairie Village, six miles west of Jenkin's Station, was the next stop on the line to receive rails. The prairie here had been named by Thomas Sudgen in 1836. Sudgen and two companions, John Coates and a Mr. Garton, had first approached the prairie from the south. Before turning back, they gave it a name: North Prairie. In 1851 North Prairie Village had over one hundred residents, as well as businesses that included a blacksmith shop and Peter Gifford's Equality Hotel.[10]

In August construction on the road slowed—the company was again short of money. After Kilbourn had issued the $150,000 of bonds in June, the market for railroad securities had plummeted and less than $50,000 of the bonds had sold. During the same period many of the company's stockholders had fallen behind in paying their stock subscriptions. Most of them were wheat farmers, and two consecutive partial crop failures combined with low prices for wheat had put them in arrears. To reduce costs and to keep the work moving forward, Edgerton ordered track to be laid without the gravel ballast normally poured between the ties to anchor them.[11]

During the long months of Kilbourn's absence, a rift had been forming in the company's directorate. There were several reasons for this. With the line to Waukesha completed, the directors had had less work to do and more time to quarrel. Then there was the polarizing effect of Kilbourn himself—his insistence on unquestioning loyalty and obedience had forced the directors to be either for or against him. The fact that Kilbourn held the offices of president, chief engineer, superintendent, and chief fiscal agent had aggravated the problem. But the main reason for the rift was the practice, common at this time, by some of the directors of engaging in "side business ventures"—ventures that did business with the company. The other directors found this practice objectionable and accused the directors involved of spending more time trying to make themselves rich than in serving the company. The rift in the Milwaukee and Mississippi Company ultimately came down to those directors allied with Kilbourn, most of whom were engaged in side ventures, and the directors opposed to the president, who were also opposed to the side ventures. The latter group, led by Kilbourn's old adversary from the Milwaukee and Rock River Canal days, Director John H. Tweedy, called for reform.

The mixing of private interest with duty to the company had been a part of the organization's makeup from the beginning. Directors Bean, Clinton, Powers, and Holton had been among the first to engage in it when they operated the Powers saw mill at Brookfield and sold lumber to the railroad—their employer as directors. They had operated under a conflict of interest: they could charge what they wished for the lumber and, as directors of the railroad, they also approved the purchases. Had they charged excessively, they would have been stealing from the company. Eventually they sold the saw mill. But then Bean, Clinton, and Powers went on to contract the building of the railroad—submitting bids and then approving those same bids in their role as directors. Even if their charges and bids were reasonable, these conflicts of interest started trouble among the directors. Director John Catlin, who opposed the practice, explained:

> It is not in the nature of the best of men to attend to the interests of others as well as to their own, when those interests come in conflict. Such conflicts will occur, and if the interests of the Company should not in some cases greatly suffer thereby, such conflicts will unavoidably produce jealousy and distrust, and disturb that mutual confidence and concert so essential to the successful prosecution of an enterprise demanding the combined energies of all concerned.[12]

In August the "jealousy and distrust" grew as the awarding of the contract for the construction of the thirty miles of railroad between Eagle and Rock River drew near. Tweedy and his followers insisted that the company should hire a contractor who was independent of the company, while Kilbourn's faction tried to obtain the contract for itself (Kilbourn and Bean were still in New York). Both factions got something, which to an extent was the same thing. On September 27 Kilbourn's faction, specifically Directors Bean, Clinton, and Powers, was awarded the contract for the first five and one-half miles between Eagle and Palmyra. Two days later Tweedy's group won a major victory when the board awarded the contract for the entire thirty miles to Joseph and Selah Chamberlain of Cleveland, Ohio, experienced railroad contractors not connected with the company. The Chamberlain contract encompassed bridging, grading, and laying the track to Rock River, which work was to be completed by November 1852. Provision was made for extending the contract to Madison, an additional thirty-four miles. The Chamberlains were to be paid twelve thousand dollars per mile in monthly installments as the work progressed, one-half in cash, the other half in company bonds. As there were now two contracts for Eagle to Palmyra, Bean, Clinton, and Powers were given preemptive rights until February 1852. The Chamberlains began work immediately at Palmyra.[13]

Meanwhile in New York, Kilbourn and Bean, a native of Vermont who had lived in Wisconsin since 1840, were plotting to take over the company.[14] Kilbourn was now obsessed with having total control of the company—simply being its president, chief engineer, superintendent, and chief fiscal agent had not given him that. He needed a board of directors that would always agree with him, and to achieve that, he would need to pick the directors. As the company's directors were elected annually by the stockholders, Kilbourn would need to control the majority of the shares in the company in order to bring his plan to fruition. And he thought he had found a way. On September 12 he issued 19,000 shares—$1,900,000 worth of the company's stock, an incredible amount—to Jacob Bean. This would represent a majority of the shares for many years to come. Kilbourn was able to do this by requiring of Bean an initial payment of only 10 cents per share ($190 in total for 1,900 shares)—not the $5.00 per share required by the charter. With these shares Kilbourn and Bean would be able to vote in their own directors, and those directors would be instructed not to ask for further payment.[15]

When Kilbourn and Bean returned to Milwaukee in October, they were dismayed to find the Chamberlain contract in place—they had been hoping to have it for themselves. All they had was the contract from Eagle to Palmyra. When Bean affixed his signature to this, he added a new condition that the company had to furnish the necessary rails and hardware. The other directors insisted that Bean had thereby invalidated the contract. Bean, Clinton, and Powers proceeded to do the work anyway and then demanded payment. Their demand was difficult to ignore—Bean, as the company's fiscal subagent, held securities that he refused to release until payment was made. All of this confirmed in the minds of the majority of the directors that the decision to contract with the Chamberlains had been correct—and that Kilbourn's influence was too great.[16]

For the remainder of the year, Kilbourn and Bean bided their time, waiting for the stockholders' meeting in January. There they would vote the shares that they had fabricated in New York, shares whose existence they were keeping secret. The board, suspecting something was amiss, repeatedly requested Kilbourn to report on his New York activities. Kilbourn ignored the requests. Tensions grew, and discussion of taking disciplinary action against the president began.

By November, Anson Buttles was no longer a surveyor. He had become an independent railroad construction contractor. He wrote his wife Cornelia on November 2, "I am fixing up my division now. . . . I hired about 35 men and am stopping with them myself so as I can have it look nice."

Four days later he wrote again, telling of a troubling incident:

Dear wife,
 . . . Yesterday morning somebody put something on the track when we were going out and the cars ran off. I was on the locomotive; it stayed on. It threw all the rest of the cars off. One man was hurt some. The Company have offered $200 reward for the man who done it. He will be found out too.

Buttles also wrote to Kilbourn at this time to discuss a business matter. Despite the fact that the Buttles family had known the Kilbourn family since they both lived in Ohio, Buttles received no special treatment when he wrote Kilbourn about receiving back pay. The following was Kilbourn's reply:

> Milwaukee, Nov 9, 1851
> Anson W. Buttles Esq.
>
> Dear Sir,
>
> Yours of 2 no. [November 2] inst. has been in hand several days, but I do not as yet see how I can favor you in the matter as requested. I would suggest that you apply to Mr. Powers to give you authority to call on his partners at Palmyra for such assistance as you may need. I presume you will not require much actual cash, and that most of all that you may want they can furnish to you from their store at that place, until we bring things about so as to pay off our indebtedness to you— This seems to me the most feasible plan of getting along for the present—If you owe Powers anything, I wish you would ascertain the amount and get a R.R. order for me for it—he is considerably in my debt, and so for as this goes, you can get your pay of the Co. and pay him and he pay me, all by the same operation. This is better than to have accounts standing all around. Perhaps you had better come in some evening and attend to it.
>
> Very Respectfully yours,
> Byron Kilbourn[17]

As 1851 drew to a close, there was little celebration in the boardroom of the Milwaukee and Mississippi Railroad. Yet its accomplishments that year had been significant. In February the company had brought Wisconsin its first railroad, completely equipped, with scheduled freight and passenger service, over a 20.5-mile line between Milwaukee and Waukesha. Over the remainder of the year it had extended the road eighteen more miles to Eagle and completed grading five miles beyond that point. In December scheduled trains were running thirty miles from Milwaukee, to a point just west of Jenkins' Station.

Since the opening of its road in March, the Milwaukee and Mississippi had netted $14,914.88 from its operations.[18] And construction costs, while they had exceeded earlier estimates, had been reasonable. The total costs of building and equipping the railroad to date (December 31, 1851) were $652,313.72.[19] This came to somewhat over $17,000 per mile—less than the cost on most other railroads. But the figures that interested the stockholders most were those telling of the return on their investment—what it was and what they could expect it to be in the future. Edgerton, preparing his report in Waukesha on the last day of the year, used a mathematical approach:

> *To the President and Directors of the Milwaukee and Mississippi Railroad Company:*
> 
> As to the probable revenues of the road, no very correct estimate can be given. . . . As a general rule, the ratio of increase in the receipts of a road in consequence of its extension, may be reckoned in proportion to the square of the distance, or, in other words, doubling the length of the road should quadruple the receipts, for there will be twice the area of country tributary, and a traffic of double the distance.—This is at least a safe rule, for it leaves out of view the business which the road of itself creates. Reckoning upon this hypothesis, and taking the receipts of the past year, which have been at the rate of $24,000 per annum, as a basis, the receipts of the road, when completed to Eagle Centre, should be $76,500; at Whitewater, $146,000; and at Rock River, $280,000 per annum. . . .
> 
> On this calculation, the net revenues of the road, when extended to the points named, will be respectively six, ten, and fourteen per cent on the total cost.[20]

Despite this optimistic report, the fact remained that the Milwaukee and Mississippi was not in good health financially, and its festering troubles were coming to a boil. Most of the directors opposed Kilbourn and were seeking to remove him, while a significant number of stockholders and employees of the road remained loyal. In a report to the board dated December 22, Kilbourn had called for unity under his leadership. Using a metaphor that Abraham Lincoln would use eight years later, he lectured the board on the price of disunity:

> How long a house divided against itself can stand, is a problem likely to be tested in the history of Milwaukee. No important measure for the improvement of the business interests of our city has ever yet been begun or proposed, without arraying against it a strong, violent, and uncompromising opposition. The history of our Harbor, Canal, and Railroad, are great and imposing instances of this spirit, whereby the welfare of our city has been compromised, by the loss of millions of capital, which, by harmony and union of councils, might have been secured to our citizens, and would have been the means of placing Milwaukee in the first rank of Lake Cities.[21]

While offering the board such sentiments, Kilbourn was also gathering forces to overthrow it. One of the road's contractors, J. H. Conkey, wrote Selah Chamberlain on December 26:

I have just returned from the country and find a bad state of affairs existing in relation to the Chamberlain contract. Old Kilbourn has been doing all that he could to prejudice the stockholders against it. He has got Bean, Clinton, and Powers with him, and they are at work in an underhanded way, in the country, doing all they can. . . . Their object is to change the Board of Directors and get in men that they can do as they please with, for they cannot manage the present board at all. Eleven of the present board are all right and are sworn to stand by the contract. Now you will at once see the importance of retaining the present board and the importance of you or Joseph being here before the 13th of January. Our friends here say you must come without fail. . . . The board have the utmost confidence in you and will stand by but want you to help them carry the election. . . .

[Y]ours truly,
J. H. Conkey[22]

From Milwaukee to Janesville, in the villages and on the farms, the stockholders of the Milwaukee and Mississippi Railroad were preparing for a showdown at Waukesha.

# Chapter 11

## Wisconsin's Only Railroad
### 1852

The new year started off with a jolt for the Milwaukee and Mississippi Railroad. On January 7 its board of directors removed Byron Kilbourn from the office of president and declared stock sales that had not been duly reported to the board—including the stock purchased by Jacob Bean in New York to secure his and Kilbourn's positions—to be void. The board had repeatedly asked Kilbourn to report on the stock he had sold in New York, and he had repeatedly refused. Within a week of these events Kilbourn had set up his own stockholders organization. As a result, in the latter part of January, there followed two stockholders meetings, held on the same day but at different locations in Waukesha.

At Kilbourn's stockholders meeting, Bean held the overwhelming majority of shares. These were the controversial shares that Kilbourn had issued to him in New York. Through Bean, Kilbourn now exercised the (questionably) enviable power to choose and vote in his own directors. Presumably wishing to avoid publicity in the matter, Kilbourn did not seek reelection as president. Instead, he and Bean elected a board of directors that chose Ashael Finch Jr. as president of the Milwaukee and Mississippi.

Simultaneously, the dissenting stockholders, led by Director John H. Tweedy, elected a board that chose John Catlin of Madison as president of the Milwaukee and Mississippi. Both groups adjourned hastily. Then there was a wild scramble back to Milwaukee to take control of the railroad's property. The *Milwaukee Sentinel* reported:

The Kilbourn party took the cars [the train] and the others started in sleighs for this city, to get possession of the books and other property of the Company. The sleighs got in a little ahead, and when the Kilbourn party entered the office, they found Dr. Weeks in possession of the books, which possession he managed to maintain for some time, while both parties indulged in severe and abusive threats. At length, Mr. Gridley came to the assistance of Dr. Weeks, who resigned his position—that of sitting on the books—and took the urn of the stove as a weapon of defense. This weapon was taken from him by the Kilbourn party, and one of the party succeeded in getting some of the books away as far as the bottom of the stairs, but here the Kilbourn party was met by the reserved force of their opponents, and by dint of some choking, it is said, were compelled to disgorge the plunder which was safely secured by the others, leaving the latter [Kilbourn's opponents] in possession of the whole, which both sides seemed to think would be "nine points in the law." Dr. Weeks received considerable injury in the way of business, but nothing of a very serious nature. This is a frolic in high life. . . . We hope there will be no lives lost, and no blood spilt! We had thought that by careful management, our Road might get along without "accidents"; but it seems "they will happen on the best of Rail Roads." But seriously, we think this mess is an unpardonable trifling with the best interests of the Road, as also with that of the traveling and business public.[1]

The attempted takeover was short lived. During the two weeks of its existence, Kilbourn's board, lacking "the books," was unable to transact business. Kilbourn finally submitted the report on his New York stock sales—which he had withheld from the previous board—to Finch, the new president Kilbourn had chosen, who owed his position to the illegal shares. The report is typical of Kilbourn. In it, he casts himself as the wronged party, placing the blame elsewhere. In the first paragraph, Kilbourn states that payment on the shares would have been made "if required by the Board"—but with Kilbourn and Bean controlling the board, that might never have happened. In the second paragraph, Kilbourn claims that voting the stock was legitimate because its owner, Bean, had bought it in "good faith," a flawed argument. Kilbourn would write similar papers, often self-published, in the years to come. Proud and dictatorial, he never gave up and he never gave in. He would rebound, only to have his habits, by now familiar to the board and to the Milwaukee public, catch up with him again.

Despite his difficult and complex personality, Kilbourn was, and still is, Wisconsin's best-known railroad pioneer of the 1850s. His report of January 19 to Finch also gives insight into his personality:

At the time of receiving [Bean's] subscription, I was in negotiation with some eminent Contractors, with a view to their taking all that part of our Road to construct, this side of Wisconsin River; and with the expectation that they would receive a considerable proportion of their payments in the Stock of the Company. . . . [T]o promote these objects, I deemed it essential . . . to endeavor to interest him personally, and to a large amount, in the success of the Company. . . .

I *may* have misjudged as to the true policy of the Company; but it is my opinion still, that if on my return home, I had not found the ground previously occupied by the Chamberlin contract, I would . . . have placed . . . a contract . . . on far better terms. . . . [M]y acts were the result of my thorough convictions as to the true policy of the Company, and the success and rapid progress of the Road.

I regret all the circumstances . . . but do not feel that I am in any manner accountable for them. . . . I have the satisfaction of knowing that in all I have done, I have been actuated solely by the paramount desire to secure the highest interests of the Company. . . . The same considerations now weigh strongly in my mind in favor of a conciliatory course towards our opponents, preferring, as I do, to allow them to manage the affairs of the Company, even in an improvident manner, rather than break down the whole enterprise. . . . I am even willing for the sake of the cause, to suffer, for the present, all the inconveniences flowing from the numerous misrepresentations which, through unworthy motives, and for unworthy purposes, have been promulgated by unworthy persons, to my prejudice, for many days past.

Respectfully submitted,
BYRON KILBOURN[2]

Kilbourn's consideration of a "conciliatory course" came when he had already lost the battle. On February 10, Bean surrendered his stock.

Catlin, the new, legitimate president of the Milwaukee and Mississippi Railroad Company, lacked the flamboyance of Kilbourn, but would make up for that with his sound business sense and dependability. Like many in Milwaukee, Catlin was native to the East, born October 13, 1803, in Orwell, Vermont. The descendent of Thomas Catlin, a colonist, Catlin was trained as a schoolteacher and lawyer. In the spring of 1836 he moved west to what was about to become Wisconsin Territory, arriving in Mineral Point. There he entered into a short-term law partnership with Moses M. Strong, one of Wisconsin's early residents. Allied with Strong, he soon shifted his interests to work that was more appropriate to the growth of the state: that of postmaster to Madison, a post he held for several years. During the 1840s Catlin became clerk to the Territorial Supreme Court, clerk to the Territorial House of Representatives, a territorial councilman, the Dane County district attorney, territorial secretary (second to the governor), and Dane County judge. On accepting the presidency of the Milwaukee and Mississippi in January 1852, he moved with his wife and daughter to Milwaukee. John Catlin was well liked and respected—just the man to restore the faith of the subscribers to the still-floundering railroad.

Catlin's 1852 board of directors boasted some men of note. Forty-year-old Director George H. Walker, recently the mayor of Milwaukee, had founded and developed the South Side of Milwaukee, the land known as "Walker's Point." He had served in the Territorial House of Representatives from 1842 to 1845 and in the State Assembly in 1851.[3] Thirty-eight-year-old Director William A. Barstow, one of Waukesha's founders, had been one of the commissioners specified in the company's charter. An active Democrat, Barstow had been elected secretary of state in 1850 but failed to earn reelection in 1851.[4] The other directors for 1852 were Tweedy, Alexander Mitchell, Edward D. Holton, Anson Eldred, Eliphalet Cramer, Joseph Goodrich, Erastus B. Wolcott, James Kneeland, Adam E. Ray, Sheldon C. Hall, Joshua Cobb, and David L. Mills. William Taintor continued as secretary, as did Walter P. Flanders as treasurer.

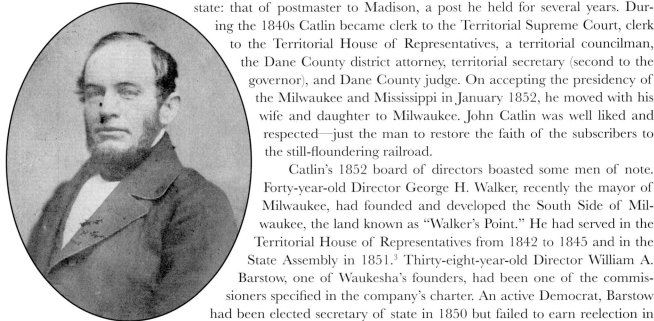

John Catlin, second president of the Milwaukee and Mississippi Railroad Company, in 1856.
WHi Image ID 27651

President Catlin inherited a railroad that was in a mess. He would describe the start of his tenure by saying that "this was at a time when the company had no money in hand to pay its laborers; quite a debt lying over and past due, and its road mortgage ten per cent bonds, without the prospect of sale, had been pledged for money to pay the January interest."[5] He soon found, however, that the railroad still had its friends—among them some of its directors:

> Several citizens of known wealth and high respectability, some of whom were not stockholders, and without the hope of gain, came forward on the 5th of February last and signed a bond with the directors for one hundred thousand dollars. . . . The names of these friends of our enterprise are Elisha Eldred, H. Crocker, W. A. Prentis, George. F. Austin, Joseph Cary, James H. Rogers, Henry Williams, C. Shepardson, and Walter P. Flanders.[6]

With its finances again under control, the tracks of the Milwaukee and Mississippi reached Eagle Centre, six miles west of North Prairie, on January 22. When pioneers Thomas Sudgeon, John Coates, and a Mr. Garton crossed this section of prairie in 1836, they had seen a large bald eagle rise up and therefore named the spot Eagle Prairie. A settlement soon followed named Eagleville, and another, in 1851, named Eagle Centre. Eagle Centre's proprietor and developer, William J. Kline, had wisely donated three acres of land to the railroad for use for a depot and yards.[7]

On May 1 Edward H. Brodhead joined the company and began his duties as superintendent and chief engineer. The directors had decided in February to hire a certified civil engineer to superintend the railroad, having until that time made do with surveyors who learned their railroad engineering on the job. Civil engineers were hard to come by at this time, West Point Military Academy being the only engineering school in the nation. Yet the directors succeeded, hiring forty-two-year-old Edward Hallock Brodhead of New York State. Brodhead was described as "[A] man . . . about 5 ft. 11 inches in height, well built, fine head,—small dark eyes, hair . . . grey . . . & in short a man of very prepossessing appearance."[8] Brodhead came from a distinguished New York family whose ancestors helped in the capture of New Amsterdam (New York City) from the Dutch in 1664. He had attended West Point's engineering school for two years as a private student, finishing in 1830. He then worked for the Ithaca and Oswego Railroad. He supervised construction on various other railroads and canals in New York before accepting the position offered by the Milwaukee and Mississippi. The company's directors awarded him a remarkably high starting salary of $3,500 per year, plus $1,000 for expenses.

The letters of Charles Linsley, a newly hired, twenty-year-old surveyor from Vermont, give insight into life on a survey crew, as well as life in Wisconsin in 1852. They also share a picture of the mismanagement the company was experiencing at that time. Linsley worked on location surveys between Whitewater and Madison. Most of his letters home were written in May, June, and July, although the earliest is dated March 10, 1852:

> Mr. Edgerton I saw a week ago today & have not seen him since. He told me to come on & take charge of the locating party from this place to Rock River & gave me an introduction to Mr. Shields, an assistant on construction who is stopping at this place. Well, I came on & made my appearance in the Engineers Office which was over a store. Among the paper bags & crockery leather flour &c a small low bench or table set near two small windows constituted the Engineers corner. Not a chair in the garret, but seats provided on raisin boxes &c if they hadn't been split into kindling wood. . . . I found Shields to be a very clever fellow, a Scotch-man

who came to this country at the time the road was commencing & has been on ever since. He commenced as chairman I believe & so along up. He is about 22 I should judge. He has charge of a division from this place east. As for the locating party I found a Mr. Little who was with me at Norwich & had been on here about a month running levels. He has been in the business about a year, is a clever fellow & a splendid mathematician. . . . They pay here Rodmen, axemen, & all $30.00 per month, making no distinction. . . .

I have thus given you a short description of the engineering on the Road, but do not think it is worse than I expected to find it or that I am at all discontented. I only write it to show how much is lost by improper management & by not having a proper head. Mr. Edgerton appears to be a very fine man, of good education, & a well read man but no experience in building Rail Roads. He came on as a land surveyor at first & knew nothing about the true practical economy of Railroading. Conkey says that when he came on here to lay track for them (that was done a year ago) he never saw so green a set, not an engineer that ever saw any track laid & all were in a fix & that is the way that he came to get the job so easily. . . . They never had an engineer on here that had ever been on another railroad. . . . It seems that the said Byron Kilbourn the former President was a scoundrel (to speak it plainly as it is said to me) & sunk a good deal of money for the Company. He appointed himself Chief Engineer & made a miserable location from Milwaukee to Waukesha, very crooked & about four miles out of the way. Everybody appears to be down on him, but Conkey says that Mr. Holton was always rather friendly to him.

On March 28, Linsley wrote:

I commenced on my own responsibility a preliminary survey to Rock River—eight miles—I commenced a new line entirely different from any that had ever been run & I think I have about the thing. . . . I find that the Co. is amazingly poor. None of the Engineers that I have seen have been paid scarcely anything for a year & they now owe them for a years work nearly, just so with the Fond Du Lac Road [Rock River Valley Union].

On April 2 he wrote:

I think I shall (if I am required) proceed towards Madison with the survey, without saying much about more wages. The distance from Rock River to Madison is 28 miles & much of the way good land, the country also is said to be somewhat settled with *"human people,"* but we should probably camp out. . . . I have been 14 miles (tramping) today in a strong cold west wind & my eyes feel sore. . . .

# WISCONSIN'S ONLY RAILROAD

On May 1 Linsley wrote from Milton:

> We are suffering much for the want of a proper head to give us directions &c & the Co. begin to find that they are a ways behind-hand in the matter of having the line ready for the contractors. Conkey & Cook were here the first of the week & they said that their horses & carts were to be shipped this week from Cleveland & put upon the work between Whitewater & Rock River. But it will take a month at least to prepare the work for them between here & Rock River and that is much the heaviest part of the work. . . .

Linsley, frustrated with management, wrote on May 14:

> They are aweful [*sic*] here in Railroading and do not manage well for their own interest. By judicious management they could have shortened the line from Milwaukee to Madison some 12 miles from what it will now be & all this deviation to hit some small village or somebody's saw mill.

On May 30, he was in Madison:

> We have continued the line westward during the week and have got as far as Stoughtonville, 16 miles from here, and last night I came in here with Mr. Temple to spend Sunday. We find a hard country between Rock River and this place; no inhabitants scarcely but Norwegians, and they live in mud houses. We have to go from four to seven miles to get from the line to a stopping place. The country through which we have passed is very poor; mostly uncultivated wild land, and a great many marshes.

Linsley's letter dated July 4 from Cooksville reveals that the company was not above deception:

> We are now running lines that we know are impracticable merely to satisfy stockholders and secure subscriptions, etc.⁹

In August, Linsley quit the company and moved to Chicago, presumably fed up with his experience working for the Milwaukee and Mississippi Railroad.

That summer revenue trains were running between Milwaukee and Eagle Prairie and construction trains were running to the railhead approaching Whitewater. In

June President Catlin issued six hundred thousand dollars worth of eight percent bonds secured by a mortgage on the entire road, from Milwaukee to Rock River. The interest would be payable semiannually in the city of New York, and the principle would be payable on July 1, 1862. President Catlin was following the precedent set by former president Kilbourn of borrowing all that could be borrowed.

July 4 was a day of celebrating independence as well as six months of rail service at Eagle Centre:

> The first celebration here was quite a notable event, as it came off on the 4th of July following the coming of the railway, and is remembered as an occasion of big doings, when every one from far and near that could come was there; and when S. S. Merrill, then a freight conductor on the road, was the ruling genius of the day, and the god of the fire-works.[10]

Five more miles of railroad, to Palmyra, were opened on August 2, making a line of forty-two miles from Milwaukee. Palmyra, named after the biblical oasis, was where railroad contractor Zebina Willson and his brother lived. The Willsons had some fifty men, as many horses, and some sixteen oxen working for them. They paid shovelers thirteen dollars per month and teamsters fifteen dollars per month, boarding included. The Willsons divided their men into two crews. Each crew would build six miles of grade at a time; when the back crew arrived at a completed section, it would move ahead six miles. Most of the right-of-way between Waukesha and Janesville was built and graded in this way. The wooden ties laid over these sections were not spaced evenly, being farther apart at the rail centers and closer together near the rail ends. In theory, this was supposed to equalize the load in supporting passing trains and minimize the wear on the end-joints.

The operations on railroads of this time, including those on the new Milwaukee and Mississippi, had the potential to be dangerous. All trains—passenger, freight, and construction, eastbound and westbound—ran over a single track, and care had to be taken to avoid collisions. Engineers were given time-cards telling them at which station and at what time they were to wait for the opposing train. The first train arriving at such a meeting place would pull into the siding. The second train, coming from the opposite direction, would stop on the main track alongside it. Passengers and freight would be discharged and taken on, and then the trains would continue in their separate directions. If, however, the second train did not show up, the first train would send a flagman ahead and then follow him at walking speed at a distance that would allow the second, oncoming train, should it appear, to stop in time. When the trains found each other in this manner, one of them would have to back to the nearest station or siding. Superintendent Brodhead wisely advised conductors to "err on the side of caution."[11] He would be able to write at the end of the year:

> I have chosen to run the trains at a moderate speed, and at times to subject the passengers to delays rather than to hazard the risk of a collision between the regular trains, and those running at all times on construction account, with no restriction as to time, but to keep out of the way of the regular trains; and I have the satisfaction of being able to say that not the slightest accident to person or property has occurred, resulting from the manner of running the trains, during this season.[12]

The tracks finally reached Whitewater in September. The line was officially opened, the completion of the first division marked, and a gala celebration held, all on September 24. A correspondent from the *Milwaukee Sentinel and Gazette* subsequently shared his observations:

> The completion of the Milwaukee and Mississippi Rail Road to Whitewater . . . was celebrated . . . Thursday last. [T]he Milwaukee Delegation, some 300 in number left our city . . . accompanied by an excellent Band of Music and a brass six-pounder, and at every stopping-place along the route, the melodious strains of the one and the thunder-tones of the other, woke up the echoes of prairie, opening and forest, and called round the train crowds of our country friends.
>
> It was nearly noon when we reached Whitewater and found assembled there two or three thousand . . . Farmers of Walworth, with their wives and children . . . the train then returned to Waukesha, giving a *free ride* to all who chose to go. About a thousand availed themselves of this offer; many of whom had never seen, or traveled upon, a Rail Road before. . . .
>
> Shortly after 2 o'clock the company were summoned to dinner . . . to the R. R. Depot where tables had been spread for 750 persons. . . . The ball was opened by the Hon. John Catlin, President of the R. R. Company. . . .
>
> The festivities within the Depot were prolonged till nearly 5 o'clock, the hour fixed for the train to start homeward. Some of the party remained to join in the dance which came off in upper story of the Depot in the evening, while the rest were brought back in good season without the least mishap and in great glee to their homes in Milwaukee.[13]

The first locomotive built in Wisconsin, the Menomonee, emerged from the shops of the Menomonee Locomotive Works in Milwaukee in October to join the company's roster. George Richardson, an employee of the Works, remembered its dimensions and characteristics well:

> The locomotive was built at the works of W. B. Walton & Co., known as the Menominee foundry, and located at the southwest corner of Reed and South Water streets. The first locomotive differed from all alleged drawings of it . . . inasmuch as it was what is known as "inside connected," that is the machinery, cylinder, etc, was all underneath the boiler, except the parallel rods connecting the two pair of driving wheels. . . . I recollect this engine as plainly as though I had seen it yesterday, and I remember that on its dome or sandbox on top of the boiler was the following: MENOMONEE LOCOMOTIVE WORKS * No. 1. * W. B. WALTON & CO., PROPRIETORS. On the side of the boiler was this word:
>
> M E N O M O N E E
>
> On Oct. 15, 1852, "Long John," with his crew of a dozen men and several yoke of oxen, began laying temporary tracks from a point at the foundry near which is now located the scales of Seeboth Brothers, and thence to Reed street, on Reed to the bridge over the Menomonee river–then a float bridge. No trouble was experienced until the bridge was reached. At that time Reed street was just about wide enough for ordinary wagons to meet and pass, and the locomotive and its tracks occupied the whole street. At the bridge all the power of men, block and tackle, as well as oxen, was needed to enable us to get the locomotive up the incline at the bridge. The engine's weight was about twenty-six tons, and under it the bridge barely escaped sinking, but it was safely landed on the north side of the river, and placed on the track, located about seventy-five feet away from the bridge, and here my connection with it ceased.[14]

The rails reached Milton, home of Director Joseph Goodrich, on December 1, with the line officially opening on December 3. It was Goodrich who had originally conceived of the farm-mortgage plan, and he had mortgaged his own farm to buy stock in the railroad. He had also donated the right-of-way and depot grounds in Milton. A remarkable pioneer, Goodrich was born in Massachusetts in 1800 and grew up in western New York, the frontier of the day. A crop failure in 1836 and the economic recession of 1837 persuaded him to look westward to Wisconsin Territory. He arrived in the spring of 1838 and chose the land he was to purchase by marking the spot where a line between Chicago and Madison crossed a line between Janesville and Fort Atkinson—Milton. That summer he built a house, sold goods, and dug a fifty-foot well by hand. He returned to New York, and on January 13, 1839, Goodrich, with his family in tow, left for Wisconsin on four teams of wagons mounted on snow-runners. After many difficulties and hardships they arrived in Milton on March 4. That summer they farmed, ran the store, and took

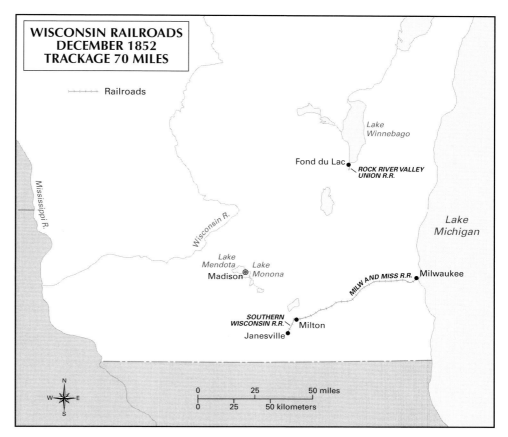

Mapping Specialists

in travelers. In time the village grew up around them. In 1844 Goodrich built his famous Milton House. It was a two-story, hexagonal building made of grout (lime, sand, broken stone, gravel, and water); today it is the oldest concrete building in the nation. Goodrich, a staunch abolitionist, would use this building and an adjacent cabin connected by a tunnel as a stop on the Underground Railroad, helping escaped slaves flee to Canada. He also founded and built the Milton Academy (later Milton College).[15]

Just beyond Milton's depot the line forked, with the main line going to Madison and a branch heading toward Janesville. Grading continued on the main line for the remainder of the year, stopping at a point where the line had not yet been located. Track laying continued, following the branch line, with the tracks reaching Janesville at the end of the year. The eight-mile branch line was initially surveyed in 1849 and had been promoted by Superintendent Brodhead as a way of realizing revenue while the line to Madison was being built. The branch actually belonged to the Southern Wisconsin Railroad Company, which on August 5 had contracted with Walter P. Flanders, treasurer of the Milwaukee and Mississippi, to have it built for one hundred thousand dollars. The money was loaned by the Milwaukee and Mississippi, which would have a fifteen-year renewable lease to operate the branch. The actual cost turned out to be $98,968.18, or $12,371 per mile.[16]

The Milwaukee and Mississippi's annual report for 1852 states that thirty-three miles of mainline and eight miles of branch line had been finished during the year. Revenues had totaled $75,310, operating expenses were $32,858, and the net profit was $42,482. On the last day of the year the directors declared a dividend to be paid to the stockholders in stock. Superintendent Brodhead reported that

> construction trains have hauled about 4,000 tons of iron an average distance of 53 miles; 93,000 cross-ties an average distance of thirty-seven miles, the weight of which is 7,000 tons; and 50,000 cubic yards of ballasting an average distance of seven and one-half miles, which reduced to weight is equal to 75,000 tons. The result of the tonnage on account of construction, is an aggregate of 85,000 tons, hauled an average distance of 12 miles.[17]

The cost of the road from Milwaukee to Janesville was $19,494 per mile, comparable to other western railroads, including the Galena and Chicago Union and the Southern Michigan. Fifty thousand miles had been run by passenger and freight trains during the year, and the company owned eight locomotives, six passenger cars, and seventy-eight freight cars (thirty-five boxcars and forty-three platform cars).

# PART THREE: NEW GROWTH

# Chapter 12

# In the Rock River Valley

### 1848–1852

At the same time that rails were being laid westward from Milwaukee, a second enterprise was underway in southeastern Wisconsin that was designed to increase trade connections with Chicago: the railroads of the Rock River Valley. The story of these railways begins with the Rock River itself. With its origins in the marshes between Horicon and Lake Winnebago, this river flows south through the present-day towns of Watertown, Jefferson, Fort Atkinson, Janesville, and Beloit, continuing southwesterly in Illinois until it empties into the Mississippi River at Rock Island. In the 1820s white settlers established mill sites and ferries on its lower, Illinois portions. Chief Black Hawk and his band ascended the Rock River in their ill-fated journey in 1832. White settlements at what would become Beloit and Janesville followed in the 1830s. An occasional steamboat would ascend the river to Janesville or Fort Atkinson, making those locations destinations for projected canals or railroads from Lake Michigan. In the mid-1840s, the Rock River Valley became the center of a new wheat-growing culture. It soon became apparent that a railroad was needed to transport the surplus wheat to market.

Early in 1847 President William Butler Ogden of the Galena and Chicago Union Railroad Company of Illinois began canvassing farmers for stock subscriptions along the Illinois-Wisconsin line. At Rockford he turned north and followed the Rock River into Wisconsin. He called on friends in Beloit and Janesville to find out if there was interest in building an extension of the Galena in Wisconsin.

Janesville, with 2,500 inhabitants, was the largest interior city in Wisconsin at the time, and was therefore a logical place for railroad promotion. Apparently Ogden found enough interest in his proposed branch line, for in early August the Galena issued a circular in which it described such a branch leaving the main line at Rockford and following the Rock River north to Beloit. Wisconsin enthusiasts responded with plans for extending the branch north from Beloit. Further assurance came in April 1848, when Ogden announced his plans for using second-hand strap-rail for the Galena and reusing it on the Beloit branch when the main line received T-rail.

One month later Wisconsin became a state. A. Hyatt Smith, a leading citizen of Janesville, took up the cause for the proposed branch line and recommended that it be continued beyond Janesville to Madison. In June the Galena Railroad Company began grading its road in Chicago and citizens in Beloit, Janesville, and Madison celebrated.

Smith had come to Janesville from New York City via Chicago in 1842, arriving in December with his family and a servant after an exhausting journey through the snow.[1] Smith was born in New York City in February 1814. He had begun studying law at age fourteen, was admitted to the bar at twenty-one, then practiced law for six years. At the age of 28, he decided to move with his family to Wisconsin in order to improve his health. After arriving, Smith became active in business and politics. He ventured into real estate and built a water-power (a dam that powers a flour mill) on the Rock River at Janesville. In 1846 he built his famous, $45,000 "big mill," which was fifty feet wide, eighty feet long, and four stories high, with six runs of stone. When the mill opened on January 26, 1847, people from as far away as the farms along the Wisconsin River came to watch the working of its machinery and to have their grain ground.[2] In 1846 Smith was elected to serve as a delegate to Wisconsin's first constitutional convention and was appointed attorney general of the territory. That year he also helped organize and became the first president of the Wisconsin Historical Society.

For the next two years, Smith drove his buggy to Madison to attend to his duties as attorney general. Occasionally he would drive up early and return to Janesville the same day. It was later said that these drives were his motivation for promoting a railroad from Janesville to Madison.[3]

On August 10, 1848, the editor of the *Beloit Journal* noted that interest in the extension of the Galena and Chicago Union Railroad in Wisconsin had spread to Watertown and Fond du Lac:

> The last Watertown *Chronicle* devotes a column to th[e] subject [of the Rock River Railroad]. It says that there is a strong and constantly increasing interest mani-

fested in favor of the road, to connect at this place with the branch of the Chicago & Galena road, and continue north to Fond du Lac. It says, also, that according to Capt. Cram's survey, the descent from Lake Winnebago to Beloit is only about two hundred feet, something less than two feet per mile. Timber is abundant along the route, no excavations of any magnitude would be required, and it is believed by the friends of the project that the General Government would grant a liberal appropriation of its unsold lands toward its construction. It has a donation of 800,000 acres to the Chicago & Galena road.[4]

Extending the road to Fond du Lac made sense. Fond du Lac, on the southern end of Lake Winnebago, would receive the trade of all the settlements on that lake and the surrounding country.

❖ ❖ ❖ ❖ ❖ ❖

Two new railroad companies—the Madison and Beloit and the Beloit and Taycheedah—were chartered by Wisconsin's legislature on August 19, 1848, to honor the wishes that the railroad from Beloit go to both Madison and Lake Winnebago. Smith was listed as a commissioner for both railroads. The Madison and Beloit Railroad Company was authorized to build a railroad from Beloit to Madison by way of Janesville. Its capital was set at $350,000, in shares of $100 each. When three hundred shares had been sold with five dollars down per share, the company could organize and the stockholders could elect nine directors to manage its affairs. Subscription payments could not be for more than twenty-five percent of the value of the share, and thirty days notice was required. The company would have fourteen commissioners: Smith, George H. Slaughter, Thomas W. Sutherland, Thomas T. Whittlesey, Nathaniel W. Dean, Daniel B. Sneden, David L. Mills, Joseph B. Doe, Edward V. Whjiton, W. H. H. Bailey, Timothy Jackman, David Noggle, Alfred Field, and John Hackett. A one-hundred-foot right-of-way was allowed for the track. As with a turnpike, any person using suitable and proper carriages and paying the legal toll had to be permitted to use the road.

The Beloit and Taycheedah Railroad Company was authorized to build a railroad from Beloit to Taycheedah, on the southern end of Lake Winnebago—a much larger project. Its charter called for nineteen commissioners and, upon organizing, nine directors. Capital was set at eight hundred thousand dollars, in shares of fifty dollars each. The company could organize when two thousand shares had been subscribed with a five dollar down payment per share. Required stock payments were limited to ten percent of the value of the share with thirty days notice given. It too was allowed a one-hundred-foot right-of-way, and in addition was required to complete ten miles of line before opening for business. As with the Madison and Beloit, any person using suitable carriages and paying the legal toll would be allowed to use the road. On September 28, the *Beloit Journal* reported:

> A meeting of the Directors of the Beloit & Fond du Lac Railroad [Beloit & Taycheedah] will be held soon at Watertown, to take the preliminary steps toward the construction of this road. We should judge from what we can learn of the feeling north that there was a full determination and confidence that the road should be speedily built. We had the pleasure, a few days since, of meeting Mr. Morgan, an engineer late in the employ of the Chicago & Galena Company, who has since then passed over the route to Fond du Lac. We find in the Watertown *Chronicle* of last week a letter from him concerning this matter. He speaks most favorably of the feasibility of the construction, and, in conclusion, remarks: "You may soon accumulate strength to complete the whole at a much earlier period than is now anticipated. A short railroad from a great market seldom pays because it does not collect sufficient business, but yours will posses all the advantages that are necessary, because however small a section you may commence with, it will be the extension of a great line. Your profits, therefore, will be realized from the first, and capitalists, having proof of the success of the undertaking, will be ready to assist to any extent that may be required."[5]

The two companies held separate conventions on December 20, 1848, the Beloit and Madison in Janesville and the Beloit and Taycheedah in Watertown. Stock subscriptions failed to materialize for either company in 1849, as it was still uncertain that the Galena would build the branch line to Beloit. In August Colonel Hugh Lee and A. T. Gray made an informal survey for the Beloit and Taycheedah, only the second railroad survey in Wisconsin (the Milwaukee and Waukesha's was done one month earlier).[6] On November 1 the Beloit and Taycheedah opened its subscription books and introduced a new player, John B. Macy of Fond du Lac, in the company's affairs. Macy, fifty years old, had been one of the founders of the city of Toledo, Ohio, and had promoted steamboating on the Great Lakes. In the 1830s he was a stockholder in the Erie and Kalamazoo Railroad. He had come to Wisconsin in 1845, settling in Fond du Lac, where he began dealing in real estate.[7]

When the tracks of the Galena reached Elgin late in 1849, Wisconsin's interested parties began requesting that its Beloit branch begin at Belvidere, Illinois, rather than at Rockford. This would give the railway a more direct line to Chicago. When the Galena failed to respond, Smith and his associates began thinking of altering the route of the Madison and Beloit and building their own railroad in

# IN THE ROCK RIVER VALLEY

Illinois. They began by lobbying the Wisconsin legislature, with almost immediate results. On February 4, 1850, the first of several charter amendments requested by the Madison and Beloit Railroad Company became law. The company was allowed to move its southern terminus to any point on the Wisconsin-Illinois line that it desired and to connect there with any Illinois railroad it chose. The company was also authorized to extend its road northward from Madison "to any point on the Wisconsin River." Five days later a second group of amendments was signed into law, changing, among other things, the name of the Madison and Beloit to the Rock River Valley Union Railroad Company. These amendments authorized the company to "extend their road from Janesville to Lake Winnebago by way of Fort Atkinson, Jefferson, and Watertown"—the route assigned to the Beloit and Taycheedah railroad. The Beloit and Taycheedah Railroad Company subsequently transferred its resources to the Rock River Valley Union.[8]

Fond du Lac became the base of operations for the Rock River Valley Union. The city was located at the southern end of Lake Winnebago, where the Fond du Lac River empties into the lake. Twenty years before Fond du Lac had been nothing more than several Winnebago villages and a trading post. The first Americans known to have come there were Judge James D. Doty, future territorial governor of Wisconsin, and his cousin, Morgan L. Martin, in 1829. They came on horseback en route between Green Bay and Mineral Point, where Doty was to hold court (possibly the first overland crossing of the territory by white men).

In 1832 Doty routed the military road through Fond du Lac, and in 1835 he and George McWilliams organized the Fond du Lac Company, purchased 3,705 acres, and platted the village. Its first residents were Colwert and Fanna Pier of Vermont, who arrived on June 6, 1836. That fall, Fond du Lac made an unsuccessful bid to become the capital of Wisconsin. In 1838 Dr. Mason C. Darling purchased eighty acres there and divided them into lots. He also donated land for a school, a courthouse, and several churches. From this the city of Fond du Lac grew. Steamboat service on Lake Winnebago began in 1843, the courthouse was built in 1844, and the population grew to more than two thousand people in 1850.

In the spring of 1850 the officers of the Rock River Valley Union began looking for a building contractor. A leading candidate was Timothy F. Strong Sr. of Bradley & Company, Vermont. Strong came to Wisconsin that summer and looked the route over, riding the entire distance from Chicago to Fond du Lac on horseback. The directors awarded him the contract. On December 19, 1850, T. L. Gillet advertised that the stock books of the new railroad were open and subscriptions could be purchased at his store in Fond du Lac. Five per cent on each share was required to be paid in advance, while the balance, in eight percent installments, would be called for quarterly.

On February 12, 1851, the state of Illinois chartered the Rock River Valley Union's partner company, the Illinois and Wisconsin Railroad Company. This company was authorized to build a railroad "from the north line of McHenry County, Illinois, to Woodstock in the same county and thence to a point on the Galena and Chicago Union Railroad in Cook, Kane, and McHenry counties and within fifty years to build into Chicago and to connect with any railroad out of Chicago and through Indiana." It was also authorized to consolidate with any Wisconsin railroad company.[9]

In March 1851 the Rock River Valley Union's charter was again amended, this time allowing the company to extend its road from Fond du Lac to Lake Superior. A subsequent amendment allowed the company to extend its western branch "from the point of intersection on the Wisconsin River to the village of La Crosse in the County of La Crosse and thence to Willow River and St. Croix Falls. There was a reason for the generosity. Senator Stephen A. Douglas of Illinois had in the prior year obtained a federal land grant from the state of Illinois to be used in aiding the construction of the Illinois Central Railroad. Wisconsin was now hoping to receive a similar grant and to bestow it on the Rock River Valley Union Railroad.

On May 12 the *Milwaukee Sentinel and Gazette* reported:

> Rock River Valley Union Railroad–dispatch from Janesville in the *Wisconsin* last evening announced that A. Hyatt Smith has lately returned from the East with contracts for building the whole of the road, 86 miles, to Fond du Lac. Our valley friends are, of course, in high feather over their prospects.[10]

Strong had received the contract. When he returned to Fond du Lac, he generated no small amount of excitement:

> When the people saw him enter the village with 160 horses, followed by loads of shovels, picks, wheelbarrows, and other tools, they aroused from their lethargy. Then there was faith; then there was enthusiasm; then there was railroad on the brain.[11]

On June 5 William B. Ogden resigned the presidency of the Galena and Chicago Union Railroad to become president of the Illinois and Wisconsin Railroad Company. Construction on that company's line began at the Chicago city limits in July. The Rock River Valley Union and the Illinois and Wisconsin were to connect at the state line between Sharon, Wisconsin, and Harvard, Illinois.

Groundbreaking ceremonies for the Rock River Valley Union Railroad took place in Fond du Lac on July 10, 1851:

People from the proposed line, from as far south as Sharon, were present. . . . At an early hour the morning of the 10th, teams began to pour into the village from all directions. Walworth, Rock, Jefferson and Dodge Counties sent large delegations. Waupun's delegation came in many conveyances, with flags flying and band playing. Most of the State officers were present. The starting of the immense procession was announced by the booming of the village cannon. A. Hyatt Smith, President of the Rock River Valley Union Railway, headed the procession. . . . Preceded by the bands, the procession marched to the spot where work was to begin—a few rods north of the passenger depot, on West Division Street, and formed a hollow square. A. Hyatt Smith, the President . . . cut the tough sod and tossed it into the air, a shout went up that made the earth tremble. . . .

John B. Macy . . . assumed the garb of a prophet on that occasion in this toast: "The Rock River Valley Union Railroad—It will be the connecting of the great chain of railroads between the Gulf of Mexico and the Pacific Ocean."[12]

Construction soon commenced. A depot and "shops" were put up at the Fond du Lac station grounds, on the west bank of the Fond Du Lac River. The shops consisted of a board shanty, a blacksmith shop, and a thirty-foot carpentry shop. The shop supervisor was, and for many years would be, Henry Hull. Hull would contribute to the company's success and progress by hiring only "sober men of the highest caliber."[13]

In 1852 Minnesota became part of the Rock River Valley Union's plans. Company representatives were busy in the lobbies of that territory's capital, and in April their efforts bore fruit. They received the legislative go-ahead for a series of rail lines that, if built in conjunction with the Wisconsin lines, would become the largest railroad system in the West:

The plan was to build a branch from Janesville to Fond du Lac, of Winnebago, and from thence to Fond du Lac of Lake Superior. Another branch was to run from Janesville to St. Croix Falls, via Madison and La Crosse; thence to St. Paul, and from St. Paul to the Red River of the North. From this point it was intended to build a branch westerly to the boundaries of Minnesota, with a fourth branch of the series to the British line, and thence back down the Red River of the North. The original, or second Janesville branch, was then to be extended easterly to the head of Lake Superior and connected with branch no. 1 at Fond du Lac (of Lake Superior). This was the most magnificent system of (paper) railroads ever built by citizens of Janesville. The Company had its head office in New York, where the material for the road, then in course of construction between Chicago and Janesville, was purchased and its bonds negotiated.[14]

The first rails of the Rock River Valley Union Railroad arrived in Fond du Lac in the spring of 1852. They had come over the lakes to Green Bay, from where they were taken by teams and wagons to Lake Winnebago; there they were loaded on scows and shipped the thirty miles up the lake to Bannister's Landing at Fond du Lac, where the first tracks were laid. The Rock River Valley Union had decided to build its track in the six-foot broad gauge, following the example of New York's Erie Railroad. This would mean using wider and heavier locomotives and cars, which would theoretically be more efficient in carrying goods and people.

The Rock River Valley Union's first locomotive, the fifteen-ton Winnebago, arrived later that year by a different route. In July the forty-five-mile Sheboygan and Fond du Lac Plank Road had been completed between the named cities. It was not a level road, but rather resembled a roller coaster. The last stretch, at Fond du Lac, consisted of a treacherous descent down the "ledge"—the high ridge of Niagara limestone that runs along the eastern shore of Lake Winnebago. The locomotive known as the Winnebago would be shipped to Sheboygan and taken to Fond du Lac over that plank road. Gustave W. Buchen, in *Historic Sheboygan County*, gave this account:

> To prevent the first machine from damaging the plank roadway the wheels were covered with wooden felloes and run on makeshift rails of long timbers laid lengthwise to the planks. Strings of as many as forty horses and oxen were hitched to the engine with ropes and chains, and with much urging and straining pulled it forward. As may be imagined, spectators along the way, especially the Indians, were struck with awe at the curious spectacle. Despite precautions, the heavy engine did considerable damage to the roadway.[15]

When the Winnebago arrived in Fond du Lac during that summer of 1852, workers had already laid some track and assembled some platform cars. They placed the Winnebago on the track, hooked up the cars, and soon were shuttling back and forth between Bannisters Landing and the end of the track, delivering construction materials. Now there were two railroads operating in Wisconsin.

# Chapter 13

## The New Contenders
### 1852

By the early years of railroad development west of Lake Michigan, both railroad promoters and the general populace visualized their railroads—even those running north-south, such as the Rock River Valley Union Railroad—as going beyond the next-nearest village or agricultural district. They hoped the lines running through their villages might reach all the way to the Mississippi River, capturing the lucrative trade of Iowa, Missouri, and Minnesota, and then continue to the Pacific Ocean. Even supporters of small railroads shared this vision, as their short lines would reap the benefits of being a link in the great chain from the East to the West.

By 1852 both Milwaukee and Chicago had built rails inland from the lake. The Milwaukee and Mississippi line had thirty miles of railroad in operation, while Chicago's Galena and Chicago Union had forty-one. The race was on to capture the trade of the Rock River Valley and, eventually, that of the Upper Mississippi Valley.

During 1851 several new railroad companies had been chartered in Wisconsin, and many more would be chartered in 1852. Though some of these would never begin construction, a number of these new contenders would build and operate railroads. Most of the new railway ventures were tied to Milwaukee or Chicago in one way or another, but some began in villages such as Sheboygan, Manitowoc, Racine, Monroe, and Mineral Point.

Milwaukee, Wisconsin's leading city in commerce and industry, was home to four of the new contenders. The first of these was the Green Bay, Milwaukee, and Chicago Railroad, which had been chartered on March 13, 1851, with allowed capital of five hundred thousand dollars. The project of Milwaukeeans Levi Blossom and Charles H. Wheeler, this railroad was to connect Green Bay, Milwaukee, and Chicago, the Illinois portion to be undertaken by the partner Illinois Parallel Railroad. From its beginning, Milwaukeeans who wanted to keep Wisconsin's business in Wisconsin opposed the project, while citizens from other villages on the proposed line, such as Kenosha, rallied behind it. In early 1852 Kenoshans voted to loan the company one hundred thousand dollars of their city's credit. In December of that year the company contracted with William Wright and J. Mallory to build the portion from Milwaukee to the Illinois state line for eighteen thousand dollars per mile, to be completed by January 1, 1854.[1]

The second Milwaukee company, the Milwaukee and Watertown, was the "sister company" of the Milwaukee and Mississippi. Early in 1851 some directors of the latter were having second thoughts about building their line to the Mississippi River in Grant County as required by their charter. They saw that La Crosse, located further north on the river, would capture the trade of St. Paul and the developing northwest and would therefore be more profitable. Rather than trying to amend the Milwaukee and Mississippi's charter, on March 11, 1851, these directors obtained a charter for a second railroad company, the Milwaukee and Watertown. This company was authorized only to build between its two named cities, but its incorporators hoped for an amendment allowing it to build to La Crosse. If such an amendment were granted, their two companies could realize the trade of both the lead country and the Mississippi above La Crosse.

Eight of the nineteen commissioners of the Milwaukee and Watertown were also directors of the Milwaukee and Mississippi: Edward D. Holton, Alexander Mitchell, James Kneeland, John H. Tweedy, Daniel Wells Jr., Byron Kilbourn, George H. Walker, and Hans Crocker. Other named commissioners were Eliphalet Cramer, Deacon Chandler, J. W. Medberry, William M. Dennis, David Jones, B. F. Fay, L. A. Cole, Simeon Ford, Peter Rogan, P. V. Brown, and E. Gilman. Capital was set at five hundred thousand dollars. The company's charter, unlike that of any other railroad, prohibited it from building through orchards or gardens, ostensibly to quiet the fears of fruit and vegetable growers along the line. The books of subscription were opened on August 14, 1851, and on February 13, 1852, its charter was amended, allowing it to build to La Crosse.

The third Milwaukee company, the Milwaukee and Horicon, was chartered on April 17, 1852, and authorized to build a railroad from Milwaukee to Iron Ridge, Horicon, and Fort Winnebago (Portage), or "to such point on the Fox River as shall be determined by a vote of the stockholders."² The charter allowed the company to later extend its road to the Mississippi River and at that time to increase its capital stock from eight hundred thousand dollars to two million dollars. The act called for nine commissioners. Shares of stock were one hundred dollars each, and when five hundred shares were subscribed and had five dollars paid on each, the company could organize and elect seven directors. Construction had to begin within five years and finish within fifteen. A five-rod-wide (or eighty-foot) right-of-way was allowed for the road. However, aside from obtaining this detailed charter, the Milwaukee and Horicon did little in 1852.

❖ ❖ ❖ ❖ ❖ ❖

The La Crosse and Milwaukee Railroad Company was the fourth and most significant of Milwaukee's new contenders. It was conceived by Kilbourn, but few people knew he was the man behind the project. Kilbourn claimed that the idea for the La Crosse and Milwaukee Railroad came to him shortly after his dismissal from the presidency of the Milwaukee and Mississippi in January of 1852: "It was after this, being free from all other railroad connection, that the scheme and the plan of the La Crosse railway was suggested."³ Kilbourn wanted a railroad that would do everything the Milwaukee and Mississippi intended to do—capture the trade of Wisconsin, Iowa, and Minnesota—but do it better. Kilbourn, however, had fallen out of favor with the legislature. To incorporate this new railroad company he would need a front man—someone who was familiar with legislative proceedings and who would act clandestinely for him. And he knew just the person: former Milwaukee and Mississippi attorney and former state assemblyman Moses M. Strong.

The forty-one-year-old Strong, a native of Vermont, had come to Mineral Point in June 1836 to practice law and to speculate in land. He had attended Middlebury College, Dartmouth, and Judge James Gould's law school in Connecticut, while also acquiring the drinking and gambling problems that would follow him for most of his life. Strong attended the territory's first legislative session at Belmont late in 1836, where he learned that legislators could be swayed by promises of reward. Six weeks later, in February 1837, he and his law partner, newly appointed territorial postmaster John Catlin, surveyed in what would become Madison's capitol square—then nothing more than a tract of wilderness—in the middle of a blizzard. A staunch Democrat, he was appointed United States Attorney for Wisconsin Territory in 1838 by President John Tyler. In 1841 he was elected as Iowa County's representative in the territorial legislature. He served five years there, including two as president of the council. He was also an influential delegate at Wisconsin's first Constitutional Convention in 1846.

Strong had achieved much of his notoriety during 1842 and '43 when he had served as the attorney for Councilman James R. Vineyard. On February 10, 1842, Vineyard had shot and killed fellow Councilman Charles C. P. Arndt of Green Bay in the capitol building's council chamber in Madison. Strong was able to get Vineyard released on bail; he then pushed through a law that allowed the trial to be held in Monroe, where there would be less prejudice against Vineyard, rather than in Madison. When the trial took place a year and a half later, Strong, with an unspoken promise of "whiskey all around" and a three-hour oration, was awarded an acquittal for Vineyard. Judge, jury, and both attorneys "adjourned" to the Monroe House, where Vineyard bought rounds of drinks into the night. For years after these events it was said that if you asked an old temperate settler "were you ever intoxicated?" he was likely to reply, "Yes, when Vineyard was acquitted."

In 1848, a year after the Milwaukee and Mississippi charter was granted, Strong, who was habitually in debt, owed Kilbourn two thousand dollars dollars on a note that Kilbourn had co-signed for him and on which Strong had defaulted.[4] When Kilbourn asked him to handle the Milwaukee and Rock River Canal Company's claims against the territory in order to work off that debt, Strong accepted. It was the beginning of a long relationship. Kilbourn kept Strong on as a lobbyist for the Milwaukee and Mississippi. Early in 1851 Strong finished his term in the legislature and lost a bid for a senate seat. In March he offered to renew his services with the Milwaukee and Mississippi but found he was no longer needed. He spent the remainder of the year in Mineral Point, waiting for something to turn up.

What turned up was a letter from Kilbourn that arrived in Mineral Point during the second week of January 1852. In it Kilbourn asked Strong to come to Milwaukee but did not say why. While Strong's wife, Caroline, objected to his going, he felt that there were other things to consider. His father and his brother George had successfully promoted railroads in the East, and Moses felt that the time had come for him to do something similar in Wisconsin. Strong surmised that Kilbourn's recent troubles with the Milwaukee and Mississippi were behind the letter and felt this could be his opportunity.

Strong took the stagecoach to Milwaukee, where he found lodging in a room at the United States Hotel. The next day he went to Kilbourn's home and office at the corner of Chestnut and Third streets. Kilbourn explained that he wanted to incorporate a new railroad company, one that would build a railroad from Milwaukee to La Crosse on the Mississippi. He told Strong that this railroad would "forever control the trade of the Upper Mississippi" and would "be worth a dozen

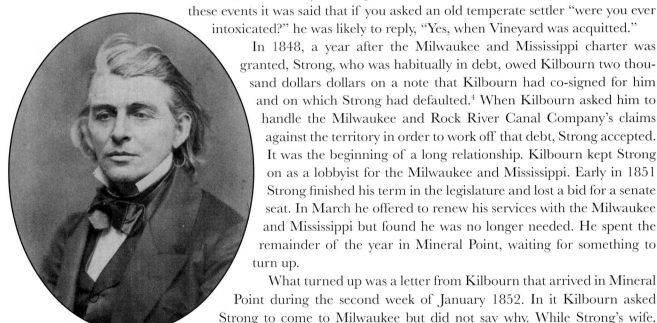

Portrait of Moses M. Strong, 1856, by Fuller and Johnson.
WHi Image ID 27749

Former Byron Kilbourn house, at the corner of Fourth and Chestnut Streets in Milwaukee, in 1870.
WHi Image ID 53673

of the Milwaukee and Mississippi." What he wanted Strong to do was to draft the charter bill and guide it through the legislature. It would be a special assignment, and the fewer people that knew of it, the better. Kilbourn's name was to be kept out of it. The new railroad would be called the La Crosse and Milwaukee to give the impression that it was a La Crosse, not a Milwaukee, venture.

At the end of the day Kilbourn and Strong had covered all the points needed to guide the La Crosse and Milwaukee Railroad on its way. Strong spent the remainder of the week in Milwaukee drafting the charter. On January 22 he took the stage to Madison and began the long and delicate process of guiding the bill through the legislature.[5]

In Madison, Strong kept in constant communication with Kilbourn by letter and telegraph. Kilbourn advised him to be guarded in talking with the legislators and warned him not to suggest anything improper. He also suggested that Strong pay a visit to the lieutenant governor, Timothy Burns, a La Crosse resident, to interest him in the La Crosse and Milwaukee, and ask him to urge it as a measure of his own. Strong followed this advice with success. He also contacted Governor Leonard J. Farwell in regard to the new railroad and convinced him to become one of the commissioners. When the bill was being debated, an amendment was offered to change the western terminus from La Crosse to Watertown. Strong successfully argued against the change.

Strong presented the petition for the La Crosse and Milwaukee as an appeal from the interests of La Crosse—a little, out-of-the-way hamlet that most of the legislators had never even heard of. Then, on February 13, the legislature amended the year-old charter of the Milwaukee and Watertown Railroad Company, allowing it to build from Milwaukee to La Crosse. Would it allow the La Crosse and Milwaukee to build from La Crosse to Milwaukee? Strong persisted, and the answer was "yes." His charter bill for the La Crosse and Milwaukee Railroad Company passed both houses of the legislature and was signed into law by Governor Farwell, one of the named commissioners, on April 2.[6] The charter authorized the company to build a railroad from La Crosse to Milwaukee or "from La Crosse to some point where the same shall intersect and connect with some other railway running to the City of Milwaukee."[7] It listed seventeen commissioners who would solicit and receive stock subscriptions and run the affairs of the company until it was organized. Among them were Lieutenant Governor Timothy Burns, Samuel T. Smith, and Benjamin F. Butler of La Crosse County; Moses M. Strong of Iowa County; Thomas J. Moorman of Portage County; John Lowth of Dodge County; Henry Weil and Patrick Toland of Washington County; Hugh McFarlane of Columbia County; Patrick Rogan of Jefferson County; Henry Shears of Waukesha County; Governor Leonard J. Farwell of Dane County; and D. C. Reed, Edwin H. Goodrich, George H. Walker, Levi Blossom, and Garret Vliet of Milwaukee County. Capital was set at four million dollars, in shares of one hundred dollars each. When five hundred shares were subscribed and five dollars paid in per share, the company could organize and elect seven directors. Construction had to begin within three years and finish within ten. A one-hundred-foot right-of-way was allowed.

Shortly after the charter passed, the Madison correspondent of the *Milwaukee Sentinel* noted,

> members [of the legislature] were at some loss to know why such a charter was asked for, where there are at least two charters already from La Crosse eastward, but Dr. Hoyt set the matter at rest, by explaining that those who had the original charters did not move quite fast enough for the La Crosse and Upper Mississippi people, and they wished another charter, so that they might begin at the western end. . . . But after all, does it not strike reasonable men rather strangely—this double and treble chartering of companies? Just as if a company had been chartered to build a road from Madison to Watertown, and the road not being completed or perhaps commenced within a year, the next Legislature charters a company to build a road from Watertown to Madison.[8]

THE NEW CONTENDERS  153

While the bill for the charter had aroused little suspicion, it had never been read aloud in either house (being part of the proposed La Crosse measure, which had not warranted much attention), and had passed into law quietly. Its official governmental publication created an uproar, however, as noted by the Madison correspondent of the *Milwaukee Sentinel*:

> There was a rich time in the Assembly Chamber last night—a combination of high tragedy, and laughter, moving farce, such as we have not before had this session. The publication of the bill chartering the La Crosse and Milwaukee railroad, disclosed the fact, to the utter astonishment of members of both Houses that, besides other obnoxious measures, it contains a section *repealing all laws which conflict* with the rights granted under the bill. Considering that charters or extensions have been granted at this session and heretofore, allowing four or five different railroads to terminate at La Crosse, you may imagine the surprise with which this surreptitious bill was read. The charter for the Milwaukee and La Crosse Rail Road Company which was discovered, after its passage, to contain two sections never dreamed of by the Legislature—the one, repealing all previous acts of incorporation, etc., clashing with this, and the other donating certain State lands in aid of the railroad—was amended by a new act repealing these two obnoxious provisions.[9]

One wonders whether Kilbourn and Strong were behaving like schoolboys having fun with the legislature or whether they were actually hoping the obnoxious sections would be enforced.

❖ ❖ ❖ ❖ ❖ ❖

On June 24 the commissioners of the La Crosse and Milwaukee Railroad Company met at La Crosse. Kilbourn, having stepped out of the shadows after the charter act passed, also attended. The official purpose of the meeting was to open the company's books of subscription. This was done at both La Crosse and Milwaukee. The second purpose was to decide who would purchase the first five hundred shares of stock. The sale of these shares was required for the company to organize; the shareholders would then vote in the first board of directors. After some bickering, a tentative agreement was reached and then finalized two weeks later. It provided Strong and Kilbourn with 100 shares each; Jasper Vliet with 50 shares; John Bracken with 41; George Strong (Moses's brother) with 20; and Timothy Burns, Jacob L. Bean, Garret Vliet, and Edwin H. Goodrich with the remaining 189 shares. Lastly, the commissioners voted to send Moses Strong to

Washington to lobby Congress for a land grant, similar to the one that Kilbourn had obtained fourteen years earlier for the Milwaukee and Rock River Canal, to help finance the railroad's construction.

Senator Isaac P. Walker's land grant bill to aid a Milwaukee-to-Mississippi railroad had been introduced in December, had passed in the U.S. Senate, and was now before the House. It was this proposed grant that the La Crosse and Milwaukee hoped to receive. Congressional land grants were the "big plums" for railroad companies at that time. In 1850 Congress had granted Illinois such a grant for the Illinois Central Railroad, which had since prospered and grown. The way these bills worked is that Congress would designate land along the proposed route of the railroad as belonging to the grant. The land would be surveyed and divided into one-mile-square sections, and the proceeds of the sales of every other section (in a checkerboard pattern) would go to the railroad for use in construction. Building and completing the railroad would raise land values, and then Congress would sell its sections, recouping the value of what it had granted.

After 1850 other states began requesting land grants, including Wisconsin with its Walker bill. The intended recipient of that bill had been and still was the Milwaukee and Mississippi Railroad Company. Kilbourn and Strong would try to change this to make the La Crosse and Milwaukee Railroad Company the beneficiary instead.

Strong left Wisconsin and arrived in Washington on July 31. He took quarters at the National Hotel and then moved to Mrs. Spaulding's boardinghouse. Soon after his arrival Strong learned in a letter from Kilbourn that his former law partner, John Catlin, now the president of the Milwaukee and Mississippi railroad, was in Washington as well. They would now be opponents. In the same letter, Kilbourn instructed Strong to "make a death struggle for a grant, and secure it if in the bounds of possibility, as with it we will put to shame the other and oust the present board."[10] The "present company" was, of course, the Milwaukee and Mississippi, and the "present board" was Catlin's. It appears that Kilbourn was still focused on getting back at the forces that had ousted him.

In Washington, Strong worked hard for the railroad bill. He reported spending two hundred and fifty dollars entertaining congressmen and was a familiar figure in the House lobby in his "broadcloth dress coat, white marseilles vest, twilled cassimere pants, plaid socks, and leather oxfords."[11] But opposition to land grant bills, mostly from the Eastern and Northeastern states, was mounting. When it appeared that all such bills would indeed be defeated, Strong's brother George advised him to persevere. But Strong's redoubled efforts were not enough. All fourteen land grant bills, including Wisconsin's Walker bill, died. In August Strong returned to Wisconsin.

Strong was in Madison on August 25 when the stockholders of the La Crosse and Milwaukee organized the company. They elected seven directors: Timothy Burns, George W. Strong, Edwin H. Goodrich, Garret Vliet, Byron Kilbourn, Jacob L. Bean, and Strong himself. Kilbourn and Bean were restored to respectable positions as officers of a railroad despite their difficulties with the Milwaukee and Mississippi in January. The directors next elected Kilbourn president. However, he immediately resigned, possibly feeling that it was too early to return to a conspicuous position as a railroad officer after his previous troubles, and Moses Strong was chosen in his stead. Having set out in January to begin a career in railroads, Strong now found himself the president of one. Bean was elected treasurer, Goodrich became secretary, and Kilbourn was appointed chief engineer.

The directors next divided the road into two parts—the ninety-five-mile eastern division, from Milwaukee to Portage City (Portage) and the 101-mile western division, from Portage City to La Crosse. On September 15 engineering parties under Jasper Vliet began the preliminary surveys of the eastern division. They surveyed two routes. The "Watertown route" ran from Milwaukee to Ixonia, Watertown, Columbus, and Portage City, was 101 miles long (coincidently the same length as the western division), and would cost $1,604,355, or $15,885 per mile. The other route, the "Iron Ridge route," ran from Milwaukee in a northwesterly direction, through Menomonee Falls, Hartford, Iron Ridge, Horicon, Beaver Dam, Pardeeville, and Portage City, was ninety-eight miles long, and would cost $1,525,558, or $15,567 per mile. Always conscious of cost, the directors chose the cheaper "Iron Ridge" route. Meanwhile, a party under John B. Vliet surveyed the western division yielding an estimated cost for 104 miles of $1,474,760, or $14,180 per mile. Thus the total estimated cost of building the railroad from Milwaukee to La Crosse was slightly over three million dollars.

For the remainder of the year, Strong was out with his horse and buggy stumping for the railroad. When the snow came he used his sleigh. He traveled along the projected line of the railroad, stopping at every tavern and village, making speeches, distributing literature, and soliciting subscriptions to the company's stock. At the end of the year he and other agents had received subscriptions to over a quarter of a million dollars worth of stock. This was heartening, and the directors predicted that they would be able to let construction contracts for the eastern division in the spring.

While Milwaukee put forth its 1852 contenders, Chicago offered one of its own. Its Galena and Chicago Union Railroad had been interested in adding a branch line in Wisconsin that would feed into its Illinois main line. It had had hopes for such with the former Madison and Beloit Railroad Company, but that company had changed its plans, had changed its name to the Rock River Valley Union Railroad Company, and was now, along with its partner the Illinois and Wisconsin Railroad Company, a competitor to the Galena. Fortunately for the Galena, the citizens of Beloit had planned another railroad to do what the Madison and Beloit had intended. In late 1850 they had offered to subscribe to $75,000 of Galena stock if the Galena would build a branch line to Beloit. The Galena's directors had accepted. At the end of 1851 they had completed their main line to Belvidere, Illinois, forty-one miles from Chicago, and began surveying three routes from there to Beloit.

On February 18, 1852, Wisconsin granted a charter for the Beloit and Madison Rail Road Company (not Madison and Beloit), authorizing it to build a railroad from Beloit, through Janesville, to Madison. This was the same route as had been designated for the Madison and Beloit Company in 1848. The act called for twenty commissioners to manage the affairs of the company until it organized, after which thirteen directors would perform that task. Capital was set at $1,200,000, in shares of $50 each. When four hundred shares were subscribed and five dollars paid per share, the company could organize. Commissioners named in the act were Chauncey Abbot, Levi B. Visas, William C. Wells, Ezra L. Varney, William H. Fox, F. G. Tibbits, John M. Keep, Hazen Cheney, George B. Sanderson, William P. Goodhue, Benjamin Durham, Lucius G. Fisher, P. C. Manchester, John Mitchell, John P. Dickinson, Volney Atwood, Charles Stevens, J. D. Ruggles, Elisha Burdick, and B. F. Pixley. These commissioners opened the books of subscription to the company's stock in Madison on May 3 and in Beloit on May 10.

Meanwhile, the Galena had decided to begin its branch to Wisconsin at Belvidere rather than at Rockford. This was good news to the citizens of Beloit. A line from their village to Chicago would be more direct via Belvidere than it would be via Rockford. An added bonus was that work on the branch would begin sooner at Belvidere with the main line not yet having reached Rockford. In June surveyors began staking out the twenty-one mile route.

On July 1 the Beloit and Madison Rail Road Company organized and elected its first board of directors. Three of the thirteen seats were given to men who were already on the board of the Galena and Chicago Union. John Bice Turner, the president of the Galena and Chicago Union, was elected the first president of the Beloit and Madison. The ties between the two companies were strong. Soon Beloit and Madison stock was being purchased at the Galena's offices in Chicago.

Turner, fifty-one years old, was an experienced railroader. Born and raised in the state of New York, he began railroading on the Ransom and Saratoga Rail

Road, beginning as a tanner's apprentice and working his way up to track layer and section foreman. In 1835 he contracted with that company to build seven miles of their road. The directors were so pleased with the results that they made him general manager of the entire line. The trains of the Ransom and Saratoga were pulled by horses, and Turner saw to it that there was a barn and a stable every ten miles. Turner next contracted to build for the New York and Erie Railroad, but the panic of 1837 put an end to the job. In 1840 he was hired to dig the Genesee Valley Canal in New York and then to build the Troy and Schenectady Railroad. With the savings realized from these jobs, Turner, with his wife and two children, headed west, arriving in Chicago on October 15, 1843. In 1845 he became the managing director of the Galena and Chicago Union Railroad, and was sworn in as its president on June 5, 1851. Now, one year later, he was the president of the Beloit and Madison Rail Road as well. In September 1852 the Galena let the contracts for the construction of the Belvidere-Beloit branch line. At the end of the year, three hundred men were grading the roadway.

Meanwhile, along Lake Michigan, the villages of Sheboygan, Manitowoc, and Racine had been interesting themselves in railroads as well. Sheboygan, 110 miles north of Milwaukee, had been taking rails seriously for some time. Founded in 1836, just one year after Milwaukee, Sheboygan had from the beginning considered itself a rival to that city. In 1845, when Sheboygan had but two hundred people, the Reverend Huntington Lyman wrote a series of articles for the *Sheboygan Gazette* discussing a great transcontinental railroad beginning at Sheboygan and running west to the Pacific Ocean. This was around the same time that Asa Whitney, the New England China merchant, was promoting a railroad from Milwaukee to the Pacific. Huntington pointed out what the people of Sheboygan already knew: that a railroad starting at Sheboygan would save lake vessels coming from the East 110 miles by bypassing Milwaukee or 200 miles by bypassing Chicago.

Two years later the citizens of Sheboygan settled for a forty-five-mile railroad to Fond du Lac. On January 25, 1847, they were granted a charter incorporating the Sheboygan and Fond du Lac Railroad Company. Capital was set at nine hundred thousand dollars to be sold in shares of one hundred dollars, with five dollars down on each share. The act called for seven commissioners to sell stock, and when five thousand shares were subscribed the company could organize and elect twelve directors to manage its affairs. Construction had to begin within five years and finish within fifteen or the company would forfeit its charter. The commissioners named in the act were Dr. Mason C. Darling (who as a legislative council member helped pass the bill); former territorial governor Nathaniel P. Tallmadge, John A. Eastman, and Moses S. Gibson of Fond du Lac; and William Farnsworth, R. P. Harriman, Henry Conklin, and Benjamin Moore of Sheboygan.[12]

On Thursday, March 11, 1847, a rally was held for the new railroad in Fond du Lac at the courthouse at which citizens of both Fond du Lac and Sheboygan counties participated. The commissioners gave speeches, formed committees, adopted resolutions, and sold stock. While the rally was a great success, it was to be the only such moment for the railroad. Fond du Lac soon lost interest in the project. With its location at the head of Lake Winnebago, it considered a plank road, the Rock River Valley Union Railroad, and the Fox River Improvement projects more worthy of its attentions and met Sheboygan's overtures to revive the railroad project with indifference.

On January 25, 1852, the five years during which construction was required to begin along the Sheboygan and Fond du Lac line expired along with the company's charter. A new group of Sheboygan promoters was granted a charter for a new railroad company—the Sheboygan and Mississippi Railroad Company—on March 8. This company was authorized to build a railroad from Sheboygan to La Crosse on the Mississippi by way of Fond du Lac. It was capitalized at three million dollars. It would have thirteen directors. There was no deadline for beginning construction, but it had to be finished in fifteen years. A 130-foot right-of-way was allowed. The commissioners named in the act were Asahel P. Lyman, Henry H. Conklin, William W. King, Charles D. Cole, Horatio N. Smith, John Bannister, A. B. Hamilton, Samuel W. Beall, John P. Sherwood, Robert Jenkinson, Benjamin F. Moore, Thomas B. Stoddard, and James M. Shafter.

Twenty miles north of Sheboygan, Manitowoc had received a charter for its Manitowoc and Mississippi Railroad Company on March 15, 1851. The act authorized the company to build a railroad from Manitowoc to a fixed terminus on the Mississippi. Capital was set at $1,500,000 in shares of $100 each. Construction had to begin within three years and the company was required to spend fifty thousand dollars by that time. Construction was to be finished within ten years. The incorporators were George Reed, Benjamin Jones, S. A. Wood, and Jarvis E. Platt of Manitowoc; Harrison Reed, Joseph Turner, and Charles Doty of Menasha; and H. L. Palmer of Milwaukee.

Racine, south of Milwaukee, had long been frustrated in its own attempts at building a railroad. In 1835 at the legislative session at Green Bay, Gilbert Knapp, the city's founder, had drawn attention to the need for a railroad along the Root [Racine] River. In 1836 Wisconsin's first legislature petitioned Congress for a railroad to connect the Mississippi with either "Milwaukee or Racine." In 1838 the Root River Rail Road Company had been incorporated to build a railroad along the Root River, but the effort came to naught, and there had been, in its stead, an effort for a railroad from Racine to Janesville. In 1847 a Representative Lovell introduced a bill in the legislature to incorporate a Racine and Mississippi Railroad Company, but the bill was laid on the table and not taken up again.

On April 17, 1852, a bill for the incorporation of a Racine, Janesville, and Mississippi Railroad Company was signed into law. The act called for thirteen commissioners until such time as the company was organized, after which thirteen directors would manage its affairs. Capital was set at three million dollars, in shares of one hundred dollars each. When three hundred shares were subscribed and five dollars paid in per share, the company could organize. Construction had to begin within five years and finish within ten years. A 130-foot right-of-way was allowed. The commissioners named in the act were Charles S. Wright, Marshall M. Strong, Samuel G. Bugh, James Catton, Peter Campbell, Henry S. Rurand, James H. Earnest, John P. Dickson, Daniel Lawson, William J. Allen, S. S. Barlow, James Neil, and William H. Lawrence.

The commissioners of the company afterward found that there was little interest in their railroad in Janesville, where residents had already invested in three other railroad companies—the Southern Wisconsin, the Milwaukee and Mississippi, and the Rock River Valley Union. So the commissioners turned their attentions to Beloit, where they found a ready welcome. Beloit had subscribed to the Galena and Chicago Union Railroad for a line to Chicago, but it also wanted a more direct line to Lake Michigan. The Racine railroad fit the bill.

In southwestern Wisconsin, in the village of Albany in Green County, citizens were also taking an interest in railroads. Early in 1852 they petitioned the legislature to charter a Southern Wisconsin Railroad Company to build a railroad from Milton, north of Janesville on the mainline of the Milwaukee and Mississippi, to the Mississippi River by way of Albany. The story goes that before the legislators could act, citizens of Monroe went to the capitol, substituted their names for those of the Albany petitioners, and substituted "Monroe" for "Albany" in the wording of the petitions. This wording of the charter, which became law on April 10, 1852, stated that the company was authorized to

> construct and erect a railroad from Milton in the county of Rock, by the way of the village of Janesville in the said county of Rock, in this state, through the counties of Green, LaFayette and Grant, to some point on the Mississippi river to be selected by the said corporation as they shall see fit.[13]

**STEAM AND CINDERS**

Capital was set at $1,500,000, to be purchased in shares of $100 each. When seven hundred shares were subscribed, the company could organize and elect nine to fifteen directors to manage its affairs. Construction had to begin within two years, and a 130-foot right-of-way was allowed the roadway. The commissioners named were Prosper Cravath, John C. Spuires, William R. Biddlecome, John Moore, Joseph B. Doe, James H. Earnest, and Ensign H. Bennett. Soon after, the stockholders met at the Stevens House in Janesville to organize the company and elect the first board of directors.

The Southern Wisconsin did not have to wait long to begin construction on the first link on its line, the eight miles between Milton and Janesville. The Milwaukee and Mississippi Company, building westward from Whitewater to Milton that summer, wanted to augment its revenues with traffic from Janesville. On August 5 the Southern Wisconsin contracted with Walter P. Flanders, treasurer of the Milwaukee and Mississippi, to build the branch for one hundred thousand dollars. The money for the work would be loaned by the Milwaukee and Mississippi, and the Southern Wisconsin would repay it by leasing the line for fifteen years to the Milwaukee and Mississippi. Track laying on the Milton-Janesville section began in December and was finished at the end of the year.

In November the Southern Wisconsin completed a survey of its route from the Mississippi to Janesville. It was described as follows:

> Beginning at Dubuque, up the river on the west, to Eagle Point, crossing the Mississippi a little below the place where a lithograph or imaginary city was laid out in 1835 or 1836, on Section 20, Township 1, Range 2; thence northwest along the east bank of said river to Sinipee, on Section 7; thence northeast to Gilmore's farm, and the place known as "Bulgero," on the Platteville and Galena road; thence east toward Janesville.[14]

The directors boasted that "the descent to the Mississippi was by easier grades and with less expense than by any route above Dubuque."

Mineral Point had been a focus of interest during the early years of railroad speculation in Wisconsin dating back to 1836, when Governor Henry Dodge, addressing the legislators at Belmont, called for a Milwaukee and Mississippi Railroad that should pass through that village. The legislature had rejected Governor Dodge's proposal, instead chartering the Dubuque and Belmont Railroad, which was allowed to build an extension to Mineral Point. Those plans were lost with the panic of 1837. Three years later the Pekatonica [sic] and Mississippi Railroad Company was chartered to build a railroad from Mineral Point to the Mississippi, but nothing became of it either. In 1849 the official plan of the Milwaukee, Waukesha and Mississippi River Railroad Company had called for building through Mineral Point, or as near to it as possible. Yet its subsequent circulars showed "near" as being far to the north of the village. By 1852 the people of Mineral Point had become convinced that if they were to have a railroad, they would have to build it themselves.

Mineral Pointers were fortunate in having Moses Strong, one of their own, in the legislative chambers in Madison to help their cause. Strong was already busy with the affairs of the La Crosse and Milwaukee, but took on the task of helping his Mineral Point neighbors as well. On April 2 he realized the passage of the La Crosse Company's charter, and on April 17 that of the Mineral Point Railroad Company. The latter named sixteen commissioners: Francis Vivian, Parley Eaton, Francis Dunn, Cyrus Woodman, John Bracken, A. Comfort, Henry Koop, and John Milton of Iowa County, and Samuel Cole, Charles Lamar, John Blackstone, H. Ladd, Edward Gratiot, Charles Dunn, James Knowlton, and Joseph Brewster of Lafayette County. The terminals of the road were stated only in general terms. Capital was set at five hundred thousand dollars, in shares of one hundred dollars each. When one thousand shares were subscribed, the company could organize and elect nine directors. Construction had to begin within three years.

On June 5 the commissioners met in Mineral Point to determine the best route for their new line. Most thought building to Janesville and connecting there with the Milwaukee and Mississippi would be best. But Strong had written the Milwaukee and Mississippi's president, Catlin, and Catlin was opposed to the idea. A committee headed by Commissioner Eaton then recommended that the Mineral Point Railroad go south in the valley of the Pecatonica to connect with the Illinois Central Railroad at Warren, Illinois. In that way the company, building only thirty-two miles of road, would have a connection east to Chicago on Lake Michigan and west to the Mississippi. Mineral ore could be carried to Chicago, and coal, which was then selling in Mineral Point at four dollars per cord, could come back in exchange. The commissioners enthusiastically adopted the committee's recommendation. On June 22, 1852, the commissioners opened the books of subscription to the company's stock in Mineral Point, receiving on that day subscriptions to over five thousand dollars' worth of stock. In two weeks the total was over $40,000, by July 1 it was $76,000, and soon after $100,000, the amount required for the company to organize.

On September 17 the stockholders met in Mineral Point to organize the company. They elected as directors Cyrus Woodman, John Bracken, Moses M. Strong, Parley Eaton, Anthony Nancolas, Francis Cholvin, John M. Keep, George

Griswold, and David A. Neal. Woodman was elected president, Francis Vivian became treasurer, and Thomas S. Allen was made secretary. Roswell B. Mason, former chief engineer of the Illinois Central, was appointed chief engineer. Mason had already conducted a rough inspection of the route and now ordered preliminary surveys. This route

> was to begin in Mineral Point a short distance east of Commerce Street, follow the valleys of the Mineral Point and Rock branches of the Pecatonica River, follow the valley of the Pecatonica, pass through the village of Darlington to the mouth of Wolf Creek at the village of Gratiot, follow the east branch of Wolf Creek to its source, near the State Line, cross the summit between Wolf Creek and Apple River, and connect with the Illinois Central Railroad about a half mile west of the village of Warren. At Gratiot the road was to cross the proposed line of the Southern Wisconsin Railroad, planned from Janesville to Dubuque.[15]

On October 22, President Woodman resigned and the directors elected Strong in his place. Shortly after assuming his new role, Strong appointed his nephew, Charles Temple, chief engineer. Temple had been an engineer on the Bennington Railroad of Vermont and would receive an annual salary of two thousand dollars.

Strong spent the remainder of the year on the road, selling stock subscriptions. The work had become routine—making the same speeches, answering the same questions, and finding accommodations for the night. He once stated that what he enjoyed most were the occasional letters from his wife that were waiting for him at the post offices along his route.

# Chapter 14

# The Scramble for New Routes
### 1853

As villagers and farmers across southern Wisconsin saw or heard about tracks being laid and trains being run, lingering doubts about the viability of railroads began to be replaced by the single desire that one should come through their community. By the winter of 1852–53 the Milwaukee and Mississippi was operating across southeastern Wisconsin, and the Rock River Valley Union was building south from Fond du Lac. In Illinois, the Galena and Chicago Union Railroad was working through the winter on a branch line between Belvidere and Beloit that would be extended in Wisconsin by the Beloit and Madison Rail Road Company. In addition, railroad surveys that had been done in 1852 held promise for new construction in 1853. The Southern Wisconsin Railroad Company had surveyed a line from Dubuque on the Mississippi to Janesville that, if built, would realize the dream of a transstate railroad passing through the southwestern Wisconsin lead region. The La Crosse and Milwaukee Railroad Company had surveyed its line from Milwaukee to La Crosse, another transstate route that would capture the trade from St. Paul, Minnesota.

On January 10, five days after the official opening of the Milwaukee and Mississippi's line to Janesville, John C. Fox pulled the first train—consisting of two twenty-six feet long, ten and a half feet wide, Menomonee-built locomotives and eighteen cars filled with eight hundred people—into town, stopping at the new depot, located north of the business district on the east side of the Rock River. The train was greeted wildly by most of the 4,200 people of Janesville. Speeches were made on the platform by John S. Jordon for Janesville and Edward D. Holton for Milwaukee and the railroad. Then everyone paraded through the streets to the Stevens House, where a great feast was held. A grand ball wound up the event.

The Monday following, the first freight train, which had twenty-one cars, left Janesville for Milwaukee, pitting its speed and efficiency against the already-running passenger trains. While the passenger train took four hours to reach Milwaukee, averaging seventeen and a half miles per hour, the freight train took six hours, and averaged only eleven miles per hour. These were acceptable times for passenger and freight trains of this period, and the directors were satisfied. The freight had shown itself a ready vehicle to transport goods to market. The end of the first month showed that there had been shipped from Janesville 140 hogs, 245 bushels of barley, 3,148 barrels of flour, 116 bushels of rye, 2,207 bushels of wheat, 1,106 hides weighing 23,018 pounds, 26,000 pounds of mill feed, eleven firkins and one barrel of butter, four barrels and fifty-two boxes of eggs, one barrel of hams, one barrel and ten half-barrels of beer, 167 barrels of high wines, 250 bushels of corn, one sleigh, forty bushels of beans, four barrels of nuts, five barrels of linseed oil, twenty-eight boxes of merchandise, three barrels of cranberries, lot boxes packages, etc.[1]

In addition to its freight capabilities, the line to Janesville gave Milwaukeeans a new route to Chicago. Superintendent Edward H. Brodhead explained:

> Passengers will be ticketed through by the stage company for $5, via Janesville, to Chicago, and by taking the 3 p.m. train from Milwaukee will arrive at Janesville at 7:20 p.m., remain overnight there, and take the stage the next morning for Belvidere or Rockford, as they may choose, the price being the same, and arrive the next afternoon at Chicago. From Chicago, they will also remain overnight at Janesville and arrive at Milwaukee at 12:30 p.m. the next day.[2]

Thus only forty miles would be spent in a stagecoach each way, rather than the one hundred miles required if traveling directly from Milwaukee to Chicago.

The Milwaukee and Mississippi, still working its way westward, resumed grading between Milton and the Rock River in the spring of 1853, the work on that section

A combination stage and train ticket from 1858.
WHi Image ID 62555

being assigned to contractors Joseph and Selah Chamberlain. On April 4 the directors awarded the contract for building the following thirty miles of road, from Rock River to Madison, to the Cooke & Sherwin contracting company. The contract specified to complete the road to Stoughton by September 1 and to Madison by January 1.

The station at Milton provides some of the more humorous stories of the early railroad. Earlier that year, Mr. Edward Barber had been appointed the station agent at Milton. But no one had told him that the residents there were Seventh Day Baptists who observed the Sabbath on Saturday rather than Sunday. Barber arrived on a Friday. All day Saturday he sat on the platform, waiting for business that never came. Passersby in their go-to-meeting clothes paid him no attention. The next day, Sunday, was the Sabbath for Mr. Barber, but it was the first day of the workweek for the people of Milton. Farmers drove teams and wagons loaded with pork, wheat, oats, and corn to the depot, but found no one there to receive them. They looked for Mr. Barber, found him at his boarding house, and requested him to open the depot, which he refused to do. The following day they complained to the railroad management, and a controversy ensued. Some officials advocated discharging Barber for having turned away business, while others supported him. Fortunately for Barber, Superintendent Brodhead was among the latter. Barber continued at Milton and was later promoted.[3]

Another story taking place at Milton concerns a standoff between Joseph Goodrich's son Ezra and the railroad at Milton. As a rule the Milwaukee and Mississippi fenced in its right-of-way to protect its trains from wandering cattle. In Milton, it extended its fence right through the village park:

> The railroad men would set in posts to set up a fence. But as fast as the posts were set, Ezra Goodrich would, with the help of village huskies [young men], yank them up again. The railroad company finally stopped trying to put up a fence when their last plan failed. They had put cross bars on the posts when they set them so they couldn't be pulled out by hand. Goodrich used a log about the height and thickness of a modern telephone pole as a lever. And the posts came out.[4]

As the road was being laid between Milton and Stoughton, the directors of the Milwaukee and Mississippi were engaged in serious discussion concerning what would happen once they reached Madison and the building of the road beyond Madison to the Mississippi. Their main concern was where they would get the money they needed to do so. Some of the directors urged operating the Milwaukee-to-Madison section of the line until Eastern capitalists could be induced to buy into the company. Others recommended stopping at the Wisconsin River and continuing with a line of steamboats to the Mississippi—an economical alternative, though not practical in winter. But the majority of the directors favored mortgaging the road and borrowing the money to finish as quickly as possible. Their motion to that effect was carried and President John Catlin was given the necessary authorization.

Former Milwaukee and Mississippi's No. 5, "E. Corning," arrived from Schenectady Locomotive Works in 1852. Note the elaborate decoration and the inclined cylinders, common in the early 1850s.
WHi Image ID 3927

There had been, since the inception of the Milwaukee and Mississippi, some uncertainty about its route to the Mississippi. Would it pass through the rough and uneven terrain of the lead region in Grant County as specified in its charter, or might it run in the level Wisconsin River Valley instead? Citizens of both regions had tried to sway the directors to adopt their route, even to the extent of chartering railroad companies to meet the Milwaukee and Mississippi part way. Lead region and Green County citizens had chartered the Southern Wisconsin Railroad Company, which in November of 1852 surveyed a line from Dubuque to Janesville, reporting that "the descent to the Mississippi was by easier grades and with less expense than by any route."[5] Yet Milwaukee and Mississippi constructing engineer Benjamin Edgerton had reported this route would be cost-prohibitive:

> The formation of the mineral region is not adapted to cheap railroad construction.... A much greater amount of excavation and embankment will be necessary than in the eastern portion of the State, and it will in most cases be rock, costing six or seven times the price per yard that gravel or sand will cost. Grades and curves must be adopted that would also be objectionable, even on a road designed for local traffic.[6]

In the meantime, Prairie du Chien residents had chartered the Madison and Prairie du Chien Railroad Company on March 24, 1852. Its incorporators included Hercules Dousman and B. W. Brisbois of Prairie du Chien and Augustus. A. Bird, Simeon Mills, and Elisha Burdick of Madison. The Prairie du Chien Railroad's route in the Wisconsin River Valley actually had easier grades, meaning the choice was made for the directors of the Milwaukee and Mississippi. And the company already had one hundred thousand dollars of subscribed stock to boot. On May 18, 1853, the Milwaukee and Mississippi and the Madison and Prairie du Chien companies merged. The resulting company took the name Milwaukee & Mississippi Railroad Company (replacing the "and" with an ampersand). It was capitalized at $4,500,000, and would terminate on the Mississippi at Prairie du Chien. Superintendent Brodhead had supported the Wisconsin River route all along, pointing out that it was

> one uniform level plain on which the road can be constructed. I have never passed over the same extent of country anywhere . . . over which a road can be constructed as cheaply. . . . It is sufficient for me to know from actual observation . . . that the route passes through a highly productive country, diversified with the riches of level and rolling prairie land, and extensive burr oak openings withal, in the midst of plenty of timber for fuel and fencing, and well supplied with pure water, and with all in a healthy climate. The soil and climate admit of raising all the varieties of farming products which the Western State are celebrated for producing in great abundance.[7]

In his report at the end of the year, Brodhead would write:

> One of the routes has a straight line of 30 miles in length, and stretches of from one to six miles each frequently occur. On about 90 miles of the distance between Madison and the Mississippi, there need not be a grade exceeding 10 feet to the mile, and on no portion exceeding 22 feet to the mile.[8]

One week after the merger, Edgerton began running preliminary surveys between Madison and Prairie du Chien.[9]

❖ ❖ ❖ ❖ ❖ ❖

Around the time of the merger, work on the Milwaukee & Mississippi had come to a halt at its Rock River crossing, two miles upstream from the village of Fulton. Construction of the bridge and of the line on either side of it languished all summer. To

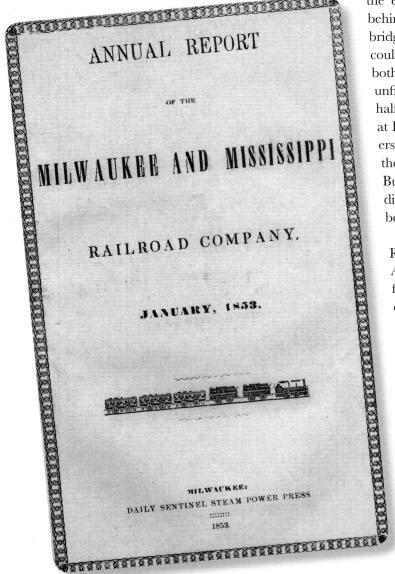

The title page of the Milwaukee and Mississippi 1852 Annual Report.
WHS Library, Pamphlet 99-5806

the east of the bridge, the Chamberlains were behind schedule laying the track; to the west of the bridge, the new contractors, Cooke & Sherwin, could not easily get the needed materials, since both tracks on the other side and the bridge were unfinished. Yet workers did grade a mile and a half past the bridge, where they erected a station at Edgerton, Fulton Station. Town site developers Page and Swift laid out a village north of the depot, and contractors Adin, Burdick, and Burdick laid out another village south of it. Ferdinand Davis put up a store and Nelson Coon began building the Exchange Hotel.[10]

The Milwaukee & Mississippi's Rock River bridge was still not usable by September. At the end of that month the Chamberlains finished their work east of the bridge. Finally, on November 25, the bridge was completed and the line to Fulton Station opened. The pace of building picked up dramatically as construction trains from Milwaukee began rumbling over the bridge. Also in November, Milwaukee & Mississippi directors William Barstow and Holton ran against each in the election for governor of Wisconsin. Barstow, a Democrat, received 30,405 votes, and Holton, of the Liberty Party, 21,886.[11] On December 15 the company initiated limited freight and passenger service to Stoughton, three months behind schedule. Most of the grading to Madison was finished by the end of the year and track laying had almost reached Stoughton. Constructing Engineer Edgerton moved with his family to a home he had purchased on Lake Mendota in Madison. It would be his base of operations until the rails reached the Mississippi. In the meantime, work began on the Madison depot:

During the fall of 1853, the company selected their depot grounds in Madison, and a depot building was put under contract; the building was to be one hundred and fifteen feet long by fifty feet wide, with walls eighteen feet high and a piazza and platform ten feet wide on each side. It was to be built of stone, and was to be completed by January 1, 1854. At the time the grounds were selected, they were covered with thick undergrowth, and the whole distance between the freight depot and Lake Monona was a dense thicket of poplar, crab, and plum trees.[12]

Operations on the Milwaukee & Mississippi continued to be simple. In Milwaukee the switching of cars in the yards was done with horses, locomotives being reserved for moving trains on the main line. The company's passenger cars, all built in its own shops, were forty feet long with low, arched-roofs and seated forty people. They had tallow candles or lanterns for lighting at night and small box stoves for heating in the winter. The cars were coupled together with iron links, and passengers tended to be jerked out of their seats whenever the train started or stopped. Fares were expensive. A one-way, twenty-mile trip from Milwaukee to Waukesha cost seventy-five cents—a day's wages for an unskilled laborer at that time. Still, those who could afford to take the train did not complain. Compared to walking, riding, or taking a carriage, the train was faster and more comfortable.

The train became a popular means of travel, while shipping by rail proved to be a profitable choice in 1853. The traffic volume during the year was considerable. Superintendent Brodhead reported:

> We have run, during most of the year, two trains each way, per day, over the road, devoted exclusively to carrying passengers, also two regular freight trains, besides a number of extra freight trains, we have also, for a large portion of the time, run two trains on construction account.[13]

Records show that westbound freight trains carried merchandise, sundries, lumber, lath, shingles, pickets, coal, posts, salt, whiskey, apples, lime, stoves, brick, and livestock. Eastbound trains carried wheat but also corn, oats, barley, rye, flax seed, grass seed, potatoes, flour, pork, lard, potash, high wines, hogs, tobacco, hides, flax, broom corn, wool, sundries, butter, livestock, stone, lumber, packing barrels, linseed oil, mill feed, lead, and shot. During the year the Milwaukee & Mississippi enlarged its inventory of freight cars from 38 to 183 and added three locomotives to bring the total to eleven.[14] The locomotives were all "eight-wheelers," having four small wheels on a leading truck and four large wheels driven by the engine.

Much wood was needed as fuel to move the trains, and the company was always advertising for it. Farmers along the line cut trees and hauled them to collection points where "wood trains" would carry them to "wood stations." There a single horse would be "plodding patiently in a circle at the end of a long sweep" to turn a circular saw that cut the wood to length. When trains stopped to "wood up," passengers who were in a hurry would help the crewmen load wood into the tender.[15]

The cost of running trains over the seventy-mile line in 1853 would total eighty-seven thousand dollars. Of this, fuel costs (in the form of wood contracts) composed 23 percent; station services 22 percent; repairs of the road 11 percent; repairs on locomotives 10 percent; and train services, repairs of cars, oil and waste, stationery and printing, taxes, and miscellaneous, the remaining 34 percent.[16]

Its line continuing to expand to the west, the company constructed a number of new buildings in 1853. In Milwaukee it built a large, two-story warehouse that allowed the transfer of freight between cars and lake vessels. Milwaukee also received a brick round house with seven locomotive stalls. New passenger and freight depots were built at Fulton, Stoughton, and Madison. The Milwaukee & Mississippi exhibited genuine concern for the safety of its passengers and employees, something lacking on most railroads of the 1850s. At the end of the year, Superintendent Brodhead reported:

> In all, we have transported over the road 75,975 passengers, and without the slightest injury or accident of any kind to one of them.... It is gratifying to add that in doing this amount of business the employees of the Company have also escaped without any injury happening to one of them of a permanent character, or any accident, which has more than for a few days at a time detained them from their regular occupation.[17]

As a result of a subtle shift in mood in the state during the winter of 1852–53, the legislature in Madison was swamped with petitions for railroad charters. They responded by introducing forty-five bills of incorporation that resulted in twenty-five actual charters. Thus, the Kenosha and Beloit Railroad Company was incorporated March 4, authorized to build a railroad "from such point in the city of Kenosha, in the county of Kenosha, to such point in the village of Beloit, upon the Rock River, as shall be determined upon by the board of directors and to connect with any other rail road running from Rock River to the Mississippi River."[18] The company was capitalized at one hundred thousand dollars and its named commissioners were Samuel Hale, Alonzo Campbell, Charles M. Baker, E. W. Evans, Josiah Bond, George Ben-

# THE SCRAMBLE FOR NEW ROUTES

nett, Henry B. Hindsdale, S. H. Stafford, Samuel R. McClelland, S. W. Benson, Joseph D. Monell Jr., Lucius G. Fisher, T. H. Fellows, and John Hackett.

Also incorporated on March 4 was the Wisconsin Central Railroad Company (not to be confused with the Wisconsin Central of 1871), capitalized at one million dollars and authorized to build a railroad from Genoa, near the Wisconsin-Illinois border, to Portage by way of Geneva, Whitewater, and Columbus. Its principal boosters were the businessmen of Walworth County. Among the twenty-three commissioners were Charles M. Baker of Lake Geneva, George Bulkley and Otis Preston of Elkhorn, Eleazar Wakeley of Whitewater, and John A. Pierce of Millard. The act called for thirteen directors; construction was to begin within three years and finish within ten. The company organized on June 30 in Elkhorn, electing Le Grand Rockwell, an Elkhorn banker, its president. On July 22 its representatives met with representatives of the Fox River Valley Railroad and Galena and Chicago Union Railroad companies of Illinois to seal an agreement that would allow the Wisconsin Central to connect with their lines, thus allowing travel to Elgin and Chicago.[19]

The charter of the Milwaukee, Fond du Lac, and Green Bay Railroad Company was signed into law on April 2. It authorized that company to build a railroad from Milwaukee to Green Bay by way of West Bend, Fond du Lac, Oshkosh, and Menasha. Among its named commissioners were James Kneeland, Herman Haertal, Alexander Mitchell, James Ludington, and Coles Bashford. This company would begin construction later in the year.

The remaining twenty-two charters were given to companies that would never lay track. Among them were the Watertown and Berlin; the Michigan and Wisconsin Transit; the Green Bay and Minnesota; the Milwaukee, Waukesha, Jefferson, and Madison (whose commissioners included Governor Leonard J. Farwell and future governor William A. Barstow); and the Fox River Valley (whose commissioners included future governors Barstow and Arthur MacArthur).[20] The editor of the *Milwaukee Sentinel* wrote:

> Our young State, thanks to the railroad mania encouraged by our Legislature, which charters improbable and impossible routes ad libitum, has authorized some 15,000 miles of Railroad, involving a capital of $300,000,000 in their construction—all to be completed immediately of course.[21]

In the early spring of 1853 the Rock River Valley Union Company sent out a party to survey the line between Fond du Lac and Janesville, from there to continue as far south as it could. One of the members of that party wrote:

We ran the preliminary line that winter from Fond du Lac through Waupun, thence skirting Winnebago Marsh on the east, through Avoca and Mayville to Horicon and Watertown. . . . We disbanded at the latter place when spring opened and the call of the plow and the hoe was heard in the land.[22]

Also that spring, the Rock River Valley Union began looking for partners. Unlike the Milwaukee & Mississippi, which was building its line in standard gauge (meaning there was four feet, eight and a half inches between the rails), the Rock River Valley Union was building its line in broad gauge (six feet between the rails). It wanted to be able to connect with and interchange cars with railroads that had the same gauge track. The company found two willing partners, the Southern Wisconsin Railroad Company and the Kenosha and Beloit Railroad Company. However, the Southern Wisconsin, despite partnering with the Milwaukee & Mississippi to build the standard gauge, eight-mile-long branch line between Milton and Janesville, wanted to build its main line between Janesville and Dubuque in broad gauge. Similarly, the Kenosha and Beloit wanted to build in broad gauge. A grand plan developed. The Rock River Valley Union and its Illinois partner, the Illinois and Wisconsin, would build a north-south trunk (or main) line between Chicago and Fond du Lac, and the Southern Wisconsin and the Kenosha and Beloit would build an east-west trunk line from Dubuque on the Mississippi to Kenosha on Lake Michigan. From this large, broad-gauge cross covering southern Wisconsin, broad-gauge branch lines would develop, and standard gauge lines, such as the Milwaukee & Mississippi, would suffer and become obsolete.[23] Or at least that was the plan. Although the final agreements were signed that May, the plan was never realized.

There were also more plans for expansion afoot. Incredibly, the Rock River Valley Union Railroad Company was pursuing an extension of its railroad to the Pacific at this time. It had been proposed by Wisconsin Congressman James D. Doty in 1852 in the *American Railroad Journal* and was to run from the head (western end) of Lake Superior to Puget Sound. Doty believed that the shipping of the Great Lakes and railroads coming from the East via Chicago would adequately feed this transcontinental line. Railroads from the East had reached Chicago in 1852, and all that was needed was the relatively short link from that city to the western end of Lake Superior—which the Rock River Valley Union Railroad could supply by extending its planned Janesville-Madison branch line northward. Edwin F. Johnson, an engineer from Vermont, even wrote a book about this project called *Railroad to the Pacific: Northern Route*. The promoters of the route had scored a victory early in 1853 when Congress authorized a survey. This survey would require an expedition to travel some 1,800 miles each way, through wilderness and Indian country, following in part the trail of Lewis and Clark. The War Department appointed army engineer Colonel Isaac I. Stevens, recently appointed governor of Washington Territory, to lead this expedition. When the group left St. Paul, Minnesota, that spring, one of its members was James Doty, son of Congressman James D. Doty.[24]

From Fond du Lac, the Rock River Valley Union Railroad was building southward towards Chester (East Waupun) twenty miles away. Track laying had commenced using broad-gauge rails. Rails were laid to Oakfield, twelve miles from Fond du Lac. Oakfield, though not much more than a cluster of cabins, was at the portage between the Fond du Lac and Rock Rivers. At one time fur traders from as far away as Montreal and St. Louis had passed this way. The track layers laid three miles of track past Oakfield, then quit. There were no more rails, and the company had run out of funds. The directors were forced to lease the line to the company's largest creditor, who was also the line's builder, Timothy F. Strong Sr. Strong would be allowed to operate the road and keep the profits until the debt was paid. Strong found that the passenger and freight receipts did not cover the cost of running the trains, so he began purchasing lumber around Lake Winnebago and shipping it over the railroad to Chester. On the last five miles, he had to run the cars over wooden sleepers that hadn't received their iron yet. According to one observer, "The rate of speed made on them was very slow, the number of miles an hour hardly exceeding the number of times a day some portion of the train was off the track."[25] At Chester the lumber was dumped into Lake Horicon and then floated down the Rock River to downstream sawmills, some as far as Janesville. Eventually Strong went to Chicago and purchased more strap iron (it can be assumed this came from the Galena and Chicago Union Railroad), which he then used to complete the track.

The Winnebago had been the road's only locomotive until this time. Strong purchased another from the Taunton Locomotive Company of Taunton, Massachusetts, for ten thousand dollars; he named it Fountain City, for the city of Fond du Lac. He had it shipped over the lakes to Sheboygan; from there he expected to transport it over the Sheboygan and Fond du Lac plank road. Author W. A. Titus wrote:

> And when the second engine was about to be similarly transported, the road owners objected. It was claimed by the railroad[,] however, that it could not legally be denied the use of the road for the purpose, pointing out that under the road's charter any ox drawn or horse drawn vehicle had the right of passage; and in order to establish that the engine was a vehicle, several men rode on it as passengers. Apparently convinced by this ingenious but specious contention, the road officials permitted the engine to proceed, but it caused great damage to the highway, which it was never possible to fully repair.[26]

STEAM AND CINDERS

The Fountain City's six week, forty-five mile passage required fourteen yokes of oxen and seven spans of horses. One writer commented:

> Some days it was not possible to haul it more than eighty rods between sun and sun. . . . It was a muddy piece of machinery when it reached Fond du Lac, having passed through more sloughs than any other locomotive which ever came to the State.[27]

Such were the affairs of the Rock River Valley Union Railroad during the summer of 1853. Meanwhile its partner, the Illinois & Wisconsin Railroad, had surveyed from Chicago to Janesville and had begun grading at Chicago.

In March the Milwaukee and Watertown Railroad began building its line between Brookfield, a stop on the Milwaukee & Mississippi fourteen miles west of Milwaukee, and Watertown, a city with three thousand inhabitants thirty-one miles to the northwest. The surveys had been completed in January. The grading now begun would continue to the end of the year. The work was difficult, as much of the country was heavily wooded, uneven, and rocky. From this time on, Brookfield would be known as Brookfield Junction. The company would use the Milwaukee & Mississippi's tracks between Milwaukee and Brookfield Junction to run its construction trains and later its passenger and freight trains. The ties between the two companies were strong. Milwaukee and Watertown president John S. Rockwell was a director of the Milwaukee & Mississippi, while Edward H. Brodhead was the superintendent and chief engineer of both railroads.

The spring of 1853 brought about several developments for the newly chartered railways. In Beaver Dam on March 30 the La Crosse and Milwaukee held its first annual meeting. Three hundred and fifty-five stockholders attended, voting their 3,620 shares. They elected thirteen directors: Timothy Burns, Joseph Kerr, Stoddard Judd, Abram Ackerman, Hiram Barber, Moses M. Strong, William Dawes, Edmund D. Clinton, Jacob L. Bean, James Ludington, Francis Huebschman, Edwin H. Goodrich, and Byron Kilbourn. This board then elected Bean president of the company (replacing Strong). Kilbourn retained his position as chief engineer.

On April 5 the Sheboygan and Mississippi Railroad Company organized in Sheboygan. Sheboygan's boosters pointed out the railroad's advantages—it was closer to the Eastern markets than either Milwaukee or Chicago and its western terminus, La Crosse, was advantageously positioned for trade with St. Paul. They again claimed that it would be Sheboygan, not Milwaukee, that would become the leading metropolis on Lake Michigan.

Later that month, on April 19, the Kenosha and Beloit Railroad Company, which had been chartered only six weeks before and whose commissioners had opened subscription books and taken in $61,000 on the first day, organized. Engineer A. C. Twining, who had examined the route between the cities, reported that there were no major obstacles to building a railroad over it. The stockholders elected as directors Samuel Hale, Alonzo Campbell, E. W. Evans, Josiah Bond, A. Leonard, Seth Doan, E. Simmons, C. C. Sholes, and H. B. Towslee of Kenosha; Charles M. Baker and C. H. Stafford of Geneva; and G. C. Davidson of Albany. Hale was chosen president of the company and Bond was named secretary. Hale was one of Kenosha's original settlers, having walked there from Chicago in 1837.

A large celebration was held in Mineral Point on May 30 by citizens wishing to mark the signing of the contract between the Mineral Point Railroad and builders Joseph and Selah Chamberlain and Carlisle D. Cooke to build and equip a thirty-two-mile railroad for $693,698.95.[28] These Mineral Point residents were joined by some eight hundred out-of-towners. They gathered at the courthouse, then followed the Mineral Point Brass Band one mile to a point south of the village. There Colonel Abner Nichols, a fiery Cornishman and the former host of the infamous Mansion House—broke first sod for the railroad. The festivities continued throughout the day and into the night.

Yet by the fall of the year, the Mineral Point Railroad was back to square one. It had been forced to cancel the Chamberlain-Cooke contract when an impending loan fell through. In August its agents succeeded in raising $602,800 in stock subscriptions—more than the estimated cost of the railroad—and President Strong began proposing an extension of the line northward to the Wisconsin River and Minnesota. Engineer Temple surveyed the proposed extension and concluded that it posed no difficulties. On October 10 President Strong signed a twenty-year agreement with the Illinois Central and the Galena and Chicago Union railroads that guaranteed the Mineral Point Railroad fifty-six thousand dollars annually, above and beyond expenses, in exchange for its exclusive business. That month the company again cancelled its construction contracts, and in December contracted a third time, with Robert & George Schuyler & Company of New York, to build its road.

❖ ❖ ❖ ❖ ❖ ❖

Summer arrived, and matters heated up in Milwaukee. On June 27 the Milwaukee, Fond du Lac, and Green Bay Company, under President James Kneeland, absorbed its rival, the Milwaukee and Fond du Lac, through a merger. It then turned against its other rival, Kilbourn's La Crosse and Milwaukee Railroad. Kneeland located his company's Milwaukee depot south of the Menomonee River, graded up 3rd

Street to the La Crosse depot, then continued grading on the La Crosse's proposed route out of the city. His audacity paid off when the city of Milwaukee awarded his company $200,000 of credit, while offering the La Crosse and Milwaukee Company only $114,000.

For the remainder of the year, the Milwaukee, Fond du Lac, and Green Bay Railroad struggled, grading just one eighteen-mile section of its route from Milwaukee to Richfield. One writer described this line as being

> of the heaviest character, costing an average of $20,000 per mile, with deep cuts and grading in some places thirty-five feet to the mile . . . the entire eighteen miles being through dense timber with a sub-soil of hard-pan, a composition of fine gravel blended with blue clay, which in most cases, was proof against plowing and blasting, and had to be loosened by manual labor. . . . Its removal was attended with more labor than the removal of solid rock. . . . A cubic foot of the solid pan weighted 130 pounds.[29]

In August the Green Bay, Milwaukee, & Chicago Railroad Company, which had been chartered two years earlier, stopped focusing on Green Bay and began working on connecting Milwaukee with Chicago. It broke ground at Kenosha at 13th Avenue south of 60th Street. The city gave the railroad the right to build through and across its streets at grade.[30] Grading proceeded northward from Kenosha (the line's ultimate destination) to Bay Shore, south of Milwaukee. Meanwhile the company's partner, the Chicago and Milwaukee Railroad of Illinois (formerly the Illinois Parallel Railroad), began grading southward from Kenosha to Chicago.[31]

❖ ❖ ❖ ❖ ❖

The fall of 1853 saw a number of railroad companies come to life. The Milwaukee and Horicon Railroad Company opened its subscription books in October, and by November enough stock had been subscribed to organize. A board of directors was elected that chose John B. Smith as president. Jesper Vliet was appointed chief engineer. The new board ordered surveys of the line and directed stock agents to solicit subscriptions along the route. The stockholders fixed the northern terminus of the line at Berlin. Also that fall, the Southern Wisconsin Railroad began its grading at Monroe, working eastward toward Janesville. It seemed to have postponed working westward through the rough terrain of the lead region.

Meanwhile, the Racine, Janesville, and Mississippi Railroad Company began grading at Racine. The company had dropped Janesville and was instead building to Beloit. In April the residents of the town of Beloit had voted to issue bonds to subscribe to one hundred thousand dollars' worth of the company's stock. In May the company had purchased its station grounds in Beloit, three blocks east of the Rock River and two blocks from the Beloit and Madison depot. The company had originally surveyed an "air line" (a railroad that is almost straight) from Racine to Delavan, but modified it to include Elkhorn and Burlington.

The fall of 1853 also occasioned a momentous event in the development of Wisconsin—the connection of the Badger State to Chicago and the East by rail. In September the Beloit and Madison Railroad Company began work on its line from Beloit to Madison. It was using third-hand strap rail purchased from the Galena and Chicago Union, which had been replacing these rails with T-rail between Chicago and Elgin since June. By November the grading extended seventeen miles north to Footville. Meanwhile, contractor J. P. Houston made progress on the wooden truss bridge over the Rock River, one thousand feet north of the state-line depot. While that was happening on the Wisconsin side, the larger work of making the connection was being done by Illinois' Galena and Chicago Union Railroad approaching from the south. On November 4 it completed its branch line from Belvidere to Beloit—the missing piece between New York and Wisconsin. One observer recalled, "Towards evening of that day the construction train stood opposite the depot on the first track which ever connected Wisconsin with the Atlantic cities."[32]

Regular service on the Beloit Branch began November 14, with trains leaving Beloit at 8:00 a.m. and 5:30 p.m. and arriving in Belvidere at 1:20 p.m. and 12:00 a.m. At Belvidere passengers had to change trains for Chicago or Freeport. The trip from Beloit to Chicago took five and a half hours, and the one-way fare was $2.50. At Beloit, stagecoaches were available for those wishing to continue to Janesville or Madison. Freight service was inaugurated as well, and with great success. On November 17 the *Beloit Journal* reported:

> The completion of the railroad is the cause of a very sensible improvement in the business and appearance of our village. The streets are full of teams, and produce is pouring in to an unanticipated extent. A great deal of grain has been held until the opening of the road, and the present high prices are hastening it upon the ground rapidly since the cars have actually made their appearance among us. Considerable quantities are coming from the region northwest of us, and from the eastern part of Green County. The termination of a road which makes us the central point and depot for a considerable territory affords a very gratifying change from the position we previously occupied, midway between the termini of two roads.[33]

❖ ❖ ❖ ❖ ❖ ❖

The year 1853 saw the appearance of many new rail lines, at least on paper. Yet only eighteen miles of new track was laid—less than half of what had been laid in 1852—and after four years of building railroads, there were only ninety miles of track in Wisconsin. But there was more to the railroad industry than mere trackage. Seven companies were now building railroads in Wisconsin, and several more were preparing to do so. The Milwaukee & Mississippi Railroad had proved itself profitable during 1853, and had been able to declare dividends. That achievement in itself would bring further investment dollars to the Milwaukee & Mississippi Railroad—and also to its rivals.

# Chapter 15

## Complete to Madison
### 1854

Luke Stoughton came to Wisconsin from Vermont in 1837. He was the founder of the village of Stoughton, located fifteen miles south of Madison, where the Milwaukee & Mississippi's tracks ended at the end of 1853. After farming and then operating a general store in Janesville over some ten years, Stoughton purchased the land at the bend of the Catfish River on which the village that bore his name would grow. He dammed the river to operate a gristmill and a sawmill. The site was first known as Stoughton Mills, and then Stoughtonville. Later Stoughton opened a general store. In 1852 he heard that the Milwaukee & Mississippi was planning to build its line through nearby Dunkirk. He promptly offered the company a large plot of land on the east side of Stoughton for its depot and rail yards. As it had with Jenkins Station, the Milwaukee & Mississippi accepted the offer and rerouted its line. It was not difficult to reroute the railroad at that time—it was simply a matter of relocating and surveying, as construction was still a year away.

On Monday, January 2, the first train steamed into Stoughton on the Milwaukee & Mississippi line, having come the full eighty miles from Milwaukee. It was pulled to the depot by the locomotive Menomonee, recently built at Milwaukee's Menomonee Locomotive Works, and was met at the station by agent Hiram Giles.

Work on the line between Stoughton and Madison continued through the winter of 1853–54 and picked up as warmer weather arrived in the spring. Tracks were

Milwaukee & Mississippi's No. 7, the "Menomonee," pulled the first train into Stoughton on January 2, 1854. She was the first locomotive built in Wisconsin, having been finished in October of 1852 by W. B. Walton & Co. in Milwaukee's Menomonee River Valley.
WHi Image ID 62051

laid eight miles to Door Creek Station—a small depot with a side track. Only eight more miles remained to Madison. Shortly after passing Lake Kegonsa, the track layers laid iron rails over a giant sinkhole. When the ground under the track disappeared, they enlisted surrounding homesteaders to cut down heavy timber and then haul, crib, and sink it into the hole. They relaid the track but found that on the next day, the cribbage had either sunk or floated away toward Lake Kegonsa and that the track was again left hanging. They repeated this process until the track finally had the support it needed.[1]

At Madison, the railroad bridge across Monona Bay, a long wooden trestle carry-

The 1857 McFarland depot is at left, William McFarland's house at right in this 1880 photograph. McFarland was 5 miles south of Madison on the former Milwaukee & Mississippi line.
WHi Image ID 27628

ing the track six feet over the water, was finished in mid-May. The first passenger train reached Madison on May 18, a full year and a half from the date originally proposed by the contractors. The track, however, was not laid up to the depot until Monday, May 22.[2] The next day was the official opening of the line between Milwaukee and Madison. The *Wisconsin State Journal* gave the following account:

> Never was the day more auspicious. The heavens were cloudless, the air warm but not sultry. . . . By ten in the morning the streets were filled with teams and the sidewalks crowded with people. Great numbers of them were men who had settled in the country at an early day and had never seen a locomotive or railroad.
>     . . . By one o'clock in the afternoon the grounds about the Depot were thronged with people. . . . We should judge that at least two thousand people from the country were about the Depot, and at the end of the bridge where the railroad crosses the bay. . . . Bright colored parasols ranged in groups along the shore lent liveliness to the scene.
>     At length the unmistakable whistle of the engine was heard, and the long train with two locomotives at its head swept grandly into sight—thirty-two cars, crowded with people. . . . At the rear of the train were several racks occupied by the Milwaukee Fire Companies in their gay red uniforms with their glistening engines. A fine band of music attended them, and, at intervals as they slowly moved across the bridge, the piece of artillery brought along by the firemen was discharged. It was a grand but strange spectacle to see this monster train, like some huge unheard of thing of life with a breath of smoke and flame, emerging from the green openings—scenes of pastoral beauty and quietude—across the Third Lake. . . . It was estimated that at least two thousand were on board.[3]

Despite this auspicious opening, the route through Madison was not without its problems. For one, the tracks east of the bridge kept sinking. The Milwaukee & Mississippi's engineers had tried to achieve a quick, level, and direct route by locating the line across marshes that had a subsoil of peat and marl, but this proved to be an unstable combination. On one day in June a large section of track sank five feet. There was nothing to do but add fill as quickly as possible until the track was properly supported and service could resume.[4]

Also in June, Madison's *Argus and Democrat* newspaper pointed out the lack of a printed schedule for Milwaukee & Mississippi trains arriving at and departing from that city:

> We have visits almost every day from persons inquiring as to the time of the arrival of the trains at Madison and the departures thence. Our Madison papers are

Group portrait of men employed with the Milwaukee and Watertown Railroad, 1855.
WHi Image ID 62098

searched in vain for the desired information. . . . We believe that the trains start about daylight in the morning, and shortly after dinner in the afternoon, but not having seen a time-table, or had occasion to look one up, we cannot say precisely.[5]

Another problem—and one more alarming to the average citizen than unpublished schedules—was the head-on collision of two freight trains in July near Palmyra due to an error in scheduling. It was Wisconsin's first such incident. Fortunately, there were no fatalities:

The station agent telegraphed from Whitewater to headquarters at Milwaukee, and then proceeded to the scene of the disaster, where he saw one of the locomotive engineers who had been involved in the disaster sitting on the side of the track and pouring sand from one hand into the other, nervously expecting, of course, that when the wrecking train arrived with the officials of the road he would be dismissed in disgrace. When Superintendent Brodhead came, all he did was to look at the wreck and observe: "That's a very bad mess. Get to work, men, and clear it away." Nobody was discharged. Nobody was even reprimanded. Brodhead was an experienced railroad man, and realized that under the conditions the employees involved in the smash-up had acquitted themselves as well as was humanly possible.⁶

The line also encouraged development of a noncommercial variety: political growth, in particular the emergence of a new political party that would prove, in time, to be one of the two major parties dominating modern American politics. On July 13 the Milwaukee & Mississippi's newly opened line to Madison facilitated this historic event by carrying car after car of disenchanted Whig, Free Soil, Liberty, and Democrat party members to Madison to attend a "People's Mass State of Wisconsin Convention." Delegates and activists assembled on the capitol grounds, where they enthusiastically organized a new party, which they named the Republican Party.⁷

Meanwhile, the Milwaukee & Mississippi Railroad had made a momentous decision to stop further construction and concentrate instead on running trains between Milwaukee and Madison. It still planned an extension to the Mississippi at Prairie du Chien, but wanted to wait to build until a few important pieces were in place. One was the purchase of charter rights from the Southern Wisconsin Railroad, which would enable it to build a second branch to the Mississippi from Milton on its main line to Dubuque, via Janesville, and the southwestern lead region. After this purchase, the company sent stock agent Deacon Edmond D. Clinton to hold meetings and encourage farmers and villagers to mortgage their properties in order to buy Milwaukee & Mississippi stock. Clinton's tour encompassed the villages of Clarno, Twin Grove, Juda, Clarence, Decatur, Sylvester, Jordan, Cadiz, Shullsburg, Benton, New Diggings, Jamestown, and Hazel Green. Clinton later recalled:

> I informed them there was so little money in the country, we could not build as rapidly as we wanted to without resorting to farm mortgages. We had taken farm mortgages and used them successfully in building the road to Janesville. [I informed them,] this is the plan, that you give your note and mortgage to the company or holder, for any amount you wish to take, to run ten years, with coupons attached, interest payable annually, at the rate of 8 per cent, for which the company authorizes me, as their agent, to give you a receipt in full for the shares of capital stock, or any number of shares, of $100 each in said company. The company will give you an indemnifying bond that they will pay the interest for ten years, also pay your 2 per cent annually, making it that the company allows you 10 per cent interest, while the coupons called for 8 per cent.⁸

That summer, Benjamin H. Edgerton had located and staked the line between Madison and Prairie du Chien. By autumn Milwaukee & Mississippi stock agent

Clinton, working along the route of the proposed southern branch, was setting stock sale records. By November he had raised $862,000. In Shullsburg he raised $127,000 in one day. Clinton had offered to have one of the company's locomotives named after the first person to mortgage their farm for ten thousand dollars. He later recalled that "John H. Bridge secured this honor, and the Company fulfilled their agreement."[9] With Clinton's success, construction of the branch seemed imminent. President John Catlin wrote optimistically:

> There is quite a flattering prospect for . . . the Southern Wisconsin road. . . . The distance from Janesville to Dubuque . . . is about 95 miles. . . . There has been subscribed nearly two millions of dollars. Its estimated cost is about $3,000,000. . . . It would form a very direct and straight road from Milwaukee to Dubuque.[10]

By year's end, however, it was obvious that the high hopes for extensive railroad construction in the state that had been held at the beginning of the year would not been realized. Milwaukee & Mississippi President Catlin was forced to explain his company's lack of progress:

> Owing to the great depression in rail road securities which has prevailed through the year, only sixteen miles have been added to the finished part of the road and brought into use . . . from Stoughton to Madison, the capital of the State.[11]

But Catlin knew that trackage alone was not an accurate indicator of the company's health. In his annual report to the stockholders he stated:

> The gross receipts of the road for the year 1854 . . . are $456,864.78; and . . . $307,632.41 net receipts. The gross receipts for 1853 were $226,918.48, and the net receipts, $134,340.14. It will be seen that although the length of the road has not been greatly increased, yet the net earnings present the very satisfactory gain of more than one hundred per cent.[12]

At the end of 1854 the company had $1,424,000 dollars' worth of stock subscribed, with $988,665 paid in, and a debt of $1,680,000. The railroad from Milwaukee to Madison had cost $2,679,082, or $25,760 per mile. The company owned twenty-two locomotives, eleven passenger and baggage cars, and 250 freight cars. The completion of the Milwaukee & Mississippi between Milwaukee and Madison in May had marked the end of an era during which Wisconsin possessed, for all practical purposes, only one railroad. That time had truly been the pioneer stage of railroading in the state. Superintendent Brodhead accurately described the line

# COMPLETE TO MADISON

as one of "about 100 miles in length, with no *through* connections, terminating in the interior of the State, where there was scarcely a white man 15 years ago."

Meanwhile, Chicago's interests were being promoted in Madison that winter. The Rock River Valley Union Railroad Company was using a house on the corner of Clymer and South Wisconsin streets (today West Doty Street and Martin Luther King Jr. Boulevard) as its headquarters to entertain legislators and further the company's interests. The reaction of the press to the strong-arming tactics of the Rock River Valley Union is telling. This house became known as "Monks' Hall," named for the impious activities that took place there, and the group that assembled there became known as the "Forty Thieves." One observer wrote that "members of the legislature were taken in and done for . . . and nights were often made hideous. . . ."[13] Newer competitors were emerging as the star players in the state, supplanting the Milwaukee & Mississippi.

Developments were brewing for other competitors as well, some positive and some negative. A few notable mergers and agreements sunk some railroads, while others profited.

On January 3 the *Racine Advocate* reported that there were from fifty to five hundred men constantly at work on the Racine, Janesville, and Mississippi line. At the end of the month, that company announced in its annual report that it would build to Beloit instead of Janesville. When the Racine, Janesville, and Mississippi Railroad Company merged with the Rockton and Freeport Rail Road Company of Illinois in February, the new company that emerged was known as the Racine and Mississippi Rail Road Company. Janesville was dropped from the name. That spring the Racine and Mississippi began grading westward from Racine through well-settled farming country that had "respectable white clapboard farmhouses every half mile or so." The line also crossed undulating tall-grass prairies, oak openings, swamps, and meadows.

The Racine and Mississippi also made headway in some significant locations, with rapid progress the result. In April the residents of the town of Beloit had voted 321 to 67 to subscribe to one hundred thousand dollars' worth of the company's stock by issuing town bonds. In May the company had purchased its station grounds in Beloit at the state line, three blocks east of the Rock River and the Galena/Beloit and Madison line's depot. On June 15, the *Racine Advocate* reported that six to seven hundred hands were being employed on the Racine and Mississippi line, and that the road was nearly graded and ready for ties as far as the Fox River (Burlington), with work going forward toward Elkhorn. On July 17 the Racine and Mississippi

Railroad Company received authorization from the legislature to build a "branch line" to Beloit. This line would, in fact, be its main line. It had abandoned all plans of building to Janesville, as originally specified. Meanwhile, the company was running trains over the first twenty miles of its line, between Racine and the Fox River.

On January 23 the La Crosse and Milwaukee Railroad Company merged with its exhausted rival, the Milwaukee, Fond du Lac, and Green Bay Railroad. The company resulting from the merger kept the name La Crosse and Milwaukee, was capitalized at $6,800,000, and owned the eighteen miles of roadway that the Milwaukee, Fond du Lac, and Green Bay had graded with such difficulty the year before. The La Crosse and Milwaukee promised to build the Fond du Lac line after the line to Portage was completed—a promise it would not keep.

In July the company let the construction contracts for its eastern division, Milwaukee to Portage, to Bradley, Whittemore & Company of Burlington, Vermont, a firm reputed to have extensive experience in railroad construction. These contractors were to be paid seven thousand dollars per mile, one-fourth in stock and three-fourths in cash—considerably less than the twenty thousand dollars per mile that had sunk the former Milwaukee, Fond du Lac, and Green Bay.[14] The company introduced its first locomotive, the Westward Ho, at Milwaukee's Fourth of July celebrations. On the following day the company executed to Francis A. Palmer of New York, trustee, a mortgage on the eastern division to secure $950,000 in railroad bonds. At the end of the year the La Crosse and Milwaukee Railroad Company had expended six hundred thousand dollars on its road. Two thirds of the line between Milwaukee and Horicon was graded and six miles of track had been laid north from the Milwaukee depot at Chestnut Street.

Also in January, the Milwaukee and Horicon Railroad Company, whose route between Milwaukee and Horicon was identical to that of the La Crosse and Milwaukee, made an agreement with the latter whereby the La Crosse and Milwaukee would pull the Horicon's passenger and freight trains over the fifty-mile distance for 80 percent of the receipts. The La Crosse and Milwaukee would provide the locomotives, and the agreement was to last for twenty years.

The company began construction that summer. A Fond du Lac County resident wrote, "The Horicon & Berlin Railroad is now in process of construction, and will accommodate the western part of the county, passing through Waupun, Alto, Metomen and Ceresco [Ripon]."[15] The company was also pursuing an extension of its line beyond Ripon to Berlin, Stevens Point, and to the junction of the Mississippi and St. Croix Rivers, as was allowed by its charter. The directors described this route as passing "through one of the richest and most fertile sections of Wisconsin, having unsurpassed agricultural, mineral, lumbering, and manufacturing resources."[16] They ordered a survey of the line to Stevens Point, and soon company agents were calling on farmers along the route to mortgage their farms to purchase railroad stock.

In March the Milwaukee and Watertown Railroad Company's charter had been amended to allow the company to extend its line from Columbus to Stevens Point, Wausau, the headwaters of the Montreal River, and Lake Superior.[17] The Milwaukee and Watertown completed the first eighteen miles of its line, from Brookfield Junction on the Milwaukee & Mississippi line to Oconomowoc, that year; the first passenger train from Milwaukee arrived in Oconomowoc on December 14.

In early summer Kenosha and Beloit Railroad Company engineer William H. Noble recorded that the grading was underway to Fox River with a workforce that averaged at various times two hundred men, sixty horses and carts, thirty cart wagons, sixteen cars, twenty wheelbarrows, and thirty additional men working on the superstructure.

The Beloit and Madison began laying strap rail at Beloit in April. This strap rail had already been twice-used—once by the Galena and Chicago Union and before that by the Michigan Southern. These rails were delivered to Beloit over the Galena's Belvidere-Beloit branch line. They consisted of iron plate $2\frac{1}{2}$ inches wide and $\frac{3}{4}$ inch thick and were laid on an oak ribbon, which in turn was laid on timbers or ties six inches square. These rails were laid from the Beloit depot across the Rock River Bridge, northward along the River's west bank, across a four-mile prairie, and through a five-hundred-foot rock cut to Afton (also known as Bass Creek), a small village with a sawmill and a public house. There the company erected a depot, an engine house, and a water station.

The Beloit and Madison had meanwhile leased its line to the Galena and Chicago Union, which on August 15 began running trains from Chicago to Afton via Belvidere and Beloit. The scheduled time from Belvidere to Beloit was four and a half hours, with one half hour more necessary to reach Afton. The fare from Beloit to Afton was forty cents—approximately half a day's wages for an average individual at that time. Stagecoaches that had previously departed from Beloit for Janesville and Madison now departed from Afton. The Beloit and Madison Railroad Company continued laying track beyond Afton, reaching Footville in December. The company now had seventeen miles of track from Beloit. The first train, which was actually owned by the Galena and Chicago Union, arrived at Footville from Chicago on December 18. The Beloit and Madison had only thirty more miles to build to reach Madison.

Other railways experienced ups and downs while struggling to get underway. The Mineral Point Railroad Company had begun building from its junction with the

Illinois Central Railroad at Warren, Illinois, northward. That company had contracted its construction work with Robert & George Schuyler & Company of New York and sent President Moses M. Strong there in the spring. Strong had tended to company business, but he also invested personal funds in Schuyler & Company. Meanwhile, Schuyler began construction at Warren, then ran out of funds and stopped paying its workers. When Strong returned from New York, a group of workers stopped him on the road to Warren and, seeing that he was carrying company funds, demanded two months back pay from him. He escaped to Warren, but the group followed him there and he was forced to pay them in the hotel lobby.[18]

On July 6 Schuyler & Co. declared bankruptcy with the Mineral Point Railroad Company owing it $75,000 for completed work. The Mineral Point Company was itself $90,000 in debt, with no means of paying. Strong lost the money he had invested in Schuyler. His nephew, chief engineer Charles Temple, hadn't been paid by the railroad in months, and told Strong that he would be looking for work elsewhere.

The Mineral Point Railroad Company took a turn for the better in December. Its directors offered $170,000 worth of new stock and received subscriptions to $78,850 of it on the first day. That amount would allow the company to carry on—for the time being.

During the fall of 1854 the Rock River Valley Union Railroad Company, once a front-runner, was teetering on the edge of bankruptcy. Timothy F. Strong Sr. continued to lease the twenty-mile line between Fond du Lac and Chester, on which he ran two trains in each direction daily. The company's creditors, including Strong himself, were calling for reorganization. A. Hyatt Smith resigned from the presidency and was replaced by Charles Butler of Chicago. Mortgages were foreclosed, and the property was purchased by Robert J. Walker, trustee for the bondholders.[19] Meanwhile the Rock River Valley Union's partner, the Illinois & Wisconsin Railroad, opened thirty-eight and a half miles of its line between Chicago and Cary, Illinois, with two broad-gauge engines from the East. Its president was William Butler Ogden, former president of the Galena and Chicago Union and brother-in-law of Butler. It was a promising shift for a railroad that was struggling to stay afloat.

Sixty-two miles of new track had been laid in Wisconsin during 1854, making for a total of 152 miles in the state. Trains were running from Milwaukee to Oconomowoc, Janesville, and Madison and from Chicago to Beloit and Footville. A graded roadway had been completed between Milwaukee and Chicago—all that was required was to lay the track. Wisconsin's economy was booming, and an increasing number of emigrants from the East were arriving every day. The stage was indeed set for further railroad development.

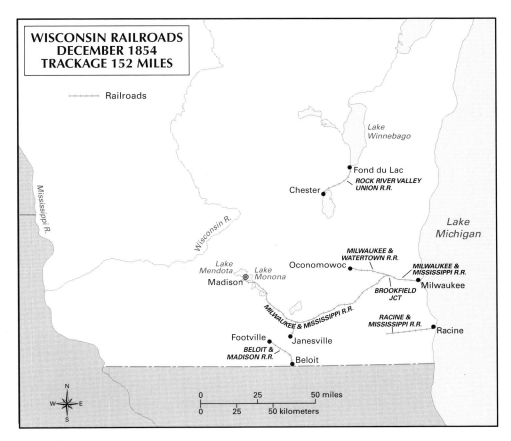

Mapping Specialists

# PART FOUR: THE GREAT BUILDING BOOM

# Chapter 16

## Western Goals and Eastern Connections

### 1855

By 1855 eight Wisconsin railroad companies were building or planning to build from Lake Michigan to the Mississippi River. The Milwaukee & Mississippi, the La Crosse and Milwaukee, the Milwaukee and Watertown, the Milwaukee and Horicon, the Racine and Mississippi, the Manitowoc and Mississippi, the Sheboygan and Mississippi, and the Kenosha and Beloit all had hopes of capturing the trade coming east from Minnesota, Iowa, and beyond as it passed through Wisconsin. But to be optimally effective, these routes needed to connect with the East, and that meant Chicago. Chicago itself had been connected by rails with the East since 1852. With a rail link from Milwaukee to Chicago imminent, Wisconsin railroads would realize that goal too.

In January, Milwaukee & Mississippi President John Catlin revealed a daring new plan for his railroad to bypass Chicago with a ferry link across Lake Michigan:

> An examination of the map of the United States will show that the city of Milwaukee is situated on the parallel of 43 deg. . . . Trace this . . . eastward . . . through Grand Haven . . . Detroit . . . Buffalo. . . . The Central Line of road through New York strikes the Atlantic Ocean . . . North of Boston.
>
> Now there only remain ninety-six miles of the Milwaukee and Mississippi, and one hundred and sixty miles of the Oakland and Ottawa roads, with the

Steam Ferry across Lake Michigan, to complete this chain of communication of about twelve hundred miles, which may be regarded as the longest stretch of Rail Road and Steamboat connection on the same general straight line. . . .

At a meeting held in Detroit in May last, it was stated that there were parties who were ready to put Steamboats on Lake Michigan, which they would *guarantee* would cross the Lake between Milwaukee and Grand Haven three hundred and thirty-six days in the year, and enable the trip to be made from Milwaukee to Detroit in ten hours.[1]

This latter goal would not be realized until 1859. The Milwaukee & Mississippi expanded its westward ambitions on February 17 by receiving authorization in its charter to purchase the Southern Wisconsin Railroad Company. It thereby acquired the southern route to the Mississippi (from Janesville and through Monroe) and Dubuque, Iowa. Capital stock was increased to eight million dollars. Ten days later the boards of both companies met; that of the Southern Wisconsin met at the Capital House in Madison, while the board of the Milwaukee & Mississippi, with President Catlin, met at their company offices in Milwaukee. Both boards approved the acquisition, and as part of the agreement, Nelson Dewey, president of the Southern Wisconsin Railroad and first governor of the state, joined the board of the Milwaukee & Mississippi.

During the spring of 1855 the Milwaukee & Mississippi contracted with the Cooke & Lockwood company to build the western half of their road between Madison and Prairie du Chien. The contract included right-of-way, fencing, road crossings, cattle guards, and buildings. It specified the use of fifty-eight-pound-per-yard rail and a completion date of November 1, 1856. The contractors were to be paid $2,014,500 in a mixture of bonds, stocks, farm mortgages, and cash. The company had been planning to locate a major rail facility with a depot, an eating house, and engine facilities at the village of Black Earth, west of Madison. These plans were suspended when the landowner there demanded too high a price for the land. The company next offered to locate the facilities at the village of Dover, but the same difficulty developed. Not being one to be put off, Milwaukee & Mississippi Superintendent Edward Brodhead resurveyed and relocated the line, bypassing Dover entirely, and then

First Governor of the State of Wisconsin, Nelson Dewey, would also be the president of the Southern Wisconsin Railroad and a director of the Milwaukee & Mississippi Railroad.
WHi Image ID 2407

located the company's new rail facilities at Mazomanie, eight miles west of Black Earth. His actions benefited not only the railroad but also himself. He was one of a group of investors who owned the land there and planned to develop a village. They had named the site Mazomanie after Man-ze-mon-e-ka, a Winnebago Indian whose name meant "Walking Iron." The Milwaukee & Mississippi Company immediately purchased eighty acres from Brodhead and his partners for its planned facilities.[2]

As superintendent, Brodhead was also responsible for drafting the railroad's annual report. That summer marked the seventh such report, and Brodhead painted a favorable picture of its accomplishments:

> Two passenger trains have run each way daily over our road, with scarcely the loss of a single trip; we have also run not less than two, and for a considerable portion of the year, five freight trains each way daily. Wood trains have been moving constantly upon the road, and for a portion of the time, construction trains also, and yet we can state, that but one slight collision has occurred, which took place between a wood and freight train, but without injury to any person. One hundred and forty-six thousand one hundred and eighty-five passengers have been transported over the road without the slightest injury to anyone, except a lady, who had her shoulder injured by reason of the breaking of an axle, which threw the passenger car in which she was sitting at the time, off the track. Extraordinary good success has attended all our operations. Our trains, both passenger and freight, have been run with great regularity and with a few unimportant exceptions, have not been thrown off the track from any cause.[3]

Brodhead also reported on several improvements made to the line, beginning with fencing its right-of-way to protect the trains from wandering livestock. Brodhead reported that "the entire line has been fenced from Rock River to Madison, about thirty miles. . . . With a few exceptions . . . the entire road is fenced from Milwaukee to Madison."[4] And now the telegraph, which had come to Wisconsin in 1849, was for the first time being routed along the railway:

> In connection with the union Telegraph Co. we have established a line of telegraph along the track of our road to Madison, and offices have been opened at nearly all the stations; and although it is not fully completed, yet it is of very great benefit to our Co. and will become more and more so, as it is perfected, and offices are opened at all the stations, which is the ultimate design.[5]

The report was also concerned with safety, in particular the speed of freight trains, which Brodhead recommended be run at eight to twelve miles per hour:

> It may be urged that freight trains running at a diminished speed, do not wear the track and rolling stock in the same degree as passenger trains. The liability to collisions and other accidents is not so great and when they occur, the loss to the Company is comparatively light. These views are worthy of consideration when we reflect how rapidly this branch of traffic has increased and will continue to increase, upon our road.[6]

In August, Rufus King, editor of the *Milwaukee Sentinel,* made a tour of inspection of the Milwaukee & Mississippi's line west of Madison. King was born in 1814 in New York, graduated from West Point, and was a successful engineer who then pursued a career in journalism. He came to Wisconsin in 1845 to assume the editorship of the *Sentinel*. King journeyed by train from Milwaukee to Madison, by horse-and-carriage from Madison to Prairie du Chien, and then by steamboat to St. Paul, Minnesota. His findings were reported to the *Sentinel* over a succession of days in the latter half of August:

> The country beyond Madison is . . . under good cultivation. For the first eight or ten miles the surface is undulatory, and there is a frequent succession of deep cuts and heavy embankments along the line of the railroad. But the soil is easily worked, and the location has been so well made that the grading is not expensive. The materials for the road-bed are excellent, the finest of gravel abounding along the line. Good stone is to be found . . . and the masonry of the culverts, bridges, etc. is of the best description. . . .
> 
> Twenty-two miles from Madison this valley opens into that of the Wisconsin. At this junction a new town has been laid out . . . Mazo-Manie, "The Iron that Walks." . . . Already some twenty buildings, including two hotels, a large store, and a church, have been put up and by November there will be a good-sized village here. . . .
> 
> We resumed our journey, following down the valley of the Wisconsin for fifty miles, crossing the river twice. . . . The valley seems to have been made for a railway. . . . It averages some three miles in width; is as level as a barn floor . . . descends toward the Mississippi at the rate of a foot and a half per mile. . . . We commenced our descent to the valley of the Mississippi . . . and shortly after, we came out upon the beautiful plain on which stands the old French town of Prairie du Chien. . . .
> 
> The Milwaukee and Mississippi Railroad . . . will shortly be . . . opened to the Mississippi. . . . The grading will be finished this year. . . . The completion of this road . . . will be a memorable event for our city and state. It has already trebled

and quadrupled the value of the farming lands along its eastern and finished division, and increased by the same amount the taxable property of the state. Its extension to the Mississippi will accomplish the like result along the western half of the line. . . . It will confer upon our city still more striking benefits . . . extending its feelers up the Mississippi and gathering in from Iowa, Minnesota, and northwestern Wisconsin rich harvests of business and golden returns of trade.[7]

❖ ❖ ❖ ❖ ❖ ❖

In October, 2,200 tons of rails, designated for the Milwaukee & Mississippi between Madison and Mazomanie, arrived at Milwaukee. But with the onset of cold weather, the directors decided to postpone laying the track until spring. The company had placed orders for 7,800 additional tons of rail, weighing fifty-eight pounds a yard, to be delivered in the spring. Progress was also made on the southern branch. President Catlin reported that

> the estimated cost of the road from Janesville to Monroe is $800,000. . . . The right of way, with the exception of about two miles, has been obtained. . . . One half of the expense of bridging Rock River at Janesville is to be born by the Chicago, St. Paul & Fond du Lac R. R. Co.[8]

In December the company contracted with Carlisle D. Cooke to build its southern branch. At the end of the year the Milwaukee & Mississippi's directors reported progress on the grading for the main line:

> From Madison to the Mississippi . . . there have been 723,689 cubic yards of earth removed and 12,180 of rock, and there has been expended for right of way, depot grounds and buildings, grading, bridging, and masonry, the sum of $630,728.15.[9]

The company now owned twenty-five locomotives, fourteen passenger and baggage cars, and 287 freight cars. Gross revenues in 1855 had been $691,843.94, while net earnings were a healthy $417,443.73. The directors had declared two 5 percent cash dividends and one 7 percent stock dividend during the year.[10]

❖ ❖ ❖ ❖ ❖ ❖

During the same time period as this successful expansion of the Milwaukee & Mississippi, several other railroads were vying for stock subscriptions, securing right of way, letting contracts, and negotiating strategic mergers and partnerships. Their eyes, like those of the Milwaukee & Mississippi, were on the goal of making connections to the East through Chicago and to the Great Lakes and shipping through Milwaukee.

The Beloit and Madison Railroad Company was seeing an increase in business in January 1855. It had leased its seventeen-mile line between Beloit and Footville to the Galena & Chicago Union Railroad. The Galena was now running two trains daily from Belvidere, Illinois, over the line, and the Beloit and Madison was receiving ten percent of the gross receipts. The Galena's rates were competitive, which had encouraged business. Now, in January, farmers west of Milton who had been shipping grain eastward on the Milwaukee & Mississippi to Milwaukee began shipping it south on the Janesville branch to Janesville instead, then taking it by wagon to Footville and shipping it on the Beloit and Madison line being run by the Galena company to Chicago.

An attempt by the Galena to try this same tactic with its westward shipments failed. It forwarded freight by wagons from the end of the line at Footville to Janesville, but there the agents of the Milwaukee & Mississippi refused to accept it. The Galena was forced to contract with an express company to haul its freight by wagons the remainder of the way to Madison, which was still the western terminus for rail traffic.[11] A new route between Footville and Janesville had the potential to solve this dilemma—but its construction was the responsibility of the Beloit and Madison. In Madison, businessman Simeon Mills began selling stock subscriptions for the company. In May the company let the four miles between Footville and Magnolia to contractors Hackett & Wells and the section between Magnolia and Evansville, which would require several difficult rock cuts, to Allen, Risley, and Perry. Both contractors began working in June.[12] By the end of the year the situation had reversed itself. Western Wisconsin farmers who had been using the Beloit and Madison to ship grain to Chicago now found the Milwaukee & Mississippi was offering a better deal. Those in the Beloit region began to take their grain in wagons to Janesville and then ship it over that line to Milwaukee. The Beloit and Madison's business suffered as a consequence.[13]

Meanwhile, the Sheboygan and Mississippi Railroad Company was successfully selling stock in the country and villages (including Sheboygan, Sheboygan Falls, and Plymouth) along its line at the beginning of 1855—but not in Fond du Lac. Fond du Lac's investors were too involved with the Rock River Valley Union Railroad and the Fox River Improvement, a project to make the Fox River more navigable through a series of locks. The *Sheboygan Lake Journal* said of Fond du Lac, "She proved herself indeed an unwilling bride."[14] And in Sheboygan, some citizens had become convinced that a railroad to Milwaukee would be more valuable than

# WESTERN GOALS AND EASTERN CONNECTIONS

one to the Mississippi. They petitioned for a Milwaukee and Superior Railroad Company, to run from Milwaukee to Michigan's upper peninsula via Sheboygan. The city of Sheboygan agreed to contribute one thousand dollars toward a survey for this proposed road. A charter was granted, and some grading was done.[15]

In March the situation of the ailing Rock River Valley Union began to look up when it was sold to William B. Ogden of Chicago, president of the Illinois & Wisconsin. On March 31, infused with $350,000 dollars from the city of Fond du Lac, it merged with the Illinois & Wisconsin to form the Chicago, St. Paul and

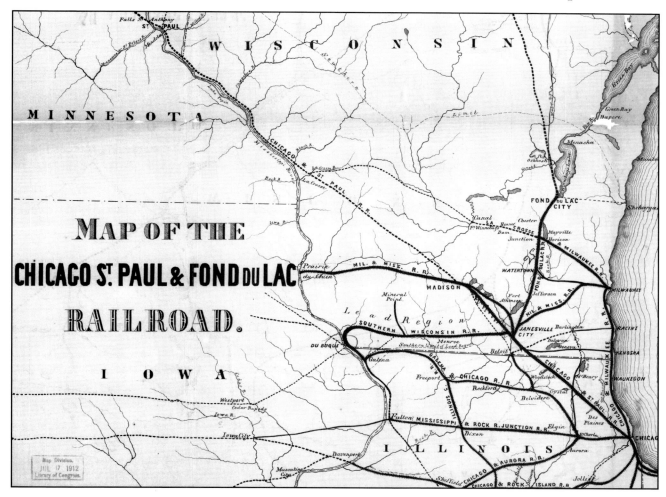

Map of the Chicago, St. Paul & Fond du Lac Railroad, 1855. The company's two branches, already begun, are shown: the "Chicago & St. Paul R. R." between those cities and the "Fond du Lac R. R." between "Janesville City," now Janesville, and Lake Superior.
IMAGE COURTESY OF THE LIBRARY OF CONGRESS

Fond du Lac Railroad Company. Its mostly north-south line, incorporating existing segments, covered a massive area: from Chicago to Janesville, then splitting with a western branch to Madison, La Crosse, and St. Paul, Minnesota, and an eastern branch to Watertown, Fond du Lac, and the upper penninsula of Michigan. It would connect with the Milwaukee & Mississippi at Janesville and Madison. Ogden became its first president, and his brother-in-law, Charles Butler, its first treasurer.[16] The company's immediate objective was to complete the line between Chicago and Janesville, thereby achieving a connection with the Milwaukee & Mississippi.

To make its lines compatible with one another, the Chicago, St. Paul and Fond du Lac changed its line in Illinois from broad gauge to standard gauge in the spring and shipped its two broad-gauge locomotives back East. That done, it began extending its tracks northwestward from Cary, Illinois, working toward Janesville. By mid-July the rails were at Woodstock, and by the end of the year they would cross the state line to reach Sharon, Wisconsin. At the same time the company extended its line in the northern division (the former Rock River Valley Union line) southward to its crossing with the La Crosse and Milwaukee Railroad at a place it called Minnesota Junction.[17]

In May the tracks of the Green Bay, Milwaukee, and Chicago Railroad, also known as the Lake Shore Line, and those of the Chicago and Milwaukee Railroad Company of Illinois were nearing the city of Kenosha on Lake Michigan. The Lake Shore Line had begun laying its rails at Bay View, south of Milwaukee, at the beginning of the year, while the Chicago and Milwaukee had continued laying its rails north from Waukegan, Illinois. Work on both lines had proceeded rapidly and the tracks approached Kenosha from both sides in May. When they met, a through line between Chicago and Milwaukee would finally be in place. On May 19 company officials of the Lake Shore Line together with Milwaukee and Bay View residents boarded a "long" train of five platform cars and made the journey to Kenosha to attend the ceremonies for the driving of the last spike. The *Milwaukee Sentinel* noted that for Milwaukee residents "it was quite a journey" to get over the marshes to the Bay View terminus on South Bay Street in Bay View.[18] In Kenosha one Mr. Frank reported:

> A great day on West Main Street. Besides more than 100 workmen on the road, large numbers of spectators filled the sidewalks. . . . The ceremony of laying the last rail on the Lake Shore Road was performed this A. M. at 10:30 o'clock. A short speech was made by the Mayor of Chicago, also the Mayor of Milwaukee. Flags were raised, cannon fired, and bells rung. A large crowd in attendance. At 11 A. M. seven passenger cars from Chicago, containing a large number of citizens

of Chicago and Waukegan, started for Milwaukee. Over one hundred went from Kenosha, myself among them. The ride was a free one; invited guests went. The excursion returned from Milwaukee at 6:00 P. M. without accident.[19]

With the completion of the line that day, the two-hundred-mile, twenty-four-hour journey that Milwaukeeans had been making to Chicago—by taking the Milwaukee & Mississippi to Janesville, and then the stage—was reduced to four hours. It would be further reduced to three hours when the road was ballasted with gravel placed between the ties to stabilize the track. Five days later, on May 24, an excursion was run from Chicago to Milwaukee. In Wisconsin, its train consisted of an engine, a tender, and five flat cars fitted with seats on which rode two hundred guests. Mr. A. Z. Blodgett was one of them. He recalled, "We stopped the train about where Zion City is now and cut pine trees and put them in the stake sockets for shade."[20]

The two lines opened for business in June. Wisconsin residents could now take connecting trains to Milwaukee, Chicago, and the East. The Green Bay, Milwaukee, and Chicago had four locomotives, eight passenger cars, and thirty-five freight cars running regularly that summer. Yet despite this success, there were inconveniences. From Milwaukee, passengers would transfer onto a barge in the Milwaukee River to be towed by the steam-tug *Tift* to the Lake Shore depot in Bay View.[21] At the state line they had to disembark, then walk down the platform with their luggage to board the Chicago and Milwaukee train for Chicago.

As the long-desired connection to the East was finally accomplished, other railways moved forward—and backward—in their plans for rollout. In April the Mineral Point Railroad Company insured its future prospects. It had received authorization from the Illinois legislature "to Extend Their Railroad from the Wisconsin State Line to the Illinois Central Railroad at Warren." This was all the permission required for Mineral Point to do trade

An 1857 advertisment of the Lake Shore and Michigan Southern Railroad.
IMAGE COURTESY OF THE LIBRARY OF CONGRESS

with Chicago. On April 25 the company renewed its agreement with the Illinois Central and Chicago and Galena Union railroads that guaranteed $56,000 per year in exchange for doing business with those two companies.[22]

In September Moses Strong resigned the presidency of the Mineral Point Railroad. The company again found itself in need of money, and convinced the town of Waldwick to buy ten thousand dollars' worth of stock, the township of Mineral Point sixty thousand dollars' worth, and the village of Mineral Point ninety thousand dollars' worth. With this new influx of cash, the directors hoped to resume construction the following spring.[23]

The former Milwaukee and Watertown's "Luther A. Cole" was built by the Menomonee Locomotive Works in Milwaukee in 1854 and stayed in service for over forty years. Pictured in 1899, she is the Milwaukee & St. Paul's "L. B. Rock."
WHi Image ID 62850

The Racine and Mississippi Railroad Company, meanwhile, began laying its tracks west from Racine in the spring. The rails reached Union Grove in August and Burlington in November. To finance further construction, on September 1 the company executed a mortgage of their entire line from Racine to Beloit to secure twenty-year, 8 percent bonds at the rate of ten thousand dollars per mile.

That summer the Milwaukee and Watertown Company extended its tracks west from Oconomowoc to Watertown, a distance of thirteen and a half miles. Before Watertown, at a section known as Richard's Cut, the company built a two-mile-long trestle. Engineer Michael O'Hara was assigned to test the bridge by driving a locomotive over it. Not convinced that the bridge would support the weight of his locomotive, O'Hara sent it across unattended and had his fireman catch it at

The former Milwaukee and Watertown's "Watertown" was built by Niles Locomotive Works in 1854. She is pictured here after being rebuilt in 1868.
WHi Image ID 62336

the far end of the bridge!²⁴ The forty-five-mile line between Milwaukee and Watertown was finished on October 1.

Kenosha's railway ambitions were not satisfied by the new Milwaukee-Chicago service passing through its town since May. No work had been done on the Kenosha and Beloit line since March because of labor disputes, but now, in July, the company's new president, Josiah Bond, was looking for new builders. A reader of the *Kenosha Tribune and Telegraph* wrote to point out that the Kenosha and Beloit, running between the Fox River and Kenosha, would be the preferred route to Chicago:

> It is twenty four and a half miles to our junction with the Fox River RR. [at the Kenosha and Beloit's crossing of the Fox River]. . . . It is about 76 miles from the junction of our road with the FRRR [Fox River Rail Road], to Chicago, via Kenosha and Beloit RR to Kenosha, thence via Lake Shore RR [to Chicago]. It is about eighty two and a half miles from the junction, over the Fox River Road

via Elgin to Chicago, or six miles shorter to Chicago, via Kenosha, on the K & B and Lake Shore Roads.[25]

The reader further pointed out that shipping over the lakes from Kenosha would be better than from Chicago:

> But when we consider the directness of our lines, their easy grades and curvatures, may there not be a decided advantage in the Kenosha & Beloit and Lake Shore Railroads to Chicago and may not the same rule hold good in traversing about thirty three miles of railroad to get to Kenosha, instead of eighty seven and a half to get to Chicago with freights? Hoping this will arouse us still more to action.[26]

The citizens of Kenosha would vote 212 to 22 to lend sixty-six thousand dollars of credit in city scrip to the railroad.

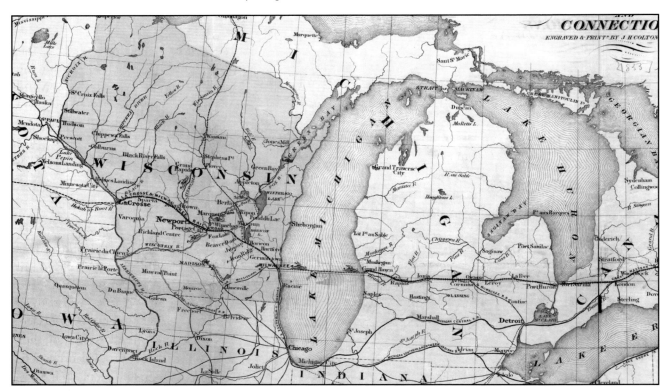

Map of the La Crosse and Milwaukee Railroad, 1855, with anticipated connections to the East via the Detroit and Milwaukee, Great Western, and New York Central railroads.
IMAGE COURTESY OF THE LIBRARY OF CONGRESS

# WESTERN GOALS AND EASTERN CONNECTIONS

Late in July the La Crosse and Milwaukee's contractor, Newcomb Cleveland, completed that road to Schleisingerville, thirty miles from Milwaukee. He was behind schedule, being required by his contract to complete the grading, furnish the ties, pay duty on the rails, and complete the road to Hartford by the first of August. Despite all efforts, Cleveland was unable to complete the four miles remaining to Hartford by the deadline. The company decided it wanted out of the contract and on August 1, it adopted a resolution forfeiting it unless Cleveland made certain concessions and performed certain tasks within twenty-four hours. It was impossible for Cleveland to comply, and the company forcibly expelled him and his men from their property. One month later, Cleveland commenced a lawsuit in the United States District Court for breach of contract and damages.[27] After removing Cleveland in August, the La Crosse and Milwaukee Railroad Company let a new contract for completing the road to Horicon to contractors Kane, Chittenden & Jackson. This firm completed the road to Iron Ridge, forty-five miles from Milwaukee, on November 21, and to Horicon, fifty-one miles from Milwaukee, on December 31.[28]

In November the Wisconsin Central Railroad began laying its track. It had finished grading the first ten miles of its line, between Genoa and Geneva, during the spring. Now it was laying used strap rail that it had purchased from the Galena and Chicago Union on that section of its line. Because the wooden ties were stockpiled at Geneva, the company hauled the strap rail there in wagons and proceeded to lay the track from north to south. The company employed numerous Irish workers, and many of them would settle with their families on farms west of Geneva, Wisconsin.[29]

The year 1855 finally saw Wisconsin bind itself in perpetuity to the other states of the nation by rail. The residents of the Janesville-Beloit region had enjoyed rail service to the East since November 1853 utilizing the Galena's Footville-Chicago trains. But now Wisconsin residents from as far west as Madison, as far north as Fond du Lac, and from any and all points between could also enjoy such service. They could ship and receive goods and products to and from the East by rail; they could also travel on business, visit friends or relatives, or travel for pleasure to Illinois, Indiana, Ohio, Pennsylvania, New York, Massachusetts, and all of their adjacent states. They could once again enjoy the security and comfort of maintaining distant business connections and social ties—a security and comfort that many had left behind when they first came to Wisconsin five, ten, or fifteen years earlier.

# Chapter 17

## An Explosion of Railroads
### 1856

The year 1855 had been a watershed for Wisconsin railroads, with the amount of track laid more than doubling the previous total. And there was little sign that things were slowing down. The Milwaukee & Mississippi, still Wisconsin's premier line, was expected to reach the Mississippi in 1856; in an unlikely alliance, it was also planning to connect with the Chicago, St. Paul, and Fond du Lac at Janesville for a line to Chicago. And, amazingly, the Milwaukee & Mississippi was planning a second line to the Mississippi, departing from the main line in Janesville and going to Dubuque via Monroe. Smaller railways were also making progress. The La Crosse and Milwaukee and the Racine and Mississippi roads were well underway, providing service on the completed portions of their lines while continuing to build westward. Railroad service was now available from Wisconsin to Chicago on three different lines—the Green Bay, Milwaukee and Chicago; the Chicago, St. Paul, and Fond du Lac; and the Beloit and Madison—and traffic was brisk and growing. The time was right for rapid growth and expansion.

In this climate of optimism, several railroad companies were building through the winter. In January, stockholders of the Beloit and Madison Railroad Company elected former Wisconsin Governor Leonard J. Farwell their president, William A.

Former Green Bay, Milwaukee and Chicago's "C.K. Watkins," built by Rogers in 1856, photographed in Chicago in 1866.
CHICAGO AND NORTH WESTERN HISTORICAL SOCIETY

Ernst secretary, and Madison merchant Simeon Mills as treasurer; all three were Wisconsin residents. The fact remained, however, that the majority of the company's directors and stockholders were from Illinois and were associated with the Illinois parent company, the Galena & Chicago Union Railroad.[1] During the year, the Galena and Chicago Union trains running into Wisconsin at Beloit did a good business. A timetable shows two trains leaving Chicago for Footville, arriving at 3:30 p.m. and 10:10 p.m., and three return trains arriving in Chicago at 11:35 a.m., 5:00 p.m., and 3:30 a.m.[2]

In February the Watertown and Madison Rail Road Company, chartered almost three years earlier on March 17, 1853, received assurance that the city of Watertown would loan it credit to an amount of two hundred thousand dollars. Its route between Watertown and Madison passed through remnants of oak openings and through the twenty-five-mile-long Sun Prairie. The city of Madison had been eager to secure a second railroad, as its shippers were being shamelessly overcharged by its only railroad, the Milwaukee & Mississippi. In March Madison voters elected an overwhelming majority of aldermen who favored a second-railroad to the city's Common Council.[3] In November the Watertown and Madison Rail Road Company's stockholders elected Madison Mayor Jairus C. Fairchild, former Wisconsin Governor Leonard J. Farwell, B. F. Hopkins, and Nathaniel W. Dean as directors of the company. The new board then elected Mayor Fairchild president. The *Madison Daily Patriot* reassured that city's citizens that "the directors of the line are sound to the core—thorough-going businessmen, perfectly reliable in all things. . . ." In December the company formally requested the city to issue one hundred thousand dollars of municipal bonds on its behalf.[4]

Besides great gains in trackage, many of Wisconsin's smaller lines were able to celebrate the victory of opening new lines in 1856, completing long-hoped-for routes, gaining new charters, or merging with existing lines. The tracks of the Racine and Mississippi Rail Road, stretching westward from Racine on Lake Michigan, reached Delavan in February. In March the company merged with the Savanna Branch Railroad Company of Illinois. The name of the new company created by the merger was the Racine and Mississippi Railroad Company (with Railroad now spelled as one word).[5] In September this new company completed its road to Beloit. In October it coordinated its schedule with that of the Chicago, St. Paul, and Fond du Lac, whose tracks it crossed at Clinton Junction, to the east of Beloit, so that Beloit residents could take the Racine and Mississippi to Clinton Junction and transfer to the Chicago, St. Paul, and Fond du Lac to reach Chicago. This service turned out to be faster than taking the established Galena and Chicago Union train from Beloit directly to Chicago.[6]

The Milwaukee and Horicon Railroad Company opened the first section of its line on February 10. This was the five miles between Horicon, a stop on the La Crosse and Milwaukee line, and Burnett, to the north. Five days later it opened ten more miles, from Burnett to Waupun. The Milwaukee and Horicon was functionally a branch of the La Crosse and Milwaukee. On October 15 it opened its line to Brandon, twenty-two miles from Horicon, and on November 15 the line was opened to Ripon, thirty miles from Horicon, where a large celebration was held.

On March 6 the La Crosse and Milwaukee reached a point fifty-four miles west of Milwaukee where its tracks crossed those of the Chicago, St. Paul, and Fond du Lac's northern division, the former Rock River Valley Union line that ran south from Fond du Lac. While the La Crosse's rails were the standard four feet, eight and a half inches apart, the Fond du Lac's were six inches apart. Nonetheless, passengers would have no trouble transferring to the other railroad with its alternate gauge at this location, designated as La Crosse Junction (later Minnesota Junction). On March 29 the company contracted with Selah Chamberlain and S. H. Alden to construct its road from Beaver Dam to Portage. The contract specified that the work had to be completed by December 31.[7] On April 24 the La Crosse and

Milwaukee's line was opened to Beaver Dam. The first train was scheduled to arrive at the Beaver Dam depot at 1:00 p.m. for the day's opening ceremonies. A procession of town residents, a marching band, and an artillery company dressed in new uniforms left downtown Beaver Dam at 12:30 and headed for the depot to meet the train. They hadn't gone far when they heard the shrill whistle of the locomotive. The marchers broke ranks, the parade turned into a stampede, and men, women, and children, all dressed in their Sunday finery, ran the ten village blocks to greet the train at the depot. They need not have done so. The engineer on the locomotive had seen the empty station platform and stopped at a distance, waiting for the celebrants to arrive.[8]

Despite its gains in trackage, the progress of the La Crosse and Milwaukee was not without incident. The original plan was for the line to cross the Wisconsin River at Newport, a village located in the Wisconsin Dells. But as the road came nearer, Newporters began demanding exorbitant prices for the land the railroad would need for its right-of-way. The company secretly surveyed a route leading to a crossing one and a half miles upstream from Newport, where narrow rock walls on either side of the river would allow a shorter bridge. As word of this leaked, Newporters led by Garret Vliet began moving to the new site, by that time designated Kilbourn City. At the end of June, the directors officially announced the route change. On July 1 the editor of the new *Kilbourn City Mirror* announced that the road had been "permanently located at Kilbourn City . . . beyond all possibility of a disturbance hereafter," referring to Newport as "a small village a mile and a half below Kilbourn City."[9]

The company employed Deacon Edmond Clinton as its stock agent in 1856. Clinton convinced farmers in Washington, Dodge, and Columbia counties to mortgage their farms for over eleven hundred thousand dollars worth of railroad stock.[10] These subscriptions helped the company as it opened its line to Fox Lake, sixty-eight miles from Milwaukee, on October 27, and Midland, eighty-seven miles from Milwaukee, on December 29. At the end of the year its tracks reached Portage. Still, it wasn't enough to secure its finances. On December 31 the La Crosse and Milwaukee Railroad Company mortgaged all of its property west of Portage (including the Madison to Portage line, the Portage and La Crosse line, and the anticipated land grant lines to the St. Croix River) to Greene C. Bronson, James T. Soutter, and Shepherd Knapp, trustees. The company thus secured a loan of ten million dollars' worth of bonds, which it then needed to sell in order to stay afloat.[11]

❖ ❖ ❖ ❖ ❖ ❖

Hopes for a transcontinental railroad originating in Wisconsin were revived on March 31 when promoters of a Northern Pacific Railroad Company were granted a charter by the Wisconsin legislature. These individuals were supporters of the Chicago, St. Paul, and Fond du Lac who wished to see that line extended to the Pacific. Among the thirty Wisconsin incorporators were former territorial governor James D. Doty, Doty's son-in-law, his brother-in-law, four former state governors, Rufus King of the *Milwaukee Sentinel*, Moses M. Strong, and Hercules Dousman. The road was capitalized at a hundred million dollars, an unheard of amount, but one that was deemed necessary for building across the western half of the continent. Its eastern terminus was defined as the head of Lake Superior or some point on the Mississippi above the Wisconsin-Illinois state line. The following winter the road was chartered on a smaller scale in Washington Territory with Doty and his two relatives among the incorporators.[12]

The Wisconsin Central Railroad finished laying its strap rails to Genoa and Richmond in Illinois in May, the result of which was an unbroken rail line from Chicago to Geneva, Wisconsin. The first train rolled into Geneva on Thursday, May 29, at 2:00 p.m. Carriages and wagons had been coming into town all morning, and were lined up in anticipation. When the flag-decorated train came into the station it was greeted by a thirteen-gun salute. Two days later the *Geneva Express* published this poem:

James Duane Doty, Territorial Governor and U. S. Congressman, in 1856.
WHi Image ID 11020

> The cars have come!
> The cars have come! Geneva shout!
> The more scarce knows what she's about!
> Shout long and loud—the whistle screams;
> We realize our wildest dreams!
> 'Tis true—'tis true! The engine's here—
> This is Geneva's happiest year.[13]

On June 3 the Geneva line's regular, scheduled service began. Fox River Valley Railroad trains left Geneva at 11:00 a.m. and 8:20 p.m. and arrived at Elgin, Illinois, at 2:45 p.m. and 11:25 p.m. There passengers took Galena & Chicago Union trains to Chicago. This made the Wisconsin Central the fourth Wisconsin railroad company to connect to Chicago by rail.[14]

The Milwaukee & Mississippi resumed construction that spring, ending the two-year hiatus that began when the line had reached Madison and expanding both its trackage and the stations and towns along the line. The tracks extended westward, the first stop being Middleton Station, which until recently had been an uninhabited stretch of small trees and brush. The company had ignored the pleas

Locomotive manufactured by Breese Kneeland and Company, one of 26 purchased by the Milwaukee & Mississippi in 1856 and 1857. It is pictured here at Middleton in 1873.
WHi Image ID 1913

of the nearby villages of Middleton (Old Middleton, on Mineral Point Road) and Pheasant Branch to the north to bring the line their way, and had instead chosen the more direct route, midway between. As the tracks neared Middleton Station, Mr. Simon Rose opened a boarding house and saloon for the railroad workers and Mr. B. C. Slaughter erected a warehouse that would serve as a depot. William McCord would be the company's first station agent there.[15]

Eight miles west of Middleton Station was the recently platted village of Christina (Cross Plains), the next stop on the line. Five miles further was Black Earth. Beyond Black Earth was Mazomanie, where the company shops and facilities were located.

That summer the workers' shanties that had lined the Milwaukee & Mississippi's tracks at Mazomanie were supplanted by houses, hotels, and stores. Mr. George Butler opened the American House, an inn and the village's first frame building.[16] The railroad built a two-story wood frame depot, an eating house, and engine facilities and appointed James Stickney as station agent. The first train steamed into town on June 7. After that, two mixed freight and passenger trains ran between Mazomanie and Madison each day.[17]

After Mazomanie the rails continued westward to Arena, a steamboat stop on the Wisconsin River. The line passed one mile south of the village, and soon its residents were hitching their possessions—sometimes entire houses—to teams of oxen, moving to be near the depot. The line crossed the Wisconsin River at Helena on a bridge located at the same site as the present-day railroad bridge (alongside the U.S. Highway 14 bridge). The company employed a resident bridge tender, who lived with his family in a house on the eastern end of the bridge. When a train passed over the bridge, the bridge tender would extinguish or remove any burning cinders left by the train that would endanger the wooden structure. When steamboats such as the *Enterprise* and the *Orinoco* whistled, he would raise the draw to allow them through. Occasionally he helped lumber raftsmen dislodge their rafts from the bridge's piers. And at night he kept lanterns lit on both ends of the bridge to guide the locals who sometimes used the structure to avoid paying fare for the ferry.

Mazomanie railroad crossing in 1869. The 1857 depot is on the left.
WHi Image ID 27213

One mile beyond the bridge, on the north side of the river, the tracks came to the village of Spring Green, which hadn't existed until that time. The intended stop for the railroad had been Jonesville, on the river. But Thomas Jones, the landowner there, had rejected the company's standard one-dollar offer (most landowners accepted these one-dollar offers, realizing that the value of their adjacent holdings would rise dramatically when the railroad was built), so the railroad rerouted its line to what would then become Spring Green. A widowed schoolteacher, Mrs. Thomas Williams, who had boarded the company's surveyors, had suggested the name Spring Green because the south-facing hollows there turned green earlier in the spring than elsewhere. The first residences there were the shanties of the railroad workers. The depot would be erected in the fall as trains commenced running.[18]

Lone Rock, seven miles west of Spring Green, was the next station. The "Rock" in the town's name refers to a sandstone formation used by the raftsmen on the river as a landmark. When the railroad surveyors first came, there was but one cabin nearby, belonging to William Perrin. Now there were several houses, a school, and a depot being built. Past Lone Rock the line crossed bridge number two, returning to the south shore of the Wisconsin River before arriving at Avoca. The village of Avoca took its name from the last stanza of Irish poet Thomas Moore's "The Meeting of the Waters":

Sweet vale of Avoca! How calm could I rest
In thy bosom of shade, with the friends I love best.

# AN EXPLOSION OF RAILROADS

The land at Avoca, like that at Mazomanie, had been purchased by Brodhead shortly before he routed the railroad through it.

In fall the Milwaukee & Mississippi's rails reached Muscoda. Here, as at Arena, villagers moved entire buildings from the riverfront to be near the depot—in this case a distance of three-quarters of a mile. The first train arrived in Muscoda on October 1. Another eight miles brought the tracks to Blue River, where the company established a flag stop, and then it was eight more miles to Boscobel.

Boscobel, meaning "beautiful woods," had been the site of a sawmill in 1846, which soon became a stop for steamboats and lumber rafts. In 1854 Brodhead, C. K. Dean, and Adam E. Ray purchased the land where the rail line and depot would be. In early 1856 they began selling lots. A Mr. Curtis then put up guests in the second story of a warehouse, and Mr. Andy Burnett erected a hotel. John Mortimer was the station agent, and the first trains arrived toward the end of the year.[19]

The tracks would proceed no farther than Boscobel until the following year. The failure to reach the Mississippi was attributed to malarial outbreaks among the railroad workers in the Wisconsin River Valley that summer, the consequent difficulties in obtaining labor, and the fact that the third and last Wisconsin River bridge, just beyond Boscobel, was not finished. Without the hoped-for revenues from a completed line and without additional loans, the company reduced the salaries and wages of its agents, clerks, and laborers by about 20 percent.[20]

At the end of the year, Superintendent Brodhead reported on the year's operations:

> We have run no less than two passenger and from three to four freight trains each way per day. We have also had from one to two wood trains per day, hauling wood to supply the stations. Not withstanding . . . I am enabled to say that it has been without accident, and in only one instance have two trains come in contact—one a wood train and the other a tie train—but with only a slight injury to the tender of one of the engines and to one or two of the platform cars.[21]

Of the company's construction he wrote that it had

> graded nearly the entire distance from Madison to the Mississippi, and laid seventy-three miles of superstructure, besides building two bridges across the Wisconsin, in length equal to 3,800 feet. We have also built about one hundred miles of fence west of Madison. . . . All the materials . . . except the bridge timber, have been hauled from Milwaukee. . . . About 200,000 ties have been hauled an average of seventy miles.[22]

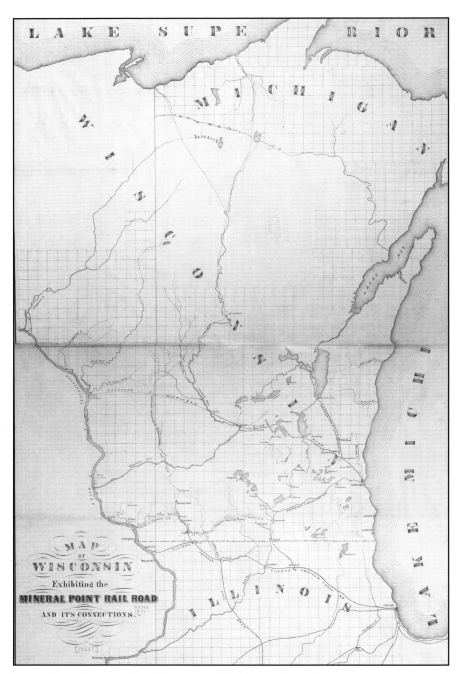

Map of the Mineral Point Rail Road, 1856. The northward extension to Lake Superior was never realized.
WHi Image ID 31173

# AN EXPLOSION OF RAILROADS

On the tasks remaining to complete the line he remarked that there remained

> a small amount of grading . . . track laying, of which there only remains about twenty-two miles—which can be laid in from six to eight weeks time. The last bridge over the Wisconsin can be completed in about two weeks' time.[23]

Concerning the proposed arrangements for the following year he wrote,

> With the Prairie du Chien and St. Paul Packet Company [would] provide two daily runs of steamers, in each direction, between Prairie du Chien and St. Paul . . . [and] can ticket passengers from Chicago via Milwaukee and via Janesville, to all points . . . on the Upper Mississippi.[24]

Of the Southern Branch, where the line had been readied for laying the track, Brodhead reported:

> Grading . . . began in February . . . [and] is nearly completed to Monroe, and the track will be laid and ready for use to Bass Creek, the first station west of Janesville, about nine miles, by April first.[25]

The directors reported a net profit of $372,691 and the paying of two 5 percent dividends to its shareholders during the year. The company now owned thirty-four locomotives, seventeen passenger and baggage cars, and five hundred freight cars. To the surprise of many, included in the report was a message from John Catlin, president of the company since 1852, who begged leave "to inform the stockholders that he does not desire a re-election to the office of President, on account of the impaired state of his health, and a desire to devote more of his time to his private affairs."[26] Catlin would, however, continue to serve on the board of directors.

The summer of 1856 saw progress on smaller lines. In June the directors of the Mineral Point Railroad Company contracted Luther Beecher of Detroit to build their road. Beecher was to complete and equip the road and pay the company's one hundred thousand dollar debt in exchange for one million dollars in cash, bonds, and stock. Beecher wasted little time. He soon had hundreds of men working at the southern end of the line, near Warren, Illinois. They worked northward into Wisconsin. By July most of the grading on the thirty-two-mile line was finished, cross ties were on the ground, and several bridges were completed. In the process, a meander of the Pecatonica River a mile and a half south of Darlington was cut off and drained. Track followed with fifty-six-pound rail and continued as funds allowed. The company erected depots at Gratiot, Darlington, and Calamine.[27] In December the Mineral Point Railroad was running freight and passenger trains between Warren, Illinois, and Darlington, Wisconsin, with stops at Gratiot and Riverside.

On June 4 the Sheboygan and Mississippi Railroad Company held its groundbreaking ceremonies in Sheboygan, a port city on Lake Michigan sixty miles north of Milwaukee. The company had recently contracted with Edward Appleton to build its first twenty miles of road, to Glenbeulah. The ceremonies were described in the *Sheboygan Times* of June 7:

> About 10 o'clock A M., the German Rifle Company, Hook & Ladder and Engine Companies, and the German Turners, in their respective uniforms, assembled in front of the National Hotel, and . . . marched in procession to the Public Square, where the citizens were provided with carriages and coaches, and the whole went in procession to the spot where the contractor intends to commence grading, near Curtis' mill.
>
> . . . Mr. [David] Taylor's remarks were brief . . . and he closed by introducing Messrs. William Farnsworth, Stephen Wolverton and Henry Otten . . . the first two being the oldest inhabitants of our city. Mr. Farnsworth then assumed the pick, Mr. Wolverton the shovel, and Mr. Otten engineered the barrow amid the repeated cheers of the assembly, whose enthusiasm augured well for the ultimate completion of the work then being commenced. . . .
>
> A. Marschner addressed the Germans present. Three times three were given for the road, and the assembly repaired to the woods nearby, where refreshments were served up.[28]

Shortly after that date the grading of the line west from Sheboygan commenced; the *Evergreen City Times* congratulated Sheboygan and Mississippi President J. F. Kirkland on his "good fortune in having the freight depot so near his warehouse and pier."[29]

On July 4 the Manitowoc and Mississippi Railroad Company, which had been chartered in 1851, held its groundbreaking ceremony in Manitowoc. It was finally getting underway. Manitowoc was a port on Lake Michigan ninety miles north of Milwaukee. The company had let contracts for grading its line to Menasha, on Lake Winnebago. Grading would progress at a healthy pace for the remainder of the year.[30] Charles Doty, son of former territorial governor James Doty and a resident of Menasha, was a leading spirit in the company.

AN EXPLOSION OF RAILROADS 217

The former Racine and Mississippi's No. 12 "Rockton," pictured at Racine in 1885, was purchased from Niles Locomotive Works in 1855.
WHi Image ID 24820

The year 1856 brought change and hope to railroads that had been struggling. The Kenosha and Beloit's new president, Josiah Bond, ended the one-year work stoppage in July by cancelling all contracts and looking for new builders. There was still confusion as to where the railroad was actually going—Beloit, Janesville, or somewhere in Illinois. This was cleared up when President Bond visited the offices of the Rockford Central Railroad Company in Rockford, Illinois, in July. Rockford Central officers returned the visit in August.

With new contracts in hand, that summer the directors of the Kenosha and Beloit placed orders for rails and locomotives. To do this they were forced to call upon some of Kenosha's more prosperous citizens, who agreed to give six-month personal notes totaling thirty thousand dollars. This would purchase twelve miles of track. Later that month the company's first two engines, the Kenosha and Silver Lake, manufactured by Richard Norris and Son of Philadelphia, were delivered by rail to Chicago. As the track had not yet been laid at Kenosha, the locomotives were kept at the state line in a car house belonging to the Chicago & Milwaukee Railroad. A third locomotive, the Genoa, arrived shortly after, and then all three were brought to Kenosha, where they sat on the side of the Lake Shore Road.

The first rails arrived at the beginning of November. They came in twenty-foot and twenty-four-foot lengths; they had been manufactured in Cambria County, Pennsylvania, and had come over the lakes from Cleveland. One of the first shipments came on the schooner *Herald*, which ran aground entering Kenosha harbor, flooded, and had to be pumped out and refloated before she could deliver her goods. Another shipment came in December on the schooner *Minnie May*, which was driven northward by a storm and ran aground while being towed into Racine harbor. The rail was rowed in on lighters, then taken to Kenosha on the cars of the Lake Shore Line.

Despite these upsets, the arrival of materials meant work could finally begin. The first rails were laid in Kenosha in mid-November between Main Street and Chicago Street, high on an overhead trestle. By the end of the month the track extended west of the Lake Shore Road's tracks by some five hundred feet. On November 27 the engine *Kenosha* was run onto the tracks and put to work hauling supplies from the dock to the end of the track. By the end of the year the Kenosha and Beloit boasted two miles of track and thirty miles of grading.[31]

For other railroads, competition drove production to a breakneck pace. In late July the track laying crews of the Chicago, St. Paul, and Fond du Lac, which had been building from Illinois into Wisconsin, and those of the Racine and Mississippi were both approaching their crossing point at Clinton Junction, ten miles northeast of Beloit. A race developed to see who would get there first. The crew winning the race would simply continue laying its track, while the second crew would have to refit rails and install "frogs" to make the crossing. The pace became frenetic when the crews came within sight of each other. On August 15 the Chicago crew beat the Racine crew to the junction by about ten minutes.[32]

In September the Chicago, St .Paul, and Fond du Lac's tracks reached Janesville, and on September 15 the first passenger train from Chicago arrived. Janesville now had two railroads—the Milwaukee & Mississippi, with its depot on the north side of town, and the Chicago, St. Paul, and Fond du Lac, with its depot on the south side. Both companies were building bridges to the west side of the Rock River. The *Janesville Gazette* reported:

> The tress bridge across the Rock River . . . is five hundred and thirty eight feet long and forty two feet above the water. . . . The structure was erected by the Chicago, St. Paul and Fond du Lac Railroad Company, and is one of the most substantial and imposing in the west. . . . The foundations were commenced by the old Valley Road Company [Rock River Valley Union]. . . .
> 
> The Milwaukee and Mississippi . . . have just completed a magnificent bridge a mile above this . . . five hundred and fifty feet in length. . . .Its height above the

# AN EXPLOSION OF RAILROADS

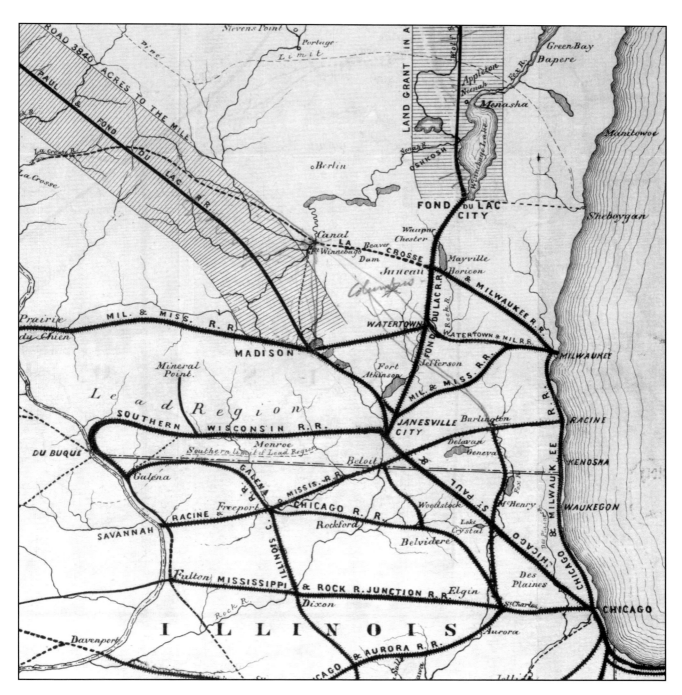

Detail of an 1856 Map of the Chicago, St. Paul & Fond du Lac Railroad.
WHi Image ID 64639

water is thirty eight feet. It was built for a double track. . . . One . . . will belong to the Chicago, St. Paul and Fond du Lac Company, which shares in the expense.[33]

The two companies would also share a depot on West Court Street. At about this time, the Chicago, St. Paul and Fond du Lac company abandoned its partially graded branch between Janesville and Madison.[34]

On the Chicago, St. Paul, and Fond du Lac's northern division (the former Rock River Valley Union line), track layers continued to lay six-foot-gauge track southward. At Burnett their rails crossed those recently laid by the Milwaukee and Horicon railroad, and a few miles further, at La Crosse Junction, those of the La Crosse and Milwaukee. By the end of the year, passengers from Fond du Lac would be able to transfer to the Horicon line for Horicon, Waupun, Brandon, or Ripon. They would also be able to transfer to the La Crosse line for Beaver Dam, Fox Lake, Portage, or Milwaukee.[35]

Between the Chicago, St. Paul, and Fond du Lac's northern and southern divisions—in other words, between Janesville and La Crosse Junction—was a fifty-seven-mile gap. Farmers living in that gap were pressured by stock agents to mortgage their farms and buy railroad stock so that the gap could be filled. Mr. Henry E. Southwell of Fort Atkinson recalled:

> The winter of 1855 and the year 1856 was noted for the excitement in rail road building and projection lines and laying out town sites and buying land on speculation. The Chicago, St. Paul, and Fond du Lac R. R. Co. had built from Chicago to Janesville and from Fond du Lac south to Watertown. To put in the link from Janesville to Watertown was the active work in sight. To further this project the Town of Koshkonong lent its credit by issuing $50,000 bonds for stock. Men mortgaged their land for stock and subscribed cash and lands to buy stock.[36]

Though 1855 had been a banner year for Wisconsin's railroads, 1856 proved to be an even better one, with 189 miles of new track laid. The state's total trackage at the end of the year was 508 miles. Ten railroad companies were now providing rail service in Wisconsin. They connected with each other in Milwaukee, Brookfield, Janesville, Clinton, Burnett, Horicon, Watertown, Racine, and Kenosha. Together, these railroads were shedding the appearance of being isolated lines and becoming a genuine rail network.

# AN EXPLOSION OF RAILROADS

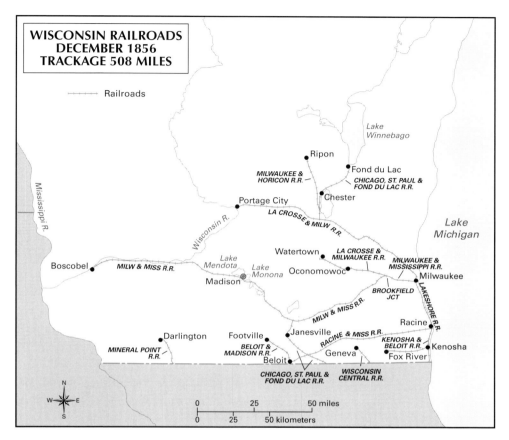

MAPPING SPECIALISTS

# Chapter 18

# The Struggle for Land Grants
### 1856

For some five years Wisconsin railroad companies had been lobbying in Washington for a federal law that would grant the lands of the public domain to Wisconsin to aid in the construction of railroads. Among these lobbyists were the Milwaukee & Mississippi, the St. Croix and Lake Superior, the La Crosse and Milwaukee, and the Rock River Valley Union, now known as the Chicago, St. Paul, and Fond du Lac. Year after year Congress had rejected these overtures, as well as those from other states, but in 1856 it had a change of heart. That spring Congress passed thirty such laws, donating nearly fifteen million acres to a number of states, among them Wisconsin.[1] Wisconsin's land grant act was largely the result of lobbying by representatives of the Chicago, St. Paul, and Fond du Lac Railroad Company—and it was this company that hoped to reap the benefits of the one million acres of prime real estate gained for Wisconsin railroads. The bill was reported on May 20, was then passed by the House and Senate, and was signed into law by President Franklin Pierce on June 3.[2]

The Wisconsin land grant act designated two rail routes, one northwestern and one northeastern. The lands along these routes would be sold and the proceeds applied toward construction of the railroad(s). The "northwestern land grant route" was designated to run "from Madison or Columbus to Portage City, thence to the St. Croix River or Lake between townships twenty-five and thirty-one, thence to Lake Superior, with a branch to Bayfield." Its Madison to St. Croix segment was already authorized in the Chicago, St. Paul, and Fond du Lac's charter, and the remainder of the route to Lake Superior reflected the ambitions of that company to connect at the western end of the lake with a Pacific transcontinental railroad. The "northeastern land grant route" was to run from Fond du Lac northward to the Wisconsin-Michigan line. This route was already in the Chicago, St. Paul, and Fond du Lac's charter and was based on its desire to build a railroad to the iron mining country of Michigan's upper peninsula. Each route would receive land for six miles on each side, of which alternate one-mile-square sections were to be sold to benefit its designated railroad. Thus the 348-mile northwestern route would receive 678,000 acres, and the 155-mile northeastern route, 380,000 acres.[3]

But for the Chicago, St. Paul, and Fond du Lac and Wisconsin's other aspiring railroad companies, the battle wasn't over—in fact, it had just begun. The federal government had donated the lands to Wisconsin, but the Wisconsin legislature still needed to decide which company or companies would build the land grant lines and receive the benefits. The stakes were high, and the railroad companies were ready to go all-out in lobbying state legislators for the prize. As mentioned, the Chicago, St. Paul, and Fond du Lac Railroad Company already held charter rights to a great deal of both of the routes. It was the company that had brought about the passage of the law, and it felt it deserved to be awarded the grants.[4] But the La Crosse and Milwaukee Railroad Company disagreed, saying that the grant was intended for Wisconsin interests, not Illinois,' and that it should be the recipient. Other contenders were the Milwaukee and Watertown Railroad Company, the Sugar Valley Railroad Company, and the St. Croix and Lake Superior Railroad Company, all with charter rights to some part of the land grant routes. The state of Wisconsin would have to decide which company would receive the grant. To that end Governor Coles Bashford called for a special six-week session of the legislature to be held in September.[5]

One week after President Pierce signed the land grant bill, a group of leading Wisconsin citizens opposed to the Chicago, St. Paul, and Fond du Lac and in favor of the La Crosse and Milwaukee met at the Wacker House in Milwaukee. In attendance were former Governor William A. Barstow, Lieutenant Governor Arthur MacArthur, former governors Nelson Dewey and Leonard J. Farwell, former Congressman James D. Doty, and James H. Knowlton, a railroad promoter from southwestern Wisconsin. Moses Strong, serving at this point as an attorney for the La Crosse and Milwaukee, presided.[6] The meeting began on June 10 with company President Byron Kilbourn stating that the La Crosse and Milwaukee was the logical choice for receiving the land grants, but that the company would concede to another railroad company if four conditions were met: 1) the company could not be in competition with the La Crosse and Milwaukee; 2) its routes could not lead more directly to Chicago than to Milwaukee; 3) it would use the grant to benefit Milwaukee; and 4) it would allow the La Crosse and Milwaukee Company to prescribe its route. These terms were accepted by the attendees, probably in the belief that there would be no alternate company and that the La Crosse and Milwaukee was the only eligible contender. The attendees then resolved to enlist influential citizens in the state to join an "association" that would further their cause. They adjourned to meet again in two months.[7]

When the group reconvened during the first week in August, they chose Strong to chair a committee assigned to draft a bill naming the La Crosse and Milwaukee the recipient of the land grant. Strong, the former speaker of the House and past president of both the La Crosse and Milwaukee and Mineral Point railroad companies, had recently moved from Mineral Point to Milwaukee to work for the "association" project.[8] There were now sixty "association" members, and each was assigned certain legislators to call on to influence the decision. Doty, one of the association members, was allotted five legislators from the northeast.[9]

In September, as promised by Governor Bashford, Wisconsin's legislators met at the capitol building in Madison for the sole purpose of assigning the land grants. At first the lobbying efforts of Milwaukee's "association" appeared to be successful. The joint legislative committee appointed to draft the bill even used Strong's draft as a template. But then things began to go wrong. It appeared that the Chicago, St. Paul, and Fond du Lac Railroad had gained the confidence of fifteen legislators, and one of them was James H. Knowlton, a member of the "association." Moreover, Knowlton was on the joint committee handling the bill. He used his influence to modify the bill to make it more favorable to the Chicago, St. Paul, and Fond du Lac—and thus unacceptable to the Milwaukeeans.[10]

On September 20 the La Crosse and Milwaukee Railroad Company strengthened its claim to the northwestern grant by merging with the Milwaukee and Watertown Railroad Company. It thereby eliminated a rival for the grant and acquired charter rights to the twenty-nine-mile Columbus-Portage segment, part of the northwestern land grant route. The Wisconsin act authorizing the merger specified that the Madison-Portage line would be used for allotting lands, but the La Crosse and Milwaukee, if it were awarded the grant, would be required to build the Madison-Portage and Columbus-Portage lines simultaneously. Kilbourn next negotiated an agreement with former governor William A. Barstow, the president of the St. Croix and Lake Superior Railroad Company, whereby the St. Croix and Lake Superior would hold the rights to the land grant between Hudson and Lake Superior, and the branch to Bayfield, but be controlled by the La Crosse and Milwaukee. As part of this deal the St. Croix and Lake Superior would convey all its property, rights, and franchises to the La Crosse and Milwaukee in return for one million dollars' worth of La Crosse Company bonds.[11]

On September 30 the Chicago, St. Paul, and Fond du Lac's president, William B. Ogden, came to Madison and addressed the legislators. He pointed out that his road was financially sound and that it had charter authorization for both the northwestern and northeastern land grant routes. He stated that the Chicago, St. Paul, and Fond du Lac had already constructed most of the road from Chicago to Fond du Lac, where it would connect with the northeastern route. And he reminded them that his company had worked long and hard to obtain this grant for Wisconsin. He asked that it be granted both routes. If that was asking too much, he said, it should at least be granted the northeastern route.[12]

Kilbourn now changed his plans, deciding to promote the La Crosse and Milwaukee to receive the northwestern grant and a new company to receive the northeastern. He had Strong draft a modified bill. He then enlisted a member of each legislative house to take charge of matters on the bill's behalf. Representative Thomas Falvey of Racine agreed to do this in the Assembly, while Senator Jackson Haddley of Milwaukee would do so in the Senate. Kilbourn, Strong, Falvey, and Haddley worked over the next several weeks to gain the support of representatives from all sections of the state. They described the benefits that the passage of this bill would bring Wisconsin, by giving the grants to Wisconsin railroads rather than to a Chicago-based railroad. Kilbourn and Strong went several steps further. They met privately with legislators, treated them to oyster dinners, and suggested that monetary rewards awaited them if they voted for the bill and it passed.[13]

In October promises of "pecuniary compliments" were extended by Kilbourn and Strong to the governor, the governor's private secretary, the lieutenant governor, the state comptroller, the clerks of the Assembly, senators, and assemblymen. Technically, they were not offering bribes, which would have meant payment *in advance* for votes. There were laws against that. Kilbourn and Strong were simply promising a "gift" to be given to those that voted for their bill *after* it passed. In the railroad business it was common, even expected, for company directors to receive gifts from contractors to whom they had awarded contracts. Why not in government? It was a "grey" area at best, and Kilbourn and Strong specialized in dealing with "grey" areas. They promised Governor Bashford fifty thousand dollars' worth of La Crosse and Milwaukee bonds, senators ten thousand dollars' worth, and assemblymen five thousand.

While most of the targets of these "gifts" were receptive to the idea, some, such as Senator C. Latham Sholes of Kenosha, who would later invent the typewriter,

Byron Kilbourn, circa 1855.
WHI IMAGE ID 9486

and Senator Amasa Cobb of Iowa County were not. Cobb related that:

> Some five or six days before the final adjournment of the said adjourned session, Mr. William Pitt Dewey, who was then the assistant clerk of the Assembly, invited me to take a walk with him, and while walking around the capital square in the city of Madison, he [Dewey] introduced the subject of the bill granting the lands which had been granted to the State of Wisconsin to aid in the construction of certain railroads, to the La Crosse and Milwaukee Railroad company, and which bill was then pending before the Legislature. During said conversation he informed me that should said bill pass, he would get a quantity of bonds. He stated the amount that he was to receive, and to the best of the recollection of this deponent, it was ten thousand dollars. He asked me what amount would induce me to cease my opposition and support the bill, or come into the arrangement. I asked him why, or by what authority he made the inquiry? He replied that he had come right from Kilbourn and was authorized by him to say that I might make my own terms. . . . He further stated that "they were bound to carry it through anyhow, and that I might as well make something out of it, as the rest of them. . . . I asked him what was the amount of the capital stock of the company? He replied[,] ten million dollars. I told him to say to Byron Kilbourn that if he would multiply the capital stock of the company by the number of leaves in the Capitol Park, and give me that amount in money, and then have himself, Moses Strong, and Mitchell blacked, and give me a clear title to them as servants for life, I would take the matter under consideration.[14]

Moses M. Strong by James Reeve Stuart, circa 1885.
WHi Image ID 2952

With offers being made to so many, word began to spread. Knowlton, by this time one of fifteen legislators in the pay of the Chicago, St. Paul, and Fond du Lac, complained on the floor of the Assembly that "men were bragging in the streets that they had bought up a majority of the legislators."[15] This so alarmed Strong that he took his bill to a printer and promised him a one hundred dollar bonus if he would work through the night. So expedited, the bill awarding the northwestern grant to the La Crosse and Milwaukee and the northeastern grant to a new Wiscon-

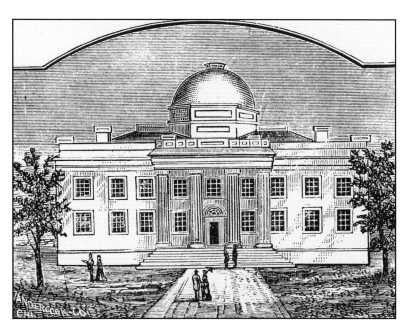

First Wisconsin Capitol Building, in Madison, 1850, where legislators met to determine land grants and railroad charters. Designed by James D. Doty, it served as the capitol from 1838 into statehood, until 1862 when it burned down.
WHI IMAGE ID 34370

sin and Superior Railroad Company that would reflect Wisconsin interests, rather than those of Chicago, came to a vote. On October 6 it passed in both the Assembly and the Senate. But to everyone's surprise, Governor Bashford vetoed it, contending that it violated the Wisconsin constitution (Article IV., Section 18, Title of Private Bills) by dealing with more than one subject—in this case, both the northeastern and northwestern routes.[16]

Kilbourn then met with the governor to discuss the changes that would need to be made in order for the bill to be signed. Two days later, assemblyman John Fox Potter of Fond du Lac introduced two bills in the Assembly. One granted the northwestern grant to the La Crosse and Milwaukee Railroad Company, its wording virtually identical to that of the earlier bill. The other granted the northeastern grant to the Wisconsin and Superior Railroad Company, incorporated in the bill. The first bill, aided by Kilbourn's promises of pecuniary rewards, passed sixty-two to seven in the Assembly and seventeen to seven in the senate. It was signed into law by Governor Bashford on October 10. When news of the law's passage reached Milwaukee, its citizens were jubilant, holding torchlight processions and lighting bonfires in celebration.[17]

This law differed from the federal grant by requiring that both the Madison-Portage City and Columbus-Portage City roads be built, and required that they be built within ten years. It specified that when twenty miles of road were completed and certified by the governor, the secretary of the interior in Washington would convey titles to 240 sections of land to the La Crosse Company. After that, for each succeeding twenty miles of completed road, another 120 sections of land would be conveyed. Once the land-grant railroad was operating, it would pay ten percent of its gross income to the state in lieu of taxes.[18] The bill for the northeastern grant had also passed the legislature, but was being held up by Governor Bashford, who was insisting that two more directors be allowed on the board of the Wisconsin and Superior and that the appointees be his brother and assemblyman Potter. The changes were made, and Bashford signed the bill.[19]

After the land grants were awarded, the recipient La Crosse and Milwaukee and Wisconsin and Superior railroad companies faced new challenges. The former had to discreetly distribute its "gifts," and the latter had to fight off a takeover. Shortly after the passage of the first bill, Kilbourn called on Governor Bashford. Kilbourn recounted:

> I called on him . . . and being informed by him that he had approved the act, I expressed to him the deep sense of gratitude which I felt. . . . I also took that occasion to express the friendly sentiments . . . and that . . . the company felt disposed to extend to him a pecuniary compliment. . . . He said that . . . he . . . would accept of it cheerfully. I then stated that I would . . . place in his hands the bonds of the company to the amount of fifty thousand dollars. . . . There was no corrupt intent in this transaction with Governor Bashford. . . . I deemed it necessary to propitiate his feelings with reference to the future operations of our company by an act of such liberality. . . . Such were my only motives. . . . On his part I believe he accepted it for the reason that he thought the company could well afford to make such a donation without doing it any material damage while to him the sum was large enough to offer a real benefit.[20]

Wisconsin Governor Coles Bashford, circa 1857.
WHi Image ID 38567

The distribution of these "pecuniary compliments," or "gifts," by the La Crosse and Milwaukee was done discreetly, which was surprising given the number of recipients involved. It had been decided that all of these recipients would go to Milwaukee to collect their rewards. There, in the company paymaster's office on Third Street, Strong would receive them. Strong made a numbered list of the recipients. He then made a second, identically numbered list, on which the recipients were not named, but the amount due them was. Strong prepared the packages, one for each claimant, each with the appropriate number of bonds. He wrapped them in plain paper and on each wrote the number of the recipient. Strong and Kilbourn then destroyed the second list so that there was no longer any record of what was in the packages. Between October 15 and 21 Strong handed packages to a steady stream of claimants. Among them were the governor, the lieutenant governor, bankers, businessmen, senators, assemblymen, clerks, jurists, various other state officials, and newspaper editors. In all, Strong distributed $862,000 worth of bonds that week.

Meanwhile the La Crosse and Milwaukee's directors had voted themselves "gifts" as well, bringing the total cost of securing the land grant to more than a million dollars. Strong received $25,000 dollars' worth of bonds for his services. All but eight of the legislators who had voted for the bill received a package, and those eight had been compensated in other ways.[21] Legislators who had not voted

# THE STRUGGLE FOR LAND GRANTS

for the La Crosse and Milwaukee bill, Cobb and Senator John Fitzgerald of Oshkosh among them, did not receive a package. Senator Fitzgerald contemptuously referred to the "gifts" as the "sweepings of the Capitol."[22]

Shortly after the legislative session ended, the Chicago, St. Paul, and Fond du Lac Company began making overtures to take control of the Wisconsin and Superior. Its intentions were revealed at board meeting in Oshkosh, at which Governor Bashford was present. Officers of the Wisconsin and Superior Company included James H. Weed of Oshkosh; Herman Haertel of Milwaukee; Benjamin F. Moore of Fond du Lac; Perry H. Smith of Appleton; and T. B. Bigelow.[23] A group of eight directors of that company, among them Doty, pledged to refuse all Chicago offers.

But these pledges, it turned out, could be bought. As more money was offered, one director after another stepped down and was replaced by a Chicago nominee. Doty succumbed after accepting forty-two shares of stock in the reorganized company and a promise of forty-one more shares if he would not make trouble. In all, William B. Ogden and the Chicago, St. Paul, and Fond du Lac Railroad Company spent $170,000 on the takeover. Many Wisconsin residents approved. They wanted the northeastern land grant railroad built as quickly as possible, and the Chicago, St. Paul, and Fond du Lac Company was in a position to do that. Also, many of them owned stock in that company, either in individual subscriptions or in the form of Janesville or Fond du Lac city bonds.

If Congressional land grants were the "big plums" for railroad companies at that time, then Kilbourn and Strong had been a long time in getting one. They had incorporated the La Crosse and Milwaukee in 1852 for the purpose of receiving a Congressional land grant and had in the same year lobbied in Washington for such a grant. But the Congressional land grant bill for Wisconsin had died in the House, and a similar measure did not come up again for several more years. Now, four years later, Kilbourn and Strong had capitalized on the lobbying efforts of the Chicago, St. Paul, and Fond du Lac, and snatched away one of its "big plums" for their La Crosse and Milwaukee railroad. Their methods had been secretive and questionable, and the monetary price they induced their company to pay in gratuities to people of influence was high. It remained to be seen whether or not they, the La Crosse and Milwaukee Railroad Company, or the citizens of Wisconsin would benefit from their actions.

# Chapter 19

# Reaching the Mississippi
### 1857

With only twenty-two miles of track left to lay, the Milwaukee & Mississippi Railroad was within spitting distance of a dream that had beguiled railroad promoters for almost a quarter of a century—completing a line connecting Lake Michigan to the Mississippi River. Unfortunately for the Milwaukee & Mississippi, its competitor, the La Crosse & Milwaukee Railroad, was about to complete its own line to the Mississippi at La Crosse. And as though that were not enough, railroad companies originating in the Lake Michigan ports of Sheboygan, Manitowoc, Racine, and Kenosha were featuring the Mississippi in their corporate names and building with the Mississippi as their goal. It appeared as though there would soon be many railroads traversing the state. Too many, perhaps. Yet some people sensed that the bottom was about to fall out from under the railroad boom due to the shaky financing and overly hasty expansion that many companies had believed was necessary in order to stay ahead of the competition. Few people had forgotten how twenty years before, during the panic of 1837, excessive borrowing had led to bankruptcy. Milwaukee & Mississippi President John Catlin certainly had not. He had bought the bonds rather than the stock of his company, becoming its lender. Yet the four-thousand-odd Wisconsin farmers who had mortgaged their farms to invest in railroad stock continued to be at risk, with some four million of their dollars at stake.[1] If the railroads failed to pay the interest on their loans, those farmers were likely to lose their farms to the creditors.

# REACHING THE MISSISSIPPI

In February a writer who signed himself "a Badger" wrote the editor of the *Milwaukee Sentinel* saying, "The thing is being overdone, and the moment confidence begins to fall, the whole fabric of our Rail Road system collapses."[2] A law enacted earlier in the year seemed to catch the metaphoric significance of such fear. It required all railroad crossings post warning signs with the words "LOOK OUT FOR THE CARS." Locomotives in cities were now expected to ring their bells before crossing streets and to limit their speed to "six miles an hour—no faster."[3]

In May a recession began that looked to last more than the remainder of the year. The bank panic that followed in August had repercussions for the railways that would soon change the course of the long railway boom in Wisconsin. In September, Karl Schurz, a German immigrant who had invested in real estate in Watertown, wrote, "Business is very quiet; money matters in the whole United States are depressed. . . . How far the financial crisis which has recently broken upon us may go is still hard to determine."[4] Sadly, in Wisconsin, it would go far, and one of its chief victims would be the railroads.

❖ ❖ ❖ ❖ ❖ ❖

The first half of 1857 was marked by growth and mergers. The Kenosha and Beloit Railroad had two miles of track out of Kenosha and a new destination—Rockford, Illinois. The company's crews had worked through the winter; the men had been forced to break up the frozen ground by driving wedges into it. In Bristol Township a Mr. John Lavell was engaged in this work when the bank of earth on which he was standing collapsed, killing him—a rare accident that reminded all involved of the dangers of railroad construction.

During the early months of 1857 the railroad went through a series of rapid mergers and name changes. On January 20 the Kenosha & Rockford Railroad Company of Illinois was chartered and authorized to build between Rockford and an undetermined connection with the Kenosha and Beloit on the state line. Eight days later the Rockford and Mississippi Rail Road Company of Illinois was chartered to build from Rockford west to the Mississippi. On February 14 Wisconsin's Kenosha and Beloit changed its name to the Kenosha & Rockford Railroad Company. On March 5 it merged with the Kenosha & Rockford of Illinois to become the Kenosha, Rockford & Rock Island Railroad Company, chartered respectively as such in the two states.

The Wisconsin Central Railroad was also looking forward to expansion. On March 2 it had its charter amended, allowing it to extend its line from Portage to Lake Superior. That month also saw President Le Grand Rockwell replaced by Rufus Cheney of Whitewater.[5]

The Watertown and Madison Railroad Company was also optimistic. In January it received a one hundred thousand dollar loan from the city of Madison. Supporters of the loan maintained that a second railroad for Madison would reduce freight and passenger bills, raise property values, and reduce the cost of living in that city. Watertown and Madison President Jarius Fairchild and former governor Leonard Farwell went to the East coast with the bonds and came back with cash. Meanwhile, company stock agents were taking mortgages on Madison properties, to a total of ninety thousand dollars, for stock. Farwell mortgaged twenty-five thousand dollars' worth of his own property to buy stock.[6] The railroad was to use East Mifflin Street coming into town, then swing south and cross the isthmus along the Lake Monona shore, and proceed to a depot on Murray Street west of downtown. On December 1 the Watertown and Madison Railroad Company executed a mortgage of its entire line, from Watertown to Waterloo, to Edwin Ludlow, trustee, to secure $340,000 of ten-year, 8 percent bonds. The company had been grading at both ends of its line and had laid track, completing twenty-four miles of its road, from Watertown to Waterloo.[7]

Other railroads also seemed to be thriving. That spring the Racine and Mississippi Railroad Company experienced a brisk business as Beloit shippers sent produce and wares over the new line to Lake Michigan. Meanwhile the company's rails entered Illinois just a few hundred feet beyond its Beloit depot. Rails were laid to Rockton and to Durand in May. By April another railway company, the Milwaukee and Horicon, had extended its line twelve miles beyond Ripon to Berlin, just forty-two miles from Milwaukee. The directors called for further expansion by extending the road to Stevens Point and Lake Superior. They ordered a survey and sent stock agents to solicit additional subscriptions along the proposed extension. The city of Milwaukee supported them. In April Milwaukee Mayor James B. Cross, addressing the common council, praised the plan:

This road seems destined to take a high rank among the railroad enterprises of this State; and will need no other than its

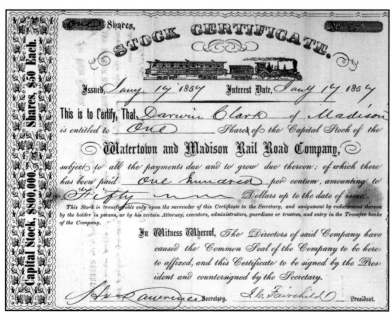

1857 stock certificate of the Watertown and Madison Rail Road Company, issued to Madison businessman Darwin Clark and signed by president of the railroad and Madison mayor, Jarius C. Fairchild.
WHi Image ID 11300

A train winds through Berlin, Wisconsin, on the former Milwaukee and Horicon line in this 1867 print by A. Ruger.
WHi Image ID 11406

own resources, to push it forward to Stevens Point, and from thence to Lake Superior. The farmers along this line, fully appreciating its importance, have stepped forward with commendable zeal and energy, and are daily furnishing available securities and means to push it onward to completion.[8]

In May, Luther Beecher, the Mineral Point Railroad's contractor, obtained ownership of the majority of the company's stock, giving him complete control of the company and allowing him to appoint a board of directors that then voted him in as president. Then, with the line between Warren and Darlington in operation and the tracks approaching Mineral Point, the company's supply of rails gave out. On May 13 the *Monroe Sentinel* reported:

> Our Mineral Point friends complain of very dull times and are anxiously waiting for completion of the road, now within two and a half miles, but delayed for the want of iron, that is expected soon.[9]

Meanwhile, building contractors completed the Mineral Point depot, a thirty by fifty foot structure of native buff limestone, an engine house, and a 2,400 square foot machine shop, the latter two buildings also made of stone. Thankfully the rail shortage did not last, and in early June the Mineral Point Railroad was able to complete its thirty-two-mile line at Mineral Point. The fenced-in line had eight wooden bridges and forty-three culverts. On June 16 the first train left Warren, Illinois, and worked its way up the Pecatonica valley to Mineral Point. Two weeks later the *Mineral Point Tribune* found that

> the business of the Mineral Point Railroad exceeds the expectations of most of our citizens. . . . We were at the depot on Friday last about the time the train was leaving and saw it start out with seven freight cars well filled, three loaded with wheat, three with lead, and one with sundries.[10]

The company had three locomotives—the John C. Freemont, the Mineral Point, and the Warren—and forty freight cars. In July the company ran several special trains to celebrate the opening of the line. The directors imposed a speed limit of sixteen miles per hour for all trains.

That summer the Green Bay, Milwaukee & Chicago shortened its name to the Milwaukee & Chicago. It opened a new station in Milwaukee by the lake at the end of Elizabeth Street (National Avenue), which became the new northern terminal of the line. To reach it, trains coming from Chicago had to pass over the marshes of south Milwaukee on a long wooden trestle. The company also kept its Bay View station, where it erected a roundhouse and freight facilities.[11]

A Milwaukee & Chicago train arrives in the Milwaukee this 1857 landscape drawing by Samuel Marsden Brookes and Thomas H. Stevenson, sketched from the perspective of the fifth ward.
WHI Image ID 23131

## REACHING THE MISSISSIPPI

❖ ❖ ❖ ❖ ❖ ❖

The success and growth of the first part of the year culminated in the achievement of a dream long held by Wisconsin citizens and railroad pioneers: by March, completion of a line between Lake Michigan and the Mississippi was imminent. The Milwaukee & Mississippi had resumed laying track at Boscobel, only twenty-two miles from Prairie du Chien. With the Wisconsin River bridge having been finished over the winter, tracks were laid to Wauzeekaw (Wauzeka), Wright's Ferry, and Bridgeport. With nine miles left to the Mississippi, the men picked up the pace. In the second week of April the last spike was driven at Lowertown, Prairie du Chien. After six and a half years the railroad from Lake Michigan to the Mississippi was finally finished. On the morning of April 15 the Milwaukee & Mississippi locomotive Prairie du Chien, pulling one baggage car and three passenger cars, left Milwaukee. It arrived at the depot in Lowertown at 5 o'clock in the afternoon and was greeted by cheers and a two-hundred-gun artillery salute. A barrel of Lake Michigan water that had been brought from Milwaukee was ceremoniously emptied into the Mississippi River. The *North Iowa Times* reported:

> Be it remembered that on Wednesday, April 15, 1857, at 5 o'clock in the evening, the cars of the Milwaukee and Mississippi Rail Road anchored on the banks of the great river. The shriek of the Lake Michigan locomotive was echoed by the bluffs and responded to by a shrill whistle of welcome from a Mississippi steamer just coming into port. Hundreds of persons were in attendance to witness the arrival of the first passenger train, and when the smoke of the engine became visible in the distance there was such an expression of anxiety as we have seen when a new and great actor is expected on the stage. As the train came in view, and the flags with which it was decorated were seen waving in the breeze, a shout of welcome broke forth from the gazers that told how many hopes of friendly reunions were awakened in the contemplation of an easy and speedy return to their eastern homes. One large banner carried on its silken folds the busy emblem of "Wisconsin, the Badger."[12]

❖ ❖ ❖ ❖ ❖ ❖

Sadly, the high note of this momentous achievement was soon overshadowed. In May, shortly after the line was opened, there was trouble when water from melting snow and ice made the Wisconsin River overflow its banks. Superintendent William Jervis reported that

An 1857 advertisement for the combined Chicago, St. Paul and Fond du Lac and Milwaukee & Mississippi service to St. Paul.
COURTESY OF THE LIBRARY OF CONGRESS

the main line west of Boscobel was interrupted 2 weeks in May by the unusual freshet in Wisconsin River. . . . No danger or interruption would have occurred from this cause, had the embankments been finished to the contemplated grade, but in many places they were 1½ to 3 feet below, and the action of the water upon the frozen lumps which had been put in during the winter, settled them one, and in some places two feet lower, making 3 to 4 feet below the elevation of the established grade. These embankments have since been raised, and in most cases protected by stone, so that no apprehension need be felt of any similar difficulty in the future.

The effect of the interruption on the business of the road was . . . serious. . . . It resulted in our losing the bulk of the through spring business.[13]

The spring freshet had also raised the water to a level that prevented lumber rafts from passing under the railroad's bridges. Raftsmen, waiting for the water to subside, threatened to dismantle the bridges. The legislature subsequently passed a law that required the company to raise its Spring Green and Lone Rock bridges by three feet.

There was still more trouble to come. In their efforts to make ends meet, summer found the Milwaukee & Mississippi charging exorbitant rates in areas where there were no competing lines. The charge for carrying wheat from Madison to Milwaukee was greater than that from Prairie du Chien to Milwaukee, Prairie du Chien having shipping on the Mississippi as an alternative. Madison's *Wisconsin State Journal* pointed out that it cost as much for Dane County growers to ship their grain to Milwaukee on the Milwaukee & Mississippi railroad as it did to ship it by wagon—meaning the only advantage of using the railroad was speed.[14] The company was increasingly pressured to resort to such measures as the economy deteriorated in May and June. In August, when runs took place on Eastern banks and Wisconsin banks suspended specie payments, the Milwaukee & Mississippi owed $4,798,705 and was committed to annual interest payments of $468,823. As its revenues dropped, the company found it more and more difficult to make those payments.[15]

❖ ❖ ❖ ❖ ❖ ❖

The La Crosse and Milwaukee Railroad Company began the year favorably, but trouble was on the horizon for them as well. On January 20 the company had contracted with Selah Chamberlain to finish its road from Portage City to La Crosse by December 31, 1858. The company opened its line to Portage City on March 16. That month the directors appointed W. R. Sill of La Crosse as engineer of the Western Division. Sill had surveyed the route between Tomah and La Crosse. Grading was commenced between Madison and Portage City—the first segment of the northwestern land grant route. Later, on August 20, the road to the village of Kilbourn (that is, the Wisconsin Dells) was also opened.

Despite this progress, the strain of continuing to finance their railroads on empty promises began to point to serious trouble ahead, even in the early part of the year. In January the La Crosse and Milwaukee Railroad Company purchased the St. Croix and Superior Railroad Company with one million dollars' worth of unsecured company bonds, thus securing the northern portion of the northwestern land grant route. These bonds, which had been issued to acquire the Milwaukee and Watertown, as well as those given out as "pecuniary compliments," committed the company to eventually redeeming some two million dollars—no incidental amount.

As word spread regarding the company's distribution of "gift" bonds, a legislative investigation was called for. On President Kilbourn's recommendation, Moses Strong ran for state assembly to block the investigation. After Strong was elected, but before he could take his seat, the Chicago, St. Paul and Fond du Lac Company, hoping to wrest away the northwestern grant, asked for an inquiry. Milwaukee Democrat Josiah Noonan wrote Assembly Clerk Horace A. Tenney that he had many Republican legislators ready to vote for an investigation. But Kilbourn and Strong were able to pay Tenney to drop the investigation. The assembly's railroad committee subsequently stated that the investigation would have been expensive and would have harmed the state.[16]

During the summer there was more and more talk of the La Crosse and Milwaukee's "gift" bonds of the year before. President Kilbourn made the statement that he and Strong should not be considered "great scamps" simply because the honorable gentlemen of the legislature had chosen "to make asses of themselves."[17] Meanwhile, the company was once more in dire need of cash. On August 17 it mortgaged its completed sections, from Milwaukee to Portage and from Watertown to Midland, to Greene C. Bronson and James T. Soutter, trustees, to secure one million dollars' worth of 8 percent bonds.

On September 26 the company leased its entire line to its contractor, Chamberlain. Chamberlain was to operate the road and apply the net receipts to 1) the

Palmer mortgage, 2) the Milwaukee city mortgages, 3) the second mortgage, and 4) the Bronson and Soutter mortgages. He could apply what was left to reduce the $629,089.72 that the company owed him.[18] The company then leased its Watertown division to D. C. Freeman; as with Chamberlain's lease, Freeman was to apply net receipts to three mortgages, then to D. C. Jackson (who was owed for grading between Madison and Portage), and then to himself. The company did complete nineteen miles of railroad between Watertown and Columbus during 1857.

On October 29 the man who had been behind the development of Wisconsin's railroads from the beginning, Kilbourn, resigned from the presidency and ended his long association with railroads. Kilbourn also confessed that the La Crosse road was on the verge of bankruptcy and that the land grant, "so eagerly sought," had, "by the expenses of the contest for its possession," contributed largely to the "present embarrassments of the Company." Stephen Clark of Albany, New York, was elected in Kilbourn's place.[19]

The La Crosse and Milwaukee's wood-and-iron bridge over the Wisconsin River at Kilbourn City (Wisconsin Dells), pictured in 1878. It was 310 feet long, 80 feet above the river, and had a lower deck for wagons.
WHi Image ID 62851

In December the La Crosse and Milwaukee's first train to cross the bridge at Kilbourn City gave its passengers a spectacular new view of the Dells. The bridge was 310 feet long, its track 80 feet above the river, and it incorporated a deck-roadway for wagons beneath the track. Chamberlain finished the line to Mauston on December 7 and to New Lisbon on December 23, making 138 miles of continuous track from Milwaukee. On December 24 the company sold its Watertown-Columbus line and the former Milwaukee and Watertown line (Brookfield Junction to Watertown) to the Madison, Fond du Lac and Michigan Railroad Company, a company which until then had owned no property.[20] The La Crosse and Milwaukee then used the proceeds to pay D. C. Jackson for grading between Madison and Portage.[21]

At the end of the month the directors requested that Governor Coles Bashford certify the forty miles that had been built on the land grant route. The governor took the opportunity to first cash in his fifteen thousand dollars' worth of "gift" bonds. Then, on December 28, he certified the forty miles between Portage City and New Lisbon and forwarded the certificate to the Secretary of the Interior in Washington.

The receipt of the granted lands was the company's last hope for survival, but with everyone involved trying to bank their bonds and get out, things did not look hopeful.

❖ ❖ ❖ ❖ ❖ ❖

The Chicago, St. Paul and Fond du Lac's fortunes also shifted over the course of the year. In January it had absorbed by merger the Wisconsin and Superior Railroad Company, thus acquiring the northeastern land grant route. In March it merged with two Michigan railroads, the Ontonagon and State Line and the Marquette and State Line, to gain access to Michigan's Upper Peninsula and Lake Superior. The directors summarized that

> the object and desire of the Chicago, St. Paul and Fond du Lac Railroad Company was the extension of their line from Janesville northwest via Madison and La Crosse to St. Paul and from Janesville north along the valley of Rock River to Fond du Lac and to the great iron and copper regions of Lake Superior.[22]

In other words, they hoped to be the first railroad to service the mining regions of the Upper Peninsula, which promised lucrative benefits.

Meanwhile, improvements were being made to the everyday workings of its existing lines. On March 19 the company implemented a new timetable between Chicago and Janesville. Trains left Chicago at 7 a.m., 8 a.m., and 2:05 p.m. for the four and a half hour journey. The 7 a.m. train stopped at Junction, Plank Road, Canfield, Des Plaines (7:50 a.m.), Dunton, Palatine, Barrington, Carey (8:55 a.m.), Crystal Lake (9:08 a.m.), Ridgefield, Woodstock (9:32 a.m.), Harvard (10:05 a.m.), Lawrence, Sharon (10:30 a.m.), Clinton (10:52 a.m.), Shopiere, and Janesville (11:30 a.m.). Return trains left Janesville at 7 a.m., 9:30 a.m., and 5:30 p.m. These improved operations were further explained:

> Trains should meet and pass at stations marked with full faced figures.
> Freight Trains will take the side track to allow passenger trains to pass.
> Passenger Trains Nos. 2 and 4 will take the side track at passing place.
> No Train will approach a station when another train is to leave within five minutes of its time of leaving. Freight Trains will pass each other at Crystal Lake.[23]

In April, the Chicago, St. Paul and Fond du Lac line became part of the through route between Chicago and St. Paul. The company's agreement with the Milwaukee & Mississippi allowed it to share the latter's line between Janesville and Prairie du Chien. At Prairie du Chien passengers continued their trip on the steamboats of the Prairie du Chien and St. Paul Packet Line to St. Paul. Author D. C. Prescott relates:

> The Fond du Lac Road connected at Janesville with a railroad called the Milwaukee & Mississippi, which extended out to Prairie du Chien on the Mississippi River and a line of passenger boats operated between that place and St. Paul, Minn., constituting a continuous line by rail and river from Chicago to St. Paul. . . . The arrangement worked nicely so long as the water in the river was high enough to permit unobstructed navigation, but in times of low water, trouble was always in store for the connecting railroad lines, because the boats were constantly getting stuck on sand bars, which invariably made them late at La Crosse and Prairie du Chien; and then the race would begin to make up time and land passengers in Chicago in time for eastern trains. . . . Arthur Hobart had the faculty of landing lady passengers at way stations actually without bringing the train to a full stop. He simply gave them a toss in such a way that they would land easily on their feet and no harm done; and of course John Hull, the baggage-man, would drop off the trunks, and all this time Hobart's hand would be in the air signaling the engineer to go ahead. This was the kind of railroad service had every time a train was late.[24]

Meanwhile, there was the business of the Chicago, St. Paul and Fond du Lac closing the gap between Janesville and Minnesota Junction. President William B. Ogden visited Wisconsin to promote stock sales in the area. L. B. Caswell of Fort Atkinson recalled:

> Mr. Ogden came here . . . in 1857, and . . . worked up large subscriptions for the stock, in the shape of mortgages and lands freely given the company for stock, and also by obtaining the towns and cities along the line to issue their bonds in large quantities, in payment for stock, and finally the town of Koshkonong, Fort Atkinson then constituting a part, issued to this company stock, $50,000, of its seven per cent, twenty year bonds, interest payable annually. Jefferson issued a large amount of similar bonds, and Watertown a much larger amount.[25]

The directors had resolved to put this part of the road under contract as soon as six hundred thousand dollars worth of stock was subscribed. This happened within a month when Fort Atkinson subscribed $100,000; Watertown, $150,000; Jefferson, $75,000; Johnson Creek, $25,000; and Juneau, $50,000. By May, however, economic conditions in the state had noticeably changed and investors had become more cautious. Henry E. Southwell of Fort Atkinson explained:

# REACHING THE MISSISSIPPI

The spring of 1857 witnessed a decided change in the outlook for business. Credits began to be looked after. Distrust was in the air. Merchants forced their goods to sale and down went the price. It was an effort to get out, with or without loss . . . Collecting agents canvassed the courts trying to force payments.[26]

The downturn, starting in May, would have a devastating effect on the railroads. Later in the year the Chicago, St. Paul and Fond du Lac found itself, along with other railroad companies, unable to pay the interest on its bonds. But it continued to run trains and do business in this state of near-bankruptcy. It owned eighteen locomotives, fourteen passenger cars, and 120 freight cars at that time. Construction work, however, stopped, and the fifty-seven-mile gap between Janesville and Minnesota Junction remained. L. B. Caswell of Fort Atkinson described the state of affairs:

> Mr. Ogden staked his entire fortune on building the road. He built on the north end from Fond du Lac to Minnesota Junction and on the south end, from Chicago to Janesville, and the company had exhausted its money and all its resources. It failed without a dollar in the treasury and no road to Fort Atkinson, none between Janesville and Minnesota Junction. Our $50,000 of town bonds were outstanding; we had the old worthless certificates of stock in the defunct road. We had helped to build some other places a road with our bonds, mortgages and lands, but had no road for ourselves. Property along the unbuilt portion was dead. Fort Atkinson was dead, for aught we could see.[27]

Undaunted, President William B. Ogden returned to Wisconsin to push for the completion of the line:

> Soon after the panic of 1857 Mr. W. B. Ogden, president of the Chicago, St. Paul and Fond du Lac Railroad, pushed the construction of the road between Janesville and Watertown. Mr. Ogden told the people of Wisconsin that a direct connection with Chicago was better for them than with Milwaukee although the distance was 60 miles farther. That Chicago was and would be the best market for farm products and was the leading city in the West. Mr. Ogden was a man of large and wide experience. A talk with him meant new ideas and enlarged views. He liked to associate with men who did things and did them well.[28]

After Ogden's visit, the company optimistically planned to resume construction in the spring.

The Milwaukee & Mississippi, which had long been Wisconsin's premier railway, was fighting to stay afloat. By September its southern branch between Janesville and Monroe had been graded and was ready for track laying. Rails were laid eight miles to Hanover (a.k.a. Bass Creek or Plymouth), where they crossed the Beloit and Madison line. From Hanover rails were laid six miles to Orfordville, then six more miles to Brodhead. Brodhead had been founded two years earlier by Superintendent Edward H. Brodhead, now president of the company. At that time the nearby villages of Clarence and Decatur were told that they would have to raise seven thousand dollars to have the railroad come their way. Confident that the railroad would come their way in any case, they did nothing. In the spring of 1856 Brodhead responded by purchasing land midway between the two villages, platting the village of Brodhead, and donating land for station grounds and right of way. Buildings then went up "as fast as workmen could be found to put them up." Soon residents of Decatur began moving their buildings to the new site. By September of 1857 Brodhead had two stores, a hotel, a lumberyard, and six hundred residents. On September 17 the editor of the *Monroe Sentinel* joined in the celebration of the opening of the line to Brodhead:

In this 1857 lithograph by Louis Kurz, a Milwaukee & Mississippi train leaves the village of Waukesha.
WHi Image ID 12176

Early on the morning of a drizzling, rainy, muddy Thursday . . . we left . . . to attend the celebration of the opening of the Southern Wisconsin [Southern Branch of the Milwaukee & Mississippi] Railroad to Brodhead. . . . An excursion train of six passenger and three or four freight cars, all crowded full, left the [Brodhead] depot to meet the excursionists from Milwaukee, Waukesha, and towns along the line of road. At Janesville, the Milwaukee train of five crowded cars was added, and the train returned to Brodhead, arriving just in time to permit the whole company to take refuge in the large depot before the approach of a passing shower. . . . The Monroe Brass Band furnished an excellent quality of music for the day. . . . The Brodhead Brass Band also played excellently. . . . There was also a martial band from Decatur that participated in all the festivities.[29]

Leaving Brodhead, the track layers came to the twin villages of Juda-Springfield, separated by Main Street. The *Monroe Sentinel* reported:

November 18: The track-layers today [Wednesday] will have the rail laid into Juda, and by Saturday night, will probably have finished all side-tracks. It is now but eight miles from Juda to Monroe, and a little more hard work will bring the cars to this point. Let every man who has a cent in money or a bushel of wheat, pay the same to B. Dunwiddie, director, or Henry Thompson, Esq., agent, and those gentlemen will faithfully apply the same to the taking of iron out of bond. It will not do to let the track-layers cease until the last switch in this town is laid.

The Milwaukee & Mississippi had defaulted on its bond interest payments in July and had also been unable to pay storage and duty charges of twenty thousand dollars on rail imported from England and now impounded in New York City. The Bank of Monroe then paid the duties so that track laying could continue.[30] The *Monroe Sentinel* continued to report on the story in installments:

November 25: Stock-holders and citizens along the line of this road are very much indebted to the Bank of Monroe, for the aid it has rendered and is now rendering, to secure the completion of our road. It has furnished money to carry on the work when no other bank in the State would loan a penny—a fact that must not be forgotten when the cars shall rumble into town.

December 6: By politeness of friend Graham, we paid another visit to the railroad, Tuesday. At the time we left, 4 o'clock p. m., the rail was laid half way across the trussel-work—which is half nearly a quarter of a mile in length. Today the train will run over it, and we have engaged a passage on the first car. The road is open within three-and-a-half miles of Monroe, and the work is progressing rapidly.

> December 23: We are in high feather, we are elated. We feel good. Why? Go with us a few rods towards the southern portion of the village, and we will show you two parallel iron rails leading to the east and connection with all her roads, over which the strong engine with its ribs and muscle of iron and steel, is hereafter to play back and forth like the weaver's shuttle, fetching and carrying its load of men and merchandise . . . The cars have come to town, and every day "Richland timber" [the trestle over Richland Creek] echoes the scream of locomotive. The facts that our people have paid the M.&M.R.R. Co., thousands of dollars within a few weeks, and that the Messrs Graham have laid the rail at the rate of about half a mile per day, throughout the worst month of the year, all go to demonstrate one thing, namely, that this village is to be a little world of bustle and activity, from this time henceforth; and here we make the assertion, which we will prove by-and-by, by the figures, that Monroe will be the heaviest produce station in Wisconsin.[31]

And so the railroad came to Monroe. And with its arrival, construction on the Milwaukee & Mississippi line ended.

In the Milwaukee & Mississippi's annual report for 1857, President Brodhead declared the road finished with 192 miles of mainline, 42 miles of branchline, and 28 miles of side track. The road with fencing, depots, telegraph, real estate, and rolling stock had cost $8,235,512, of which $3,674,673 had come from stockholder contributions and $4,560,839 was borrowed. Construction proper had cost $7,703,330, or $32,863 per mile—exceeding estimates, yet comparable to other railroads. In the report, the directors revealed what everyone already knew—that the railroad was in trouble:

> The past year, as is well known to you, has been one of great financial embarrassment. The railroad interest of the country, generally, has suffered severely from its effects. To these financial difficulties may be attributed, in a great measure, the increased cost of your road over previous estimates. The ruinous rates of interest, commissions, and exchange, the company have been obliged to pay, in order to carry a very large floating debt; the losses upon securities, sold to meet pressing engagements, and the sacrifice of others (pledged for temporary loans) upon forced sales, constitute large items in that increase.[32]

The directors also confessed that there was "a large amount due to employees, that has accumulated during the past four or five months," and that "during the last three

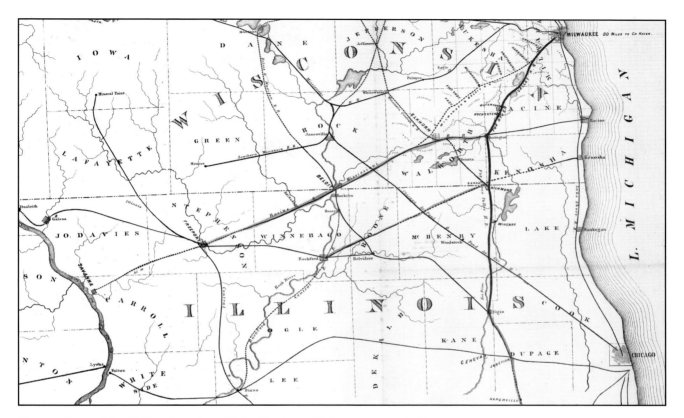

The Fox River Valley Railroad ran from Elgin, Illinois, to Richmond, near the Wisconsin state line. Its extension into Wisconsin and to Milwaukee, prominently displayed in this 1857 map, was never realized.
IMAGE COURTESY OF THE LIBRARY OF CONGRESS

months a reduction of about 20 per cent has been made in salaries of agents and clerks, and in wages of laborers . . ."[33] This despite the fact that the Milwaukee & Mississippi's net earnings in 1857, $470,617, exceeded those of the previous year.

Late in the year the Mineral Point Railroad began running its trains on a regular schedule. It left Mineral Point at 6:45 a.m. and reached Warren at 8:45 a.m. It returned leaving Warren at 9:45 a.m. and arriving back in Mineral Point at 11:45 a.m. The company did well despite the depression due to the guaranteed $56,000 it received annually from the Illinois Central and Galena and Chicago Union companies.

Most companies, however, did not fare so well. During 1856 and 1857 the Manitowoc and Mississippi Railroad Company had graded its roadway between Manitowoc and Menasha but now, like many companies responding to the financial crisis, it suspended all work.

Late in 1857 Racine and Mississippi President H. S. Durand stated what many felt to be true of the railway's immediate future:

> The fact is the state of the times for railroad operations is frightful and the prospect is dubious in the extreme. It makes no difference how low you offer securities, nobody wants them. People have been swindled so much and disappointed so often in railroad investment that they have come to regard them all as valueless.[34]

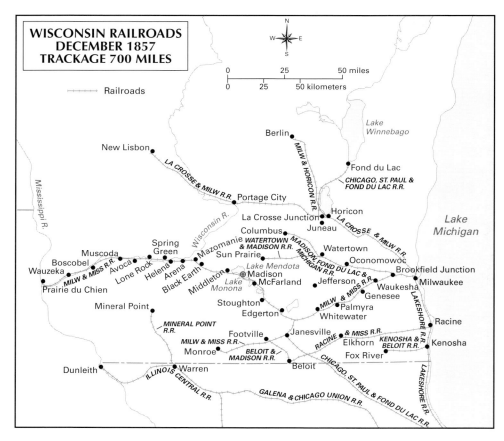

MAPPING SPECIALISTS

President Durand's statement captured the extent to which the high hopes held by most at the beginning of 1857 had fallen. Looking back, the euphoria of a Wisconsin railroad reaching the Mississippi in April had died with the economic recession that began in May. It was true that with the transstate line operating, shipping by rail quickly came to predominate shipping by steamboat as measured at Prairie du Chien and at McGregor, Iowa, on the Mississippi—but the total volume of shipping dropped dramatically. Milwaukee & Mississippi superintendent William Jervis reported at the end of 1857:

> The freighting business on the Upper Mississippi river during the past season was much larger than the previous or any former year. But the increase was all in the earlier part of the season, at the time when we were not ready for it . . . so that in reality we had only the benefit of through business about six months of the current year, when business of all kinds suffered from . . . the commercial crisis.[35]

That said, revenues were being earned on the line between Milwaukee and the Mississippi as general merchandise, coal, iron, brick, and lumber were carried westward and wheat, corn, hay, barley, oats, hides, and pork were carried eastward.

Despite the economic recession and the bank panic that had occurred in August, 192 miles of track had been laid in Wisconsin during 1857—more than in any previous year—bringing the state's total to slightly over 700 miles. Lines were extended from Boscobel to Prairie du Chien, from Midland to New Lisbon, from Watertown to Columbus and Waterloo, from Ripon to Berlin, from Janesville to Monroe, and from Darlington to Mineral Point. Through-service had been established from both Milwaukee and Chicago to the Mississippi at Prairie du Chien. But the construction of these extensions had been achieved with borrowed money, and with the decline in business, the ability of the railroads to repay that money was diminishing. The Milwaukee & Mississippi was a case in point. Knowing it could not rely on revenues to make timely payments on its debts, in September it executed a second mortgage on its entire line from Milwaukee to Prairie du Chien.[36] At the end of the year, the company reported holding capital stock of $3,674,672 and outstanding bonds (loans to the company) of $3,735,500—a balance that could not have made stockholders comfortable.

And so it was that Wisconsin's railroads arrived at the Mississippi and promptly fell into hard times.

# PART FIVE: HARD TIMES AND RECOVERY

# Chapter 20

## A Peculiar Hardship
### 1858

Wisconsin's economic depression deepened in 1858, and railroad revenues continued to fall—in fact, they were often so low that that the railroad lines could not pay the interest on their loans. When that happened, the companies fell into bankruptcy, as one, the Rock River Valley Union Railroad, already had in 1855. However, even in bankruptcy, companies kept trains running and continued to earn revenues, although not to an amount that would enable them to meet their debt obligations. At the end of 1858, Milwaukee & Mississippi President John Catlin wrote to his company's stockholders: "The year just closed has been one of great depression in this State, operating with peculiar hardship upon railroads."[1] This would indeed be a year of "peculiar hardship," one that would make or break many of Wisconsin's railways. Clearly, under such conditions, financial adjustments were called for—more borrowing, renegotiation of loans, or even sale or reorganization of railroads.[2] Adjustment was also called for in sectors beyond the financial; at the beginning of the year one railroad company was deep in the throes of a major bribery scandal whose outcome would have more financial repercussions for railroads—and for the reputation of Wisconsin.

In January the La Crosse and Milwaukee Company's alleged bribery of the previous year's legislature was brought up by Governor Alexander Randall in his inaugural speech. The governor said that the people of the state had the right to know whether their representatives could be "bought and sold like slaves in the market or like cattle in the shambles."[3] He continued, saying that

> grave charges have been made in the past year . . . [including] corrupt conduct in the Legislature. . . . Good citizens have become alarmed at such official misconduct, and the reputations of the members of that Legislature, and of the State have naturally suffered in consequence. . . . The man who would dare to approach a sworn public officer with a bribe to turn him from his honest conviction of duty, should be hunted down by the law and severely punished."[4]

The legislature agreed to investigate.

On February 4 Governor Randall wrote United States Secretary of the Interior Jacob Thompson requesting that no land patents be issued the La Crosse and Milwaukee until he could determine whether or not the company had indeed fulfilled the conditions of the grant.[5] A joint legislative committee was formed to investigate; its chairman was James H. Knowlton, the assemblyman from Janesville who had, while serving on the 1856 select committee that had disposed the grants, changed sides from supporting the La Crosse and Milwaukee to opposing it. Knowlton would do most of the interrogating himself. He subpoenaed Byron Kilbourn, the former president of the La Crosse and Milwaukee who had masterminded the alleged bribery; when Kilbourn refused to appear, Knowlton had him taken into custody, arraigned before the assembly, and cited for contempt. Kilbourn subsequently appealed to the Wisconsin Supreme Court, which upheld Knowlton and his committee.

Knowlton also cited Moses Strong for contempt and had him jailed until he agreed to testify two days later. Strong then inadvertently admitted distributing the bribes, referred to as "the package," when he testified:

> I cannot and do not pretend to any perfect recollection of the names of the persons to whom I delivered the "package." I preserved no memorandum of the matter and have nothing with which to refresh my recollection. It has been the habit of my life to make and preserve written memoranda of all events or circumstances that I desired to remember. I had no desire to remember anything about the delivery of the "package." My office for a day or two was thronged with members of

the legislature and others, who I suppose came to receive their "package." I got rid of them as soon as possible. I was acting as a ministerial officer of the company and delivered to the different members of the legislature, whose names were written upon them, and to others, the several packages in my possession. It would be invidious to mention the few, whose names accident enables me to recollect, and having already stated that I delivered all which were left at my office, I desire to be excused from making any more personal answer to this interrogatory. I delivered the "package" in person and took no voucher or receipt from any person.[6]

After questioning forty witnesses, Knowlton's committee concluded that Kilbourn, Strong, and other La Crosse company officials had distributed more than eight hundred thousand dollars worth of bonds. These bonds were distributed to fifty-nine assemblymen and thirteen senators, all of whom had voted for the company's bill, as well as former Governor Bashford, the clerks of the two houses, and others. By that time Bashford, who had cashed in fifteen thousand dollars' worth of his bonds with Kilbourn the previous April, had moved to Arizona Territory, thereby escaping the repercussions of the public outcry.[7] The committee published a fifty page report of its findings; this report had several results, foremost among them the passage of a law that prohibited officers of railroad companies from having money interests in company contracts and from disposing company securities for any but legitimate purposes—violation of which would constitute a felony and be punishable by one to five years' imprisonment.[8] Of course, the law was not retroactive; no one in this case was fined or punished. Still, the repercussions of such a case coming to trial were grave. By the time the new laws were passed, Wisconsin's reputation had been marred and the value of Wisconsin railroad securities in the East fell. The *Madison Argus and Democrat* said that the investigation

> proved what everybody knew long ago, but have done nothing about it. They wasted public funds, about $30,000, to prove people rascals, proved it, and left the rascals just where they found them.[9]

Not surprisingly, the persons named in the report did all they could to remove blame from their shoulders, including buying all the copies of the report they could find and destroying them.[10] Kilbourn was unrepentant and subsequently published a pamphlet in which he claimed that he had been forced to take such actions to counteract similar methods used by the rival Chicago, St. Paul and Fond du Lac Railroad Company. The Chicago company allegedly had fifteen legislators in its pay during that session, among them Knowlton. Knowlton's committee did not investigate the Chicago, St. Paul and Fond du Lac. Kilbourn argued that he had only acted in the best interests of Wisconsin by thwarting the Chicago company's aspirations to the grant. He asked his readers, "Suppose we had failed, and offered as an excuse that it would have cost a million dollars to have secured the grant, while at the same time by the expenditure of a million and a half, payable in its stock, the Chicago Company should have secured the prize? Would not every citizen and every stockholder have blamed us for our stupidity? Would they not have taunted us with the loss of land worth ten or twelve millions?" Whatever Kilbourn's intent, his actions had resulted in a flood of La Crosse and Milwaukee "gift" bonds on the Eastern markets in 1857 that undermined the value of all the company's securities and contributed to ultimately placing it in the hands of Eastern creditors in 1858.[11]

❖ ❖ ❖ ❖ ❖ ❖

Despite this looming setback, the La Crosse and Milwaukee continued to move forward on its lines. In April work commenced at the western end of the La Crosse and Milwaukee at La Crosse. Grading began between La Crosse and the tunnel forty miles to the east.[12] Grading between Tomah and La Crosse had begun in April, the month Nehemiah P. Stanton became the company's new president. On August 1 the company failed to pay the interest due on the bonds secured by its land grant mortgage of 1856. On August 3, still hoping to acquire the granted lands, it filed a certificate with the governor's office in Madison stating that it had completed sixty miles of land grant road between Portage City and Tomah. However, Governor Randall maintained that the law required the company to commence the construction of the land grant road at Madison and Columbus, not Portage City, and that no lands should be granted until both the Madison and the Columbus roads to Portage were complete.[13] The Department of the Interior would only grant the lands if requested by the state, so the La Crosse company was effectively blocked from receiving them. While the governor's objections were based on the stipulations in the grant, it may be assumed that he was opposed to the La Crosse company benefiting from a grant that it had obtained through underhanded methods.

On October 6 the La Crosse and Milwaukee finished its line to the Mississippi. Celebrations were held in

Governor Alexander Randall, painted by William Cogswell in 1862.
WHI IMAGE ID 2885

A La Crosse and Milwaukee train leaves Milwaukee in 1858 lithograph by Louis Kurz.
WHi Image ID 23130

La Crosse on October 14, with military, fire, and civic associations in attendance and trips to St. Paul offered by steamer. Regular service followed, with two trains leaving La Crosse at 12:30 a.m. and 6:30 a.m. for Milwaukee. Passengers taking the former train could arrive in Chicago in time for the 5:30 p.m. trains to the East, seventeen hours after leaving La Crosse.[14] The new line lacked one critical feature—at Tunnel City, forty miles east of La Crosse, there was a north-south range of hills that separated the Mississippi and Wisconsin watersheds and blocked the railroad line, but there was as yet no tunnel. Eastbound or westbound, passengers had to descend from the trains and climb or be carried with their luggage over the hills through which the tunnel was to be made. Before the year was over, the company would install a great capstan on the brow of the hill. Oxen hitched to poles would turn this enormous pulley device, which in turning, would wind the cables fastened to the cars, drawing them up the hill. Upon reaching the top, the process would be reversed to lower the cars to the tracks and waiting locomotive on the other side. This would be the working arrangement for three years until the tunnel was completed.[15]

❖ ❖ ❖ ❖ ❖ ❖

Meanwhile, the Milwaukee & Mississippi, the only railway company that could boast of a line that connected the bodies of water for which it was named, continued to lead the way in 1858—at least in terms of the way it handled its mounting debt. In February Edward H. Brodhead resigned the presidency of the company and John Catlin was called back to that office. Catlin would guide the company through its troublesome last years. For now, he borrowed money to pay back previously borrowed money, keeping the company out of bankruptcy. In March the directors executed another mortgage on all of the company's property to secure $1,800,000 worth of bonds that would be used to reduce the company's floating debt and pay off earlier bonds.[16]

The Milwaukee & Mississippi ballasted its line between Janesville and Monroe early in 1858. Trains began running on January 12, leaving Monroe at 8:15 a.m. and returning at 6:00 p.m. On January 19 the grand celebration of the opening of the line took place. From 5 a.m. to 7 a.m., Monroe shook and rattled due to the cannons being fired in the public square. A train left early that morning for Janesville, where it was joined with trains from Milwaukee and Prairie du Chien into one train that then made the trip back to Monroe. Passengers were taken on at Hanover, Orfordville, and Brodhead to number more than one thousand, with many standing in the aisles. Conductor George Church ordered the engineer to reduce speed because of the load and the still-settling road bed. Many of the passengers were frightened as the train traversed the quarter-mile-long, forty-foot-high Richland Creek trestle, just east of Monroe. The train arrived at 2:30 p.m. and was received by station agent William B. Strong and a large crowd. Although only twenty years old at this time, Strong had been with the company for three years, having previously served as station agent at Janesville, Milton, and Whitewater.[17] The *Monroe Sentinel* reported the day's events,

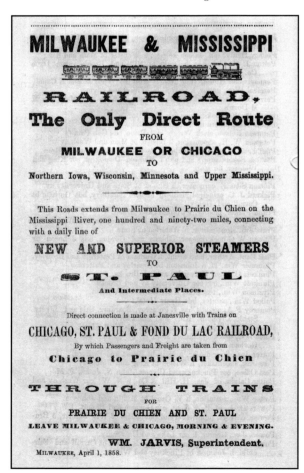

This 1858 advertisement for the Milwaukee & Mississippi boasts steam and rail service.
WHi Image ID 62123

including the train to Janesville, the combined return train, the cheerfulness of the guests, the speeches, and the fare at the American Hotel where celebrants gathered. It finished with praise for one of the company's employees:

> We cannot close without giving in our testimony to the very affable, kind and courteous manner in which Conductor Sanburn discharged all the duties of his station. He never wearied in answering the thousand questions that were given him by inquisitive folks unaccustomed to railroad travel, greeted all with same unvarying politeness, and assiduously labored for the comfort and safety of the large family he had to provide for. It is of vast importance to a railroad corporation to have obliging and courteous employees, such as we feel and know Mr. Sanburn to be, and we are twice glad that we have such upon the Southern Wisconsin Railroad [Milwaukee & Mississippi].[18]

With the route between Lake Michigan and the Mississippi complete and trains running regularly, President Catlin closed the Milwaukee & Mississippi's construction account in April. The costs of building and equipping the entire road, from Milwaukee to the Mississippi were:

| | |
|---|---|
| Iron rails, ties, and track laying | $2,168,544 |
| Grading | 1,468,856 |
| Equipment (locomotives, rolling stock, etc.) | 1,006,100 |
| Discount on bonds | 890,069 |
| Loss on hypothecated stock | 547,592 |
| Bridging | 426,419 |
| Interest | 402,504 |
| Buildings | 288,621 |
| Real estate, including depot grounds | 286,776 |
| Right of way | 220,642 |
| Original cost of Southern Wisconsin Railroad | 124,569 |
| Engineering | 98,180 |
| Discount negotiations | 94,660 |
| Salaries and expenses of directors and officers | 67,070 |
| Shop tools | 23,521 |
| Total | $8,114,126, or $34,615 per mile.[19] |

April's schedule showed that the trip from Milwaukee to Prairie du Chien took thirteen and a half hours, while traveling from Milwaukee to Monroe took seven hours. Fares varied. A ticket from Stoughton to McFarland, a distance of nine miles, cost twenty-five cents; going to Edgerton, another nine-mile journey, was thirty-five cents; and a ticket to Madison, which was sixteen miles away, cost fifty cents. Yet a ticket to Janesville, twenty-five miles away, cost one dollar, and a ticket to Milwaukee, an eighty-five mile trip, cost two dollars.[20]

Despite a steady flow of passengers, there were still complaints concerning the Milwaukee & Mississippi's transfer schedule at Milton. Milwaukee passengers felt the company was giving Chicago passengers special treatment. The *Milwaukee Free Democrat* editorialized on June 21:

> The mismanagement of this road is beyond human endurance. Milwaukee first breathed the breath of life into this road and has loaned its credit for over $530,000 to build it, and now that it is completed to the Mississippi, it is virtually a Chicago road, controlled by Chicago interests, and runs to Janesville half the time as a branch of the Chicago & St. Paul road, and passengers are duped there and compelled to lie over for the Chicago train. The Milwaukee trains east and west that connect with the boats on the Mississippi from St. Paul, and the upper towns, stop at Janesville *five* hours, while the Chicago trains go straight through. By this Chicago arrangement, passengers can start from Chicago some five or six hours later than from Milwaukee, and reach Prairie du Chien at the same time, and passengers from Prairie du Chien reach Chicago before the train leaves Janesville for Milwaukee. The result is, nearly all the trade of Minnesota and Iowa, which would naturally come to this city goes to Chicago, because it can go there directly. And the citizens have the satisfaction of seeing the road, which they have been mainly instrumental in getting built, act as a feeder to Chicago. We venture to say that if a Chicago railroad had treated Chicago as shabbily as this road is now treating Milwaukee, public meetings would have been promptly called, to devise some remedy.[21]

The company at this time decided to compare its service between Chicago and La Crosse (they actually compared the Chicago, St. Paul and Fond du Lac railroad from Chicago to Janesville, the Milwaukee & Mississippi railroad from Janesville to Prairie du Chien, and contracted steamboats on the Mississippi from Prairie du Chien to La Crosse) to that of its competitor, the La Crosse and Milwaukee (the Lakeshore Railroad from Chicago to Milwaukee and the La Crosse and Milwaukee Railroad from Milwaukee to La Crosse). In December constructing engineer Benjamin Edgerton measured the distance a steamboat would have to travel between Prairie du Chien and La Crosse on the Mississippi and found it to be sixty-five miles. The directors then compared the two routes between Chicago and La Crosse:

From Chicago via Janesville to Prairie du Chien . . . 230 miles. Thence to La Crosse by Miss. River 65 miles. Total 295 miles [via Milwaukee & Mississippi]. . . . From Chicago via Milwaukee & La Crosse road, 285 miles [via La Crosse and Milwaukee]. Savings of distance by La Crosse road, 10 miles.

The time . . . between Chicago and La Crosse . . . at twenty miles per hour including stops, is [as follows]. . . . From Chicago to Prairie du Chien, 11.5 hours. Thence to La Crosse by boat, 4 hours. Total 15.5 hours [using the Milwaukee & Mississippi]. . . . Time via Mil. & La Crosse, 14.25 hours miles [using the La Crosse and Milwaukee] . . . making no allowance for . . . transporting passengers by teams, from the Lake Shore railroad to the La Crosse road . . . say three quarters of an hour.

The fact is that whatever difference of opinion there may be as to the real time saved by the La Crosse road, it, at all events, is so small, that that road can never make a connection at Chicago that cannot be made by the Milwaukee & Mississippi road via Janesville, as in all probability through trains will never leave Chicago for the east within an hour of each other, and therefore, for all practical purposes, the time is the same.[22]

❖ ❖ ❖ ❖ ❖ ❖

Per new governmental regulations, the tenth annual report of the Milwaukee & Mississippi Railroad Company listed any accidents involving injuries or death that the company had been involved in that year. Two casualties were reported that spring. On March 30 Matthew Connell, a switchman in the yard at Milwaukee, attempted to cross the track as an engine was backing; he tripped and was run over, dying two days later from his injuries. On April 23 fireman Joseph Westbury was killed at Waukesha while attempting to board a moving engine.[23] Several more accidents were reported that summer and fall, as the report detailed:

On the 19th of June, an Irish boy in attempting to jump from a freight car, where he had secreted himself, fell upon the track, and was run over and killed as the train was starting from Janesville Station.

On the 14th of July, Matthew Sullivan was killed at Milwaukee while engaged loading lumber into a car. The train was backing towards him, and failing to get out of the way, he was knocked down and run over by a freight car.

On the 14th of July, the passenger train ran into a wagon on road crossing, near Middleton Station. The driver, name unknown, was slightly injured.

On the 25th of August, a woman was killed in attempting to cross the track ahead of a passenger train at a road crossing one mile west of Madison. She was in a wagon drawn by two horses, driven by her son. Whistle was sounded and bell rang as usual.

On the 23d of November, Lorenzo Wiltzer, a brakeman, was struck by a road bridge, two miles east of Palmyra, and so injured that he survived but four hours. He was standing at the time upon the top of the baggage car.

On the 11th of December, Jacob Snyder was killed about one mile west of Genesee. He was leading a cow along the track. After the engine passed, the cow was struck by a car, and the man was thrown under the train and instantly killed.[24]

The report also listed the cost of these casualties, followed by final commentary:

The amount of loss to the company from casualty, is $421.25.

Whole number killed 7, of whom 3 were employees of this company, (passengers none), and 4 persons not in the employ of this company. Of the above casualties, none resulted from the carelessness of employees of this company.[25]

As accidents such as these became a more regular occurrence, safety was becoming a bigger concern for all the rail lines. Following the current trends of other railways, the Mineral Point company had strict regulations regarding safety and speed. Instructions stated that "[t]rains must be run at such speed as to enable the mail to be exchanged at Stations where there are Post-offices" and required trains to "[r]educe speed to eight miles per hour over all Bridges, and Trestle work, and shut off Steam and close ash pan." It also provided the following directions concerning signals:

1st. One Red Flag by day, or one Red Light by night, carried upon an engine, indicates that another engine is following, which engine will be allowed all the rights and privileges of the engine bearing such.

2nd. Two Red Flags by day, or two Red Lanterns by night, carried upon an engine, indicate that another engine or train is following, which must be treated as part of the forward train. No train, after meeting two flags or Lanterns upon an engine, will leave the station where it meets the two Flags or Lanterns so carried, until the flagged train arrives, or is positively heard from.

3rd. It must be distinctly understood that when such Flags or Lights are carried, the train for which they are carried must be in sight at every station. If it is not in sight, then the forward train must leave a written communication to that effect for the following train with the station agent, and then the following train must run under the rule of signals.

4th. A Red Flag by day, or Lantern by night, waved upon the track, signifies that a train must come to a full stop.

# A PECULIAR HARDSHIP

5th. A stationary Red Flag signifies that the track is not in perfect order, and must be run over with great caution.

6th. Two Red Signal Lights must be exhibited on the rear of each Passenger train in the night time and one on Freight trains, until the train arrives at its destination.

7th. One puff of the steam whistle is a signal to Brake; two puffs is the signal to loose the brakes; three puffs is the signal to back; five or more rapid puffs is the signal for Wooding up, or calling in Signal men stationed out on the road.

8th. A Lantern swung over the head is the signal to go forward; raised and lowered perpendicularly, to stop; swung sideways, to back.[26]

The revenues of the Mineral Point Railroad fell sharply during the year. This was due to the poor economy, a poor wheat harvest, and the failing lead mines. During the year the Mineral Point had carried ten million pounds of freight and nine thousand passengers. The revenues more than met operating expenses but fell short of paying the interest on the company's loans—a common fate for many of the railroads that year.

At the end of 1858 it was obvious to Milwaukee & Mississippi President Catlin that his company would not be able to pay the half a million dollars in interest that it owed at that time—this despite the fact that the Milwaukee & Mississippi had transported over two million bushels of wheat during the year. The company's annual report for 1858, like those of all other Wisconsin railroad companies, followed a new format required by Wisconsin law:

*First.* The whole length of the road in operation is 234 41/100 miles.
*Second.* The amount of capital actually subscribed is 38,556 shares, $3,855,600.
*Third.* The whole cost of the road is $8,114,126.43.
*Fourth.* The amount of indebtedness is 4,809,852.64.
*Fifth.* The amount due the corporation on bills, accounts, &c., is $61,141.56.
*Sixth.* The amount received for transportation is as follows: $883,186.02.
*Seventh.* The amount expended for the year is as follows:

| | |
|---|---|
| Operating costs and salaries | 443,242.49 |
| Interest on debts | 487,321.96 |
| Interest on Construction accounts; sinking fund | 330,945.18 |
| Total | $1,261,509.63 |

*Eighth.* No dividends have been paid or declared during the year.

*Ninth.* The number of passengers transported and rate of fare is as follows:
Through passengers, 24,829. Rate per mile, 3.03 cents.
Way passengers, 143,081. Rate per mile, 3.40 cents.

*Tenth.* The amount of freight transported over the road during the year is 163,917 tons.[27]

❖ ❖ ❖ ❖ ❖ ❖

The fate of smaller companies such as the Mineral Point Railroad—and uncertainty over the larger ones—was of central concern as the financial crisis deepened. Many railways were making changes due to the financial crisis. Earlier in the year the Beloit and Madison had made arrangements with the Milwaukee & Mississippi to allow use of its tracks between Hanover Junction (Plymouth) and Janesville. This agreement went into effect on May 17. Galena trains now left Chicago at 9:30 a.m. and 5:00 p.m., arriving at Janesville at 2:40 p.m. and 10:00 p.m., respectively. Return trains left Janesville at 12:00 a.m. and 11:30 a.m., arriving in Chicago at 5:30 a.m. and 4:20 p.m., respectively. The Galena trains shared the Janesville depot with those of the Milwaukee & Mississippi and the Chicago, St. Paul, and Fond du Lac. Despite these arrangements, the Beloit and Madison would not be able to meet its obligations in 1858. It continued to lease the finished portion of its line to the Galena and Chicago Union Railroad Company, which responded to the hard times by dropping the Chicago-Beloit passenger fare from $3.00 to $2.35.

The investors of the Chicago, St. Paul, and Fond du Lac were also suffering. Henry Southwell of Fort Atkinson commented:

> This road, like most other roads, was built to develop the country and relied on the country filling up to give it support. Failing to get this, the road was forced into bankruptcy. The bonds sold at 30 cents and the stocks at 5 cents on the dollar.
>
> Farm mortgages and town bonds given for stock were put up as collateral to the Company's notes and sold out at a small percent of their face value. Most of the Towns repudiated their bonds and judge Nagle of the circuit court declared the farm mortgages given for stock illegal and uncollectable.
>
> From the panic of 1857 to the civil war, farm products were low in price and general business very dull. Failures were a common occurrence and labor commanded very low price.[28]

Meanwhile, Fond du Lac trains, like those of Wisconsin's other troubled lines, continued to run and earn revenues.

❖ ❖ ❖ ❖ ❖ ❖

The Chicago, St. Paul and Fond du Lac responded to the crisis by becoming more competitive. In October it began extending its tracks north from Janesville. They crossed those of the Milwaukee & Mississippi at what would be called Milton Junction, one mile west of Milton. There, on the northwest quadrant of the crossing, Mr. G. W. Mathews erected a small, one-story frame house, which he opened as a depot and hotel. Several of the Irish railroad workers' families settled at the junction and established the village of West Milton (Milton Junction). While the road was being constructed, an engine went through a bridge over Otter creek and sank in the quicksand. It was never recovered.[29] Meanwhile, work began at Fond du Lac to extend the road to Oshkosh, and that extension was completed by the end of the year.[30]

In June the Kenosha, Rockford & Rock Island began using a two-story, forty-foot-long boarding-house car for its workers on the line. The company had begun operating twelve miles of track out of Kenosha at the beginning of the year and had purchased more rails earlier in the spring. It ran its first passenger train on July 5, a special, taking Kenoshans to the Independence Day celebrations at the Linus Woodworth farm in Bristol Township. The thirteen-car train made four additional runs that day, stopping at all stations, a round-trip ticket costing 25 cents. On one of these runs the train carried one thousand passengers. There were more excursions that summer, one taking a large group of school children to Bristol for an outing. More rails arrived at Kenosha in mid-July. The company advertised for one hundred laborers, and track laying resumed. The rails of the Kenosha, Rockford & Rock Island reached Silver Lake in mid-September and Fox River at the end of the month, where they stopped because the bridge was not finished. The bridge was completed in November, and rails were laid for a few more miles before the supply ran out.

At about this same time the Galena & Chicago Union Railroad decided to demonstrate that its new Chicago-Janesville service was better than the Chicago, St. Paul, and Fond du Lac's. Janesville was at this time becoming a major hub. On June 5 an observer noted rail cars in the yards belonging to eight different companies—the Milwaukee & Mississippi; the Chicago, St. Paul, and Fond du Lac; the Galena and Chicago Union; the Racine & Mississippi; the Milwaukee and Watertown; the Chicago, Burlington and Quincy Illinois Central; and the Fox River Valley. As author D. C. Prescott explains, each of these companies wanted to dominate:

> About this time the Chicago & Galena Union R. R. looked with covetous eyes upon this St. Paul business, and proceeded hurriedly to arrange a connection for

the purpose of gathering in a share of it. To that end they built a line from Belvidere to Janesville, meeting the Milwaukee & Mississippi road at that place and coming in on the opposite side of the same depot occupied by the Fond du Lac road and the M. & M. road. They advertised extensively their ability to put trains into Janesville as quickly as the Fond du Lac, though they had some twelve miles further to run; still with this handicap they lowered the scheduled time usually made by the Fond du Lac road, and a train hauled by a big engine called the Whirling Thunder started in on the run. The Fond du Lac train leaving Chicago at the same time arrived thirty minutes ahead, and the boys lined up on the platform to welcome the Galena train. It came in with a scream and a rush and a roar, rounding the curve at full speed, fetching up at the depot almost with a bang. The engineer hauled his lever over to reverse and applied steam in order to stop at the depot. It was a great event and the Fond du Lac boys cheered; but the scheme did not work; the Galena did not have an engine that could turn its wheels fast enough to make the run as advertised, and they did not get the business; but it caused lively railroading, as will be understood.[31]

The Kenosha, Rockford & Rock Island inaugurated regular service from Kenosha on December 7. The end of the tracks now lay two miles beyond the Fox River bridge. Its train, consisting of ten new freight cars and one new passenger car, would leave Kenosha at 5:00 p.m., stay overnight, and leave Wheatland Township the following morning at 8:00 a.m. Westbound freight could be routed to Milwaukee or Chicago, the cars being transferred onto the Milwaukee & Chicago track in Kenosha and reaching their destination the same day. Sadly, the company ended its first week of service with a derailment. On December 11 the eastbound train went off the tracks one mile west of the Fox River bridge. The locomotive and twelve cars of wood stayed on the track, but the freight car and the passenger car derailed. Brakeman Harry Clark, who had been riding on top of the freight car, was shaken up but soon recovered. The passengers were unhurt.

Despite a few success stories, the forecast for the rest of the railroad industry and its partners was grim. By 1858 nearly four thousand Wisconsin farmers had mortgaged their farms to buy railroad stock. Eastern investors had loaned the money and held these mortgages. Railroad companies with reduced revenues were defaulting on their loans and the value of their stock was plummeting. The Eastern creditors now began to foreclose. Faced with losing their farms, Wisconsin's farmers blamed the railroads,

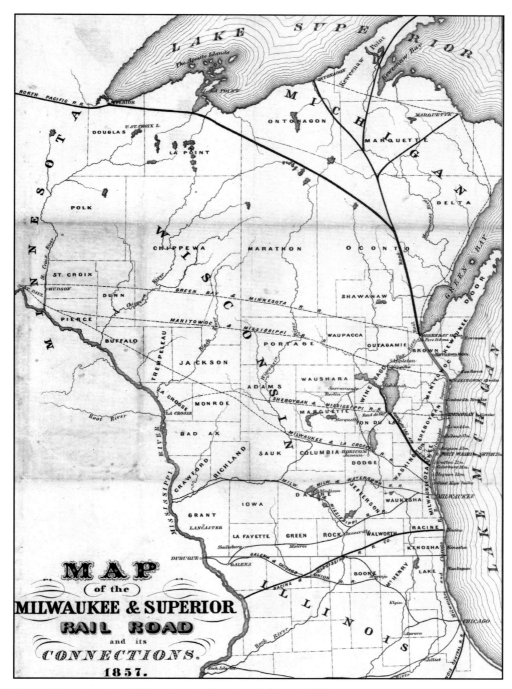

Map of the completed Milwaukee & Superior Railroad, 1857.
IMAGE COURTESY OF THE LIBRARY OF CONGRESS

whom they claimed had misled them into mortgaging their farms. They cited excessive freight rates, mismanagement, corruption, and fraud. They claimed that railroad directors had watered down stock, misused corporate funds, and contracted with construction firms in which they held an interest. The Milwaukee and Superior and Milwaukee and Beloit companies had actually dissipated all of their money without laying a single mile of track.[32]

Farm foreclosures were often met with resistance. Local officials delayed proceedings. As a last resort, mortgagor's friends and neighbors sometimes packed foreclosure sales to intimidate prospective bidders. Wisconsin's legislators aided this effort by passing a law that delayed actual foreclosure for at least a year and another law that stopped foreclosure proceedings altogether when a mortgagor proved that he had signed his note because of "fraudulent representations by the railroad agent." In 1858 and for some time following, these laws gave farmers relief.[33]

It was an odd state of affairs: railroads were in bankruptcy and farmers were losing their farms, yet so much wheat was flowing into Milwaukee by the fall of 1858 that new methods for handling it were needed. Earlier in the year the Board of Trade and the Corn Exchange had consolidated to form Milwaukee's Chamber of Commerce, which had implemented improved grading and weighing standards. This year saw the first large grain elevators erected in Milwaukee that were specifically designed to handle wheat shipped in bulk (not bagged) by rail. L. J. Higby built the first such elevator on the Milwaukee & Mississippi property on the Menomonee River. It had a capacity of fifty thousand bushels, which soon proved inadequate. Angus Smith built a giant grain elevator to serve the La Crosse and Milwaukee line on the Milwaukee River at Chestnut Street. Smith's elevator, when finished, would have a capacity of four hundred thousand bushels and would be able to receive and ship one hundred thousand bushels per day.[34] Gone were the days when commission buyers met farmers coming into town to purchase wheat on the wagons. Now they assembled each morning at Higby's warehouse, where they traded, then made the rounds to the other warehouses. In the afternoon they would take care of paper work, but after supper they would be found in the lobby of the Newhall House, buying and selling again.[35]

An 1858 advertisement for the Racine & Mississippi Railroad.
WHi Image ID 62095

The Watertown and Madison tried to save their company with a second mortgage in 1857.
WHI IMAGE ID 38559

By the end of the year, as financial reports started to be filed, the repercussions of the financial downturn became clear in the number of railways that were forced to sell or close. On October 1 the Watertown and Madison Railroad Company was sold by the court to Russell Sage of New York. The company had defaulted on its debt payments in January and a trustee for the bondholders had filed for foreclosure on April 21. On October 12 Sage "quit-claimed" the property to the Milwaukee, Watertown and Baraboo Valley Railroad Company, which owned the Brookfield Junction–Watertown–Columbus and the Watertown-Waterloo lines. On December 20 that company leased those lines back to the La Crosse and Milwaukee. The Racine and Mississippi had only laid a few miles of track in 1858. On December 3 the bondholders of its 1855 mortgage filed suit to foreclose the company's Wisconsin property from Racine to Beloit. The Milwaukee and Horicon, along with its partner in operation, the La Crosse and Milwaukee, had defaulted on interest payments on its bonds in 1858. A receiver was appointed on behalf of its bondholders and several lawsuits were filed to foreclose the different trust deeds given to secure their bonds.

The Wisconsin Central Railroad Company had also failed. It had finished most of the grading between Geneva and Whitewater in 1857 and its officers had already placed orders for the rails when the bottom fell out due to the recession. The company would build no more. A two-mile spur of rail had been built southward from the line's junction with the Milwaukee & Mississippi in Whitewater to receive the rails when they arrived from the East over the latter line. But the spur would remain unused and would eventually be disassembled by one of the company's creditors.[36]

The continuing depression, along with its attendant bankruptcies, unemployment, the evaporation of travel for pleasure, and reduced demand for merchandise and lumber, had taken an incredible toll on Wisconsin's railroads in 1858. Almost all of them—the Milwaukee & Mississippi; the La Crosse and Milwaukee; the Milwaukee and Horicon; the Mineral Point; the Chicago, St. Paul, and Fond du Lac; the Watertown and Madison; the Racine and Mississippi; and the Wisconsin Central—had defaulted on loan payments and now faced foreclosure.[37] The state legislature had contributed to these problems by chartering competing railroads in the same region or along the same route. A case in point was the extension of the charter of the Milwaukee and Watertown Railroad in 1856, which allowed that company to build from Watertown to Madison and then to the Mississippi. Although the company wasn't actually prepared to build such a route at that time, the authorization highlighted the fact that this proposed route was twenty-two miles less from Milwaukee to Madison and fifty miles less from Milwaukee to the Mississippi than the Milwaukee & Mississippi's lines. This information permanently damaged the latter company's credit and lowered the value of its stocks and bonds, contributing, ultimately, to its bankruptcy. However, it was the national state of depression, more than any other factor, which caused Wisconsin's railroads to fail.

Still, there was a bright side amidst all this bad news. In 1858, despite the nation's financial struggles, there had been construction, and trains were kept running. The La Crosse and Milwaukee had completed its line to the Mississippi (the line that would carry Chicago–Twin Cities Amtrak trains 150 years later), and the Kenosha, Rockford & Rock Island opened twenty-two miles of its line out of Kenosha in December. Sixty-one miles of track had been laid in Wisconsin during the year, bringing the state's total to 762.

# Chapter 21

## Reorganization
### 1859

The depression that had crippled Wisconsin's economy for two long years reached a tipping point in 1859, when several major railroads defaulted on their loans and were forced to declare themselves bankrupt or sell, paving the way for new ownership. Their stories followed a similar pattern: as railroads continued to default on the interest payments of their bonded debts, Eastern creditors or bondholders took steps to recover the money they had loaned out. They filed suits in the courts of the state of Wisconsin to foreclose on the different trust deeds or mortgages that the railroad companies had given to secure their bonds. After issuing decrees of foreclosure and sale, the court would auction the railroad's property. Invariably, the purchaser would be a representative of, or an association of, the bondholders that had filed suit. As new owners, they held the power and privileges previously enjoyed by the former executives and directors. Section 1, Chapter 121 of the general laws of the state of Wisconsin stated that the new owners

> should exercise and enjoy thereafter all and the same rights, privileges, grants, franchises, immunities and advantages . . . which belonged to and were enjoyed by the company making such trust deed or mortgage . . . and that such purchasers, their associates, successors or assigns might proceed to organize anew and elect directors, distribute and dispose of the stock, take the same or another name, and

conduct their business generally and in the manner provided in the charter of such railroad company.¹

The stock in the reorganized company was then distributed by giving the former bondholders an amount equivalent to what had been owed them (thereby making sure they suffered no financial loss), while the former stockholders of the old company divided whatever was left. The latter group's loss was the result of their borrowing more than they could repay, a bitter pill to swallow for many who had invested heavily or against good judgment. The beauty of these procedures was that the reorganized companies were virtually debt free.

Though not every railroad was forced to sell and reorganize, many of the companies that had laid the first tracks in Wisconsin did find themselves under new ownership—and operating under new names—by the end of the year. In a few cases this led to expanded, not diminished, dividends—an unexpected but welcome effect of turnover. Despite those few cases, the economic depression in Wisconsin would continue through the year, exacerbated by another difficult winter and spring. It wouldn't begin to lift until the following year, and would still be lingering at the beginning of the Civil War in 1861.

Credit must be given to the people who kept the trains running during these hard economic times. Railroad presidents, board members, investors, lenders, shippers, and passengers all did their part, but it was the employees of the railroads—station and shop hands, line-maintenance workers, and train crews—who deserved the most thanks. Then, as now, they often worked long hours in uncomfortable and dangerous conditions to keep people and freight moving over the line. Author D. C. Prescott described the trying conditions on the Chicago, St. Paul and Fond du Lac Railroad during the winter of 1858 to 1859:

> The winters of those years were longer and colder, there was then more snow to contend with. There were no such things as overshoes or underclothing as we now have. Vulcanized rubber goods and machine knit wearing apparel were unknown then. Railroad men wore cowhide boots in winter with two or three pairs of woolen socks (hand knit) inside of them, although Mr. Tarrant always held that a man's feet would be warmest with no socks on at all. Then they wore at least two pairs of pants, two or three blue flannel shirts, blue drilling overalls and shirts, buckskin mittens, cloth caps, and any old thing for a coat.²

One awful winter these Fond du Lac men had a terrible time. A storm set in and raged nearly a week, a blizzard with the mercury way below zero. Every road was blocked, and there was little use in trying to put a train through. As quickly, however, as it was thought wise four engines were coupled and pushed out up the line with a snow plow attached ahead. They were nearly a week in getting through to Janesville. They left the engine, Walter S. Gurnee, partly on its side in the ditch at Crystal Lake, and the N. K. Wheeler in the ditch between Shopierre and Janesville. It was too cold to do anything more than to blow them out, shove the track over and run around them. The other engines had to be kept alive all the time to prevent freezing, and at night had to run out on the road to pump up water into the boilers. The men had little sleep, not much food, and were very cold. At work these engines would back off a mile, and when all was ready they ran for the snow drifts, going a mile a minute when they struck; and as they went in every damper and every throttle was closed; it was like going into a great cushion. Of course that snow flew, and when the avalanche stopped and the snow settled so one could see, the engineers poked their heads out to inquire if all was well along the line, and if so all would reverse and go back a mile for another onward rush. Just think of a week's work like this. Other engines were sent to replace those in the ditch.[3]

❖ ❖ ❖ ❖ ❖ ❖

The Chicago, St. Paul and Fond du Lac had defaulted on its interest payments in 1858 and was for all purposes bankrupt at the beginning of 1859. Its bonds were selling at thirty cents on the dollar, and its stocks at five cents on the dollar. In February the Illinois legislature authorized the sale and reorganization of the company in Illinois, and a few weeks later Wisconsin's legislature followed suit. L. B. Caswell, a Fort Atkinson businessman, attended a meeting of the Chicago, St. Paul and Fond du Lac Railroad Company in New York City in March at which the stockholders and creditors allowed that company to die and the Chicago and North Western Railway Company to rise from its ashes:

> Charles Butler . . . the Treasurer of the late company . . . called . . . a meeting . . . to see if a new company could not be organized to go on and construct the unbuilt portion of the road and if possible realize something on the old stock, now considered worthless. . . . There were just five of us that answered the call. . . . Everyone . . . except the five mentioned, were so completely discouraged, that they did not risk the expense of the journey. We sat down around the table at number four Wall Street. Charles Butler took up his pen to write, he hardly knew what. He finally said and wrote with his pen: We, the stockholders and creditors of the late

Chicago, St. Paul and Fond du Lac Railroad Company, do hereby organize and constitute a new railway company for the purpose of completing the road already begun; and the stockholders of said old company shall be entitled to sixty per cent of their old stock, in the new company, and the creditors shall be entitled to forty per cent of the new stock for their claim against said old company. . . . Then came the question of a name for the new company. . . . Finally someone said, name it the Chicago and North Western Railway Company. All agreed to this. We separated leaving Charles Butler to complete the organization; but that was all we expected it would amount to, the interest taken in the enterprise was so small.[4]

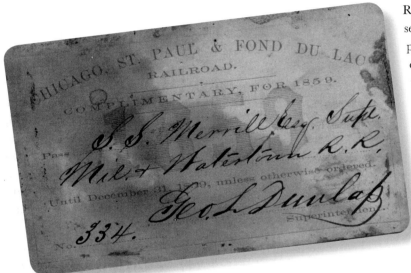

Chicago, St. Paul & Fond du Lac Railroad ticket issued to Sherburn S. Merrill, superintendent of the Milwaukee and Watertown Railroad from 1857 to 1862.
WHi Image ID 62556

The signal to proceed with the Chicago and North Western Railway Company was given by the legislatures of Illinois and Wisconsin on February 19 and March 14, respectively.

On June 7 the Chicago and North Western Railway Company was organized in Janesville. It occurred as a result of the sale of the Chicago, St. Paul and Fond du Lac on June 2. The latter had been sold by the trustees for the bondholders to Samuel J. Tilden and O. D. Ashley for $10,849,938, paid in stocks and bonds. William B. Ogden, who had been the president of the Chicago, St. Paul and Fond du Lac, was now elected the first president of the Chicago and North Western. E. W. Hutchins, G. M. Bartholomew, Charles Butler, Thomas H. Perkins, Mahlon D. Ogden, A. C. Courtney, Henry Smith, J. R. Young, J. R. Pease, M. C. Darling, and Albert Winslow constituted the board of directors. Tilden and Ashley proposed that the former bondholders—who now owned forty percent of the new company—advance six hundred thousand dollars with which to place the company on a paying basis.

The new company had ninety-eight miles of road in service between Chicago and Milton Junction and fifty more miles from Minnesota Junction to Oshkosh, with a fifty-mile gap in between. The bondholders advanced the money and the company began closing that gap, with crews working from both ends. The track between Minnesota Junction and Fond du Lac, which had been laid by the Rock River Valley Union in 1852, was changed from broad gauge to standard, as was the locomotive Winnebago and the northern division's rolling stock—the hope being that a through railroad between Oshkosh and Chicago might be realized within the year.[5]

❖ ❖ ❖ ❖ ❖ ❖

On February 1 the La Crosse and Milwaukee company defaulted on its interest payments on the mortgage organized by trustee William Barnes made in June of the prior year. Seven days later the Wisconsin Legislature passed an act that allowed the trustee of a railroad mortgage to become the purchaser for the benefit of the bondholders at any sale of the railroad on the mortgage of which he was trustee. On February 11, Barnes, the trustee who was behind this measure, foreclosed on the mortgage given him by the La Crosse and Milwaukee. The company's property was then advertised for sale at public auction in the city of Milwaukee. On May 21 it was purchased by Barnes for the benefit of the bondholders for $1,593,333.33, which was 75 percent of what was due on the bonds. No money was exchanged, the payment being made in bonds. On May 23 the bondholders filed articles of organization under Chapter 79 of the statutes of Wisconsin to organize the Milwaukee & Minnesota Railroad Company and transferred to that company the entire property of the La Crosse and Milwaukee that had been mortgaged to Barnes. Russell Sage of New York was elected president of the Milwaukee & Minnesota. Although this new corporation owned the property, Selah Chamberlain continued in his lease to operate the line and apply all profits toward what was still owed him. As long as this situation continued, the Milwaukee & Minnesota company would not be able to earn a profit.

On May 25 two rather meaningless elections were held for the now propertyless La Crosse and Milwaukee Railroad Company. Newcomb Cleveland, the contractor who had been forcibly expelled from the property in a labor dispute in 1856, was elected president by one group. The other faction of stockholders elected Daniel Wells Jr. of Milwaukee. But with nothing but a company on paper to work with, their reactionary efforts soon stopped. Neither board ever met again. The records and books of the La Crosse and Milwaukee company were kept by Dwight W. Keyes, who was both Chamberlain's bookkeeper and the Milwaukee & Minnesota's secretary.

❖ ❖ ❖ ❖ ❖ ❖

The Milwaukee & Mississippi, realizing it too would soon be defaulting on its interest payments, prepared itself for change. In February the company's stockholders elected a new board of directors that included many "old timers." Hercules

Dousman of Prairie du Chien, the wealthiest man in Wisconsin, had been on the board since 1853. Nelson Dewey, who had been the first governor of the state of Wisconsin, had served since 1855. George H. Walker, former two-term mayor of Milwaukee, had served since 1852. And Joseph Goodrich, Erastus B. Walcott, and Edward D. Holton had served since the beginning of the company in 1849. The new board reelected John Catlin to the presidency of the company.

The Milwaukee & Mississippi—now in competition with the La Crosse and Milwaukee/Milwaukee & Minnesota for the Mississippi River trade to St. Paul and the trans-Mississippi trade to Iowa and Minnesota—strengthened its water connections. In the summer, it purchased Alexander McGregor's steam ferry, used for ferrying freight and passengers across the Mississippi between Prairie du Chien and McGregor, Iowa. With this purchase, the Milwaukee & Mississippi effectively terminated on the western side of the Mississippi. The company also made arrangements to operate director Dousman's magnificent steamboat, the *Alamakkee*, between Prairie du Chien and St. Paul. This action affirmed its belief that it could compete in the Chicago–St. Paul trade with its competitor upriver at La Crosse.

For seven years Milwaukee's railroads had been at a disadvantage with Chicago's railroads when it came to transporting passengers and freight to the East. With Lake Michigan as a barrier, Milwaukee's eastbound traffic had to go south through Chicago before going east. But now steamships became a factor in the Milwaukee & Mississippi's bid to compete with Chicago as a center of trade with the East. For a number of years, the Milwaukee & Mississippi had been waiting for the Detroit & Milwaukee Railroad Company to finish its line across the lower peninsula of Michigan and to extend it with ferries across the lake to Milwaukee. On August 31 the editor of the *Milwaukee Sentinel* heralded the arrival of the *Detroit* and the *Milwaukee*, two large, ocean-class steamers that finalized the connection. Designed by H. O. Perry and built at Buffalo, New York, by the Mason and Bidwell company, these 1,100-ton vessels were powered by both sail and steam and were the only ocean-style steamships with side-paddlewheels on the Great Lakes. The editor predicted that

> a large share of travel to and from the Northwest . . . hitherto gone by way of Chicago, will henceforth follow the more direct route through Milwaukee, across Lake Michigan and over the Detroit and Milwaukee and Great Western Railways. . . . [It is] clearly the interest of our business men to give this route the bulk of their patronage.[6]

The Detroit & Milwaukee's lake-and-land route to the East had been the hope of several Milwaukee-based railroads for competing with Chicago for the trade of the Eastern states. In the fall the first shipment of grain from Minnesota to the East arrived at Prairie du Chien. It was loaded onto ten of the Milwaukee and Mississippi's cars and taken to Milwaukee.

Steam service proved to be a good move for the railway, garnering the attention of newspapers far and near. In December, the Prairie du Chien *Leader* noted that the inventor Norman Wiard of New York would be bringing the *Lady Franklin*, a twenty-passenger water-and-ice steamboat to work the Milwaukee & Mississippi's Prairie du Chien–St. Paul service division in winter:

> His twenty-passenger boat can be raised or lowered, while in motion or at rest, to . . . pass through . . . snow of three feet. . . . It is an amphibious machine. . . . It can be run off the ice at a speed of twenty miles an hour into the water with safety; and it can propel itself across the water to contact with the ice on the other side, and get out upon the ice and be put again in operation without any material delay. It is, also, almost danger-proof; for, if it should be thrown into the water by accident, on its side, or even bottom up, it would right itself instantly; and about thirty holes would have to be broken in the hull before it could be sunk, even if it were full of water.[7]

Former Milwaukee & Mississippi grounds in Milwaukee, circa 1865. From left to right are freight house no. 1, the 1850 depot, and the freight office (three buildings from the depot). Behind the depot are the shops building and roundhouse.
WHI Image ID 24900

At the end of the year Milwaukee & Mississippi President Catlin addressed the stockholders of his company, commenting on the competition their company faced and its effects:

During the past year, the Racine and Mississippi road has been opened to Freeport, forming connection with the North-Western and the Illinois Central Roads, thus opening another route to the Mississippi River. The Milwaukee, Watertown and Baraboo Valley Railroad has been extended to Sun Prairie, within twelve miles of Madison. The Chicago and North-Western Road has also been opened during the year from Janesville through to Oshkosh. These roads *indirectly*, and, at points, *directly*, come in competition with your road, and tend to reduce rates and divert business. The worst effect of competition, however, is in the reduction of rates.[8]

The year 1859 was not without its tragedies for the Milwaukee & Mississippi. In March Conductor George E. Price died of injuries suffered at Milton on the Milwaukee & Mississippi's Janesville branch. On Monday evening, March 7, Price was in charge of a train that consisted of a single, occupied passenger car pushed by a locomotive from Janesville to Milton, there to be joined to the train going to Milwaukee. As the locomotive pushed the car round the curve at Milton, Price, partially blinded by the setting sun, noticed an unexpected platform car loaded with lumber sitting on the track. Price stood by his station, immediately setting the hand brake of his car to slow it and the pushing locomotive down. But his efforts came too late. The train slammed into the lumber car with an explosive sound. All twenty-five passengers were thrown from their seats, but none suffered more than minor injuries. Price, at the front of the car, was hurled into the lumber car, suffering extensive injuries. He died two weeks later. Funeral services were held in Janesville on Friday, March 25. Three special mourning trains, draped in black, arrived from Milwaukee—no fares were charged. Descending from these trains were President John Catlin, Superintendents William Jervis, Sherbourne S. Merrill, and many other officers of the company. The pallbearers that day were D. A. Olin, L. B. Rock, E. C. Brown, George Redington, E. J. Sweet, George Church, George Sandborn, and William B. Strong.

George Price had often expressed his love of the countryside along the line at North Prairie, and had said that when he died he wished to be buried there. This wish was honored, and his body was taken on board one of the mourning trains to North Prairie. There he was buried on railroad property. A monument with a ten-foot marble shaft and a railway coach engraved at the base was paid for and erected by his friends. On it was the simple inscription:

GEORGE E. PRICE
DIED AT MILTON MARCH 23, 1859
LATE CONDUCTOR ON M AND M RR[9]

A more lighthearted story comes from the residents who lived near Fulton Station. Inhabitants of the Rock River region had been requesting the company to change the name of Fulton Station. A committee decided to name the station "Edgerton," after Benjamin H. Edgerton, the company's constructing engineer; the committee then thought to ask his permission. When asked if he objected, Edgerton replied, "Better wait until I am dead. I might do something in the meantime to discredit the name." The committee had no such concerns, and "Edgerton Station" it was. The adjoining village also adopted the name "Edgerton."

# REORGANIZATION

❖ ❖ ❖ ❖ ❖ ❖

For some railroads, it was expansion, not dissolution or reorganization, which marked the year 1859. The Sheboygan and Mississippi's rails reached Plymouth in June. Sheboygan's *Evergreen City Times* ran the following article on June 25:

> When the road reached Plymouth in June, 1859, the event was celebrated by an excursion of the members of Sheboygan Deluge Fire Company No. 2 to that village as the special guests of Mr. Appleton, the railroad contractor. Marching to the depot on Indiana Avenue in full uniform and regalia, to the music of the German Band, and the fife and drum corps, they placed their engine aboard a platform car, boarded the train and moved gaily out of the station. At Plymouth they were welcomed by a large delegation of citizens; and R. H. Hotchkiss furnished a pair of horses to haul the engine through the streets, although the men would have preferred to draw it by hand. "On arriving at the Quitquioc House," says a journal of the time, "Foreman Brown gave the word, the Delugers [firemen seized the ropes, and in about two minutes were playing with great force on the flouring mill of Hotchkiss & Puhlmann some 15 rods distant, getting their suction from the mill pond. A powerful stream was thrown, through 150 feet of hose, and a 1¼ inch nozzle, entirely over the mill, three stories high and 50 feet across." Then, after partaking of a banquet in Concert Hall prepared by the ladies of Quitquioc, came the toasts, sentiments, speeches, &c., &c. . . .
>
> At 5 o'clock the company gave three times three and a "tiger" for their entertainers, and then marched back to the depot to the exhilarating music of their bands, and in due time were again home, having enjoyed their excursion to its full extent with a *rational* enjoyment.[10]

The company owned, at this time, two twenty-two-ton locomotives, the Sheboygan and the Cape Cod, two passenger cars, fifteen platform cars, five box cars, and two four-wheeled construction cars. Its Sheboygan depot, round house, and machine shops were located on the south side of the river near the lake shore.

That summer the Milwaukee, Watertown and Baraboo Valley Railroad extended the former Watertown and Madison line from Waterloo to Deansville and Sun Prairie:

> A line of railroad having been projected from Milwaukee to the Baraboo valley had been completed as far as Watertown, and located and graded on a line about three miles south of the village of Sun Prairie. . . . Meetings were held, committees appointed and negotiations entered into with S. L. Rose, president

of the railroad company, S. S. Merrill, general manager, D. C. Jackson and other influential railroad men, with the object of securing a change in the location of the road so as to bring it to Sun Prairie. . . . A bill for this purpose was introduced . . . and defeated. Strategy, however, which more often than valor, wins victories, succeeded in procuring the necessary legislation under which the desired change could be made. A clause was introduced into a bill then pending, which provided that no valid injunction could be served upon a railroad company to restrain them from doing any act unless thirty days previous notice had been served upon such company. The bill to which this provision was attached passed the legislature and became a law before those who were opposed to the desired change of route were aware that under it the change could be made. Thus protected from restraint by injunction, the company hastened the laying of the track without unnecessary delay, in some places not even grading the road-bed, and in less than thirty days the route was changed, and the triumph of Sun Prairie secured. In November, 1859, the railroad was completed to that point. For ten years, Sun Prairie was the western terminus of the Milwaukee and Baraboo Valley Railroad, and was one of the largest and most flourishing inland grain markets in the state.[11]

Also that summer the bondholders of the former Racine and Mississippi Railroad Company completed the line to Freeport, Illinois. The mortgages of the Racine and Mississippi had been foreclosed the prior year. The bondholders had acquired the property on May 10, 1859.

By June the Kenosha, Rockford and Rock Island was unable to pay the interest it owed on the bonds loaned by the city of Kenosha. The city agreed to pay the interest by levying a special tax on its citizens. Kenosha's mayor, Michael Frank, wrote in his diary:

> The citizens of Kenosha are desponding on account of the business prospects this fall. Grain market does not compare with other places; people predict the ruin of the city on account of taxes to pay for a railroad which does no business.[12]

In September the Kenosha, Rockford and Rock Island placed purchasing orders for five miles' worth of iron rail to extend their track to Genoa. There the track would cross that of the Wisconsin Central, changing Genoa Station to Genoa Junction. The rails arrived at Kenosha in November on the "propeller" vessels

*Racine* and *Forest Queen*. But the company was out of money, so the rails just lay in storage in Kenosha. The editor of Kenosha's *Tribune and Telegraph* summarized the state of affairs:

> The subscription of new Railroad stock . . . is probably impossible; the further issuing of bonds . . . is out of the question. . . . But if there are no available means at the disposal of the Company, we doubt not it would be the general sentiment of those interested in the Road—stockholders and all, that the entire property be consigned to any party who will complete the work, and put the Road in a working condition through to Rockford. It is hazardous to delay in expectation of more auspicious times; interests are accumulating and debts increasing; better therefore give the Road to any responsible party on almost any condition, rather than suffer the consequences of an unproductive investment.[13]

While no tracks would be laid by the Kenosha, Rockford and Rock Island in Wisconsin, the company's Rockford division did better in 1859, laying tracks from its junction with the new railway the Chicago & North Western at Harvard to Rockford—the last rail being spiked on November 21. The company then leased the line to the Chicago & North Western to expedite business—a measure of good faith in a reorganized company that was already doing well. Scheduled passenger service between Rockford and Harvard, with connections available to Chicago, began at the end of the year.

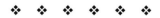

Just a few months after the date of its reorganization, The Chicago and North Western was making great progress on its own lines. In September the Chicago and North Western Railway's construction crews of the northern and southern division were approaching each other between Fort Atkinson and Jefferson. On September 29 the *Fort Atkinson Standard* reported that

> the iron is laid to the south bank of the Rock River, at this place. And there is something less than ten miles of track to put down to finish the Chicago and North Western Railroad to Oshkosh. The bridge here will be ready for the rail by the time the switches and sidetrack are completed, when the gap will be speedily closed up.

On October 4 the North Western began running trains from Janesville to Fort Atkinson. The *Standard* caught the spirit of the event:

# STEAM AND CINDERS

Hurrah! 10,000 Cheers!

The Railroad has come!! Rejoice!!!

Nobody need think that we are going to write like a deacon or a judge. We shan't do it. The steam is up, and we must "blow off" or explode!

The whistle soundeth in our ear, and our hearts dance to its music. The giant steed which will cross a continent without weariness, has come to our doors. Chicago shakes hands with us through a telegraph of iron, and the balance of creation will hereafter acknowledge our acquaintance.

The day so long looked for, and at times hopelessly, has dawned, and it brings with it pleasure, heightened by delay. Our streets are throbbing with new life and our people are animated with a hope, new, large and healthful. Enthusiasm, music and the booming gun, are the features of the day, and the screech of the locomotive responds right cheerily. The appearance of our military company adds much interest to the occasion. . . . It is only necessary for our citizens to put forth all their energies for the improvement of the advantages thus placed within reach, to make the 29th of September a day long to be remembered and celebrated as the harbinger of improvement and prosperity.[14]

Two weeks later the two crews met one and a half miles south of Jefferson. The result was a 194-mile continuous, standard-gauge railroad between Chicago and Oshkosh that would operate on a paying basis. Incredibly, the company was able to return an unused portion of the six hundred thousand dollars it had borrowed for the project.[15] L. B. Caswell of Fort Atkinson would say of the completed railroad that it "revived the spirit and energy of our people, and all went to work with renewed courage."[16]

The Chicago and North Western's completed line between Chicago and Oshkosh proved to be a financial success in the midst of what was for most railway companies another disheartening year. Soon after its opening, a Menasha manufacturer, wishing to see if it was more expedient to ship by way of Green Bay and Lake Michigan to Chicago or by the railroad, tried both methods. He sent one shipment of wooden pails and tubs by way of the Fox River to Green Bay, and another over Lake Winnebago to Fond du Lac, and then by rail. He found that the goods that went by rail cost less to ship, took half the time to get there, and arrived in better condition.[17]

Sheet music cover for the 1859 "North Western Railway Polka." Polkas have remained popular in Wisconsin since.
WHi Image ID 62096

Sadly, the joy of opening the Chicago-Oshkosh line was to last for only a few short weeks. The celebration came to an abrupt end when Wisconsin's first major train wreck occurred on the North Western in November. While the decade of the 1850s had been one of horrific train wrecks in other states, Wisconsin had until this time maintained an exceptional safety record. All of that changed on November 1, one month after the Chicago and North Western's line to Oshkosh opened. Celebrating the line's first month of operation, some six hundred people took an excursion train from Chicago to Fond du Lac. On the morning of November 1 they climbed back on board the twelve-coach train to return to Chicago. All was well as far as Watertown, but as the train proceeded toward Belleville (Johnson Creek), disaster struck:

> The train was running at a rate of fifteen miles an hour, and slackening speed to stop at the Bellville depot, when cattle were discovered some distance ahead, close beside the track. The whistle alarmed one of them, which immediately ran off into the woods. A large white steer remained until the locomotive came up, then attempted to cross the road but was caught and carried a short distance, when he partially fell through a culvert, thus causing sufficient obstruction to force the engine off the rails. The momentum of the train was so great, before the engineer could apply the brakes, the locomotive plunged off the track and was firmly embedded in the swampy roadside. The crash that followed was too horrible to contemplate. The first passenger car was driven against the express car with such force that the floor and the roof of the latter went crashing through its entire length, demolishing every seat, and carrying with it the inmates, mails and baggage, and all precipitated into a broad ditch on the north side of the road where the water was over a foot in depth. The only car that resisted the shock, among the six that were hurled together, was the fourth, which was too strongly built to yield to the pressure. This caused the next to be held so firmly that it was driven halfway through the fifth passenger car, crushing everything in its course. Of the seven other cars in the train, four were more or less damaged, platforms being demolished and ends broken in. All this ruin was wrought in an instant, without any warning to those on board, and the escape of so many persons alive, and unharmed, seems miraculous.
>
> There were at least six hundred persons on the train, of whom eight were instantly killed, and about thirty-five seriously wounded. The latest reports are that seven have died since the calamity.[18]

Miraculously, the final death toll of this crash, which came to be known as the "Belleville disaster," was only fourteen.

A Chicago and North Western train steams away from Fond du Lac in this 1867 drawing by A. Ruger.
WHi Image ID 11412

The year 1859 saw two new, reorganized railroad companies emerge in Wisconsin—the Milwaukee & Minnesota and the Chicago and North Western. The Milwaukee & Minnesota now owned one of the state's major through lines—the one built by the La Crosse and Milwaukee from Milwaukee to La Crosse—but its hands were tied. Its title was being challenged in the courts by former mortgagers Greene C. Bronson, James T. Soutter, and Sheppard Knapp, and it was unable to derive any profits from its property, as the railroad was still being operated by former contractor Chamberlain to recoup his expenses in building the railroad. More effective and vigorous than the Milwaukee & Minnesota was the Chicago and North Western, which completed its continuous 198-mile line between Chicago and Oshkosh on Lake Winnebago during the year.

There had been successes among the smaller railroads as well. The Sheboygan and Mississippi extended its line to Plymouth and the Milwaukee, Watertown and Baraboo Valley Railroad connected Milwaukee with the central Wisconsin wheat entrepôt of Sun Prairie (but still didn't reach Madison). The bondholders of the former Racine and Mississippi extended that line to Freeport, Illinois.

Though the railroads weren't out of the woods yet, such progress was heartening. Eighty-eight miles of track had been laid in Wisconsin during the year, bringing the grand total to 850 miles of track in the state.

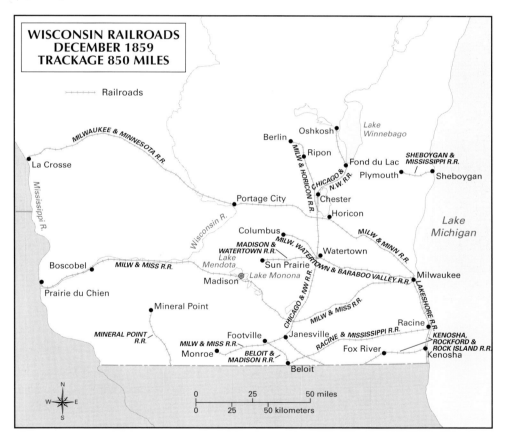

MAPPING SPECIALISTS

# Chapter 22

## New Beginnings

### 1860–1861

As Wisconsin entered a new decade, some citizens viewed the railroads that were now crisscrossing the landscape as a blessing and a harbinger of better things to come. The railroads made it easier, and sometimes cheaper, for farmers to transport their crops to distant markets, and immigrants found it easier to reach new lands to the west. On the other hand, many farmers had lost their land entirely due to the financial difficulties of the lines in which they had invested. And for every town on the line that boomed, another withered as the rails passed it by. Some investors and financiers got rich in the course of various stock manipulations, while others lost their shirts. It was clear that the railroads could pay their way, once the enormous costs of development had been covered. But it was no less obvious that many lines were still in need of a painful financial reorganization if they were to remain viable.

❖ ❖ ❖ ❖ ❖

The stockholders of the Milwaukee & Mississippi were made aware of the dire state of the company's affairs by President John Catlin in his 1859 annual report. In it, he noted that there was $144,480 of outstanding interest, $107,000 of which was due to the company's sinking fund (a fund built over several years to pay the principle of mortgage debts when they came due), and $38,740 of additional mortgage interest due since January 1. He recommended that the stockholders relinquish control and place their road in the hands of a trustee who would attempt to pay the company's mortgage interest with its earnings and stave off foreclosure by the bondholders:

> Under so discouraging a statement, it is evident that without a vigorous effort, or an arrangement preventing competition, or a revival of business, the road cannot long be retained by the stockholders, and it is submitted to you whether it is not advisable, under the circumstances, to let the trustee of the sinking fund and second mortgage bonds enter into the possession, under an arrangement, or with the understanding that he shall forbear a foreclosure while there is a reasonable prospect that the net earnings will pay up all the mortgage interest now due, within the next two years.[1]

Unfortunately, President Catlin's proposal was not realistic—the net earnings of the company were not sufficient to pay off its mortgage interest within a set amount of time, let alone within two years. Recognizing this, the company's board of directors, its bondholders, and Wisconsin's representatives in government proceeded to prepare for foreclosure. On March 30 the state of Wisconsin passed a law "to facilitate and authenticate the formation of a corporation by the purchase of the Milwaukee and Mississippi Railroad Company."[2] This law spelled out in detail the process that should be followed in foreclosure, the sale of the Milwaukee & Mississippi company to a trustee of the bondholders, the creation of a new corporation to receive the railroad from the trustee, and the reorganization process through which the bondholders of the old company would become the stockholders of the new. A key feature was that the number of shares in the new company would be reduced in order to increase their value.

Preparations for the sale of the Milwaukee & Mississippi continued in the spring of 1860. A preliminary plan was drawn up, and on April 25 the directors offered to relinquish control to the bondholders:

> Should the plan proposed be acceded to, as the Directors have reason to believe it will be, their connection with the road will soon cease . . . and grateful to the Bondholders for the forbearance which they have shown during the past two years of trial and disappointment . . . they tender to their successors all the aid and cooperation in their power, to restore the road to that degree of prosperity which the revival of business, and the return of prosperous times will most surely produce.[3]

At the end of April, the bondholders of the Milwaukee & Mississippi agreed to purchase the road and form a new company:

> THIS AGREEMENT, made the 30th day of April, 1860, witnesseth:
> That whereas, the Milwaukee and Mississippi Rail Road Company is embarrassed and unable, at present, to pay its mortgage or other debts . . . And whereas suits of foreclosure have been commenced in the United States Court . . . And whereas, the said Company are willing to surrender the road and all its property . . . Now therefore, if the said Company shall, on or before the tenth day of May, 1860, surrender the possession of the Road . . . Then, we the undersigned, as holders of the different classes of mortgage bonds of the said Company . . . do hereby severally agree . . . that we will purchase said road and all its property . . . and that we will form and organize a new Company. The name of the corporation shall be "The Milwaukee and Prairie du Chien Railway Company."[4]

At this time, the stockholders of the Milwaukee & Mississippi had put $3,500,000 into the company with their stock purchases and had borrowed almost $6,000,000 to build the railroad. The property was valued at $8,125,839.[5] Subtracting the debts from the value of the railroad left $2,125,839 for the stockholders of the old company—a $1,374,161 loss.

On May 9 Isaac Seymour, trustee for the bondholders on the so-called second mortgage (taken in 1857 for six hundred thousand dollars), who had initiated foreclosure proceedings, was appointed by the United States District Court for the state of Wisconsin to be the receiver of the company. As receiver he would become responsible for the road's maintenance, repair, and continued operations until such time as the property was conveyed to the new Milwaukee and Prairie du Chien Railway Company. On July 31 Seymour reported to the bondholders the debts and expenses the Milwaukee & Mississippi had incurred under his receivership:

> To the Mortgage Bondholders of the Milwaukee and Mississippi Railroad Company:
> The subscriber respectfully reports . . . that . . . there was not due for supplies and for unpaid wages to the employees of the road, so large a sum as was supposed. . . . I have reduced the above indebtedness to the sum of $35,111.62, of which $26,652.60 is yet due to employees.[6]

Further, Seymour called for necessary improvements to the line, citing these as preventative measures:

# NEW BEGINNINGS

1860 photograph of the Milwaukee & Mississippi's bridge across Monona Bay at Madison, along with the depot and rail yards, by John S. Fuller.
WHi Image ID 27107

The legislature . . . enacted a law . . . for railroad companies . . . to erect and maintain fences along the lines. . . . It will be the means of preventing accidents . . . and . . . law-suits, for cattle killed on the track from time to time. . . . Also . . . an elevator should be erected at Prairie Du Chien, for the purpose of facilitating the transit of grain on the road from that point to Milwaukee.[7]

By summer's end, the Milwaukee & Mississippi, under receivership, had defaulted on all of its remaining mortgages. That fall Seymour and the trustee to the bondholders of one of the company's other mortgages, George S. Coe, commenced foreclosure suits in the United States District Court for the District of Wisconsin on the four remaining mortgages. All told, there were five suits:

1. A June 15, 1852 mortgage on the road from Milwaukee to Rock River, given to George S. Coe, trustee, to secure $600,000 of 10-year, 8% bonds.
2. An April 21, 1853 mortgage on the road from Rock River to Wisconsin River, given to Isaac Seymour, trustee, to secure $650,000 of 10-year, 8% bonds.
3. A June 1, 1855 mortgage on the main road from Milwaukee to the Mississippi River, given to Isaac Seymour, trustee, to secure $2,500,000 of 22-year, 8% bonds.
4. A June 3, 1856 mortgage on the southern branch from Janesville to the Mississippi River, given to Isaac Seymour, trustee, to secure 8% bonds at $10,000 per mile.
5. A September 16, 1857 mortgage on the main road from Milwaukee to the Mississippi River, given to Isaac Seymour, trustee, to secure $600,000 of 5-year, 10% bonds.[8]

On October 5 the court issued the final decrees of foreclosure and sale on all five mortgages.

On January 21, 1861, the Milwaukee & Prairie du Chien Railway Company was organized to succeed the Milwaukee & Mississippi. The bondholders, unsecured creditors, and stockholders of the Milwaukee & Mississippi had formed an

Former Milwaukee & Mississippi passenger cars steam past Civil War soldiers in training in this 1862 lithograph of Camp Randall, drawn by Louis Kurz in 1862.
WHi Image ID 1838

association at the beginning of the month to purchase and reorganize the company, with Lewis H. Meyer, L. A. Von Hoffman, William Schall, and Allen Campbell, all of New York, and President John Catlin as trustees. The trustees purchased the road for $7,500,000 at a court-ordered marshal's sale held on January 18. Three days later they organized as the Milwaukee & Prairie du Chien with Meyer, William Pitt Lynde, Campbell, Schall, John Wilkinson, Catlin, Hercules L. Dousman and N. A. Cowdrey as directors. It had been a requirement that the majority of the directors be "citizens or residents of New York." Only Catlin and Dousman were from Wisconsin. This board elected Meyer president of the new company and Catlin vice president.[9] The new company was capitalized at $7,500,000, divided into 75,000 shares of $100 each. The city of Milwaukee would be fully indemnified for the credit it had loaned the old company.[10]

The only railroad company to weather the hard times unscathed was the Galena and Chicago Union, which had followed a policy of limited borrowing and reduced costs. In January the company decided to reduce the number of trains it ran between Beloit and Janesville from two to one. The remaining train left Beloit at 5:12 p.m. and arrived in Janesville at 6:15 p.m., then left Janesville at 8:00 a.m.

the next morning, returning to Beloit at 9:15 a.m. This change did not leave the Galena and Chicago Union in the black, but it did lower its debt significantly enough for the company to forego foreclosure.

The Galena and Chicago Union was also able to strengthen its holdings by repossessing other lines, in particular that of the Wisconsin Central Railroad. On February 29 the directors of the Wisconsin Central Railroad Company held their last board meeting. The company was in debt and without revenues. The Galena and Chicago Union had already repossessed its line from Richmond, Illinois, to Geneva Lake. All future business would consist of creditors trying to reclaim what they had loaned.[11] That fall the last train ran over the Wisconsin Central's line to Geneva Lake—a Galena train riding on strap rail. A Mr. Ben Fish was then allowed to operate over the line with a flat car pulled by a team of mules. Some time later one of the mules would be killed in an accident, and Fish would continue with the single mule. The track would wear out completely by 1862 and would be removed.[12]

In April, its prospects looking brighter, the Galena and Chicago Union reinstated two-train service between Beloit and Janesville. On May 25 some forty Janesville high school students and their teachers hired a coach from the Milwaukee & Mississippi for a field trip to Beloit. The car was placed under the authority of the Galena company, which provided a captain (conductor), crew, and the locomotive Cloud. The party left Janesville on the Milwaukee & Mississippi's southern branch and then, after reaching Hanover Junction, followed the Beloit and Madison tracks to Beloit. In Beloit the Janesville students and teachers picnicked with a similar group from Beloit. Their return trip to Janesville, however, turned out to be no picnic—the Cloud pulled them at speeds that often exceeded sixty miles per hour. Still, they fared better than a group of passengers on the Racine & Mississippi line a few months later. On September 18 the *Burlington Gazette* reported an accident on the Racine & Mississippi Railroad at Delavan. Five people had been killed and twenty-five injured. Many were coming home from the Walworth County Fair. This was Wisconsin's second major rail accident, the first having been the Belleville disaster of the previous year.

With its two-train run between Janesville and Beloit successful, the Galena and Chicago Union decided to extend this service to other lines. In the June 31 *Burlington Gazette* the company placed an advertisement announcing that it would run two trains daily from Janesville to Chicago. The morning train would leave Janesville at 10:30 a.m., arriving in Chicago at 5:30 p.m., and the evening train would leave at 8:39 p.m., arriving in Chicago at 4:05 a.m. These trains would run over Milwaukee & Mississippi tracks to Plymouth, then on Beloit and Madison tracks to Beloit, and from there on Galena and Chicago Union tracks to Chicago.

A Chicago and North Western train crosses the Rock River at Watertown in 1860 in this lithograph by Louis Kurz.
WHi Image ID 37447

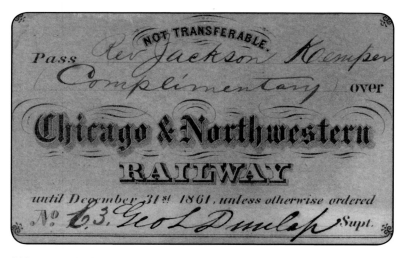

Chicago & North Western Railway Pass, 1861. Passes such as this were issued to guests of the railroad, allowing them to travel free of charge.
WHi Image ID 62553

Meanwhile, some smaller companies were making progress while others were slipping in the continuing wake of the financial crisis. In March the Sheboygan and Mississippi's tracks reached Glenbeulah, west of Sheboygan, which event was celebrated on March 28. During the ensuing summer, Sheboygan County farmers began shipping their wheat by rail to Sheboygan for the first time, where it was transferred to lake vessels headed for Buffalo in the East.

In April the Chicago and North Western Railway Company was authorized to extend its road from Appleton to Green Bay, then on to the state line with Upper Michigan. However, although it had been reorganized less than a year before, the company was already having trouble making interest payments.[13]

Over the summer the Beloit and Madison replaced most of the timbers in its eight-year-old bridge over the Rock River in Beloit. During July and August it laid four more miles of track, extending the road beyond Footville to Magnolia.

On June 12 the former La Crosse and Milwaukee's properties, both those in the eastern and the western divisions, were placed in the hands of Hans Crocker, receiver. The eastern division was now owned by the Milwaukee & Minnesota Railroad Company. With Crocker's appointment, Selah Chamberlain relinquished the lease he had held since 1857 and ceased operating. Though charged with maintaining the existing property, Crocker immediately requested and obtained permission from the court to build a grain elevator at La Crosse for receiving and dispatching bulk shipments of wheat (the company had previously shipped all wheat in bags).

Meanwhile, the Milwaukee and Horicon Railroad Company had defaulted on interest payments for its 1856 mortgage; on July 12, 1860, it faced foreclosure. Unfortunately, two courts became involved, one appointing Lindsey Ward of Milwaukee the receiver of the property and the other appointing Jarius Fairchild of Madison. The result was a disagreement that was to become known as the "Horicon Railroad War." With use of force that was reported to include "a large number of men well-armed" and "a canon or two from Milwaukee," Ward won the dispute.[14]

Thus Ward would operate the Milwaukee and Horicon Railroad in receivership until it was sold to the Milwaukee & St. Paul Railway Company in 1863.

In the midst of continuing struggle, there was some hopeful news—the Ripon and Wolf River Railroad, which would branch off from the Milwaukee and Horicon line at Rush Lake Junction near Ripon, began construction. This company was the promotion of Captain David Mapes, a New Yorker who had come to Wisconsin in 1846 and had helped found the city of Ripon as well as Ripon College. Mapes had been an active promoter of the Milwaukee and Horicon, and had helped bring that line to the city. Around 1855 he began contemplating building a railroad from Ripon to Oshkosh, but with the proximity of the Chicago, St. Paul and Fond du Lac at Fond du Lac, he settled instead on a railroad from Ripon to Winneconne on the Wolf River. He had obtained a charter for the Ripon and Wolf River Railroad Company on March 31, 1856. The charter granted the company authorization to build a railroad from Rush Lake Junction to Winneconne via Omro. Mapes hoped that the railroad would make Winneconne a center of industry that would receive lumber floated down the Wolf River, process it into various wood products, and then ship both raw lumber and lumber products over the new railroad to Ripon, Horicon, and Milwaukee. During 1860 the company completed the first fifteen miles to Omro and graded and set ties on the remaining line to Winneconne. Unfortunately the company did not have any money left with which to buy rails to complete the line.[15]

Despite the continuing economic hard times, a few companies were still able to extend their debts. At the beginning of 1860, the Kenosha, Rockford and Rock Island Railroad Company was out of cash and without credit. Its new president, Z. G. Simmons,

## THE CITY.

**Arrival and Departure of Railroad Trains, and Hour of Closing Mails.**

```
              MILWAUKEE & CHICAGO.
Depart.              Arrive.           Mails Close.
10:15 A. M. ......... 1:15 P. M ...... 9:30 A. M.
3:15 P. M. .........12:30 A. M. ......2:00 P. M.
6:30 P. M. Mixed train to Chicago.
  Trains on this road leave on Chicago time, which is
15 minutes ahead of Milwaukee time.
              LA CROSSE & MILWAUKEE.
1:15 A. M............ 9:40 A. M ......9:00 P. M.
1:55 P. M............ 2:35 A. M ......12:30 P. M
              MILWAUKEE & MISSISSIPPI.
10:45 A. M. .........11:45 A. M......9:30 A.M.
4:00  " ............. 6:00 A. M ......3:15 P.M.
9:00 P. M ........... 5:30 P. M.......9:00 P.M.
              MILWAUKEE & HORICON.
1:45 A. M ........... 9:30 A. M.......9:00 P.M
1:55 P. M ........... 2:35 P. M......12:30 P.M.
       MILWAUKEE, WATERTOWN & BARABOO VALLEY.
4:15 P. M............ 10:40 P. M .....3:30 P.M.
              DETROIT & MILWAUKEE.
8:00 P. M............ 11:00 P. M .....7 P. M.
```

**Departure of Steamers.**

FOR TWO RIVERS.

The steamer *Huron* leaves Olmsted's dock, every evening at 8 o'clock, for Port Washington, Sheboygan, Manitowoc and Two Rivers.

FOR BUFFALO.

Screw steamers, with good accommodations, leave the different transportation docks every day, for Buffalo.

FOR OSWEGO AND OGDENSBURGH.

One of the Northern Transportation Co's screw teamers sails for the above ports every day, from the he Company's dock at the M. & Miss. R. R. depot, touching at nearly all intermediate ports.

FOR COLLINGWOOD.

The Collingwood Line of screw steamers leave semi-weekly from Dousman's dock, foot of East Water Street, connecting at Collingwood with the Northern Railway of Canada, for the East.

FOR GREEN BAY.

The screw steamer *Ogonts* makes weekly trips to the above port starting from Olmsted's dock.

This railway timetable appeared in the *Milwaukee Daily Sentinel* on October 10, 1860.

disposed of his private business interests in order to devote his full attention to the problem. Simmons appealed to Kenosha's common council to free up the mortgage it held, which it did on February 13. He then had some New Jersey investors inspect the line and issue a favorable report. On March 8 the company issued 800 five hundred dollars bonds and 3,200 one hundred dollar twenty-year bonds, which afterwards sold quickly on the Eastern market.

With new investors to back it, the company was even able to expand. In July the Kenosha, Rockford and Rock Island Railroad Company purchased the iron to lay fifteen miles of track—the amount needed to close the gap between the Wisconsin and Illinois segments of the line. The ties were delivered at Kenosha in June and July, and the first shipment of iron arrived in August. The company contracted with A. E. Cromwell of Syracuse, New York, to lay the track. Cromwell advertised for workers, and as harvesting finished, he was able to hire some five hundred men. That summer Cromwell began laying track west from Fox River to Genoa using the rails that had lain in storage for almost a year. In September the tracks reached Genoa Junction, where the tracks of the Wisconsin Central railroad had deteriorated beyond use, having been abandoned when that company ran out of funds. All the same, the Kenosha company now boasted twenty-eight miles of continuous railroad from Kenosha to the Illinois state line. To celebrate, it ran a series of excursion trains, one of which was described as follows:

The train was made up of flat cars with seats of plank along the side, shade being afforded by oak and poplar saplings from the woods nailed to the edge of each car. The ladies on the excursion went dressed in their prettiest clothing, [and] many wore white dresses. In the open cars, with the wood burning engine belching smoke and cinders, these dresses were in a deplorable condition on their return.[16]

Regular service between Kenosha and Genoa Junction began on October 1 with a single train that left Kenosha at 3:00 p.m. and arrived at Genoa at 6:00 p.m. It returned the following morning, leaving Genoa at 7:30 a.m. and arriving at Kenosha at 10:30 a.m. In November an excursion was run for the company's bondholders, who reported that they were pleased with the progress of the work and the scenery viewed from the line. At the end of December, the Kenosha's tracks entered Illinois.

❖ ❖ ❖ ❖ ❖ ❖

Meanwhile, for the farmer-mortgagors fighting to keep their farms, the situation was becoming grim. Wisconsin's Supreme Court declared the "stay laws," which had protected the farmers from foreclosure by "staying" the procedures for two years, to be unconstitutional. In Clark v. Farrington and Blunt v. Walker, the court held that the farm mortgages were valid contracts and that their holders were entitled to foreclose. The farmers responded by organizing the "Grand State League," an organization which published a weekly paper called the *Home League*. Editor Alexander M. Thomson saw the situation as a struggle between "five or six thousand men who have been cheated and defrauded in the most shameful and disgraceful manner" and the "railroad thieves and their apologists . . . in the pay of Wall Street." He asked his adversaries, "Will you force us from our homes?" If so, he warned, "We will meet that force in kind." Thomson listed seven illegal means that railroads had employed to swindle farmers:

1. They took stock of the farmers upon the express condition that the roads should be laid in certain localities, and after the stock was thus obtained, the right of way was altered to suit the private speculations of the directors.
2. They made out false reports and false statements in order to show the road to be in a better condition than it really was, and to induce the famers from such statements to mortgage their farms for stock.
3. They issued large amounts of bogus and fictitious stock in order to overshadow the Farm Mortgage interest, and perpetuate themselves in office.
4. They sold the capital stock of the Company at a ruinous discount in order to raise money with which to pay semi-annual dividends that they had declared, falsely representing that the money thus paid out was the legitimate earnings of the road over and above expenses.
5. They colluded with each other and made contracts with themselves for the building and operating of the road at the most extravagant prices.
6. They bought up large tracts of real estate, and then altered the line of the road so as to accommodate their own land and enhance the value of their own property.
7. They continued to take Farm Mortgages when they knew that their corporations were bankrupt.[17]

Given such practices, Thomson held that Eastern investors holding mortgages were little more than accessories to the swindle.

Without the "stay-laws," farmers relied on foot-dragging by local officials and intimidation of creditors at foreclosure sales to prevent the loss of their farms. Eventually the majority of creditors would come to some kind of settlement with their debtors, typically cancelling about fifty percent of the debt, which in most cases allowed the farmers to retain their land and their homes.[18]

That fall the three-year economic depression was lifted by a bumper crop of wheat. In 1857 the state's wheat harvest had been slightly above average—fourteen million bushels—but prices were low. The years 1858 and 1859 were years of drought. But in 1860 everything was right for a good growing season. There had been a mild winter, which was followed by an early spring, and the growing season had abundant rainfall. The result was a crop of twenty-nine million bushels—twice that of any previous harvest. And the market was paying farmers a better price for their wheat than it had since before the panic. This harvest was called the "golden harvest." It benefited farmers, railroads, buyers, storage operators—everyone.[19] It wasn't surprising that no matter what the financial outlook was, the first upgrades along many lines were improvements to grain elevators (as with the Milwaukee & Mississippi and the Milwaukee and Minnesota).

March 1861 marked the end of another of Wisconsin's earliest railroads. In 1860 and 1861 the Sheboygan and Mississippi found itself unable to pay the interest due on its loans. While it had subscriptions to four hundred thousand dollars' worth of its stock, its revenues from twenty miles of road were inadequate.[20] Its bondholders now filed suit to foreclose on the property, and a receiver was appointed to operate the road. The company was sold, and on March 2, 1861, the bondholders reorganized a new company, the Sheboygan and Fond du Lac Railroad Company. Among its incorporators were J. F. Kirkland, Harrison Barrett, Edward Appleton, and J. O. Thayer.

On March 16, 1861, the Milwaukee, Watertown and Baraboo Valley Railroad Company, under the superintendency of Sherburn S. Merrill, who had been assistant superintendent of the Milwaukee & Mississippi from 1853 to 1857, changed its name to the Milwaukee and Western Railroad Company. Its lines ran from Brookfield Junction to Columbus, with a branch from Watertown to Sun Prairie.

No one could have foreseen at the time that these many railroads—the Milwaukee & Prairie du Chien, the Milwaukee & Minnesota, the Milwaukee and Horicon, the Milwaukee and Western, and the Racine and Mississippi—would

> **RAILWAY MATTERS.**
>
> **RAILROADS IN THE UNITED STATES.**
>
> The progress of Railroads in the United States, during the past twenty years, is shown in the following table. In 1831 there were but 54 miles in operation:
>
> | Year. | Miles. | Year. | Miles. |
> |---|---|---|---|
> | 1842 | 3,817 | 1852 | 10,849 |
> | 1843 | 4,174 | 1853 | 13,315 |
> | 1844 | 4,311 | 1854 | 15,511 |
> | 1845 | 4,522 | 1855 | 18,153 |
> | 1846 | 4,870 | 1856 | 21,440 |
> | 1847 | 5,336 | 1857 | 24,390 |
> | 1848 | 5,682 | 1858 | 26,210 |
> | 1849 | 6,350 | 1859 | 27,857 |
> | 1850 | 6,475 | 1860 | 29,401 |
> | 1851 | 8,356 | 1861 | 31,179 |
>
> The cost of all the railroads in this country is stated at $1,177,993,818.

*Milwaukee Daily Sentinel*, February 16, 1861.

together become the company most associated with Wisconsin's railroads in the second half of the century, the Chicago, Milwaukee and St. Paul Railway Company, consolidating more than half of the original lines under one company and ensuring the financial future of all the railroads. This would not have been possible without another event in the spring of 1861, one that divided—and eventually united—all of the United States into one America.

On April 12, 1861, Confederate troops at Charleston, South Carolina, fired upon Fort Sumter, beginning a war that would change America forever. With that event the era of antebellum railroads in Wisconsin came to a close. By the time those fateful shots were fired, Wisconsin's railroad companies had laid almost nine hundred miles of track to form a rail network within the state and to connect Wisconsin to the rest of the nation. Railroads had not only arrived in Wisconsin; they had established themselves in a form that has survived in much the same structure to the present day.

# Epilogue

Wisconsin's railroads had been built just in time. When the Southern states closed the Mississippi River to traffic at the beginning of the Civil War, those railroads carried the trade of the upper Mississippi to the East, supplying produce, materials, and cash from exported wheat, all of which aided the war effort. They also helped to send Wisconsin's soldiers to the Southern battlefields and to bring those that survived home again. With a reorganized capital structure, bountiful crops, and war contracts, Wisconsin's railroads were finally able to repay their construction debts.

With the war, Wisconsin's railroads began a twenty-year period of consolidation. The prices paid for failed railroads were relatively low, and those buying them recognized that economies of scale made larger rail systems more profitable. They saw that Wisconsin needed a unified rail network to be able to compete in interstate trade. Those railroads originating in Milwaukee were acquired by the Milwaukee & St. Paul Railway Company, organized from the western division of the La Crosse and Milwaukee on May 8, 1863, and those originating or tied to Chicago were acquired by the Chicago and North Western Railway Company. The pioneer companies that were acquired by the Milwaukee & St. Paul were as follows:

On January 21, 1861, the Milwaukee & Mississippi was deeded to the Milwaukee & Prairie du Chien Railway Company, organized by the purchasers of the Milwaukee & Mississippi three days previously. The Milwaukee and Prairie du Chien was sold on December 31, 1867, to the Milwaukee & St. Paul.

The Milwaukee and Watertown and the Watertown and Madison railroads had been acquired by the Milwaukee, Watertown and Baraboo Valley Railroad Company, which changed its name to the Milwaukee and Western on March 16, 1861. This company was deeded to the Milwaukee & St. Paul on May 8, 1863.

The La Crosse and Milwaukee's western division, between Portage and La Crosse, was reorganized into the Milwaukee & St. Paul Railway Company in 1863. Its eastern division, between Milwaukee and Portage, was operated by the

Milwaukee & Minnesota Railroad Company, which was acquired by the Milwaukee & St. Paul in March 1868.

The Milwaukee and Horicon was purchased by the Milwaukee & St. Paul on June 23, 1863. The Ripon and Wolf River was purchased by the Milwaukee & St. Paul on October 3, 1863.

The Western Union Railroad Company, successor of the Racine and Mississippi, was leased by the Chicago, Milwaukee & St. Paul in 1879 (it would be purchased on September 1, 1901). The Milwaukee & St. Paul had added Chicago to its name in 1874.

Finally, on September 29, 1880, the Mineral Point Railroad Company was deeded to the Chicago, Milwaukee & St. Paul.

By 1900 the Chicago, Milwaukee & St. Paul had pushed westward into the Dakotas, and five years later it began building its Pacific extension to Puget Sound, which it finished in 1909. The company reorganized in 1927, changing its name to the Chicago, Milwaukee, St. Paul & Pacific Railway Company, commonly referred to as the "Milwaukee Road."

In 1970 America's railroad passenger lines were reduced in number and those remaining, including the Milwaukee Road's Chicago–Puget Sound "Olympian," were relegated to Amtrak. In 1985 the company became bankrupt, and its Wisconsin lines were acquired by the Soo and Canadian Pacific railroad companies.

The pioneer companies that were acquired by the Chicago and North Western were as follows:

The Milwaukee & Chicago and the Chicago and Milwaukee railroads merged in 1863, taking the name Chicago and Milwaukee. This meant that passengers were finally able to travel between the two cities without changing trains at the state line. The Chicago and Milwaukee was leased by the Chicago and North Western in 1866, and purchased by that company in 1883.[1]

The Sheboygan and Fond du Lac, successor to the Sheboygan and Mississippi, was acquired by the Chicago and North Western in 1879. By that time it had extended the original road from Glenbeulah to Fond du Lac, Ripon, and Princeton.

The Chicago and North Western Railway Company extended its Chicago-Oshkosh line northward to Appleton and Green Bay in 1861. It also acquired the Kenosha, Rockford and Rock Island line in January 1864.

The Galena and Chicago Union Railroad merged with the Chicago and North Western on June 2, 1864. The new company kept the name Chicago and North Western. With 860 miles of track, the merger made the new company the largest railroad in the world.

# EPILOGUE

The Beloit and Madison completed its line to Madison in August 1864 and shortly thereafter became the Beloit Division of the Chicago and North Western Railway.

The Chicago and North Western Railway Company survived, with several reorganizations, until it was sold to the Union Pacific Railroad Company in 1995.[2]

Wisconsin's railroad pioneers lived out their lives in the late nineteenth and early twentieth centuries.

### PIONEERS OF THE 1830s

Henry Rowe Schoolcraft, who visited the lead region in 1831, discovered the source of the Mississippi River at Itasca Lake in 1832. He was appointed superintendent of Michigan's Indian Agency in 1836 and wrote a six-volume reference guide on Indian tribes published in several volumes between 1847 and 1857. Schoolcraft died on December 10, 1864, in Washington, D.C.

Colonel Henry Dodge, Wisconsin's territorial governor from 1836 to 1841 and again from 1846 to 1848, and United States Senator from 1848 to 1852, retired in 1857 and moved to Burlington, Iowa, where he died on June 19, 1867, at the age of eighty-four.

James Doty, who obtained Wisconsin's first railroad charter on December 3, 1836, for his La Fontaine railroad, was territorial governor from 1841 to 1845, and became director of the Wisconsin and Superior in 1857. In 1861 he was appointed Indian Agent in Utah Territory and in 1863 became the governor of that territory, where he died shortly after.

Solomon Juneau, founder and first mayor of Milwaukee, opened a store in Theresa, Wisconsin, in 1848, and moved there with his family in 1852. Juneau died while attending a government payment of annuities to the Menomonee Indians on their Keshena reservation on November 14, 1856. He was sixty-three years old.[3]

Increase Lapham, chief engineer of the Milwaukee and Rock River Canal, became well known as Wisconsin's first scientist. In 1836, his first year in Wisconsin, he published a book titled *A Catalogue of Plants and Shells Found in the Vicinity of Milwaukee*. Over the years Lapham authored some eighty more titles, served as president of the State Historical Society of Wisconsin from 1862 to 1871, was instrumental in establishing the national weather service, and was Wisconsin's official chief geologist from 1873 to 1875. He died September 14, 1875.

### DIRECTORS OF THE MILWAUKEE & MISSISSIPPI

William A. Barstow, director from 1852 to 1855 and governor of Wisconsin in 1854 and 1855, raised a cavalry regiment at the beginning of the Civil War and served as the regiment's colonel. His health failing, he spent most of the war in hospitals. Barstow never fully recovered his health before he died on December 13, 1865, at the age of fifty-two.

Edward H. Brodhead, superintendent and chief engineer from 1852 to 1856 and president of the company in 1857, retired the following year to attend to his business interests. He became president of Milwaukee's Farmers and Millers Bank in 1865 and later of the First National Bank. Brodhead died December 20, 1890, at the age of eighty-one.

John Catlin, president of the Milwaukee & Mississippi from 1852 to 1861, became vice president of the company's successor, the Milwaukee and Prairie du Chien line, a post he held until 1863. He retired to Elizabeth, New Jersey, where he died August 4, 1874, at the age of seventy-one.

Nelson Dewey, first governor of the state of Wisconsin from 1848 to 1852, and director of the Milwaukee & Mississippi from 1855 to 1861, was active in many other railroad companies, notably the Potosi & Dodgeville, the Southern Wisconsin, the Northern Pacific, the Western Wisconsin, the Platteville & Calamine, and the Military Ridge & Grant County. Dewey lost badly in the financial panic of 1873. He resumed his legal practice until his death in 1889.

Hercules Dousman, director from 1853 until 1861, was one of Wisconsin's wealthiest men. He served as a director of the Milwaukee and Prairie du Chien from 1861 to 1866. He spent his declining years on his large Prairie du Chien estate, giving lavish parties and entertaining distinguished visitors. He died in Prairie du Chien on September 12, 1868.

Ashael Finch Jr., who was named president of Kilbourn's breakaway faction of the Milwaukee and Mississippi company in January 1852, stayed on as a director through 1861. Finch was an abolitionist, was active in the temperance movement, and ran for mayor of Milwaukee in 1867. He died April 4, 1883, at the age of seventy-four.

Joseph Goodrich, director from 1852 to 1861, was an abolitionist and stationmaster on the underground railroad at Milton, helping runaway slaves escape to Canada. He died in Milton, the village he founded, in 1867.

Edward D. Holton, director from 1849 to 1861, was an active abolitionist for whom Holton, Kansas, was named. He unsuccessfully ran for governor for the Free Soil Party in 1853 and was president of Milwaukee's Farmers' and Millers' Bank from 1854 to 1863. During the Civil War he served as state allotment officer with Wisconsin soldiers in the field. Holton spent his last years traveling. He died in Savannah, Georgia, on April 21, 1892, at the age of seventy-seven.

# EPILOGUE

Byron Kilbourn, president of the Milwaukee and Mississippi until 1852, then president of the La Crosse and Milwaukee, retired from railroading in 1857. In 1860, with real estate holdings and a flouring mill in Milwaukee, Kilbourn was the fourth-wealthiest person in Milwaukee. In 1868 he moved to Jacksonville, Florida, to receive treatment for rheumatism. He died there on September 16, 1870. In the 1990s, the Historic Milwaukee organization brought his remains back to Milwaukee.

Alexander Mitchell, director from 1849 through 1854 and again in 1858, became president of the Milwaukee & St. Paul in 1865. Over the next sixteen years, the Milwaukee & St. Paul under Mitchell absorbed other companies until it had over five thousand miles of track in seven states. Mitchell died on April 19, 1887. His grandson, Billy Mitchell, was a famed aviator for whom Milwaukee's botanical domes are named.

Alexander Randall, who drafted the Milwaukee and Waukesha charter and, as governor of Wisconsin, initiated the investigation of the La Crosse and Milwaukee, was reelected to the governorship in 1859. He vigorously organized the state for participation in the Civil War and was appointed United States Postmaster General by President Andrew Johnson after the war. Randall retired to practice law in Elmyra, New York, where he died in 1872.

John H. Tweedy, director in 1850, 1852, and 1858 and leader of the movement that ousted Kilbourn from the presidency in 1852, retired from active business and politics in the 1860s and continued to live in Milwaukee, where he died at the age of seventy-seven on November 12, 1891.

George H. Walker, director from 1852 to 1860 and two-term mayor of Milwaukee in 1851 and 1853, organized Milwaukee's mule-powered streetcar service in 1859. He died on September 20, 1866, at the age of fifty-four.

Erastus B. Wolcott, M.D., director from 1849 until 1861, became Wisconsin's surgeon general during the Civil War. He served as vice president of the State Historical Society of Wisconsin in 1861, and became manager of the National Home for Disabled Volunteer Soldiers after 1866. He married Dr. Laura Ross in 1869 and championed equal rights for women in the medial profession. He died in Milwaukee on January 5, 1880.

## OTHER EMPLOYEES OF THE MILWAUKEE & MISSISSIPPI

John Bailie, master car builder at Waukesha in 1850, built railroad cars for the company and its successors, the Milwaukee and Prairie du Chien and the Milwaukee & St. Paul, over a period of thirty years.[4]

Edwin Bridgeman, the first train conductor in Wisconsin, left the Milwaukee & Mississippi for the La Crosse and Milwaukee in 1853. He worked for the La Crosse until shortly before his death on October 17, 1859.

Joseph Cochrane, the first passenger train locomotive engineer in Wisconsin, left the Milwaukee & Mississippi about 1853 to engage in brick making. He ran street-sprinkling wagons in Milwaukee until 1877. Cochrane died March 19, 1879.[5]

Benjamin Edgerton, constructing engineer from 1851 until 1861, for whom Edgerton, Wisconsin, is named, continued with the successor Milwaukee and Prairie du Chien in the early 1860s. He later became chief engineer of the McGregor & Western Railway in Iowa, and established the city of Cresco, Iowa. The town of Edgerton, Kansas, was named after him during his tenure as chief engineer of the Kansas Southern Railroad. In the early 1870s Edgerton became chief engineer for the Milwaukee and Northern Railroad, building between Milwaukee and Green Bay on many of the Indian trails he had trod in 1835 after first coming to Milwaukee. Edgerton died in Chicago on December 9, 1886, and was buried in Forest Home Cemetery in Milwaukee.

John C. Fox, the young engineer who brought the first train into Janesville, later became foreman of the Janesville roundhouse. He was then made master mechanic with supervision over the shops in Janesville, Rockford, Beloit, Monroe, and Mineral Point, a post he held until 1909, when a sudden illness forced him to retire after fifty-eight years of active service. In 1919 Mr. Fox suffered from a broken hip, from which time he was confined to his home. In March 1921 the *Janesville Gazette* featured the following article:

> President of St. Paul greets John Fox, 94, oldest living employee
>
> In his little home at 118 Madison Street where from his bed he can look out at the passing trains, 94-year old John C. Fox, oldest living employee of the Chicago, Milwaukee & St. Paul Railway, is happy. He has felt another touch of human kindness, greater than all that have gone before. His 69 years of loyal service as a railroader were rewarded Monday. None other than H. E. Byrnam, president of the St. Paul, called upon him. It was the tribute from a great heart to a faithful worker, and it touched the aged man. Tears of joy dimmed for a moment the sparkle of his blue eyes. . . . It was payment for the labor of a lifetime loyally done. Perhaps no more touching scene has been enacted in Janesville. Lying upon his bed, the grand old man replied to the president's greeting with the satisfied statement: "I wondered, sir, if you would find time to see me." The formality of introduction was over. An immediate friendship was cemented, and as friends of old, the chief of one of the biggest railroad systems in the country and the man who holds the distinction of having run the first St. Paul engine into Janesville chatted about "their" railroad. History they related; anecdotes they told, and jokes they swapped. . . . "What we need today," says Mr. Fox, "is more love of our Saviour, more love of

# EPILOGUE

our country and more loyalty for our boss and our work." As he concluded, there was a murmur of "Amens" from the distinguished visitors.[6]

John C. Fox died in June of the following year, 1922.

Edwin Kittredge, who built Wisconsin's first railroad passenger car, left the Milwaukee & Mississippi to work for the La Crosse and Milwaukee in 1853. He would build railroad cars for that company and its successors for the next thirty years.[7]

Walter Kittredge, master car builder at Waukesha, was superintendent of the La Crosse and Milwaukee from 1854 to 1859. In 1865 he became the station agent at Portage for the successor Milwaukee & St. Paul. He died on March 19, 1867.[8]

Sherburn S. Merrill, foreman of a section crew in 1850 and freight conductor in 1851, served as assistant superintendent from 1853 to 1857. Between 1857 and 1862 he was superintendent of the Milwaukee, Watertown and Baraboo Valley line. He moved to Minnesota for his health, but in July 1865 returned to Milwaukee to become the general manager of the Milwaukee & St. Paul Railway, a post he would hold for twenty years. In 1881 the city of Merrill, Wisconsin, was named for him. He died on February 8, 1885, at the age of sixty-six.

James Stickney, depot agent at Mazomanie in 1856, continued in that position for many years. He was a staunch Republican, a supporter of Lincoln, an investor in real estate, a breeder of racehorses, and, for a time, village president. In 1907, when he was seventy-nine years old, Stickney was recognized as the oldest railroad agent in the United States. He would serve another three years in that capacity. The company named Stickney, South Dakota, after him.

William B. Strong, station agent at Monroe in 1857, was transferred to Janesville in 1858, where he would serve as station agent for seven years. Strong then worked for the McGregor & Western in 1865; the Chicago & North Western from 1866 to 1870; the Burlington & Missouri River from 1870 to 1872, and the Chicago, Burlington and Quincy from 1872 to 1878. In 1878 Strong joined the Atchison, Topeka & Santa Fe Railroad, of which he became president in 1881. Under his eleven-year administration, the road grew from 637 miles to an incredible 9,000 miles. In 1889 Strong retired and returned to Beloit, where he aided building projects for churches and hospitals.[9]

### PIONEERS ASSOCIATED WITH OTHER LAKE MICHIGAN–
### MISSISSIPPI RIVER RAILROADS

Jacob Linsley Bean, former financial agent for the Milwaukee & Mississippi and president of the La Crosse and Milwaukee in 1853, began iron mining and smelting in 1854 at Iron Ridge. He died on May 8 of the following year at the age of forty-six.

Jairus C. Fairchild was Wisconsin's first state treasurer in 1848 and Madison's first mayor in 1856. He was a director and then president of the Watertown and Madison in 1857, and the disputed receiver of the Milwaukee and Horicon railroad from 1860 until his death at the age of sixty on July 18, 1862.

Zalmon G. Simmons, president of the Kenosha, Rockford & Rock Island Railroad in 1860 and 1861, was also president of the Northwestern Telegraph Company of Kenosha. In 1884 he became a director of the Western Union Company. In 1889 Simmons organized the Manitou and Pike's Peak Railroad Company in Colorado, and two years later saw the completion of the cog-railway to the top of Pike's Peak. Simmons was president of the First National Bank of Kenosha from 1871 to 1909. He was best known for organizing the Northwestern Wire Mattress Company of Kenosha, which eventually became the Simmons Manufacturing Company, one of the largest producers of wire mattresses, steel springs, and iron and steel beds in the world. Simmons died in Kenosha on February 11, 1910, at the age of eighty-one.

Moses M. Strong, president of the Mineral Point Railroad and attorney for the La Crosse and Milwaukee, led Wisconsin's "copperhead" Democrats, who were critical of the Lincoln administration, during the Civil War. Strong served as president of the State Bar Association form 1878 to 1893 and as vice president of the State Historical Society of Wisconsin from 1871 until his death, at the age of eighty-four, in 1894.

### PIONEERS ASSOCIATED WITH CHICAGO-CRIENTED RAILROADS

Edwin F. Johnson, an engineer from Vermont who wrote the book *Railroad to the Pacific, Northern Route* in 1853, became the chief engineer of the Chicago, St. Paul, and Fond du Lac in 1855. In 1867 Johnson was appointed chief engineer of the Northern Pacific Railroad.

John B. Macy, promoter for the Rock River Valley Union and a United States Congressman from 1853 to 1855, drowned on September 24, 1856, after attempting to jump into a lifeboat from the steamer *Niagara*, which burned on Lake Michigan off Port Washington.

William B. Ogden, president of the new Chicago and North Western in 1859, extended the company's lines to Green Bay by 1862 and engineered its merger with the Galena and Chicago Union in 1864. In September of 1862 he became the first president of the Union Pacific Railroad, a post from which he resigned after eight months. Ogden retired from the North Western on June 4, 1868. In 1871 he suffered over two million dollars in losses in the Chicago and Peshtigo fires. He returned to New York, where he died on August 3, 1877.

A. Hyatt Smith, president of the Rock River Valley Union Railroad from 1850 to 1854, retired to manage his Janesville and Chicago real estate holdings. He oper-

# EPILOGUE

ated the Hyatt House in Janesville, one of the largest and most luxurious hotels in the West, until it burned down in 1867. Smith continued to practice law in Janesville, where he passed away on October 17, 1892.[10]

John Bice Turner, president of the Beloit and Madison from 1852 until 1855, purchased the company in 1862. Turner represented the Galena and Chicago Union in its merger with the Chicago and North Western in 1864 and subsequently served as a director of the North Western.

Leonard J. Farwell, president of the Beloit and Madison and a stockholder in the Watertown and Madison, was ruined by the financial the panic of 1857. Farwell was a state assemblyman in 1860 and served as an examiner in the U.S. Patent Office from 1863 to 1870. He was credited with saving Vice President Andrew Johnson's life by warning him of a possible attack on the night that President Lincoln was assassinated. Farwell moved to Chicago, then to Grant City, Missouri, where he engaged in banking and real estate until his death on April 11, 1889.

## LOCOMOTIVES

No. 1., Wisconsin's first locomotive, which was purchased by Kilbourn for the Milwaukee and Mississippi in 1850, was subsequently designated as the Iowa, the Bob Ellis, and the No. 71, serving the Milwaukee & Mississippi, Milwaukee and Prairie du Chien, and Milwaukee & St. Paul companies before it was put out of commission in 1886. Its boiler was used to heat the round house in Waukesha as late as 1898.

The Spring Green, Milwaukee & Mississippi's engine No. 40, was one of seventeen locomotives purchased from Breese, Kneeland & Company of New York in 1856. It became No. 105 on the Milwaukee & St. Paul line and was sold in 1889 to the El Paso & Southwestern Railroad Company, becoming that company's No 1. until it was retired in 1909. We have the following account from a Mr. L. A. Curtis:

> In 1912 . . . I was approaching the railroad one night in El Paso when I saw before me a little locomotive of very familiar outline. Surely those high set slanting cylinders, those big drivers and the contour of the dome and sand box spelled Breeze Kneeland, 1857. The little engine was not on the road but sat within a railing on a grass plot, she was painted maroon, striped and lettered in gold, bore the number one, and a brass plate proclaimed her to be the first locomotive of the El Paso and South-Western and the first locomotive to enter Bisbee, Arizona. Sure enough, there was the Breeze Kneeland badge plate on the steam-chest, dated 1857. She had the plain wooden cab without panel below the windows used by the Chicago Milwaukee and St. Paul in the seventies and the old St. Paul tender with a heavy

wooden frame and a tool box behind, the St. Paul headlight brackets of short box days kept in use over the extension front. Yes, there in the dark on the Rio Grande was one of the old Chicago, Milwaukee and St. Paul Breeze Kneelands that used to pull the Rockford passenger out of Madison, Wisconsin.[11]

The Spring Green was placed in the Centennial Museum in El Paso, Texas, in 1960, where it can be seen today. The Spring Green is one of only twenty surviving 4-4-0 locomotives (a car with four wheels on the leading truck; four large, driving wheels; and no trailing wheels—the most common configuration on nineteenth century locomotives). There were approximately 25,000 of these locomotives built in the nineteenth and early twentieth centuries.

The Winnebago, the Rock River Valley Union's first locomotive, was changed to standard gauge in 1859 by the successor Chicago and North Western. The Winnebago was serving as a switch-engine in 1880 at the Green Bay yards, having more years of continuous service at the time than any other locomotive in the state.[12]

## BUILDINGS AND OTHER STRUCTURES

Unfortunately, very few pre–Civil War railroad stations are left in Wisconsin. Sadly, Wisconsin's oldest railroad station, the Milwaukee & Mississippi's Waukesha station, was demolished in the 1990s to make way for a parking lot. The Milwaukee & Mississippi depots at Mazomanie and Boscobel have survived, as has the Mineral Point depot at Mineral Point.

The La Crosse and Milwaukee's tunnel at Tunnel City was finished in 1861. It was used for only thirteen years because the rumble of the trains caused sand-falls. A new, higher, more solidly built tunnel with a brick lining was built alongside the old one in 1874 and 1875. That tunnel is still in use today.[13]

## RAILROAD BEDS, CUTS, AND EMBANKMENTS

We finish our tome with the humble, lowly, often-overlooked railroad bed—the smooth, graded beds of earth and gravel on which tracks are laid. Railroad beds, especially where they pass through cuts in hills or on embankments over low areas, are the most common and visible remains of Wisconsin's early railroads. Like Native American burial mounds, they hold their shape and seem to defy weather and time. Driving through the undulating landscape west of Madison on U.S. Highway 14, one sees mile after mile of the old Milwaukee & Mississippi roadway staying level alongside the highway as one's car goes up and down. Built in 1855 by men using picks, shovels, wheelbarrows, horses, oxen, and plows, it has had regularly scheduled trains running over it for over 150 years. There are many other roadbeds like it, some still in use and others long abandoned, throughout southern Wisconsin.

# EPILOGUE

These roadbeds are the permanent and unique legacy of Wisconsin's railroad pioneers—pioneers who, although motivated by profit, knew that their work would result in better lives for their families, their communities, and the future citizens of Wisconsin. One wonders how many of them, especially the axe men, the grubbers, the diggers, and the graders who worked on railways for seventy-five cents or a dollar a day, imagined that their labor would outlast both their century and the next.

# Afterword

The story of Wisconsin's first railroads—from Schoolcraft's proposed railroad for the lead region in 1831, to the premature charters of Wisconsin's territorial years, to the opening of the state's first railroad in 1851, to the federal land grants and political corruptions of 1856, to the economic boom and the recession that followed, and to the bankruptcies and reorganizations at the end of the decade—is a story of people, their ideas and ambitions, and their successes and failures. It's a story of lead, lumber, and wheat being transported to markets near and far; a story of farms, villages, and cities growing in a virgin environment; and a story of tracks and trains tying it all together. As with most train stories, there is an element of romance—the romance of pioneers in a new land; of men spiking iron rails in place; of locomotives, passenger and freight cars, conductors, engineers, train crews, stations and station masters. The story of Wisconsin's first railroads is a rich one and can be enjoyed for what it is—a good story.

The story also offers historical insights and meaning. Most of them pertain to the years in which the story takes place, from 1831 to 1861. It was not coincidental that the thirty years in which Wisconsin's railroads first developed were the same years in which Wisconsin changed from a home to tribal peoples that hunted, gathered, and subsistence farmed to a home for a modern, expanding, industrialized society. The former existed for 11,000 years, while the latter has now existed for 160 years. Remarkably, the underlying economic structure of the latter society has changed little. The inflated housing prices and foreclosures of property in Milwaukee in 1837 are startlingly similar to those of 2008. What has changed is the size of the society. Since 1850 Wisconsin's population has more or less doubled every fifty years—from 300,000 in 1850; to 2,100,000 in 1900; to 3,400,000 in 1950; and to 5,400,000 in 2000—and its consumption of resources has increased even more. But since Wisconsin's size is obviously fixed, this growth cannot continue indefinitely. To achieve stability, at some point Wisconsin will need a new, significantly different economy—one that adapts to the environment, ensures earth-friendly jobs, and does not depend on growth.

We may, at the beginning of the twenty-first century, be seeing the beginnings of such an economy. People are beginning to demand locally produced food, energy-efficient housing, and fuel-efficient transportation, not just to lower their own expenses but also to reduce their "carbon footprint." People are beginning to want to live in a sustainable world that they can pass on to the next generation. And what does this have to do with railroads? Just as they supported the change in Wisconsin from a subsistence society to our industrialized modern world, railroads will support the change from environmental depletion to sustainability. Achieving sustainability will require new levels of efficiency in production, distribution, consumption, regeneration, trade, and transportation. And there is nothing as efficient for moving people and goods as a wheel on a rail.

# Notes

**Chapter One**
1. Frederic L. Paxson, *History of the American Frontier 1763–1893* (Boston: Houghton Mifflin Company, 1924), 258–285.
2. Ray Allen Billington, *Westward Expansion: A History of the American Frontier* (New York: Macmillan Company, 1967), 229–331.
3. Harry Sinclair Drago, *Canal Days in America: The History and Romance of Old Towpaths and Waterways* (New York: Clarkson N. Potter, Inc., 1972), 87, 103–205.
4. Billington, *Westward Expansion*, 332–333.
5. C. Hamilton Ellis, *The Lore of the Train* (New York: Madison Square Press, 1971), 50–51.
6. Alice E. Smith, *The History of Wisconsin, Volume I: From Exploration to Statehood* (Madison: State Historical Society of Wisconsin, 1973), 178–180.
7. Ibid., 181–182.
8. Ibid., 162; see also Doty's letter to Moses Strong, December 25, 1827, Wisconsin Historical Collections XIII, "Papers of James Duane Doty," Wisconsin Historical Society, Madison, WI, 241.
9. Smith, *History of Wisconsin*, 196.
10. Ibid., 182–186.
11. Workers of the Writer's Program of the Work Projects Administration of the State of Wisconsin, *The Story of Mineral Point: 1827–1941* (Mineral Point, WI: Mineral Point Historical Society, 1979), 21, 33–34.
12. Moses M. Strong, *History of the Territory of Wisconsin from 1836 to 1848* (Madison: Democrat Printing Co., 1885; Bowie, MD: Heritage Books, 2002), 175. Citations are to the 2002 edition of the book.
13.. Henry Rowe Schoolcraft, *Personal Memoirs* (Philadelphia: Lippincott, Grambo, and Co., 1851), 392.
14.. Henry Rowe Schoolcraft, *Summary Narrative of an Exploratory Expedition to the Sources of the Mississippi River in 1820: Resumed and Completed, by the Discovery of Its Origin in Itasca Lake, in 1832* (Philadelphia: Lippincott, Grambo, and Co., 1855), 562.
15. Ibid, 562.
16.. Ibid, 563.

**Chapter Two**
1. Seymour Dunbar, *A History of Travel in America* (Indianapolis: Bobbs-Merrill Co., 1915), 725–737.

2. George Fiedler, *Mineral Point: A History* (Mineral Point, WI: Mineral Point Historical Society, 1962), 47.
3. Alice E. Smith, *The History of Wisconsin, Volume I: From Exploration to Statehood* (Madison: State Historical Society of Wisconsin, 1973), 228–229.
4. Peter L. Scanlan, *Prairie du Chien: French, British, American* (Menasha, WI: George Banta Publishing Co., 1937), 148–150.
5. Fiedler, *Mineral Point*, 53.
6. James L. Clark, *Henry Dodge, Frontiersman* (Madison: State Historical Society of Wisconsin, 1957), 2–8.
7. *Green Bay Intelligencer*, February 5, 1834.
8. Western Historical Company, *History of Milwaukee, Wisconsin*, Vol. 1 (Chicago: Western Historical Company, 1881), 135.
9. Scanlan, *Prairie du Chien*, 199.
10. Leland L. Sage, *A History of Iowa* (Ames: Iowa State University Press, 1974), 50–53.
11. Western Historical Company, *History of Grant County, Wisconsin* (Chicago: Western Historical Company, 1881), 480.
12. Joseph Schafer, *Four Wisconsin Counties: Prairie and Forest* (Madison: State Historical Society of Wisconsin, 1927), 47.
13. William R. Smith, *Observations on the Wisconsin Territory: Chiefly on That Part Called the "Wisconsin Land District"* (Philadelphia: E. L. Carey & A. Hart, 1838), 78–79.
14. Wisconsin Historical Company, *History of Milwaukee*, 200.
15. Carrie Cropley, *Kenosha: From Pioneer Village to Modern City 1835–1935* (Kenosha, WI: Kenosha Historical Society, 1958), 2–7.
16. Increase Allan Lapham, *Wisconsin: Its Geography and Topography, History, Geology, and Mineralogy: Together with Brief Sketches of Its Antiquities, Natural History, Soil, Productions, Population, and Government* (Milwaukee, WI: I. A. Hopkins, 1846; New York: Arno Press, 1975), 169. Citations are from the 1975 edition of the book.
17. Alice E. Smith, *History of Wisconsin*, 189, 190.
18. Henry Rowe Schoolcraft. *Personal Memoirs* (Philadelphia: Lippincott, Grambo, and Co., 1851), 520.
19. Elizabeth T. Baird, *O-de-jit-wa-win-ning, or, Contes du Temps Passe: The Memoirs of Elizabeth T. Baird* (Green Bay, WI: Heritage Hill Foundation, 1998), 32.
20. Goodwin Berquist and Paul C. Bowers Jr., *Byron Kilbourn and the Development of Milwaukee* (Milwaukee, WI: Milwaukee County Historical Society, 2001), 1–5.
21. Ibid., 6–9.
22. Ibid., 13.
23. Ibid., 35.
24. Ibid., 38.
25. Ibid., 51–58.
26. Balthasar Meyer, *History of Transportation in the United States before 1860* (Washington, DC: Carnegie Institution of Washington, 1948), 496–498, 506, 510.
27. Dunbar, *History of Travel*, 267–268.
28. Rudolf A. Koss, *Milwaukee* (Milwaukee, WI: Herald Press, 1871), 36, 37.
29. Willis F. Dunbar, *Michigan: A History of the Wolverine State* (Grand Rapids, MI: William B. Eerdmann's Publishing Co., 1980), 243–249.

30. Moses M. Strong, *History of the Territory of Wisconsin* (Madison, WI: Democrat Printing Co., 1885; Bowie, MD: Heritage Books, 2002), 194–197. Citations are to the 2002 edition of the book.
31. Joseph Schafer, *The Wisconsin Lead Region* (Madison: State Historical Society of Wisconsin, 1932), 61.
32. "Benjamin Hyde Edgerton: Wisconsin Pioneer," *Wisconsin Magazine of History*, Vol. 4, no. 3 (March 1921): 355.
33. Ibid., 354–358.
34. Balthasar Meyer, "A History of Early Railroad Legislation in Wisconsin," *Wisconsin Magazine of History* 14 (1931): 209–211.
35. Alice E. Smith, *History of Wisconsin*, 235–238; Strong, *History of Territory of Wisconsin*, 207.

**Chapter Three**
1. Alice E. Smith, *The History of Wisconsin, Volume I: From Exploration to Statehood* (Madison: State Historical Society of Wisconsin, 1973), 238–240.
2. Western Historical Company, *History of Milwaukee, Wisconsin*, Vol. 1 (Chicago: Western Historical Company, 1881), 154.
3. Jack Rudolf, *Birthplace of a Commonwealth: A Short History of Brown County, Wisconsin* (Green Bay, WI: Brown County Historical Society, 1976), 15, 18.
4. Carrie Cropley, *Kenosha: From Pioneer Village to Modern City 1835–1935* (Kenosha, WI: Kenosha Historical Society, 1958), 4.
5. Peter L. Scanlan, *Prairie du Chien: French, British, American* (Menasha, WI: George Banta Publishing Co., 1937), 200.
6. Ibid., 199–200.
7. David V. Mollenhoff, *Madison: A History of the Formative Years* (Madison: University of Wisconsin Press, 2003), 21.
8. Joseph Schafer, *Four Wisconsin Counties: Prairie and Forest* (Madison: State Historical Society of Wisconsin, 1927), 59, 60.
9. George Fiedler, *Mineral Point: A History* (Mineral Point, WI: Mineral Point Historical Society, 1962), 59.
10. Western Historical Company, *The History of Grant County* (Chicago: Western Historical Company, 1881), 537, 538.
11. Rudolf, *Birthplace*, 84–85.
12. Western Historical Company, *History of Milwaukee, Wisconsin*, Vol. 2 (Chicago: Western Historical Company, 1881), 1319, 1320.
13. Ruben G. Thwaites, *The History of Winnebago County and the Fox River Valley 1541–1877* (Winnebago County, WI: Winnebago County, 1984), 20.
14. John Porter Bloom, ed., *The Territorial Papers of the United States*, Vol. XXVII (Washington, DC: U.S. Government Printing Office, 1969), 93.
15. Smith, *History of Wisconsin*, 251–254.
16. Mollenhoff, *Madison*, 22.
17. *Milwaukee Advertiser*, December 10, 1836.
18. Joseph Schafer, *The Wisconsin Lead Region* (Madison: State Historical Society of Wisconsin, 1932), 71, 72.
19. Moses M. Strong, *History of the Territory of Wisconsin* (Madison, WI: Democrat Printing Co, 1885; Bowie, MD: Heritage Books, 2002), 231. Citations are to the 2002 edition of the book.

20. Alice E. Smith, *James Duane Doty: Frontier Promoter* (Madison: State Historical Society of Wisconsin, 1954), 185.
21. Strong, *History of Territory of Wisconsin*, 226.
22. Western Historical Company, *History of Grant County*, 537–538.
23. Balthasar Meyer, *History of Transportation in the United States before 1860* (Washington, DC: Carnegie Institution of Washington, 1948), 293–294.
24. Shafer, *Wisconsin Lead Region*, 69.
25. Frank H. Lyman, *The City of Kenosha and Kenosha County, Wisconsin: A Record of Settlement, Organization, Progress, and Achievement* (Chicago: S. J. Clarke Publishing Co., 1916), 150–153.
26. Shafer, *Wisconsin Lead Region*, 69–70.
27. Western Historical Company, *History of Grant County*, 43–44.

**Chapter Four**

1. Alice E. Smith, *The History of Wisconsin, Volume I: From Exploration to Statehood* (Madison: State Historical Society of Wisconsin, 1973), 277.
2. Glyndon G. Van Deusen, *The Jacksonian Era, 1828–1848* (New York: Harper, 1959), 117.
3. William R. Smith, *Observations on the Wisconsin Territory: Chiefly on that Part Called the "Wisconsin Land District"* (Philadelphia: E. L. Carey & A. Hart, 1838), 44, 45.
4. Goodwin Berquist and Paul C. Bowers Jr., *Byron Kilbourn and the Development of Milwaukee* (Milwaukee, WI: Milwaukee County Historical Society, 2001), 142.
5. John Porter Bloom, ed., *The Territorial Papers of the United States*, Vol. XXVIII (Washington, DC: U.S. Government Printing Office, 1969), 976–980.
6. William F. Raney, "The Building of Wisconsin Railroads," *Wisconsin Magazine of History*, Vol. 19, No. 6 (June 1936), 387.
7. *Milwaukee Sentinel*, September 18, 1838.
8. Bloom, *Territorial Papers*, 1150.
9. Increase Allan Lapham, *Wisconsin: Its Geography and Topography, History, Geology, and Mineralogy: Together with Brief Sketches of Its Antiquities, Natural History, Soil, Productions, Population, and Government* (Milwaukee: I. A. Hopkins, 1846; New York: Arno Press, 1975), 44, 45. Citations are to the 1975 edition of the book.
10. Milwaukee Grain Exchange, *Commercial History of Milwaukee: Opening of the Chamber of Commerce: Addresses by Hon. Edward D. Holton* (Madison: State Historical Society of Wisconsin, 1859), 254.
11. Lapham, *Wisconsin*, 45.
12. Bloom, *Territorial Papers* Vol. XXVII, 222.
13. William Fiske Brown, *Rock County, Wisconsin: A New History of Its Cities, Villages, Towns, Citizens, and Varied Interests, from the Earliest Times up to Date* (Chicago: C. F. Cooper & Co., 1908), 529.
14. Alice E. Smith, *History of Wisconsin*, 326.
15. Lapham, *Wisconsin*, 113.
16. Bloom, *Territorial Papers* Vol. XXVII, 308–309.
17. Ibid., 112.
18. John G. Gregory, *History of Milwaukee* (Chicago: Clarke Publishing Co., 1931), 345–346.
19. Balthasar Meyer, *History of Transportation in the United States before 1860* (Washington, DC: Carnegie Institution of Washington, 1948), 210.
20. Lapham, *Wisconsin*, 42–48.
21. Ibid., 445–446. Citations are to the 2002 edition of the book.

22. Moses M. Strong, *History of the Territory of Wisconsin from 1836 to 1848* (Madison, WI: Democrat Printing Co., 1885, Bowie, MD: Heritage Books, 2002), 445.
23. Strong, *History of the Territory of Wisconsin*, 445–446.
24. Joseph Schafer, *A History of Agriculture in Wisconsin* (Madison: State Historical Society of Wisconsin, 1922), 81–96.
25. Bayrd Still, *Milwaukee: The History of a City* (Madison: State Historical Society of Wisconsin, 1965), 182.
26. Milwaukee Grain Exchange, 261.
27. Balthazar Meyer, "A History of Early Railroad Legislation in Wisconsin," *Grant County Herald*, September 5, 1846.
28. Strong, *History of the Territory of Wisconsin*, 498.
29. Meyer, "A History," 212.
30. Strong, *History of the Territory of Wisconsin*, 533–537.
31. Ibid.
32. Ibid.
33. Ibid.
34. Milwaukee, Waukesha, and Mississippi Railroad Company, *Acts Incorporating the Milwaukee, Waukesha, and Mississippi River Rail Road Company: Together with a Report of the Committee Relating to a Plan of Operations, Adopted by the Board of Directors, Milwaukee, May 19, 1849* (Milwaukee, WI: Sentinel and Gazette, 1849).
35. Alice E. Smith, *History of Wisconsin*, 445.

**Chapter Five**
1. Moses M. Strong, *History of the Territory of Wisconsin from 1836 to 1848* (Madison, WI: Democrat Printing Co., 1885), 591.
2. Western Historical Company, *History of Milwaukee, Wisconsin* Vol. 2, (Chicago: Western Historical Company, 1881), 1322.
3. Ibid., 129–133.
4. August Derleth, *The Milwaukee Road: Its First Hundred Years* (New York: Creative Age Press, 1948), 26, 27.
5. Ibid., 27.
6. Ibid., 648–679.
7. Ibid., 669.
8. *Milwaukee Sentinel and Gazette*, January 6, 1848.
9. Balthasar Meyer, *History of Transportation in the United States before 1860* (Washington, DC: Carnegie Institution of Washington, 1948), 299.
10. Ibid., 299.
11. Ibid., 304.
12. Milwaukee Grain Exchange, *Commercial History of Milwaukee; Opening of the Chamber of Commerce; Addresses by Hon. Edward D. Holton* (Madison: State Historical Society of Wisconsin, 1859), 254.
13. Ibid., 274.
14. Western Historical Company, *History of Milwaukee* Vol. 2, 1586.
15. Milwaukee, Waukesha, and Mississippi Railroad Company, *Acts Incorporating the Milwaukee, Waukesha, and Mississippi River Rail Road Company: Together with a Report of the Committee Relating to a Plan of*

*Operations, Adopted by the Board of Directors, Milwaukee, May 19, 1849* (Milwaukee, WI: Sentinel and Gazette, 1849).
16. Western Historical Company, *History of Milwaukee*, Vol. 2, 999.
17. Milwaukee, Waukesha, and Mississippi Railroad Company, *Acts Incorporating*.
18. Ibid.

**Chapter Six**
1. Milwaukee, Waukesha, and Mississippi Railroad Company, *First Annual Report of the Directors of the Milwaukee, Waukesha, and Mississippi Rail-Road Company to the Stock-holders* (Milwaukee, WI: Milwaukee, Waukesha, and Mississippi Railroad Co., 1850), 3.
2. Goodwin Berquist and Paul C. Bowers Jr., *Byron Kilbourn and the Development of Milwaukee* (Milwaukee, WI: Milwaukee County Historical Society, 2001), 6–9, 28, 29.
3. Milwaukee, Waukesha, and Mississippi Railroad Company, *First Annual Report*, 3.
4. Paul R. Wolf and Russell C. Brinker, *Elementary Surveying* (New York: Harper & Row, 1989), 112.
5. Byron Kilbourn, *Report Made by Byron Kilbourn* (Milwaukee, WI: Free Democrat Print, 1853), 21.
6. Milwaukee, Waukesha, and Mississippi Railroad Company, *First Annual Report*, 3; Kilbourn, *Report Made by Byron Kilbourn*, 21.
7. *Milwaukee Daily Wisconsin*, June 10, 1849.
8. *Milwaukee Daily Sentinel and Gazette*, October 26, 1849.
9. *Milwaukee Daily Sentinel and Gazette*, June 6, 1849.
10. Berquist and Bowers, *Byron Kilbourn*, 147.
11. Bayrd Still, *Milwaukee: The History of a City* (Madison: State Historical Society of Wisconsin, 1965), 170.
12. Kilbourn, *Report Made by Byron Kilbourn*, 21, 22.
13. H. Roger Grant, *The North Western: A History of the Chicago & North Western Railway System* (DeKalb, IL: Northern Illinois University Press, 1996), 10.
14. Wolf and Brinker, *Elementary Surveying*, 529–530, 567–569; R. M. Rylatt, *Surveying the Canadian Pacific: Memoir of a Railroad Pioneer* (Salt Lake City: University of Utah Press, 1991), forward, ix.
15. Kilbourn, *Report Made by Byron Kilbourn*, 21, 23.
16. Ibid., 21–24.
17. Western Historical Company, *History of Milwaukee, Wisconsin*, Volume 2 (Chicago: Western Historical Company, 1881), 1072–1077; Alice E. Smith, *George Smith's Money* (Madison: State Historical Society of Wisconsin, 1966), 35–36; John G. Gregory, *History of Milwaukee, Wisconsin* (Chicago: Clarke Publishing Co., 1931), 190–192.
18. *Waukesha Democrat*, August 21, 1849.
19. Milwaukee, Waukesha, and Mississippi Railroad Company, *First Annual Report*, 3.
20. Kilbourn, *Report Made by Byron Kilbourn*, 21–24.

**Chapter Seven**
1. *Milwaukee Daily Wisconsin*, Sept. 24, 1849.
2. Milwaukee, Waukesha, and Mississippi Railroad Company, *First Annual Report of the Directors of the Milwaukee, Waukesha, and Mississippi Rail-Road Company to Stock-holders* (Milwaukee, WI: Milwaukee, Waukesha, and Mississippi Railroad Company, 1850), 4–5.
3. *Milwaukee Sentinel and Gazette*, November 28, 1849.
4. *Watertown (WI) Chronicle*, December 5, 1849.

5. Western Historical Company, *History of Milwaukee, Wisconsi*, Vol. 2 (Chicago: Western Historical Company, 1881), 1323.
6. Milwaukee Grain Exchange, *Commercial History of Milwaukee; Opening of the Chamber of Commerce; Addresses by Hon. Edward D. Holton*, Vol. 4 (Madison: State Historical Society of Wisconsin, 1859), 275–277.
7. *Waukesha (WI) Democrat*, October 16, 1849.
8. *Wisconsin Democrat*, Oct.16, 1849.
9. *Milwaukee Sentinel and Gazette*, October 31, 1849.
10. *Milwaukee Sentinel and Gazette*, December 18, 1849.
11. Ibid.
12. *Milwaukee Sentinel and Gazette*, October 31, 1849.
13. *Milwaukee Sentinel and Gazette*, November 17, 1849.
14. *Milwaukee Sentinel and Gazette*, November 28, 1849.
15. Milwaukee, Waukesha, and Mississippi Railroad Company, *First Annual Report*, 7–8.
16. Anson Buttles Papers, Wisconsin Historical Society, Madison, WI.
17. Milwaukee, Waukesha, and Mississippi Railroad Company, *First Annual Report*, 3.
18. Ibid., 5.
19. John F. Stover, *The Routledge Historical Atlas of American Railroads* (New York: Routledge, 1999), 17.
20. Ibid.
21. Ibid., 5–6.
22. Ibid., 6.
23. *Waukesha (WI) Democrat*, July 31, 1849.
24. Western Historical Company, *History of Milwaukee*, Vol. 2, 1017.
25. Alice E. Smith, *George Smith's Money: A Scottish Investor in America* (Madison: State Historical Society of Wisconsin, 1966), 11; Western Historical Company, *History of Milwaukee*, Vol. 2, 1072.
26. *Milwaukee Daily Wisconsin*, Oct. 1, 1849.
27. *Milwaukee Sentinel and Gazette*, October 19, 1849.

**Chapter Eight**
1. August Derleth, *The Milwaukee Road: Its First Hundred Years* (New York: Creative Age Press, 1948), 28.
2. Ibid., 30, 31.
3. Goodwin Berquist and Paul C. Bowers Jr., *Byron Kilbourn and the Development of Milwaukee* (Milwaukee, WI: Milwaukee County Historical Society, 2001), 149.
4. Derleth, *Milwaukee Road*, 31.
5. Ibid., 25.
6. Edward D. Holton, *Reply to the Address of the Farmers' General Home League by the Milwaukee and Mississippi Rail Road Company* (Milwaukee, WI: Daily Press and New Steam Printing, 1861), 43.
7. Milwaukee Grain Exchange, *Commercial History of Milwaukee; Opening of the Chamber of Commerce; Addresses by Hon. Edward D. Holton*, Vol. 4 (Madison: State Historical Society of Wisconsin, 1859), 275–277.
8. Holton, *Reply to the Address*, 43, 44.
9. *Milwaukee Daily Wisconsin*, June 14, 1850.
10. *Milwaukee Sentinel and Gazette*, June 22, 1850.

11. Milwaukee and Mississippi Railroad Company, *Circular to Capitalists Relative to Milwaukee City Loan for the Benefit of the Milwaukee and Mississippi Rail Road Company: Together with the Acts and Ordinances Authorizing Said Loan* (Milwaukee, WI: Daily Sentinel and Gazette Print, 1850), 24.
12. Berquist and Bowers, *Byron Kilbourn*, 151.
13. Ibid.
14. Ibid.
15. C. H. Carruthers, *Railway and Locomotive Historical Society's Bulletin Number 10* (Boston: Railway and Locomotive Historical Society, 1925).
16. Ibid.
17. Derleth, *Milwaukee Road*, 32.
18. *Milwaukee Daily Sentinel and Gazette*, September 25, 1850.
19. John G. Gregory, *History of Milwaukee, Wisconsin* (Chicago: Clarke Publishing Co., 1931), 349.
20. Ibid., 350.
21. *Milwaukee Daily Sentinel and Gazette*, November 20, 1850.
22. Wisconsin Historical Company, *History of Milwaukee, Wisconsin*, Vol. 2 (Chicago: Western Historical Company, 1881), 1334.
23. Milwaukee and Mississippi Railroad Company, *Engineer's Report of the Milwaukee and Mississippi Rail Road for the Year 1850* (Milwaukee, WI: Sentinel and Gazette Steam Press, 1851), 15.

**Chapter Nine**
1. Milwaukee and Mississippi Railroad Company, *Engineer's Report for the Year 1850* (Milwaukee, WI: Daily Sentinel and Gazette Print, 1850), 6.
2. Western Historical Company, *The History of Waukesha County, Wisconsin* (Chicago: Western Historical Company, 1880), 730–731.
3. The Anson Buttles Papers, Wisconsin Historical Society Archives, Wisconsin Historical Society, Madison, WI.
4. Milwaukee and Mississippi Railroad Company, *Engineer's Report*, 8.
5. Western Historical Company, *History of Milwaukee, Wisconsin*, Vol. 2 (Chicago: Western Historical Company, 1881), 1348.
6. John G. Gregory, *History of Milwaukee, Wisconsin* (Chicago: Clarke Publishing Co., 1931), 358–359.
7. Samuel Freeman, *The Emigrant's Hand Book and Guide to Wisconsin* (Milwaukee, WI: Sentinel and Gazette Power Press Print, 1851; Madison: State Historical Society of Wisconsin, 1968), 110. Page number refers to 1968 edition.
8. August Derleth, *The Milwaukee Road: Its First Hundred Years* (New York: Creative Age Press, 1948), 33.
9. Derleth, *Milwaukee Road*, 33–34.
10. Western Historical Company, *History of Milwaukee*, 1331.
11. *Milwaukee Daily Wisconsin*. February 26, 1851.
12. Milwaukee and Mississippi Railroad Company, *Reports of the Board of Directors and Engineer of the Milwaukee and Mississippi Rail Road, January, 1852* (Milwaukee, WI: Daily Sentinel Steam Power Press Print, 1852), 7–8.
13. Ibid., 9.
14. Derleth, *Milwaukee Road*, 35.
15. Ibid., 35–36.

16. *Milwaukee Daily Sentinel and Gazette*, May 10, 1851.
17. Western Historical Company, *History of Milwaukee*, 1333.

**Chapter Ten**

1. Byron Kilbourn, *Report Made by Byron Kilbourn* (Milwaukee, WI: Free Democrat Print, 1853), 13–14.
2. Ibid., 3.
3. Ibid.
4. Ibid., 3–8, 11–15; August Derleth, *The Milwaukee Road: Its First Hundred Years* (New York: Creative Age Press, 1948), 39–42.
5. Derleth, *Milwaukee Road*, 29.
6. Milwaukee and Mississippi Railroad Company, *Reports of the Board of Directors and Engineer of the Milwaukee and Mississippi Rail Road, January, 1852* (Milwaukee, WI: Daily Sentinel Steam Power Press Print, 1852), 29–30.
7. Ibid., 29.
8. Ibid., 11, 20.
9. Western Historical Company, *The History of Waukesha County, Wisconsin* (Chicago: Western Historical Company, 1880), 741.
10. Ibid., 742.
11. Milwaukee and Mississippi Railroad Company, *Reports*, 11.
12. Ibid., 24.
13. Ibid., 12–17.
14. Dwight L. Agnew, ed., *Dictionary of Wisconsin Biography* (Madison: State Historical Society of Wisconsin, 1960), 31.
15. Goodwin F. Berquist and Paul C. Bowers Jr., *Byron Kilbourn and the Development of Milwaukee* (Milwaukee, WI: Milwaukee County Historical Society, 2001), 152–153.
16. Milwaukee and Mississippi Railroad Company, *Reports*, 4–5.
17. The Anson Buttles Papers, Wisconsin Historical Society Archives, Wisconsin Historical Society, Madison, WI.
18. Milwaukee and Mississippi Railroad Company, *Reports*, 4.
19. Ibid., 5–6.
20. Ibid., 34.
21. Kilbourn, *Report*, 4.
22. The Carlisle D. Cooke Papers, Wisconsin Historical Society Archives, Madison, WI.

**Chapter Eleven**

1. August Derleth, *The Milwaukee Road: Its First Hundred Years* (New York: Creative Age Press, 1948), 43–44.
2. Byron Kilbourn, *Report Made by Byron Kilbourn* (Milwaukee, WI: Free Democrat Print, 1853), 9–10.
3. Dwight L. Agnew, ed., *Dictionary of Wisconsin Biography* (Madison: State Historical Society of Wisconsin, 1960), 364.
4. Ibid., 28–29.
5. Milwaukee and Mississippi Railroad Company, *Annual Report of the Milwaukee and Mississippi Railroad Company* (Milwaukee, WI: Daily Sentinel Steam Power Press, 1853), 5.
6. Ibid., 5–6.

7. Western Historical Company, *The History of Waukesha County, Wisconsin* (Chicago: Western Historical Company, 1880), 737–738.
8. Derleth, *Milwaukee Road*, 49.
9. Alice E. Smith, ed., "Wisconsin's First Railroad: Linsley Letters, 1852," *Wisconsin Magazine of History* 30, no. 3 (1917): 335–352.
10. Western Historical Company, *History of Waukesha County*, 741.
11. Milwaukee and Mississippi Railroad Company, *Annual Report*, 13.
12. Ibid.
13. *Milwaukee Daily Sentinel and Gazette*, October 3, 1852.
14. Old Settlers' Club of Milwaukee, *Early Milwaukee: Papers from the Archives of the Old Settler's Club of Milwaukee County, 1830–1890* (Madison, WI: R. Hunt, 1977), 101–104.
15. Milton Bicentennial Committee, *The Bicentennial History of Milton* (Milton, WI: Milton Bicentennial Committee, 1977), 5.
16. Milwaukee and Mississippi Railroad Company, *Annual Report*, 8.
17. Ibid., 12–13.

## Chapter Twelve

1. William Fiske Brown, *Rock County, Wisconsin: A New History of Its Cities, Villages, Towns, Citizens and Varied Interests, from the Earliest Times up to Date* (Chicago: C. F. Cooper & Co., 1908), 535–536.
2. Ibid., 539.
3. Ibid., 548
4. Western Historical Company, *History of Rock County, Wisconsin* (Chicago: Western Historical Company, 1879), 382.
5. Ibid., 382–383.
6. Brown, *Rock County*, 542.
7. Dwight L. Agnew, ed., *Dictionary of Wisconsin Biography* (Madison: State Historical Society of Wisconsin, 1960), 236.
8. Robert J. Casey and W. A. S. Douglas, *Pioneer Railroad: The Story of the Chicago and North Western System* (New York: Whittlesey House, 1948), 78.
9. Western Historical Company, *History of Rock County*, 176.
10. *Milwaukee Daily Sentinel & Gazette*, May 12, 1851.
11. Western Historical Company, *History of Fond du Lac County, Wisconsin* (Chicago: Western Historical Company, 1880), 425.
12. Ibid.
13. Stewart M. Rich, "Railroad Shops and Car Building in Fond du Lac," *Railway and Locomotive Historical Society Bulletin* 135 (Fall 1976): 9.
14. Western Historical Company, *History of Rock County*, 386.
15. Gustave W. Buchen, *Historic Sheboygan County* (Sheboygan, WI: Sheboygan Historical Society, 1944), 174.

## Chapter Thirteen

1. Carrie Cropley, *Kenosha: From Pioneer Village to Modern City 1835–1935* (Kenosha, WI: Kenosha County Historical Society, 1958), 27.
2. Herbert W. Rice, "Early History of the Chicago, Milwaukee and Saint Paul Railway Company" (PhD diss., State University of Iowa, n.d.), 71.

3. Ibid., 60.
4. Kenneth W. Duckett, *Frontiersman of Fortune: Moses M. Strong of Mineral Point* (Madison: State Historical Society of Wisconsin, 1955), 111.
5. Ibid., 113, 127.
6. Ibid., 114.
7. Rice, "Early History," 61.
8. Ibid., 59.
9. Ibid., 77, 78.
10. Moses M. Strong Railroad Papers, Wisconsin Historical Society Archives. Letter from Kilbourn to Strong, August 9, 1852.
11. Duckett, *Frontiersman of Fortune*, 117.
12. Gustave W. Buchen, *Historic Sheboygan County* (Sheboygan, WI: Sheboygan Historical Society, 1944), 180.
13. *Charter of the Southern Wisconsin Railroad Company* (Wisconsin: Southern Wisconsin Railroad Company, 1852).
14. Western Historical Company, *History of Grant County, Wisconsin* (Chicago: Western Historical Company, 1881), 539.
15. Daniel J. Lanz, *Railroads of Southern & Southwestern Wisconsin: Development to Decline* (Blanchardville, WI: Ski Printers, 1985), 15.

**Chapter Fourteen**
1. *Janesville (WI) Gazette*, June 24, 1853.
2. John G. Gregory, *History of Milwaukee, Wisconsin* (Chicago: Clarke Publishing Co., 1931), 351.
3. Gregory, *History of Milwaukee*, 359–360.
4. Milton Bicentennial Committee, *The Bicentennial History of Milton* (Milton, WI: Milton Bicentennial Committee, 1977), 13.
5. August Derleth, *The Milwaukee Road* (New York: Creative Age Press, 1948), 51.
6. Ibid.
7. Ibid., 52.
8. Milwaukee & Mississippi Railroad Company, *Fifth Annual Report of the Directors of the Milwaukee & Mississippi Rail Road Company, to the Stockholders: Together with the Reports of the Treasurer, Secretary, and Superintendent* (Milwaukee, WI: Daily Sentinel Steam Power Press, 1854), 38.
9. Derleth, *The Milwaukee Road*, 51–52.
10. Western Historical Company, *History of Rock County, Wisconsin* (Chicago: Western Historical Company, 1879), 675.
11. Wisconsin Legislative Reference Bureau, *State of Wisconsin 2001–2002 Blue Book* (Madison, WI: Joint Committee on Legislative Organization, 2001), 707, 710.
12. Western Historical Company, *History of Dane County, Wisconsin* (Chicago: Western Historical Company, 1880), 608–609.
13. Milwaukee & Mississippi Railroad Company, *Fifth Annual Report*, 35.
14. Ibid., 40.
15. Gregory, *History of Milwaukee*, 358–359.
16. Milwaukee & Mississippi Railroad Company, *Fifth Annual Report*, 51.
17. Ibid.

18. Paul L. Behrens, *The KD Line* (Hebron, IL: Paul L. Behrens, 1986), 3–4.
19. Paul L. Behrens, *Steam Trains to Geneva Lake* (Hebron, IL: Paul L. Behrens, 2002), 22–23.
20. Western Historical Company, *The History of Waukesha County, Wisconsin* (Chicago: Western Historical Company, 1880), 392.
21. Richard N. Current, *Wisconsin: A History* (Champaign, IL: University of Illinois Press, 2001), 29.
22. Roger H. Grant, *The North Western: A History of the Chicago & North Western Railway System* (DeKalb, IL: Northern Illinois University Press, 1996), 25.
23. William Fiske Brown, *Rock County, Wisconsin* (Chicago: C. F. Cooper & Co., 1908) 545.
24. Alice E. Smith, *James Duane Doty, Frontier Promoter* (Madison: State Historical Society of Wisconsin, 1954), 327, 328.
25. Western Historical Company, *The History of Fond du Lac County Wisconsin* (Chicago: Western Historical Company, 1880), 426.
26. W. A. Titus, "Three Pioneer Taverns," *Wisconsin Magazine of History* Vol. 17, No. 2 (1933): 179.
27. Western Historical Company, *History of Fond du Lac County*, 426.
28. Daniel J. Lanz, *Railroads of Southern & Southwestern Wisconsin: Development to Decline* (Blanchardville, WI: Ski Printers, 1985), 15.
29. Western Historical Company, *The History of La Crosse County, Wisconsin* (Chicago: Western Historical Company, 1881), 43.
30. Carrie Cropley, *Kenosha: From Pioneer Village to Modern City 1835–1935* (Kenosha, WI: Kenosha County Historical Society, 1958), 27.
31. Bernard C. Korn, *The Story of Bay View* (Milwaukee, WI: Milwaukee County Historical Society, 1980), 45.
32. Behrens, *Steam Trains to Geneva Lake*, 25–26.
33. Ibid., 26.

**Chapter Fifteen**
1. Barbara Houghton and Jane Nielsen Margaret Licht, *City of the Second Lake: A History of McFarland, Wisconsin* (McFarland, WI: Community Publications, 1976), 18.
2. Western Historical Company, *History of Dane County, Wisconsin* (Chicago: Western Historical Company, 1880), 608–609.
3. *Wisconsin State Journal*, May 24, 1854.
4. David V. Mollenhoff, *Madison: A History of the Formative Years* (Dubuque, IA: Kendall/Hunt Publishing Company, 1982), 51.
5. August Derleth, *The Milwaukee Road* (New York: Creative Age Press, 1948), 54
6. John G. Gregory, *History of Milwaukee, Wisconsin* (Chicago: Clarke Publishing Co., 1931), 357–358.
7. Alice E. Smith, *James Duane Doty, Frontier Promoter* (Madison: State Historical Society of Wisconsin, 1954), 335.
8. Helen M. Bingham, *History of Green County, Wisconsin* (Milwaukee: Burdick & Armitage, 1877), 392.
9. Ibid.
10. Milwaukee & Mississippi Railroad Company, *Sixth Annual Report of the Directors of the Milwaukee & Mississippi Rail Road Company, to the Stockholders: Together with the Reports of the Treasurer, Secretary, and Superintendent* (Milwaukee, WI: Daily Sentinel Steam Power Press, 1855), 13–14.

11. Ibid., 8–9.
12. Ibid.
13. Daniel S. Durrie, *A History of Madison, the Capital of Wisconsin* (Madison, WI: Atwood & Culver, 1874), 361–363.
14. Herbert W. Rice, "Early History of the Chicago, Milwaukee and Saint Paul Railway Company" (PhD diss., State University of Iowa, n.d.), 65.
15. Western Historical Company, *The History of Fond du Lac County, Wisconsin* (Chicago: Western Historical Company, 1880), 424.
16. Rice, "Early History," 72.
17. Wisconsin Railroad Commissioners Department, *Annual Report of the Railroad Commissioners of the State of Wisconsin* (Madison, WI: R. Bolens, 1854), 294.
18. Daniel J. Lanz, *Railroads of Southern & Southwestern Wisconsin: Development to Decline* (Blanchardville, WI: Ski Printers, 1985), 16.
19. Western Historical Company, *History of Rock County, Wisconsin* (Chicago: Western Historical Company, 1879), 382.

**Chapter Sixteen**

1. Milwaukee & Mississippi Railroad Company, *Sixth Annual Report of the Directors of the Milwaukee & Mississippi Rail Road Company, to the Stockholders: Together with the Reports of the Treasurer, Secretary, and Superintendent* (Milwaukee, WI: Daily Sentinel Steam Power Press, 1854), 12–13.
2. Allen Ruff, *Black Earth, a History* (Madison: Wisconsin Power and Light Co., 1992), 16–18.
3. Milwaukee & Mississippi Railroad Company, *Seventh Annual Report of the Directors of the Milwaukee & Mississippi Rail Road Company, to the Stockholders* (Milwaukee, WI: Daily Sentinel Steam Power Press, 1856), 41.
4. Ibid., 43.
5. Ibid., 42–43.
6. Ibid., 33.
7. *Milwaukee Sentinel*, August 17, 21, and 23, 1855.
8. Milwaukee & Mississippi Railroad Company, *Seventh Annual Report*, 16–17.
9. Ibid., 42.
10. Ibid.
11. Paul L. Behrens, "Galena Railroad Days at Beloit," *North Western Lines* (Spring 1998): 26.
12. Ibid., 26.
13. Ibid.
14. Gustave W. Buchen, *Historic Sheboygan County*, rev. ed. (Sheboygan, WI: Sheboygan Historical Society, 1944), 184.
15. Ibid., 192.
16. Western Historical Company, *History of Rock County, Wisconsin* (Chicago: Western Historical Company, 1879), 386.
17. Ibid., 382.
18. *Milwaukee Sentinel*, May 18, 1855.
19. Carrie Cropley, *Kenosha: From Pioneer Village to Modern City 1835–1935* (Kenosha, WI: Kenosha County Historical Society, 1958), 27.
20. John G. Gregory, *History of Milwaukee* (Chicago: S. J. Clarke Publishers, 1931), 333.

21. Bernard C. Korn, *The Story of Bay View* (Milwaukee, WI: Milwaukee County Historical Society, 1980), 45.
22. Daniel J. Lanz, *Railroads of Southern & Southwestern Wisconsin: Development to Decline* (Blanchardville, WI: Ski Printers, 1985), 16.
23. Ibid., 17.
24. August Derleth, *The Milwaukee Road* (New York: Creative Age Press, 1948), 56.
25. P. L. Behrens, *The KD Line* (Hebron, IL: P. L. Behrens, 1986), 9.
26. Ibid.
27. John W. Cary, *The Organization and History of the Chicago, Milwaukee and St. Paul Railway Company* (Milwaukee: Cramer, Aikens, and Cramer, 1892), 16.
28. Ibid., 16.
29. Behrens, "Galena Railroad Days at Beloit," 24.

**Chapter Seventeen**
1. Paul L. Behrens, "Galena Railroad Days at Beloit," *NorthWestern Lines* (Spring 1998): 27.
2. Ibid.
3. David V. Mollenhoff, *Madison: A History of the Formative Years* (Madison: University of Wisconsin Press, 2003), 75–76.
4. Ibid.
5. Behrens, "Galena Railroad Days," 27.
6. Ibid.
7. John W. Cary, *The Organization and History of the Chicago, Milwaukee & St. Paul Railway* (New York: Arno Press, 1981), 16.
8. Roger Noll, *Beaver Dam: 1841–1941* (Chicago: Arcadia Publishing, 2003), 28.
9. *Kilbourn (WI) City Mirror*, July 1, 1856.
10. Cary, *Organization and History*, 17.
11. Ibid., 21.
12. Alice E. Smith, *James Duane Doty: Frontier Promoter* (Madison: State Historical Society of Wisconsin, 1954), 337.
13. Geneva Lake Train Project, *Tracks through Time: A Community Remembers* (Lake Geneva, WI: The Project, 1989), 3.
14. Paul L. Behrens, *Steam Trains to Geneva Lake* (Hebron, IL: P. L. Behrens, 2002), 24.
15. Western Historical Company, *History of Dane County, Wisconsin* (Chicago: Western Historical Company, 1880), 905–906.
16. Ibid., 935.
17. Frank E. Wolf, ed., *Mazomanie Landmarks: Village of Mazomanie, Dane County, Wisconsin* (Mazomanie, WI: Mazomanie Historical Society, 1990), 4, 5.
18. August Derleth, *The Milwaukee Road: Its First Hundred Years* (New York: Creative Age Press, 1948), 60.
19. Western Historical Company, *History of Grant County, Wisconsin* (Chicago: Western Historical Co., 1881), 789.
20. Derleth, *The Milwaukee Road*, 62.
21. Milwaukee & Mississippi Railroad Company, *Eighth Annual Report of the Directors of the Milwaukee & Mississippi Rail Road Company to the Stockholders* (Milwaukee, WI: Daily Sentinel Steam Power Press, 1857), 29.

22. Ibid., 27, 28.
23. Ibid., 29.
24. Ibid., 15, 16.
25. Ibid., 30.
26. Ibid., 24.
27. Daniel J. Lanz, *Railroads of Southern & Southwestern Wisconsin: Development to Decline* (Blanchardville, WI: Ski Printers, 1985), 15.
28. Gustave W. Buchen, *Historic Sheboygan County*, rev. ed. (Sheboygan, WI: Sheboygan Historical Society, 1944), 185, 186.
29. *Sheboygan (WI) Evergreen City Times*, June 28, 1856.
30. Western Historical Company, *History of Milwaukee, Wisconsin*, vol. 2 (Chicago: Western Historical Co., 1881), 397.
31. Ibid., 14–17.
32. Western Historical Company, *History of Rock County, Wisconsin* (Chicago: Western Historical Co., 1879), 387.
33. *Janesville (WI) Gazette*, May 3, 1856.
34. Elvera K. Belden, *History of Racine and Kenosha Counties, 1879* (Racine, WI: Racine County Historical Society, 1980), 177.
35. "National Railway and Locomotive Historical Society Bulletin," *Railroad History* 135 (Fall 1976): 5.
36. Hannah Swart, *Koshkonong Country: A History of Jefferson County, Wisconsin* (Fort Atkinson, WI: W. D. Hoard & Sons, 1975), 135.

**Chapter Eighteen**
1. Alice E. Smith, *James Duane Doty: Frontier Promoter* (Madison: State Historical Society of Wisconsin, 1954), 337.
2. Kenneth W. Duckett, *Frontiersman of Fortune: Moses M. Strong of Mineral Point* (Madison: State Historical Society of Wisconsin, 1955), 127.
3. John W. Cary, *The Organization and History of the Chicago, Milwaukee & St. Paul Railway Company* (Milwaukee, WI: Cramer, Aikens & Cramer, 1892; New York: Arno Press, 1981), 10. Citations are to the 1981 edition of the book.
4. Smith, *James Duane Doty*, 337.
5. Duckett, *Frontiersman of Fortune*, 127.
6. Smith, *James Duane Doty*, 337.
7. Duckett, *Frontiersman of Fortune*, 128.
8. Ibid., 127.
9. Ibid., 337.
10. Ibid.
11. Ibid., 128.
12. Ibid.
13. Ibid., 129.
14. Ibid.
15. Ibid.
16. Ibid.
17. Bayrd Still, *Milwaukee: The History of a City* (Madison: State Historical Society of Wisconsin, 1948), 173.

18. Duckett, *Frontiersman of Fortune*, 129.
19. Ibid.
20. Robert S. Hunt, *Law and Locomotives: The Impact of the Railroad on Wisconsin Law in the Nineteenth Century* (Madison: State Historical Society of Wisconsin, 1958), 34.
21. Duckett, *Frontiersman of Fortune*, 130.
22. Smith, *James Duane Doty*, 342.
23. Western Historical Company, *History of Milwaukee, Wisconsin*, vol. I. (Chicago: Western Historical Co., 1881), 1380.

**Chapter Nineteen**
1. Wisconsin Railroad Commissioners' Department, *Annual Report of the Railroad Commissioners of the State of Wisconsin* (Madison, WI: Atwood & Culver, 1874), 250, 251.
2. Richard N. Current, *Wisconsin: A History*, Vol. 2 (Champaign, IL: University of Illinois Press, 2001), 41.
3. August Derleth, *The Milwaukee Road: Its First Hundred Years* (New York: Creative Age Press, 1948), 62.
4. Current, *Wisconsin*, 237.
5. Paul L. Behrens, *Steam Trains to Geneva Lake* (Hebron, IL: P. L. Behrens, 2002), 26.
6. David V. Mollenhoff, *Madison: A History of the Formative Years* (Madison: University of Wisconsin Press, 2003), 75–76.
7. Ibid.
8. *Milwaukee Sentinel*, April 23, 1857.
9. Daniel J. Lanz, *Railroads of Southern and Southwestern Wisconsin: Development to Decline* (Blanchardville, WI: Ski Printers, 1985), 18.
10. Ibid., 19.
11. John G. Gregory, *History of Milwaukee* (Chicago: Clarke Publishing Co., 1931), 352.
12. Derleth, *Milwaukee Road*, 60.
13. Milwaukee & Mississippi Railroad Company, *Ninth Annual Report of the Directors of the Milwaukee & Mississippi Rail Road Company to the Stockholders* (Milwaukee, WI: Daily Sentinel Steam Press Print, 1858), 18.
14. Current, *Wisconsin*, 242.
15. Gregory, *History of Milwaukee*, 361.
16. Kenneth W. Duckett, *Frontiersman of Fortune: Moses M. Strong of Mineral Point* (Madison: State Historical Society of Wisconsin, 1955), 128–132.
17. Ibid.
18. John W. Cary, *The Organization and History of the Chicago, Milwaukee & St. Paul Railway Company* (New York: Arno Press, 1981), 24.
19. Current, *Wisconsin*, 245, 246.
20. Robert S. Hunt, *Law and Locomotives: The Impact of Railroads on Wisconsin Law in the Nineteenth Century* (Madison: State Historical Society of Wisconsin, 1958), 15.
21. Cary, *Organization and History*, 22.
22. Robert J. Casey and W. A. S. Douglass, *Pioneer Railroad: The Story of the Chicago and North Western System* (New York: McGraw Hill, 1948), 79.
23. Charles T. Knudsen, *Chicago and North Western Railway Steam Power 1848–1956 Classes A–Z* (Chicago: Knudsen Publications, 1965), 10.

24. Ibid., 47.
25. Hannah Swart, *Koshkonong Country: A History of Jefferson County, Wisconsin* (Fort Atkinson, WI: W. D. Hoard & Sons, 1975), 141.
26. Ibid., 136.
27. Ibid., 141.
28. Ibid.
29. *Monroe (WI) Sentinel*, September 23, 1857.
30. Edmund C. Hamilton, *The Story of Monroe: Its Past and Its Progress Toward the Present* (Monroe, WI: Monroe Public Schools Print Shop, 1976), 43.
31. Lanz, *Railroads of Southern & Southwestern Wisconsin*, 10.
32. Milwaukee & Mississippi Railroad Company, *Ninth Annual Report*, 10.
33. Ibid., 20, 21.
34. Lee D. Dahl, "The Origins of Conflict between Southport and Racine," in *Kenosha Historical Sketches* (Kenosha, WI: Kenosha County Historical Society, 1986), 61.
35. Milwaukee & Mississippi Railroad Company, *Ninth Annual Report*, 18.
36. Ibid., 7.

**Chapter Twenty**

1. Milwaukee & Mississippi Railroad Company, *Tenth Annual Report of the Directors of the Milwaukee & Mississippi Rail Road Company to the Stockholders* (Milwaukee, WI: Jermain & Brightman, 1859), 9.
2. Richard N. Current, *Wisconsin: A History*, Vol. 2 (Madison: State Historical Society of Wisconsin, 1976), 237.
3. Ibid., 267.
4. Gordon Berquist and Paul C. Bowers Jr., *Byron Kilbourn and the Development of Milwaukee* (Milwaukee, WI: Milwaukee County Historical Society, 2001), 172.
5. August Derleth, *The Milwaukee Road: Its First Hundred Years* (New York: Creative Age Press, 1948), 85.
6. Ibid., 82.
7. Ibid., 84.
8. Ibid., 82.
9. Ibid., 85.
10. Ibid., 82.
11. Current, *Wisconsin*, 245, 246.
12. Western Historical Company, *History of La Crosse County, Wisconsin* (Chicago: Western Historical Company, 1881), 585.
13. John G. Gregory, *History of Milwaukee* (Chicago: Clarke Publishing Co., 1931), 367–369.
14. Albert H. Sanford and H. J. Hirshheimer, *A History of La Crosse, Wisconsin 1841–1900* (La Crosse, WI: La Crosse Historical Society, 1951), 79.
15. Monroe County Wisconsin Bicentennial Committee, *Monroe County, Wisconsin, Pictorial History 1976* (Tomah, WI: Tomah Journal Printing Co., 1976), 202.
16. Milwaukee & Mississippi Railroad Company, *Tenth Annual Report*, 11.
17. Western Historical Company, *History of Rock County, Wisconsin* (Chicago: Western Historical Co., 1879), 191–192.
18. *Monroe (WI) Sentinel*, January 20, 1858.
19. Milwaukee & Mississippi Railroad Company, *Tenth Annual Report* 3–4.

20. Ferd Homme, *Oak Opening: The Story of Stoughton* (Stoughton, WI: Stoughton Centennial History Committee, 1947), 31.
21. Derleth, *Milwaukee Road*, 62–63.
22. Milwaukee & Mississippi Railroad Company, *Tenth Annual Report*, 19–20.
23. Ibid., 3.
24. Ibid, 3–8.
25. Ibid, 7, 8.
26. Daniel J. Lanz, *Railroads of Southern and Southwestern Wisconsin: Development to Decline* (Blanchardville, WI: Ski Printers, 1985), 20.
27. Milwaukee & Mississippi Railroad Company, *Tenth Annual Report*, 3–7.
28. Hannah Swart, *Koshkonong Country: A History of Jefferson County, Wisconsin* (Fort Atkinson, WI: W. D. Hoard & Sons, 1975), 137.
29. Milton Bicentennial Committee, *The Bicentennial History of Milton* (Milton, WI: Milton Bicentennial Committee, 1977), 91.
30. Railway and Locomotive Historical Society, Inc. *Railroad History* 135 (Fall 1976): 5.
31. D. C. Prescott, *Early Day Railroading from Chicago* (Chicago: David B. Clarkson Co., 1910), 51–52.
32. Current, *Wisconsin*, 244.
33. Ibid., 248; Robert S. Hunt, *Law and Locomotives: The Impact of Railroads on Wisconsin Law in the Nineteenth Century* (Madison: State Historical Society of Wisconsin, 1958), 48, 49.
34. Dale E. Treleven, "Railroads, Elevators, and Grain Dealers: The Genesis of Antimonopolism in Milwaukee," *Wisconsin Magazine of History* 52, no. 3 (1969): 206.
35. Bayrd Still, *Milwaukee: The History of a City* (Madison: State Historical Society of Wisconsin, 1948), 175.
36. Paul L. Behrens, *Steam Trains to Geneva Lake* (Hebron, IL: P. L. Behrens, 2002), 26.
37. Current, *Wisconsin*, 237.

**Chapter Twenty-One**
1. John W. Carey, *The Organization and History of the Chicago, Milwaukee & St. Paul Railway Company* (Milwaukee, WI: Cramer, Aikens & Cramer, 1892), 11–12.
2. D. C. Prescott, *Early Day Railroading from Chicago* (Chicago: David B. Clarkson Co., 1910), 12.
3. Ibid., 37–38.
4. Hannah Swart, *Koshkonong Country: A History of Jefferson County, Wisconsin* (Fort Atkinson, WI: W. D. Hoard & Sons, 1975), 144.
5. Western Historical Company, *History of Fond du Lac County, Wisconsin* (Chicago: Western Historical Company, 1880), 427.
6. Bayrd Still, *Milwaukee: The History of a City* (Madison: State Historical Society of Wisconsin, 1965), 175.
7. *Prairie du Chien (WI) Leader*, December 8, 1859.
8. Milwaukee & Mississippi Railroad Company, *Eleventh Annual Report of the Directors of the Milwaukee & Mississippi Rail Road Company to the Stockholders* (Milwaukee, WI: Daily News Book and Job Steam Printing Office, 1860), 17.
9. Donald J. Kabitzke, *North Prairie: An Historic Wisconsin Village, 1834–1950* (Milwaukee, WI: D. J. Kabitzke, 1983), 27.
10. Gustav W. Buchen, *Historic Sheboygan County* (Sheboygan, WI: Sheboygan County Historical Society, 1976), 187.

11. William J. Park & Co., ed., *Madison, Dane County and Surrounding Towns* (Madison, WI: W. J. Park & Co., 1877), 318, 319.
12. Paul L. Behrens, *The KD Line* (Hebron, IL: Paul Behrens Publishing, 1986), 20.
13. Ibid., 20–21.
14. *Fort Atkinson (WI) Standard*, October 4, 1859.
15. Western Historical Company, *History of Rock County, Wisconsin* (Chicago: Western Historical Company, 1879), 386.
16. Swart, *Koshkonong Country*, 144.
17. Richard N. Current, *The History of Wisconsin, Volume II: The Civil War Era* (Madison: State Historical Society of Wisconsin, 1976), 35.
18. Swart, *Koshkonong Country*, 145.

**Chapter Twenty-two**
1. Milwaukee & Mississippi Rail Road Company, *Eleventh Annual Report of the Directors of the Milwaukee & Mississippi Rail Road Company to the Stockholders* (Milwaukee, WI: Daily News Book and Job Steam Printing Office, 1860), 18–19.
2. Milwaukee & Mississippi Railroad Company, *Plan for the Reorganization of the Milwaukee & Mississippi Railroad Company* (Milwaukee, WI: Milwaukee & Mississippi Railroad Company, 1860), 1.
3. Ibid., 1–2.
4. Ibid., 9.
5. August Derleth, *The Milwaukee Road: Its First Hundred Years* (New York: Creative Age Press, 1948), 65.
6. Isaac Seymour, *To the Mortgage Bondholders of the Milwaukee and Mississippi Railroad Company* (Milwaukee, WI: Milwaukee & Mississippi Railroad Company, 1860), 1–2.
7. Ibid.
8. John W. Cary, *The Organization and History of the Chicago, Milwaukee & St. Paul Railway Company* (Milwaukee, WI: Cramer, Aikens & Cramer, 1892), 85.
9. Derleth, *Milwaukee Road*, 66.
10. Ibid.
11. Paul L. Behrens, *Steam Trains to Geneva Lake* (Hebron, IL: P. L. Behrens, 2002), 28.
12. Ibid., 29.
13. Robert J. Casey and W. A. S. Douglas, *Pioneer Railroad* (New York: Whittlesey House, 1948), 81.
14. Western Historical Company, *History of Milwaukee, Wisconsin*, vol. II (Chicago: Western Historical Company, 1881), 1330.
15. Michael J. Goc and Geraldine N. Driscoll, *Winneconne: History's Crossing Place* (Winneconne, WI: New Past Press, 1987), 11.
16. Carrie Cropley, *Kenosha: From Pioneer Village to Modern City, 1835–1935* (Kenosha, WI: Kenosha County Historical Society, 1958), 29.
17. Derleth, *Milwaukee Road*, 78.
18. Ibid., 74–77, 79.
19. Richard N. Current, *The History of Wisconsin, Volume II: The Civil War Era* (Madison: State Historical Society of Wisconsin, 1976), 241.
20. Gustav W. Buchen, *Historic Sheboygan County* (Sheboygan, WI: Sheboygan County Historical Society, 1976), 192.

## Epilogue

1. Robert J. Casey and W. A. S. Douglas, *Pioneer Railroad* (New York: Whittlesey House, 1948), 128.
2. John F. Stover, *The Routledge Historical Atlas of the American Railroads* (New York and London: Routledge, 1999), 100–101.
3. Dwight L. Agnew, ed., *Dictionary of Wisconsin Biography* (Madison: State Historical Society of Wisconsin, 1960), 198.
4. Western Historical Company, *History of Milwaukee, Wisconsin*, Vol. 2 (Chicago: Western Historical Company, 1881), 1350.
5. Ibid., 1331.
6. *Janesville (WI) Gazette*, March 22, 1921.
7. Western Historical Company, *History of Milwaukee*, 1352.
8. Ibid., 1348.
9. William Fiske Brown, ed., *Rock County, Wisconsin* (Chicago: C. F. Cooper & Co., 1908), 192–195.
10. Brown, *Rock County*, 548.
11. Lawrence A Curtis, "The Previous History of El Paso and South-Western No. 1 and Something of Her Contemporaries on the Saint Paul," *Railway and Locomotive Historical Society Bulletin* 15 (1927): 60, 62.
12. Western Historical Company, *History of Milwaukee*, 1379.
13. Monroe County Wisconsin Bicentennial Committee, *Monroe County, Wisconsin: Pictorial History, 1976* (Tomah, WI: Tomah Journal Print, 1976), 202.

# Subject Index

*Following the Subject Index is a People and Place Name Index. Italicized page numbers indicate illustrations.*

## A

*Abiah* (brig), 99
accidents, 182, 259–261, 264, 276, 281, 289
African Americans, 3, 135
*American Railroad Journal*, 172
*American Traveler*, 15
Army Ordinance Bureau, 8

## B

*Badger* (steam launch), 25
Baltimore and Ohio Railroad, 5, 25
bankruptcy, 251–268
Battle of the Bad Axe, 17, 19
Beaver Dam Railroad, 57
Belmont and Dubuque Railroad, 34–35, 40, 44, 45
Beloit and Madison Rail Road, 157, 163, *189*, 198, 206, *221*, *283*, 290
Beloit and Taycheedah Railroad, 141–143. *See also* Rock River Valley Union Railroad
*Beloit Journal*, 140–141, 142, 177
Best Friend of Charleston (locomotive), 5
Black Hawk Purchase, 18, 20
Black Hawk War, 17, 21, 29, 32, 35
Bob Ellis (locomotive), 100. *See also* No. 1
British, 3, 5–6, 15, 20
bribery, 252–254
bridges, 180–181, 236
*Burlington Gazette*, 289

## C

*C. K. Watkins* (locomotive), *207*
Camden and Amboy Railroad, 5, 25
canals, 4–5, 74
celebrations (railroad), 175, 235
Charleston and Hamburg Railroad, 5
charters, *31*, 33–34, 47–49, 55–58, 170
Chicago, Milwaukee and St. Paul Railway, 294–295
Chicago, St. Paul and Fond du Lac Railroad, *199*, 199–200, 206, 208, 210, 218–223, *219*, *221*, 225–226, 229, *236*, 239–241, *246*, 253, 262–263, 270–272, *272*
Chicago and Galena Railroad, 86, *246*
Chicago and Milwaukee Railroad, 176, 217
Chicago and North Western Railway, 271–272, 279–282, *280*, 282, *282*, *283*, *290*
Chicago and Sheboygan Railroad, *283*
Chippewa (tribe), 6, 8
Civil War, 270, *288*, 295, 297
competition with other transportation, 5, 54–55, 67–68, 75–76
consolidations (railroads), 297–299
construction (railroads), 70, 81–85, 102, 180, 306–307

## D

depression (economic), 42, 45, 47, 58, 251, 268, 288, 291
Detroit and Pontiac Railroad, 10, 12

## SUBJECT INDEX

Detroit and St. Joseph Railroad, 17, 26
*Detroit* (steamer), 274
Dubuque and Belmont Railroad, 160

### E

E. Corning (locomotive), *166*
Eastern railways, 88, 142, 157, 193
*Emigrants Handbook and Guide to Wisconsin* (Freeman), *111*
*Enterprise* (steamboat), 212
Erie and Kalamazoo Railroad, 142
Erie Railroad, 88
expansion (railroads), 37, 206–221, 230–247

### F

fares, 5, 104, 258
farm mortgages, 75–76, 93, 95–96, 119, 230, 266, 284, 293–294
farming/farmers, 4, 15, 53–55, 58–59, 119, 139, 284, 290
*First Steam Passenger Train in America* (Brown), 15
Fond du Lac and Beaver Dam Railroad, 57
founding of Milwaukee, 18, 22, 23–25, *24*
founding of Madison, 37–39, *38*
*Forest Queen* (propeller vessel), 279
*Fort Atkinson Standard*, 279
Fountain City (locomotive), 173–174
Fox River Valley Railroad, 171, *245*
Fox-Wisconsin (waterway), 6–7, 13, 22, 27, 35, 39, 41
Fox (tribe), 18
fur trade, 6–7, 21, 23

### G

Galena and Chicago Union Railroad, 77, 89–90, 112, 118, 136, 139, 144, 155–157, 171, 177, 198, 207, 245, 263–264, 288–289
*Geneva Express*, 210
Genoa (locomotive), 217
Granite Railway, 34
*Grant County Herald*, 55
Great Western Railway, 25–26
Green Bay, Milwaukee, and Chicago Railroad, 148, 176, 200–201, *207*, 234
Green Bay and Minnesota Railroad, 171

*Green Bay Intelligencer*, 18
*Green Bay Intelligencer and Democrat*, 22

### H

*Herald* (schooner), 218
Hetton Rail-Road, 15
*Historic Sheboygan County* (Buchen), 146
*History of the Territory of Wisconsin* (Strong), 57
Ho Chunk (tribe). *See* Winnebago
*Home League* (weekly), 293
horse-powered railroads, 5
Hudson River Railroad, 77

### I

Illinois and Wisconsin Railroad, 144, 156, 188, 199
Illinois Central Railroad, 144, 154, 161, 188, 201, 245, *246*
immigrants, 6, 25, 53, 91, 93, 284
Ithaca and Oswego Railroad, 129
Indian Removal Act of 1830, 4
Iowa (locomotive), 100. *See also* No. 1
Ithaca and Oswego Railroad, 129

### J

*Janesville Gazette*, 218, 302
John C. Freemont (locomotive), 234

### K

Kenosha, Rockford & Rock Island Railroad, 263–264, 268, 278–279, *283*, 291–293
Kenosha and Beloit Railroad, 170, 172, 175, *221*, 231, *283*
Kenosha (locomotive), 217, 218
*Kenosha Tribune and Telegraph*, 203, 279
*Kilbourn City Mirror*, 209

### L

L. B. Rock (locomotive), *202*
La Crosse and Milwaukee Railroad, 149–155, 163, 175, 186, *204*, 205, 208, *221*, 223–230, 237, *238*, *246*, 252–256, *255*, 267–268, 282, 290

## SUBJECT INDEX

La Fontaine Rail Road, 35, 39, 44
*Lady Franklin* (steamboat), 275
Lake Michigan and Mississippi Railroad, 56, 57
Lake Shore and Michigan Southern Railroad, *201*
Lake Shore Line. *See* Green Bay, Milwaukee, and Chicago Railroad
Lakeshore Railroad, *221, 246, 283*
land grants, 70, 90, 222–229, 154, 222–229
land sales, 22-25
lead mining, 7–13, 18, 20–21, 28, 32, *44*; map of mines, *7*
locomotives, 99–100, 305. *See also individual locomotives*
Luther A. Cole (locomotive), *202*

## M

Mad River and Lake Erie Railroad, 26
Madison and Beloit Railroad, 141–143, *143*, 156. *See also* Rock River Valley Union Railroad
Madison and Prairie du Chien Railroad, 167. *See also* Milwaukee & Mississippi Railroad
*Madison Argus and Democrat*, 181, 253
*Madison Daily Patriot*, 208
Manitowoc and Mississippi Railroad, 158, 246
"Meeting of the Waters" (Moore), 212
memorials to Congress, 27–28, 41, 45–46
Menomonee (locomotive), 133, *180*
Menomonee Locomotive Works, 133–134, *180*, *202*
Menomonee (tribe), 6
Michigan Militia, 17
Michigan Territorial Council, 10, 12, 26
Milwaukee, Fond du Lac, and Green Bay Railroad, 171, 175–176, 186
Milwaukee, Watertown and Baraboo Valley Railroad, 277–278, 283, *283*, 294. *See also* Milwaukee and Western Railroad
Milwaukee, Waukesha, and Mississippi River Railroad, 161
Milwaukee, Waukesha, Jefferson, and Madison Railroad, 171
Milwaukee & Mississippi Railroad, 167, *168*, 178, *180*, 206, 235–236, *236, 242, 256, 275*, 284–288, *287, 288*, difficulties of, 242–245, 256–259, 261–262; expanded routes of, 193–200; to Madison, 179–189; map of, *189*, *221, 246, 283*; reorganization of, 273–276. *See also* Milwaukee and Mississippi Railroad; Milwaukee and Prairie du Chien Railway
*Milwaukee Advertiser*, 36, 39
Milwaukee and Beloit Railroad, 266
Milwaukee and Chicago Railroad, 234, *234*. *See also* Green Bay, Milwaukee, and Chicago Railroad
Milwaukee and Fond du Lac Railroad, 175
Milwaukee and Horicon Railroad, 148–149, 176, 186, 208, *221, 233*, 267–268, *283*, 291
Milwaukee and Minnesota Railroad, 282, *283*
Milwaukee and Mississippi Railroad, 35–37, 39, 41, 44–46, 48–49, 51–53, 56, 95, *103, 111*, 127–129, 131–136, *135*, 159, *166*, 167, difficulties at, 115–124, 125–127, 129–131; expanded routes of, 163–170; first train on, 99–104; funding of, 53, 93–99. *See also* Milwaukee & Mississippi Railroad; Milwaukee and Waukesha Railroad
Milwaukee and Prairie du Chien Railway, 286–288. *See also* Milwaukee & Mississippi Railroad
Milwaukee and Rock River Canal, *48–49*, 49–51, 56, 65, 67, 70, 74, 119, 150
Milwaukee and St. Paul Railroad, *202*
Milwaukee and Superior Railroad, 36, *265*, 266
Milwaukee and Watertown Railroad, 148, 174, *182, 189, 202*, 202–203, 223, 224, *246*, 268, *272*
Milwaukee and Waukesha Railroad, 57–58, 63–72, 73–80, 81–91, 95
Milwaukee and Western Railroad, 294. *See also* Milwaukee, Watertown and Baraboo Valley Railroad
*Milwaukee Daily Sentinel*, 292, 295
*Milwaukee Daily Wisconsin*, 75, 82, 97
*Milwaukee Free Democrat*, 258
*Milwaukee Sentinel*, 46, 82, 85–86, 91, 99–100, 125–126, 152–153, 196, 200, 210, 274
*Milwaukee Sentinel and Gazette*, 67, 75–76, 86, 98, 101, 103, 112–113, 133, 144
*Milwaukee* (steamer), 274
Mineral Point, Wisconsin, 16, 18, 22, 27, 35–37, 39, 147, 160–162
Mineral Point (locomotive), 234
Mineral Point Railroad, 160–162, 175, 187–188, 201–202, *214*, 215–216, *221*, 233–234, 245, 260–261

# SUBJECT INDEX

*Minnie May* (schooner), 218
Mississippi River, expansion to, 37, 59, 230–247
Mohawk and Hudson Railroad, 5, 15, *16*, 25
*Monroe Sentinel*, 233–234, 242–244, 256–257

## N

N. K. Wheeler (locomotive), 271
name changes (railroads), 297–299
Native Americans, 3–4, 6. *See also* Chippewa, Fox, Menomonee, Ottawa, Potawatomi, Sauk, Winnebago
New York and Erie Railroad, 88, 157
Niles Locomotive Works, *203, 217*
No. 1 (locomotive), 99–101, *101*, 110, *275*, 305
Norris Locomotive Works, 99–100
Northern Pacific Railroad, 209

## O

Ohio Railroad, 25
Ojibwa (tribe). *See* Chippewa
*Orinoco* (steamboat), 212
Ottawa (tribe), 8

## P

Pacific Railroad Convention, 90
Panama Rail Road, 91
*Patrick Henry* (schooner), 99, 101
Pekatonica and Mississippi Railroad, 48, 49, 161
plank roads, 67–68
Potawatomi (tribe), 6, 8
*Prairie du Chien Leader*, 275
"Project for a Railroad to the Pacific" (Whitney), 90

## R

Racine, Janesville, and Mississippi Railroad, 159, 176–177, 185
*Racine Advocate*, 185
Racine and Mississippi Rail Road, 185–186, *189*, 202, 208, *217, 221*, 246, *266*, 267, 278, 289
*Racine* (propeller vessel), 279
*Rail-Road Journal*, 15

*Railroad to the Pacific: Northern Route* (Johnson), 172
Rainhill Trials, *16*
Ransom and Saratoga Railroad, 157
reorganization (railroad companies), 269–283
Ripon and Wolf River Railroad, 291
roads, 4, 7–8, 34, *51*, 67–68
*Rock County Badger*, 82
Rock River Valley railroads, 139–146
Rock River Valley Union Railroad, *68*, 118, 130, *135*, 143–147, 156, 158–159, 163, 171–174, 185, 188, *189*, 198–200, 208, 251
"Rocket" (Stephenson), *16*
Rockton and Freeport Rail Road, 185
Rockton (locomotive), *217*
Root River Rail Road, 47, 158–159
rump territory, 26, 29

## S

Sauk (tribe), 17–18
Savanna Branch Railroad, 208
Schenectady Locomotive Works, *166*
school funds, 93–95
Sheboygan and Fond du Lac Railroad, 56, 57, 157, 158
Sheboygan and Mississippi Railroad, 174, 198, 216, 277, 283, 290, 294
*Sheboygan Democrat*, 94
*Sheboygan Evergreen City Times*, 216, 277
*Sheboygan Gazette*, 157
*Sheboygan Lake Journal*, 198–200
*Sheboygan Times*, 216
Silver (locomotive), 217
shot tower, 20–21
Southern Michigan Railroad, 136
Southern Wisconsin Railroad, *135*, 136, 159–160, 163, 166, 172, 194
Spring Green (locomotive), 305–306
St. Croix and Lake Superior Railroad, 223, 224, 237
stage travel, *51, 68*
statehood, 66
steam travel, 4–6
stocks, 34, 63–64, 85–87, 89, 95–96, 188
Stockton and Darlington Railroad, 5
Sugar Valley Railroad, 223
surveys (land), 23-24, 27
surveys (railroad), 47, 73–78, 86–87, 155

## SUBJECT INDEX

### T

Taunton Locomotive Company, 173
tickets, *165, 272, 290*
*Tift* (steam-tug), 201
Tom Thumb (locomotive), 5
tramways, 20–22
*Treatise on Rail-Roads Compiled from the Best and Latest Authorities* (Earle), 15
Treaty of Rock Island, 17
transportation: plank roads, 67–68; stage coaches, *51, 68*; tramways, 20–22; wagons, 4, 7–8, 34, 54; waterways, 4–7, 13, 22, 27, 35, 39, 41
Troy and Schenectady Railroad, 157

### U

Utica and Schenectady Railroad, 25

### V

*View of the Lead Mines of Missouri* (Schoolcraft), 10

### W

W. B. Walton & Co. *See* Menomonee Locomotive Works
wagons, 4, 7–8, 34, 54
Walter S. Gurnee (locomotive), 271
Warren (locomotive), 234
Watertown and Berlin Railroad, 171
Watertown and Madison Rail Road, 207, 232, *232, 246,* 267, *267,* 277
*Watertown Chronicle*, 82
Watertown (locomotive), *203*
*Waukesha Democrat*, 84–85, 90
Westward Ho (locomotive), 186
wheat, 15, 53–55, 119, 266
Winnebago (locomotive), *68*, 173, 306
Winnebago (tribe), 6, 8, 17, 195
Winnebago War, 8
Wisconsin and Superior Railroad, 226–227, 228, 229, 239
Wisconsin Centennial Mural, *9*
Wisconsin Central Railroad, 171, 210, 268
Wisconsin Historical Society, 140, 299, 304
*Wisconsin State Journal*, 181, 236
Wisconsin Territory, 17, 25, 29–32; capital selection for, 26–27, 32, 37–39, 41; map of, *43*; statehood of, 66
Wisconsin (train), 101, 103

# People and Place Name Index

*Preceding the People and Place Name Index is a Subject Index. Italicized page numbers indicate illustrations.*

## A

Abbot, Chauncey, 156
Ackerman, Abram, 174
Albany, Wisconsin, 159–160
Alden, S. H., 208
Allen, Thomas S., 162
Allen, William J., 159
Appleton, Edward, 216, 277, 294
Arndt, Charles C. P., 150
Arndt, John P., 38
Ashley, O. D., 272
Astor, Wisconsin, 18, 35, 37, 39
Atchison, John, 32, 34, 40
Atkinson, Henry, 17
Atwood, Volney, 156
Austin, George F., 128

## B

Bailey, W. H. H., 141
Bailie, John, 109, 301
Baird, Elizabeth T., 23
Baird, Henry S., 37
Baker, Charles M., 170, 171, 175
Bannister, John, 158
Barber, Edward, 165
Barber, Hiram, 174
Barlow, S. S., 159
Barnes, William, 273
Barnum, P. T., 117
Barrett, Harrison, 294
Barstow, Samuel H., 107
Barstow, William A., 57, 107–108, 114, 128, 168, 171, 223, 224, 300
Bartholomew, G. M., 272
Bashford, Coles, 171, 224, 225, 227–229, *228*, 238, 253
Beall, Samuel W., 158
Bean, Jacob L., 107, 115, 119–121, 124, 125–127, 153, 155, 174, 303
Beecher, Luther, 215, 233
Belleview, Wisconsin, 39
Belleville, Wisconsin, 281
Belmont, Wisconsin, 32–35, *33*, 37, 39, 40
Beloit, Wisconsin, 47, 139–140, 159, 177, 208
Bennett, Ensign H., 160
Bennett, George, 170–171
Benson, S. W., 171
Benton, Thomas Hart, 29
Bequette, Pachall, 35
Berlin, Wisconsin, *233*
Biddlecome, William R., 160
Bigelow, T. B., 229
Bird, Augustus A., 167
Birkinshaw, John, 5
Black Hawk (Sauk leader), 17–18, *18*, 139
Blackstone, John, 161
Blodgett, A. Z., 201
Blossom, Levi, 148, 152
Blue Mounds, Wisconsin, 41, 45
Bond, Josiah, 170, 175, 203, 217
Bowman, James, *31*
Bracken, Charles, 35, 45
Bracken, John, 153, 161
Brewster, Joseph, 161

# PEOPLE AND PLACE NAME INDEX

Bridge, John H., 184
Bridgeman, Edwin, 102, 110, 111, 301
Bridgeport, Wisconsin, 30
Brisbois, B. W., 167
Brodhead, Edward Hallock, 129, 132–133, 135–136, 164, 165, 167, 169–170, 174, 182, 184–185, 194–196, 213, 215, 242, 256, 300
Bronson, Greene C., 209, 237–238, 282
Brookfield Junction, 174, *189*, *221*
Brown, E. C., 276
Brown, J., 111
Brown, P. V., 148
Brown, Sam, 36
Brown, William, 15
Brown, William Jr., 52
Buchen, Gustave W., 146
Bugh, Samuel G., 159
Bulkley, George, 171
Burdick, Elisha, 156, 167
Burnett, Andy, 213
Burnham, H., 26
Burns, Timothy, 152, 153, 155, 174
Butler, Benjamin F., 152
Butler, Charles, 188, 271, 272
Butler, George, 211
Buttles, Anson, 87, 108, 114, 121–122
Buttles, Cornelia Mullie, 87, 108, 121–122

## C

Campbell, Allen, 288
Campbell, Alonzo, 170, 175
Campbell, Peter, 159
Carley, Quartus, 18
Cary, Bushnell B., 47
Cary, Joseph, 128
Cassville, Wisconsin, 27, 32, 37, 39
Caswell, L. B., 240, 241, 271, 280
Catlin, John, 120, 125, 128–133, *129*, 149, 154, 161, 166, 184, 193–194, 197, 215, 230, 251, 256–257, 274–276, 284–285, 288, 300
Catton, James, 159
Cawker, E., 95
Chamberlain, Joseph, 120, 121, 124, 127, 165, 168, 175
Chamberlain, Selah, 120, 121, 123–124, 127, 165, 168, 175, 208, 290

Chandler, D., 101, 148
Chandler, R. W., *7*
Chase, Horace, 36
Cheney, Hazen, 156
Cheney, Rufus, 111, 231
Cholvin, Francis, 161
Church, George, 276
City of the Four Lakes, Wisconsin, 38, 45. *See also* Madison, Wisconsin
Clark, Darwin, *232*
Clark, Harry, 264
Clark, Stephen, 238
Clayton, John, 29
Cleveland, Newcomb, 205, 273
Clinton, Dewitt, 25
Clinton, Edmond D., 68, 69, 75, 82, 86, 107, 114, 119–120, 124, 174, 183–184, 209
Clinton, Norman, 57
Coates, John, 119, 128
Cobb, Amasa, 226, 229
Cobb, Joshua, 128
Cobb, S. E., 95
Cochrane, Joseph, 102–103, 302
Coe, George S., 287
Cole, Charles D., 158
Cole, L. A., 148
Cole, Samuel, 161
Comfort, A., 161
Conkey, J. H., 123–124, 130, 131
Conklin, Henry H, 158
Connell, Matthew, 259
Cooke, Carlisle D., 175, 197
Coon, Nelson, 168
Cooper, Peter, 5
Courtney, A. C., 272
Cowdrey, N. A., 288
Cramer, Eliphalet, 128, 148
Cravath, Prosper, 160
Crocker, Charles, 115–116
Crocker, Hans, 36, 45, 128, 148, 290–291
Crocker, Oliver, 18, 22
Cromwell, A. G., 292
Cromwell, Charles T., 117
Cross, James. B., *232*
Cryder, McKay, and Jaudon (investors), 116
Currier, R. J., 18
Cutler, Alonzo R., 18, 107
Cutler, Morris D., 18, 107

# PEOPLE AND PLACE NAME INDEX

## D

Darling, Mason C., 58, 143, 157, 272
Davidson, G. C., 175
Davis, Ferdinand, 168
Dawes, William, 174
Dean, C. K., 213
Dean, Nathaniel W., 141, 207
Dennis, William M., 148
Detmold, C. E., 5
Dewey, Nelson, 66, 89, 95, *194*, 223, 274, 300
Dewey, William Pitt, 226
Diamond Grove, Wisconsin, 35
Dickinson, John P., 156
Dickson, John P., 47, 159
Doan, Seth, 175
Dodge, Henry, 8, 11–12, 17, 19, 21, 29–32, *31*, 35, 37, 39, 48–50, 58, 66, 160, 299
Dodgeville, Wisconsin, 17, *43*
Doe, Joseph B., 141, 160
Doty, Charles, 158, 216
Doty, James (son), 173
Doty, James D. (father), 22, 31, 35, *38*, 38–40, 51, 143, 172, 173, *210*, 216, 223, *227*, 299
Dougherty, Robert, 32
Dousman, Elizabeth, 70
Dousman, George D., 52
Dousman, Hercules L., 30, 157, 210, 273–274, 288, 300
Dousman, Michael, 70
Dunbar, S. W., 36
Dunn, Charles, 161
Dunn, Francis, 161
Dunwiddie, B., 243
Durand, H. S., 246–247
Durham, Benjamin, 156
Durkee, Charles, 41
Dye, Asael, 30

## E

Eagle, Wisconsin, 86, 120
Eagle Centre, Wisconsin, 128–129
Earle, Thomas, 15, *16*
Earnest, James H., 159, 160
Eastman, John A., 158
Eaton, Parley, 161

Edgerton, Benjamin H., 27–28, 35–36, 70, 74, 77–78, 114, 117–119, 129–130, 166–168, 183, 276, 302
Eldred, Anson, 69, 78, 128
Eldred, Elisha, 69, 128
Ellis, Albert G., 26, 39, 41
Engle, Peter, 37
Ernst, William A., 206–207
Evans, E. W., 170, 175

## F

Fairchild, Jairus C., 207–208, 232, *232*, 304
Falvey, Thomas, 225
Farnsworth, William, 22, 30, 158, 216
Farwell, Leonard J., 151–152, 171, 206–207, 223, 232, 305
Fay, B. F., 148
Fellows, T. H., 171
Field, Alfred, 141
Fillmore, Millard, 27
Finch, Ashael Jr., 125, 126, 300
Fisher, Lucius G., 156, 171
Fitzgerald, John, 229
Flanders, Walter P., 70, 115–117, 128, 136, 160
Foley, John, 35
Follett, Emmons, 30
Fond du Lac, Wisconsin, 37–39, 140–146, 158, 173, 198, *282*
Ford, Simeon, 148
Foster, Mary Stuart, *44*
Fowler, Albert, 18, 22, 35
Fox, John C., 163, 302–303
Fox, William H., 156
Freeman, D. C., 238
Freeman, Samuel, *111*
Fuller, John S., *287*

## G

Galena, Illinois, 12, 32, 34
Gardner, William N., 36–37
Garton (Mr.), 119, 128
Gibson, Moses S., 158
Gifford, Peter, 119
Giles, Hiram, 179
Gillespie, Eugene, 47
Gillet, T. L., 143
Gilman, E., 148

# PEOPLE AND PLACE NAME INDEX

Gilmore, James, 35
Goodhue, William P., 156
Goodrich, Edwin H., 152, 153, 155, 174
Goodrich, Ezra, 165
Goodrich, Joseph, 95–96, *96*, 111, 114, 128, 134–135, 165, 274, 300
Gould, James, 149
Gratiot, Edward, 161
Gray, A. T., 142
Green Bay, Wisconsin, 6, 23, 27–28, 35
Griswold, George, 161–162

## H

Hackett, John, 141, 171
Haddley, Jackson, 225
Haertal, Herman, 171, 229
Hale, Samuel, 170, 175
Hall, Sheldon C., 1258
Hamilton, A. B., 158
Hamilton, Alexander, 26
Hamilton, William S., 26–27
Harriman, R. P., 158
Hathaway, Joshua, 52
Hazel Green, Wisconsin, 8
Heath, Consider, 47
Helena, Wisconsin, 20, 37, 39, 212
Higby, L. J., 266
Hindsdale, Henry B., 171
Hollister, D. S., 36
Holmes, Thomas, 37
Holton, Edward D., 47, 54–55, 57, 68–69, 70, 73, 78, 83–84, 90, 95, 102, 107, 110–111, 114, 128, 130, 148, 164, 168, 274, 300
Hopkins, B. F., 207
Horner, John S., 26, 32
Hotchkiss, R. H., 277
Houston, J. P., 177
Hubbard, Henry, 22, 42
Hubbell (Judge), 110
Huebschman, Francis, 174
Hustis, John, 50
Hutchins, E. W., 272
Hyer, N. F., 36

## I

Irwin, David, 32

## J

Jackman, Timothy, 141
Jackson, Andrew, 3, 25, 29, 42
Jackson, D. C., 238, 278
Janes, Henry F., 47
Janes, Lorenzo, 47
Janesville, Wisconsin, 47, 86, 139–140
Jenkins, Benjamin A., 118
Jenkinson, Robert, 158
Jervis, William, 235–236, 247, 276
Johnson, Andrew, 305
Johnson, Edwin F., 172, 304
Jones, Benjamin, 158
Jones, David, 40, 148
Jones, George Wallace, 29, 45
Jones, Thomas, 212
Jordon, John S., 164
Judd, Stoddard, 174
Juneau, Peter, *19*
Juneau, Solomon, 18, *19*, 23–25, *24*, 27, 36, 45, 102–103, 114, 299
Juneautown, Wisconsin, 25, 65, 70

## K

Keep, John M., 156, 161
Kerr, Joseph, 174
Kilbourn, Byron, 18, 23–25, *24*, 35–37, 41, 46, 49–51, 56–57, 63, 65–66, 69–70, *70*, 73–80, 82, 85, 87, 90, 94–95, 97–100, 102, 104–105, 108–109, 111, 114, 115–127, 130, 132, 148–155, *151*, 174, 223, *225*, 225–229, 237, 252–254, 301
Kilbourntown, Wisconsin, 25, 35, 65, 70
King, Rufus, 196, 210
King, William W., 158
Kirkland, J. F., 294
Kittredge, Edwin, 109, 303
Kittredge, Walter, 109, 303
Kline, William J., 129
Knapp, Gilbert, 18, 22, 26, 158
Knapp, Shepherd, 209, 282
Kneeland, James, 69, 95, 114, 128, 148, 171, 175
Knowlton, James H., 161, 223, 224, 226, 252–253
Koop, Henry, 161

# PEOPLE AND PLACE NAME INDEX

Koshkonong, Wisconsin, 39
Kurz, Louis, *242, 255, 288, 290*

## L

La Crosse, Wisconsin, 148
Ladd, H., 161
Lamar, Charles, 161
Lansing, Andrew J., 18
Lapham, Increase, *48–49*, 50–53, 299
Lavell, John, 231
Lawrence, George, 95
Lawrence, William H., 159
Lawson, Daniel, 159
Lee, Hugh, 142
Leet, Charles, 47
Leonard, A., 175
Linsley, Charles, 129–131
Longstreet, William R., 36
Lowth, John, 152
Lucas, Betsey, 54
Ludington, Harrison, 52
Ludington, James, 171, 174
Lyman, Asahel P., 158
Lyman, Huntington, 157
Lynde, William Pitt, 288
Lyon, Lucius, 16

## M

MacArthur, Arthur, 171, 223
Macy, John B., 142, 145, 304
Madden, William I., 35
Madison, Wisconsin, 37–39, *38*, 41, 86, 179–189, *227, 287. See also* City of Four Lakes
Mallory, J., 148
Manchester, P. C., 156
Manitowoc, Wisconsin, 147, 157–158
Mapes, David, 291
Marschner, A., 216
Martin, Morgan L., 17, 18, *19*, 23, 40, 143
Mason, Roswell B., 162
Mason, Stevens T., 31
Mathews, G. W., 263
Mazomanie, Wisconsin, 195–197, 211–212, *212*
Mazzuchelli, (Reverend), 37
McClelland, Samuel R., 171
McCloy, W. A., *9*

McCord, William, 211
McFarland, William, *180*
McFarland, Wisconsin, *180*
McFarlane, Hugh, 152
McGregor, Alexander, 274
McKinn, Richard, 35
McWilliams, George, 143
Medbery, J. W., 148
Menomonee, Wisconsin, 35
Merrill, S. S., 102, 114, 132, *272*, 276, 278, 294, 303
Mexico, territory of, 3
Meyer, Lewis H., 288
Michigan (state), 64, 66, 239, 274
Michigan Territory, 3, 5, 7, 9, 16, 20, 26
Middleton, Wisconsin, 45, 210–211, *211*
Miller, E. L., 5, 41, 234
Mills, David L., 128, 141
Mills, Simeon, 167, 198, 207
Milton, John, 161
Milton, Wisconsin, 86, 134, 159–160, 164–166
Milwaukee, Wisconsin, 37, 39, 54, 56, *94*, 148, *151, 255, 275*; development of, 18, 22, 23–25, *24*; map of, *19, 24*
Mitchell, Alexander, 69, 78–79, 90, 114, 128, 148, 171, 226, 301
Mitchell, John, 156
Mitchell, Martha Reed, 78
Monell, Joseph D., 171
Monroe, James, 10
Moore, Benjamin, 158, 229
Moore, John, 160
Moore, Thomas, 212
Moorman, Thomas J., 152
Morgan, Richard P., 77, 78, 114, 142
Mortimer, John, 213
Morton, A. B., 36
Mullie, Jacob, 87

## N

Nancolas, Anthony, 161
Navarino, Wisconsin, 18, 21, 26, 30
Neal, David L., 162
Neil, James, 159
Newcomen, Thomas, 5
Nichols, Abner, 18, 175
Noble, William H., 187
Noggle, David, 141

# PEOPLE AND PLACE NAME INDEX

Noonan, Josiah, 237
Norris, Richard, 217

## O

O'Hara, Michael, 202
O'Conner, M. L., 82
O'Farrall, Francis K., 35
Ogden, Mahlon D., 272
Ogden, William B., 23, 139, 144, 188, 199, 225–226, 229, 240–241, 304
Olin, D. A., 276
Otten, Henry, 216

## P

Paine, William, 18, 22
Palmer, Francis, 186, 238
Palmer, H. L., 158
Palmer, Strange M., 34
Parkinson, Peter, 45
Parsons, J., 95
Pease, J. R., 272
Perkins, Thomas H., 272
Perrin, William, 212
Perry, H. O., 274
Phelps, Walter, 99
Philips, John, 22
Phoenix, Samuel F., 47
Picett, Alexander F., 57
Pier, Colwert and Fanna, 143
Pierce, Franklin, 222, 223
Pierce, John A., 171
Pike, Wisconsin, 22, 30, 41
Pixley, B. F., 156
Pixley, Maurice, 52
Platt, Jarvis E., 158
Platteville, Wisconsin, 8, 32, 37, 39
Plumbe, John, 46
Polk, James K., 66
Potter, John Fox, 227
Potter, Paraclete, 52, 57
Powers, David J., 95, 107, 119–120, 124
Prairie du Chien, Wisconsin, 18, 30, 90
Prairie Village, Wisconsin, 44, 107
Prairieville, Wisconsin, 58, 107
Prentiss, William A., 36, 51–52, 128
Prescott, D. C., 263, 270

Preston, Otis, 171
Price, George E., 276
Putnam, Osgood, 90

## R

Racine, Wisconsin, 26, 37, 39, 47, 54, 56, 147, 157–159
Randall, Alexander W., 57, 63, 108, 111, 114, 254, *254*, 301
Randall, F., 52
Ray, Adam E., 128, 213
Redington, George, 276
Reed, D. C., 152
Reed, George, 158
Reed, Harrison, 158
Richardson, George, 133
Rock, L. B., 276
Rockwell, John S., 174
Rockwell, Le Grand, 171, 231
Rogan, Patrick, 152
Rogan, Peter, 148
Rogers, James H., 36, 52, 128
Rose, Simon, 211, 278
Ross, Laura, 301
Ruger, A., *233*, *282*
Ruggles, J. D., 156
Rurand, Henry S., 159

## S

Sage, Russell, 267
Sandborn, George, 276
Sanderson, George B., 156
Schafer, Joseph, 27, 41, 54
Schall, William, 288
Schoolcraft, Henry Rowe, *10*, 10–13, *11*, 17, 23, 299, 308
Schurz, Karl, 231
Seymour, Isaac, 286–287
Shafter, James M., 158
Shears, Henry, 152
Sheboygan, Wisconsin, 30, 147, 157–158, 198
Sheldon (Representative), 41
Shepardson, C., 128
Sherwood, John P., 158
Shew, William, 58

# PEOPLE AND PLACE NAME INDEX

Shields, Robert, 129–130
Sholes, C. C., 175
Sholes, C. Latham, 225
Sill, W. R., 237
Simmons, E., 175
Simmons, Z. G., 291–292
Simmons, Zalmon G., 304
Sinipee, Wisconsin, 45–46
Slaughter, B. C., 211
Slaughter, George H., 141
Smith, A. Hyatt, 140–142, 145, 188, 304–305
Smith, Alice E., 58
Smith, Elias, 47
Smith, George, 23
Smith, Henry, 272
Smith, Horatio N., 158
Smith, John B., 176
Smith, Perry H., 229
Smith, Samuel T., 152
Smith, William R., 21, 42, 44
Sneden, Daniel B., 141
Snyder, Jacob, 260
Southport, Wisconsin, 47, 54. 56
Southwell, Henry E., 220, 249
Soutter, James T., 209, 237–238, 282
Spuires, John C., 160
Stafford, C. H., 171, 175
Stanton, Nehemiah P., 254
Stephenson, Robert, *16*
Stevens, Charles, 156
Stevens, Isaac I., 173
Stickney, James, 211, 303
Stoddard, Thomas B., 158
Stoughton, Luke, 179
Strong, Caroline, 150
Strong, George, 153, 154, 155
Strong, Marshall M., 159
Strong, Moses M., 42, 52, 55, 57, 94, 127, 149–155, *150*, 161, 174, 138, 202, 210, 223, 225–226, *226*, 228–229, 237, 252, 304
Strong, Timothy F. Sr., 143, 173, 188
Strong, William B., 256, 276. 303
Sudgeon, Thomas, 119, 128
Sullivan, Matthew, 259
Sully, Robert M., *18*
Sutherland, Thomas W., 141

Suydam, John, *38*
Sweet, Alanson, 41
Sweet, E. J., 276

## T

Taintor, William, 128
Tallmadge, Nathaniel P., 110, 158
Taylor, David, 216
Taylor, Zachary, 17, 89
Teas, Joseph, 38
Temple, Charles, 188
Tenney, Horace A., 237
Thayer, J. O., 294
Thompson, Henry, 243
Thomson, Alexander M., 293–294
Tibbits, F. G., 156
Tilden, Samuel J., 272
Titus, W. A., 173
Toland, Patrick, 152
Towslee, H. B., 175
Trevethick, Richard, 5
Turner, John Bice, 156–157, 305
Turner, Joseph, 158
Tweedy, John H., 69, 78, 95, 114, 119–120, 125, 128, 148, 301
Twining, A. C., 175
Tyler, John, 149

## U

Underwood, W. O., 95
Upham, Don A. J., 77, 89, 103, 110, 111

## V

Van Buren, Martin, 50
Van Dorn, Charles, 30
Varney, Ezra L., 156
Veiu, Jacques, *19*
Vineyard, James, 26–27, 27, 150
Visas, Levi B., 156
Vivian, Francis, 161, 162
Vliet, Garret, 152, 153, 155, 209
Vliet, Jasper, 153, 155
Vliet, Jesper, 74, 78, 101, 176
Vliet, John B., 155
Von Hoffman, L. A., 288

## PEOPLE AND PLACE NAME INDEX

## W

Wade House, *68*
Wakeley, Eleazar, 171
Walcott, E. B., 70, 73
Walker, George H., 90–91, 128, 148, 152, 274, 301
Walker, Isaac P., 154
Walker, Robert J., 188
Walker, Isaac P., 66
Ward, Lindsey, 291
Warren, Lyman, 21
Watt, James, 5
Waukesha, Wisconsin, 44, 107, *242*
Weed, James H., 229
Weeks, Lemuel W., 45, 57, 63, 69, 78, 126
Weil, Henry, 152
Wells, Daniel, 57
Wells, Daniel Jr., 148, 273
Wells, William C., 156
Wengler, John B., *94*
Westbury, Joseph, 259
Wheeler, Charles H., 148
Whitney, Asa, 90, 157
Whitney, Daniel, 18, 20–21, 22
Whittlesey, Thomas T., 141
Whjiton, Edward V., 141
Wiard, Norman, 275

Wilkinson, John, 288
Williams, Henry, 128
Williams, Micajah T., 18, 23–25, 26
Williams, Mrs. Thomas, 212
Willow Springs, Wisconsin, 11
Willson, Zebina, 132
Wiltzer, Lorenzo, 260
Wing, Austin E., 17
Winnebago City, Wisconsin, 35, 40
Winslow, Albert, 272
Wisconsin City, Wisconsin, 37, 39
Wisconsin Heights, Wisconsin, 17, 36
Wisconsin Territory, 17, 25, 29–41, *31*, *43*, 47, 49, 53, 55, 66–67, 127, 149, 153
Wisconsinapolis, Wisconsin, 37, 39
Wolcott, Erastus B., 69, 70, 108, 128, 274, 301
Wolverton, Stephen, 216
Wood, H. D., 47
Wood, S. A., 158
Woodman, Cyrus, 161–162
Wright, Charles, 159
Wright, Hoel, 30
Wright, William, 148
Wrightstown, Wisconsin, 30

## Y

Young, J. R., 272

**DeSoto Public Library**

AP 1 8 '15